Islam, Causality, and Freedom

In this volume, Özgür Koca offers a comprehensive survey of Islamic accounts of causality and freedom from the medieval to the modern era. Based on this examination, Koca identifies and explores some of the major currents in the debate on casuality and freedom. He also discusses the possible implications of Muslim perspectives on causality for contemporary debates on religion and science. The book is an invitation for Muslims and non-Muslims to explore a rich, but largely forgotten, aspect of Islamic intellectual history.

Özgür Koca is an assistant professor of Islamic Studies and Philosophy at Bayan Claremont Islamic Graduate School. His research focus is on Islamic philosophy, theology, Sufism, and discussion of science and religion.

Islam, Causality, and Freedom

From the Medieval to the Modern Era

ÖZGÜR KOCA
Bayan Claremont Islamic Graduate School

CAMBRIDGE
UNIVERSITY PRESS

CAMBRIDGE
UNIVERSITY PRESS

Shaftesbury Road, Cambridge CB2 8EA, United Kingdom

One Liberty Plaza, 20th Floor, New York, NY 10006, USA

477 Williamstown Road, Port Melbourne, VIC 3207, Australia

314–321, 3rd Floor, Plot 3, Splendor Forum, Jasola District Centre, New Delhi – 110025, India

103 Penang Road, #05–06/07, Visioncrest Commercial, Singapore 238467

Cambridge University Press is part of Cambridge University Press & Assessment, a department of the University of Cambridge.

We share the University's mission to contribute to society through the pursuit of education, learning and research at the highest international levels of excellence.

www.cambridge.org
Information on this title: www.cambridge.org/9781108791977

DOI: 10.1017/9781108866965

First published 2020
First paperback edition 2023

A catalogue record for this publication is available from the British Library

Library of Congress Cataloging-in-Publication data
NAMES: Koca, Ozgur, 1977– author.
TITLE: Islam, causality, and freedom : from the medieval to the modern era / Ozgur Koca.
DESCRIPTION: 1. | New York : Cambridge University Press, 2020. |
Includes bibliographical references and index.
IDENTIFIERS: LCCN 2019056223 (print) | LCCN 2019056224 (ebook) |
ISBN 9781108496346 (hardback) | ISBN 9781108791977 (paperback) |
ISBN 9781108866965 (epub)
SUBJECTS: LCSH: Islamic philosophy. | Cosmology. | Causality (Physics) |
Causation (Islamic law) | Liberty–Religious aspects–Islam.
CLASSIFICATION: LCC B745.C6 K63 2020 (print) | LCC B745.C6 (ebook) |
DDC 122.088/297–dc23
LC record available at https://lccn.loc.gov/2019056223
LC ebook record available at https://lccn.loc.gov/2019056224

ISBN 978-1-108-49634-6 Hardback
ISBN 978-1-108-79197-7 Paperback

To my loving and supportive wife Ayşin and
to my three wonderful children, Berrin, Reyyan, and Alp Eren.

Contents

Conventions *page* ix
Acknowledgments xi

Introduction 1

1 Causality in the Early Period: Muʿtazilites and the Birth of Ashʿarite Occasionalism 16

2 Toward a Synthesis of Aristotelian and Neoplatonic Understandings of Causality: The Case of Ibn Sīnā 40

3 Occasionalism in the Middle Period: Ghazālī's and Rāzī's Responses to Ibn Sīnā 60

4 The First as Pure Act and Causality: The Case of Ibn Rushd 83

5 Light, Existence, and Causality: The Illuminationist School and the Case of Suhrawardī 100

6 The World as a Theophany and Causality: Sufi Metaphysics and the Case of Ibn ʿArabī 116

7 Continuities and Developments in Sufi Metaphysics: The Cases of Qūnawī and Qayṣarī 135

8 Toward an Occasionalist Philosophy of Science: The Case of Jurjānī 159

9 Causality and Freedom in Later Islamic Philosophy: The Case of Mullā Ṣadrā 183

10 Occasionalism in the Modern Context: The Case of Said Nursi 200

11 Islamic Theories of Causality in the Modern Context: The Religion and Science Debate 231

Conclusion 255

Bibliography 262

Index 279

Conventions

I have simplified Arabic names by removing the definite article (for example Ashʿarī for al-Ashʿarī, Ghazālī for al-Ghazālī). Certain commonly used Arabic words that appear in Merriam-Webster's dictionary have not been transliterated or italicized, such as "Allah" and "hadith." I have preserved *ʿayn* and *hamza*, for example in "Qurʾan" and "shariʿa." However, I have removed initial *hamza*s (for example *Islamiyyīn* for *ʾIslamiyyīn*).

I use both my own and existing translations throughout this study. I have also modified some existing translations. These are indicated in the footnotes.

My transliteration of Arabic, Persian, and Turkish words is based on the chart developed by the *International Journal of Middle East Studies*. I have fully transliterated technical terms, Arabic book titles, and Arabic names with diacritical marks (macrons and dots). After introducing works in the footnotes, I refer to them by a single significant word in the title (for example *Maqālāt* for *Maqālāt al-Islamiyyīn wa-l-Ikhtilāf al-Muṣallīn* or *al-Milal* for *Kitāb al-Milal wa-l-Niḥāl*).

Said Nursi's writings present a particular challenge for transliteration. Nursi wrote in Ottoman Turkish, which borrows extensively from Arabic and Persian and today is written in the Modern Turkish alphabet. To transliterate his works, I have used modern Turkish orthography. Moreover, despite the fact that modern Turkish orthography no longer includes hatted vowels (â, î, û), I have elected to use them, because it is quite common to see hatted vowels in Turkish texts written during the first half of the twentieth century, as is the case for Nursi's writings. The following characters appear in the transliterations of this scholar's writings.

c = j, as in joke
ç = ch, as in change
ğ = unpronounced, elongates the preceding vowel
ı = as in io of action
ö = as in French peu
ş = sh, as in shark
ü = as in French rue

Acknowledgments

Research and rewriting for this book were accomplished over several years in the friendly environment of Bayan Islamic Graduate School; I am grateful to all of my colleagues at Bayan. I am especially indebted to Jihad Turk and Munir Shaikh who worked actively to provide me with the protected academic time and scholarly environment. I am honored to have had their competent assistance and enthusiastic support.

I would like to thank Professors Ahmet Kuru, Gökhan Bacık, Ahmad Alwishah, Zayn Kassam, Stefano Bigliardi, Nazif Muhtaroğlu, and Ensar Demirkan for their valuable help in the preparation of this book as well as their insightful comments and help during the preparation process of this book. My special thanks to Professor Philip Clayton. The value of his guidance, knowledge, and support has been immeasurable to my work. My deep gratitude to the personnel of the library at Claremont School of Theology: They have provided competent assistance and have promptly obtained sources I needed from different parts of the world. I am grateful to the anonymous readers of Cambridge University Press who read the manuscript very carefully and provided detailed and insightful comments.

Nobody has been more important to me than the members of my family in the pursuit of this project. My wife, Ayşin Koca, is on every single page of this study; her love and patience permeate the whole work. Without her support and respect for my work, I would not be able to do anything an academic is expected to do. I will always remember her kindness and patience during my studies, as well as her dedication to our three wonderful children, Berrin, Reyyan, and Alp Eren.

Introduction

You threw not, when you threw.

(Qur'an 8:17)

God's free will has given existence to our free will / His free will is like a rider beneath the dust / His free will creates our free will / His commands are founded upon a free will within us.

(Rūmī, *Mathnawī*, V. 3087–3038)

In this book, I examine different accounts of causality formulated by Muslim theologians, philosophers, and mystics. The book also includes examinations of how they established freedom in the created order as an extension of their perception of causality. Based on this examination, I identify and explore some of the major currents in the debate on causality and freedom. I also discuss the possible implications of Muslim perspectives on causality for contemporary debates over religion and science. The central figures examined in this book are early Muʿtazilite and Ashʿarite theologians, Ibn Sīnā (980–1037), Abū Ḥāmid al-Ghazālī (1058–1111), Shihāb al-Dīn Suhrawardī (1154–1191), Ibn Rushd (1126–1198), Fakhr al-Dīn al-Rāzī (1149–1209), Muḥyiddīn Ibn ʿArabī (1165–1240), Ṣadraddīn al-Qūnawī (1210–1274), Dāwūd al-Qayṣarī (1260–1350), al-Sayyīd al-Sharīf al-Jurjānī (1340–1413), Mullā Ṣadrā (1571–1640), and Said Nursi (1877–1960).

WHY CAUSALITY AND FREEDOM?

What is the nature of relationship between cause and effect?[1] Is this relationship necessary or contingent? To what extent do humans and other entities have causal efficacy? What is the metaphysical basis of the causal efficacy of entities? How can one square the divine will, knowledge, and omnipotence with human freedom? These and similar questions about causality and freedom are fundamentally important for any religion for many reasons, a few of which can be mentioned here.

First, the way one understands causal relations in the natural world has fundamental implications for many contentious theological and philosophical questions. This understanding informs one's perception of the God-and-cosmos relationship. This perception, in turn, has important implications for one's conception of the relationship between God and the individual. Our convictions as to whether causal relations are necessary or contingent shape our thinking about freedom and consciousness

[1] The word for cause is *sabab* or *ʿilla*. *Sabab* in classical dictionaries means a "bond," a "rope," or a "way" that is used to connect or tie two things together. Cause (*sabab*) is that to which effect is tied or with which one could attain or arrive at effect (*musabbab*, *muʾaththir*). See, for example, Tahānawī, *Kashshāf Iṣṭilāḥāt al-Funūn*, ed. Ali Dahruj (Beirut: Maktabat Lubnan, 1996), II, 924; Ibn al-Manẓūr, *Lisān al-ʿArab* (Beirut: Dar Sadr, n.d.), I, 458–459; Jurjānī, *Kitāb al-Taʿrīfāt* (Lipsiae: Sumptibus F. C. G. Vogelii, 1845), 121; Fīrūzābādī, *al-Qāmūs al-Muḥīṭ* (Beirut: Muassasat al-Risala, 1986), I, 295; Ibn Fūrak, *Kitāb al-Ḥudūd fī-l-Uṣūl*, ed. Muhammad Sulaymani (Beirut: Dar al-Gharb al-Islami, 1999), 159–160. The word *sabab* is used in the Qurʾan in both singular (*sabab*) and plural form (*asbāb*). Again, in the Qurʾanic context, it usually means that which relates two things to each other (22/15; 18/84–85, 89–92; 2/166; 38/10, 40/36–37). *ʿIlla* means "illness," "cause," "genesis," "excuse," etc. The term is not mentioned in the Qurʾan. Ashʿarite and Muʿtazilite theologians generally use the concepts of *sabab* and *ʿilla* interchangeably. Qāḍī ʿAbduljabbār and Nīsābūrī, however, make a distinction between *sabab* and *ʿilla* on the basis of the notion of necessity. *ʿIlla* implies a necessary relationship between cause and effect, whereas *sabab* refers to a volitional relationship. See, for example, Qāḍī ʿAbduljabbār, *al-Mughnī fī Abwābi al-ʿAdl wa-l-Tawḥīd*, 16 vols. ed. Ibrahim Madkur, Taha Husayn, and various editors (Cairo: al-Dar al-Misriyya, 1962–5), IX, 48–50; Nīsābūrī, *al-Masāʾil fī-l-Khilāf bayn al-Baṣriyyīn wa-l-Baghdādiyyīn*, ed. Ridwan Sayyid and Maʿn Ziyada (Beirut: Maʿhad al-Inma al-Arabi, 1979), 70. Similarly, Ibn Ḥazm (994–1064) argues that the concepts of *sabab* and *ʿilla* can be distinguished on the basis of their separability from the effect. *Sabab* can be separated from effect, as is the case in the relationship of an agent and his acts. *ʿIlla*, however, occurs necessarily together with its effect such as fire-flame or fire-heat. It appears that *ʿilla* has more necessitarian implications than *sabab*. *Sabab* refers to an agent who could exist separately before and after its effect, whereas *ʿilla* necessitates and occurs together with its effects. See Ibn Ḥazm, *al-Iḥkām fī Uṣūl al-Aḥkām* (Beirut: Dar al-Afak al-Jadid, 1980), I, 41. Cf. Osman Demir, *Kelamda Nedensellik: Ilk Dönem Kelamcılarında Tabiat ve İnsan* (Istanbul: TC Kültür ve Turizm Bakanlığı, 2015), 23–24.

and the answers we give to theological problems of theodicy and eschatology.

Second, the question of causality bears significantly on spiritual and mystic tendencies that are usually distinguished by their accentuation of the divine presence in the world, a presence that is itself grounded in a particular conception of causality. A distant God located at the origin of a long chain of causality is usually rejected by mystics of most religions. Since our perception of causality also shapes our understanding of the God-and-individual relationship, it influences one's spiritual state in religious observances and rituals.

Third, the question of causality is linked with discussions of logic and epistemology. For example, one of the premises of classical logic is that the consistent sequential relationships between cause and effect constitute a valid basis for demonstrative syllogism. Ashʿarite occasionalism, however, is skeptical about the necessity of these relations due several theological reasons examined in this book. In the case of Muslim occasionalists, their doubt regarding the necessary connection between cause and effect appears to have led to a type of "empiricism" in which the deductive tendencies of Aristotelian logic and the concept of universals were questioned and finally rejected. This also led to lively discussion on the difference between mental constructions and extramental reality.

Fourth, the question of causality bears significantly on debates over religion and science. One of the challenges in this field is to have theories of causality that preserve the rigor of the scientific method as well as a sense of the divine presence in the world. Construction of such theories requires a solid understanding of the profound nature of causality.

The question of how to establish freedom in the created and divine order is also fundamentally important for any religion to ground human autonomy, moral agency, and responsibility. Reconciliation of creaturely freedom with God's omniscience, omnipotence, omnipresence, and predestination is one of the main problems heavily debated among Muslim theologians, philosophers, and mystics for centuries. This is one of the cornerstones of all theological and philosophical thinking, for without freedom, concepts such as accountability, judgement, revelation, the divine commands-prohibitions, and justice appear to collapse.

One can also trace the implications of convictions about causality and freedom to such diverse fields as politics and economics. It would not be an exaggeration to say that conscious or unconscious presumptions about causality and freedom form an ever-present background and influence one's answers to these and similar questions in many areas of life.

THE SELECTION OF THE THINKERS

There are several reasons why I have chosen the abovementioned thinkers as the focus of this study. First of all, these exceptional figures have long received and will likely continue to see extensive attention throughout the Muslim world. Their viewpoints, therefore, are particularly significant.

Second, these scholars can be seen as some of the most important representatives of the best-known philosophical, theological, and spiritual schools and tendencies in the Islamic tradition. For instance, the early Muʿtazilite and Ashʿarite theologians Ghazālī, Jurjānī, Rāzī, and Nursi could be included in the category of the *mutakallimūn*, usually translated as "the theologians." Ibn Sīnā and Ibn Rushd are regarded as the major representatives of the Peripatetic school of Islamic philosophy (*mashshāʾiyyūn*), which attempts to synthesize the tenets of Aristotelianism, Neoplatonism, and Islamic revelation. Suhrawardī and Mullā Ṣadrā belong to the Illuminationists (*ishrāqiyyūn*), who aim to harmonize experiential aspects of spirituality and theoretical aspects of philosophy. Ibn ʿArabī, Qūnawī, and Qayṣarī are considered among the most illustrious representatives of Sufi metaphysics and theosophy. A study of their thought will thus contribute to our understanding of how major schools in the Islamic tradition approach questions of causality and freedom.

Third, as will be argued, these scholars make significant contributions to the debate on causality and freedom. To explore the emergence and development of occasionalist accounts, I examine the earlier discussion among Muʿtazilite and Ashʿarite theologians. Ibn Sīnā's philosophy offers an analysis of the issue from both metaphysical and physical perspectives. His concepts of existence (*wujūd*) and essence (*māhiyya*) provide a metaphysical framework that deeply influenced the Philosophers' and Sufis' accounts in later centuries. Ghazālī's writings show how an occasionalist response can be formulated against Ibn Sīnā. Although Ghazālī mostly repeats previous Ashʿarite theologians' arguments, he also introduces a novel application of the principle of "preponderance without reason," which then becomes one of the backbones of occasionalism in the middle period. He also manages to raise some important challenges to Ibn Sīnā's synthesis of Aristotelian and Neoplatonic ideas on causality, which in turn influenced Ibn Rushd's thought. Ghazālī focuses on the theological aspect of the discussion and remains uninterested in the cosmological challenges of Ibn Sīnā's physics. Rāzī takes up the challenge and responds to Ibn Sīnā's hylomorphism by using Euclidian geometry and develops a list of novel arguments for a defense of atomism. Rāzī's response and Jurjānī's contributions led to the emergence of an occasionalist philosophy of science marked by a pragmatic-cum-skeptic attitude toward dominant scientific models. Ibn Rushd was important for reformulating and developing certain aspects of Ibn Sīnā's synthesis after Ghazālī's criticism. Suhrawardī's writings provide an evaluation of the issue through the use of the analogy of light and suggest that the ground of all causality is the radiation of the divine light upon the essences and that secondary causality is efficacious due to those essences' participation in the divine light. Ibn ʿArabī presents a participatory account of causality by starting from the concept of existence and also integrates certain occasionalist elements within the larger context of his metaphysics. Ibn ʿArabī's followers Qūnawī and Qayṣarī offer in their writings more philosophical evaluation of some ideas attributed to the Philosophers, such as secondary causality and emanation, and of ideas attributed to Ashʿarites, such as continuous creation, breaks in the divine habits, and preponderance. Their writings suggest that later representatives of Sufi metaphysics selectively appropriated ideas defended by different schools by using the philosophical possibilities suggested by the concepts of existence and essence. Mullā Ṣadrā's writings provide insights into how the questions of causality and freedom were evaluated in later Islamic philosophy. Nursi's account is an interesting case in terms of its contemporary appropriation of occasionalism. Nursi also puts occasionalism in conversation with Sufi metaphysics and elaborates the concept of causal disproportionality, which can be regarded as a novel development within the occasionalist tradition. These cases, it is hoped, will allow us to see the emergence, development, continuities, discontinuities, and adaptability of the occasionalist and participatory accounts of causality and more synthetic approaches.

I have tried to follow a contextualist approach while examining these scholars. When I explore occasionalist accounts, for example, I have attempted to describe the salient features of the larger theological framework in which this theory of causality emerged and developed. Hence, the emergence of the occasionalist theory is examined from the perspective of the general Ashʿarite conception of the God–cosmos relationship and from the perspective of the overall tendency of the 'Ashʿarite' school to transform the notion of "possibility" into a modus operandi for thinking about all theological, philosophical, and cosmological questions in order to preserve both the divine will and freedom. Similarly, I have sought to understand participatory accounts and other hybrid models within the larger metaphysical framework in which they were constructed. Hence, in all these cases, I start my analyses from the notions of existence (*wujūd*) and essence (*māhiyya*), which provide rich perspectives on the questions of causality and freedom, allow interesting interactions between different accounts of causality, and lead to powerful syntheses.

I am aware that my treatment of the questions of causality and freedom in this book is neither definitive nor exhaustive. Many more books and articles will be needed before justice is done to a subject as complex as this one. However, I am confident that this book will advance our understanding on the topic. By the end, I hope to have convinced the reader that discussions of causality and freedom in Islamic intellectual history are wide ranging, important, and still relevant.

A SPECTRUM OF THEORIES ON CAUSALITY

It will be argued in the forthcoming pages that Muslim philosophers, theologians, and mystics elaborated an array of theories on causality. A closer study of these theories allows us to identify and explore certain major trends among them.

The first of these trends is the *occasionalist* tradition. The emergence and development of this tradition will be examined extensively in the following chapters. Occasionalist accounts often claim that finite beings do not have causal efficacy. God creates both cause and effect and attaches them to each other in a self-imposed habitual pattern. There is no necessary connection between cause and effect; there is only constant conjunction. As examined in the Chapter 1, the development of these accounts was closely linked to discussions taking place in the early period on the relationship between the divine attributes and God, the Qurʾanic emphasis on divine freedom and sovereignty, and an atomistic cosmology. The accentuation of the divine will and freedom leads to denial of any type of necessity in God or in the world. The idea of necessity is replaced with the notion of possibility. The concept of possibility, then, becomes the central tenet of the occasionalist worldview, shaping its convictions from epistemology and eschatology to morality and prophetology.

There are also different versions of *participatory* accounts. These accounts usually assimilate Aristotelian understanding of causality within the larger context of participatory understanding of causality. How Muslim philosophers and mystics have integrated these accounts within larger metaphysical frameworks will be examined in detail in the following chapters. At this point, a short introduction to some of the basic convictions of Platonic and Neoplatonic participatory and Aristotelian accounts may prove beneficial for grasping the spectrum of ideas about causality examined in this book.

Different versions of participatory accounts can be found in Platonic and Neoplatonic thought. Plato accepts the existence of the Forms such as the Beautiful, the Good, the Just, and so on, and employs them as explanations for all other things. "When it was agreed that each of the Forms existed," then "other things acquire their name by having a share in them."[2] Things are the way they are because they participate in the Forms.[3] A thing is beautiful because it partakes in the Beautiful, or because the Beautiful is present in that beautiful thing.[4] The Beautiful is "itself by itself with itself, it is always in one form; and all the other beautiful things share in that, in such a way that when those others come to be or pass away, this does not become the least bit smaller or greater nor suffer any change."[5] Hence "all beautiful things are beautiful by the Beautiful,"[6] and all free things are free by the Free, all powerful things are powerful by the Powerful, and so on. This logic implies that the Forms are causes of their manifestations in the sensible realm: "Once one has seen it (the form of the Good), one must conclude that it is the cause of all that is correct and beautiful in anything."[7]

What exactly is the participation of the object in the Form? Some of Plato's writings and the later Neoplatonic tradition do attempt to answer this question. At the beginning of *Parmenides*, Parmenides asks Socrates how the Forms participate in individual entities.[8] If they do so as a whole then the Forms are separate from themselves. Therefore, the Forms must exist in entities only in part. This also suggests a gradational structure in the world, in which entities participate in the Forms in differing degrees.

2 Plato, *Complete Works*, ed. John M. Cooper with introduction and notes, ass. ed. D. S. Hutchinson (Cambridge, UK: Hackett, 1997), *Phaedo*, 102b.

3 The Forms also make knowledge possible. There has to be something permanent in this world of flux: "it is not even reasonable to say that there is such a thing as knowledge, Cratylus, if all things are passing on and none remain ... But if there is always that which knows and that which is known, if there are such things as the beautiful, the good, and each one things that are, it does not appear to me that these things can be all like flowings or motions as we were saying just now they were." *Cratylus*, 440. b.

4 Plato, *Complete Works*: *Phaedo*, 100d.

5 Plato, *Complete Works*: *Symposium*, 211b.

6 Plato, *Complete Works*: *Phaedo*, 100d.

7 Plato, *Complete Works*: *Republic*, 517b.

8 "Tell me this: it is your view that there are certain forms from which these other things, by getting share of them, derive their names..." "It certainly is," Socrates replied. Plato, *Complete Works*: *Parmenides*, 131a.

For instance, not everything participates in the Beautiful to the same degree. This is why one can "start from the beautiful things" and use them like "rising stairs"[9] to "see the divine Beauty in itself," which is "absolute, pure, unmixed, not polluted by human flesh, colors, or any other great nonsense of mortality."[10] Thus, someone who "believes in the beautiful itself can see both it and the things that participate in it and does not believe that participants are it or that it itself is the participants." This person "is very much awake."[11]

In *Parmenides*, Plato introduces the One as the ground of the Forms. To participate in the Forms is to participate in the One. Yet, this participation does not make entities identical with the One. They are situated between being and not-being, for entities participate simultaneously in being and not-being. "Or, can you find a more appropriate place to put them (beings) then intermediate between being and not being? So, they cannot be more than what is or not be more than what is not, for apparently nothing is darker than what is not or clearer than what is."[12] Because of this intermediacy, entities do not belong to either being or not being. "What participates in both being and not being and cannot correctly be called purely one or the other."[13] This implies a shadow-like quality in entities between pure and unpolluted being and absolute not-being. Entities participate in being but are not the absolute and pure being. "In between the being that is indivisible and always changeless, and the one that is divisible and comes to be in the corporeal realm, he mixed a third, intermediate form of being, derived from the other two ... each part remaining a mixture of the Same, the Different, and of Being."[14]

We see a similar approach in the Neoplatonic tradition to the question of participation. Plotinus writes that all beings (*panta ta onta*) owe their being to the One (*toi eni esti onta*).[15] The One continuously gives us participation in its being, because the One is what it is. The One's being is the being of all existing things. The One is "all things and none of them."[16] It is none of

[9] Plato, *Complete Works*: *Symposium*, 211c. [10] Ibid., 211e.

[11] Plato, *Complete Works*: *Republic*, 476d [12] Ibid., 479d. [13] Ibid., 478e.

[14] Plato, *Complete Works*: *Timeaus*, 35a–b.

[15] Plotinus, *The Enneads*, trans. Stephen MacKenna. Abridged and edited by John Dillon (London: Penguin Books, 1991), VI. 9. 1. 1–2

[16] Plotinus, *Enneads*, V. 2. I. 1–3 and VI. 7. 32. 12–14. Also in Plato, "Insofar as it (the One) is in the others, it would touch the others; but insofar as it is in itself, it would be kept from touching the others," Plato, *Complete Works*: *Parmenides*, 148e; "the One both touches and does not touch the others and itself." *Parmenides*, 149d.

them, because the One is undifferentiated unity and beyond multiplicity. It is all, because it must also contain them all. This makes the One "everywhere and nowhere" without qualification. Similar to Plato, Neoplatonism situates the world between the two absolutes, the One and nothingness. The world participates in both the One and nothingness.

Why do entities participate in the One? It is because they cannot be deprived of the One, for "nothing prevents it [the One] from partaking of many things."[17] Entities are also not the same as the One. "But clearly a being would partake of the One, while being something other than the One. Otherwise, it would not partake, but it would itself be the One."[18] The best way to think about this ambiguity is through the idea of participation. "And yet the others are not absolutely deprived of the One, but somehow partake of it."[19] The idea of participation suggests things are neither identical nor separate from the One. They merely participate in the One. Plotinus writes that "if anything comes from the One, it must be something different from it, and in being different, it is not one: for if it was, it would be that One."[20]

In *Timeaus*, Plato also asserts that the Good shares its being with other entities to bring them into being. It is in the definition of the Good to share its goodness and its being. "Don't you in fact call getting a share of being 'coming to be'?"[21] Being is, then, something given to things. "So, has being been distributed to all things, which are many, and is it missing from none of the beings, neither the smallest nor the largest? . . . How could being be missing from any of the beings? In no way . . . So being is chopped up into beings of all kinds from the smallest to the largest possible, and is the most divided thing of all; and parts of being are countless."[22] Neoplatonism agrees with this account. The world proceeds from the Good, as "good diffuses itself" (*bonum diffusivum sui*). The One does not keep its perfection to itself and does not begrudge possible beings a share in its perfection.[23] It is this act of bestowal of being that allows entities to participate in the being of the One.

[17] Plato, *Complete Works: Parmenides*, 160e. [18] Ibid., 158a.

[19] Ibid., 157c. "Therefore, the One will be like and unlike the others – insofar as it is different, like, insofar as it is like, different." *Parmenides*, 148c.

[20] Plotinus, *Enneads*, V. 3. 15. 35–41. [21] Plato, *Complete Works: Parmenides*, 156 a.

[22] Plato, *Complete Works: Parmenides*, 144b.

[23] Plotinus, *Enneads*, V. 4. 1. 23. ff. This process is likened to the outflow of light from the sun. *Enneads*, V. 1. 6. 28–40, V.3.12.39–44, V. 4. I. 23–41. This also explains how unity gives rise to multiplicity. What proceeds from the One must be different from the One, and hence there is a multiplicity of things. See, for example, V. 3. 15. 1–11 and VI. 7. 8.

Moreover, it is this participation in the being of the One that is the basis of entities' causal efficacy and freedom. Even Plato's Forms rest on the ground of causality of the One. The omnipresence and immanence of the One introduces the causality of the One into all levels of the world-process.[24] This is why Plotinus remarks that "the One is power of all things" (*dynamis panton*). Similarly, for Plato, getting a share of being is the cause of the world-process. There is change in the world because "it partakes of (the One's) being."[25]

The Aristotelian account of causality has profoundly influenced Muslim scholars' perception of causal relations. One of the most influential of Aristotle's ideas holds that causality is the fundamental condition of proper knowledge. The four causes (material, formal, efficient, and final) are indispensable tools for any meaningful investigation of the physical world around us.[26] One cannot have knowledge of a thing without grasping why a thing is what it is, the way it is, and why it cannot be other than it is.[27] Any student of nature has to bring the "why-question" back to all natural phenomena in the way appropriate to this causal investigation.[28]

17–32. Matter is the point where emanation fades away into complete darkness. The outflow from the One cannot terminate until all possibilities come into existence. *Enneads*, IV. 8. 6.; V. 2. 2. 1 ff.

[24] This is what R. Wallis calls eidectic causality in *Neoplatonism*, 2nd ed. (London: Duckworth, 1995), 126, 155. See also, Costa D'Ancona, "Plotinus and Later Platonic Philosophers on the Causality of the First Principle," in *The Cambridge Companion to Plotinus*, ed. Lloyd P. Gerson (Cambridge, UK: Cambridge University Press, 1996), 361.

[25] Plato, *Complete Works*: *Sophist*, 256a.

[26] Aristotle, *The Complete Works of Aristotle*, ed. Jonathan Barnes, 2 vols (Princeton, NJ: Princeton University Press, 1984), *Physics* II 3 and *Metaphysics* V 2.

[27] Aristotle, *Posterior Analytics*, 1 b 9–11; *Physics*, 194 b 17–20.

[28] Aristotle, *Physics*, 198 a 21–23. A good summary of Aristoelian theory of causality can be found in Andrea Falcon, "Aristotle on Causality," *The Stanford Encyclopedia of Philosophy* (Spring 2015 Edition), ed. Edward N. Zalta https://plato.stanford.edu/archives/spr2015/entries/aristotle-causality/. See also Mary Louise Gill, "Aristotle's Theory of Causal Action in *Physics* III. 3," *Phronesis*, 25 (1980), 129–147; Cynthia A. Freeland, "Aristotle on Bodies, Matter, and Potentiality," in *Philosophical Issues in Aristotle's Biology*, ed. Allan Gotthelf and James Lennox (Cambridge, UK: Cambridge University Press, 1987), 392–407; Julia Annas, "Aristotle on Inefficient Causes," *Philosophical Quarterly*, 32 (1982), 311–326; Ursula Coope, "Aristotle's Account of Agency in *Physics* III.3," *Proceedings of the Boston Area Colloquium in Ancient Philosophy*, 20 (2004): 201–221.

A central Aristotelian concept relevant to our discussion is "nature." Things have natures that necessitate their behavior.[29] The occasionalist tradition rejects this idea due to its necessitarian implications. If the active and passive actions of entities were *determined* by and directly flow from natures of beings, that might imply limits to God's free action and creative power over the created order. It is this very idea that the occasionalist project aims to refute. To this end, it attempts to construct alternative notions and a new cosmology to replace the idea of necessity with the idea of possibility.

Aristotle's concepts of potentiality and actuality are also important for the present study. The world-process is a movement from potentiality into actuality. Things pass from potentiality to actuality. This is to say, potentiality is prior to actuality. Things are realized in accordance with the kind of potentiality they have. This concept provides the grounding for the explanation of motion and rest, and hence physical causality. The more important element here, however, is the theological implication of this conception of potentiality and actuality. The First is pure action without potentiality. The First must of necessity be pure action, for there can be no unrealized potentiality waiting to be actualized or realized in the First. Such a condition would be contrary to the utmost perfection. In the created order, things pass from potentiality to actuality. Therefore, potentiality is prior to actuality in this domain. Yet, actuality must in fact be prior to potentiality, since something potential can only be actualized by something else that is already actual. God is the First being and there is nothing prior to God. Hence, there can be no potentiality in God. God is pure act and complete self-fulfillment. As such, God is the first cause, the unmoved mover, the eternal. God is also the final cause, for the world is progressing toward becoming more actual and, thus, more like God.

Numerous Muslim thinkers attempt to integrate these accounts into larger, coherent metaphysical frameworks. In Sufi metaphysics, one also observes the tendency to absorb certain occasionalist ideas within the larger context of participatory accounts. The Muslim theological

[29] Aristotle, *Metaphysics*, 1049b5–10 and 9.1, 1046a11–13; *Physics*, 192b 20–23, 198a 24–27. See also Sarah Waterlow, *Nature, Change, and Agency in Aristotle's* Physics (Oxford: Clarendon Press, 1982); Stasinos Stavrineas, "Nature as a Principle of Change," in *Aristotle's* Physics: *A Critical Guide*, ed. Mariska Leunissen (Cambridge, UK: Cambridge University Press, 2015), 46–65; Richard Sorabji, *Matter, Space, and Motion: Theories in Antiquity and Their Sequel* (London: Duckworth or Ithaca, NY: Cornell University Press, 1988); Andrea Falcon, *Aristotle and the Science of Nature: Unity without Uniformity* (Cambridge, UK: Cambridge University Press, 2005).

tradition remains occasionalist for the most part. However, in some cases, occasionalist thinkers have appropriated certain elements from Sufi metaphysics. We thus find a spectrum of accounts accentuating certain tendencies more than others, without necessarily excluding or rejecting other currents.

The metaphysical frameworks created by the aforementioned Muslim thinkers have enabled conversation between and in some cases reconciliation of participatory, Aristotelian, and occasionalist currents. The concepts of existence (*wujūd*) and essence (*māhiyya*) have been integral to these frameworks. It is this integrative aspect of the Islamic tradition that appears to be quite original and innovative.

THE QUESTION OF FREEDOM

The book attempts to understand the approaches of the various scholars discussed above to the question of *freedom*. Freedom, throughout this study, is understood as an entity's quality and capacity of being an *uncaused cause* of itself. This quality will be regarded as the ground of autonomy, moral agency, and the absence of coercion in God and in the created order. Described as such, the question of freedom is closely related to the question of causality, and the two will therefore be considered in relation to each other in the following chapters.

My conviction is that the positions of the scholars examined in this book on causality to a great extent informed their answers to the question of freedom. Occasionalist accounts frequently use the theory of acquisition (*kasb*), which posits a *possible* relationship between human acquisitive power and divine creative power. This accords with the general tendency of occasionalist accounts to replace the notion of necessity with possibility. The theory of acquisition attributes creative power to God and acquisitive power to the created order. The role of human power is to acquire an act that is created by God. God's will and power create all objects, and acquisition becomes an "occasion" for the divine creative act. However, occasionalists do seem to imply that human will and power are still controlled by divine will and power. The question of whether this account attributes genuine causal efficacy and freedom to human individuals has been widely discussed and will also be evaluated in this book.

Participatory accounts establish human freedom in a way quite different from occasionalist ones. Again, the concepts of existence and essence play an important role here. One way of establishing human freedom starts from the concept of existence. Human individuals are free by participating in the divine existence, because by participating in the divine existence they also participate in the divine freedom. Another way to establish human freedom starts from the concept of essence. Essences are uncaused objects of the divine knowledge. God knows these essences but does not cause what type of essence an entity has. God brings essences into being by sharing its own existence. Thus, in order to exist these essences are absolutely dependent on God's existentiating act. However, as objects of the divine knowledge, essences remain uncaused causes of themselves. It is this uncaused nature of essences that allows creaturely freedom.

SUMMARY OF THE CHAPTERS

Chapter 1 explores the development of Muʿtazilite and Ashʿarite theories of causality, with a focus on their theological concerns and philosophical underpinnings. It will be argued that there is a close connection between the way the early schools perceive the relationship of the divine attributes to God and how they formulated divine causality and creaturely agency. Due to the importance of this connection, the chapter begins with an examination of Muʿtazilite and Ashʿarite positions on the relationship between the divine attributes and God. The chapter then elucidates how these discussions led to the emergence of Ashʿarite occasionalism, in which accentuation of the divine will became the central concern.

Chapter 2 examines Ibn Sīnā's account of causality and freedom. It offers an extensive analysis of the concepts of existence (*wujūd*) and essence (*māhiyya*) and explores how these concepts allow him to approach the question of causality from both physical and metaphysical perspectives to synthesize Aristotelian and Neoplatonic currents. My conviction is that Ibn Sīnā ultimately introduced a participatory theory of causality with a strong presence of Aristotelian elements that affirms freedom both in the created order and in the First.

Chapter 3 introduces Ghazālī's and Rāzī's responses to Ibn Sīnā's theological and cosmological challenges to the occasionalist worldview. Ghazālī's response is heavily influenced by Ashʿarite theology's emphasis on the divine will and freedom. In this discussion, Ghazālī harkens back to the earlier Ashʿarite tradition, offers novel applications of old arguments, and raises important challenges to Ibn Sīnā. Rāzī formulates a list of arguments for the defense of Ashʿarite cosmology based on a discrete and atomistic model of the universe. Rāzī's atomistic arguments can be seen as a novel development in the occasionalist tradition. Rāzī's use of Euclidian geometry for and against atomism also led to emergence of an occasionalist philosophy of science marked by pragmatic and skeptic attitude toward dominant scientific models.

Chapter 4 examines Ibn Rushd's take on causality. Ghazālī's challenges to Ibn Sīnā prompted Ibn Rushd to make several modifications to Ibn Sīnā's synthesis. It was this conviction that led to certain divergences between Ibn Rushd's and Ibn Sīnā's thought. In this chapter, it will be argued that Ibn Rushd's theory of causality comes very close to Neoplatonistic participatory accounts, despite his strong Aristotelian tendencies.

Chapter 5 considers Suhrawardī's account of causality and the way he establishes freedom in accordance with that account. I contend that Suhrawardī suggests a participatory account of causality and freedom in which causal efficacy of entities is established through participation in divine causality. This account follows from Suhrawardī's continuous-cum-gradational ontology, the salient features of which will also be examined in the chapter.

Chapter 6 outlines Ibn ʿArabī's relational, processual, and gradational metaphysics and its relationship to the question of causality. The chapter argues that, from the perspective of the dominant tendencies of Sufi metaphysics, causality describes the regularity and predictability of the related societies of theophanies. The chapter also examines how Ibn ʿArabī appropriates certain occasionalist elements within his participatory account of causality. It then explains his account of freedom in accordance with his understanding of *wujūd* and the fixed archetypes.

Chapter 7 examines later developments in Sufi metaphysics regarding the question of causality and freedom. It focuses on the two influential followers of Ibn ʿArabī: Qūnawī and Qayṣarī. The chapter looks more specifically at how both Qūnawī and Qayṣarī reevaluated certain ideas attributed to the Philosophers and Ashʿarites in light of the central concepts of their metaphysics – existence and essence.

Chapter 8 focuses on the thought of Jurjānī to understand later developments in the occasionalist tradition. Jurjānī was one of the most important Ashʿarite theologians, who transformed occasionalism from a theory of causality into the central axis of all theological thinking. The notion of possibility made central by Ashʿarite occasionalism became the modus operandi for thinking about questions from prophetology and eschatology to theodicy and free will. More importantly, Jurjānī develops a critical philosophy of science to appropriate and criticize Aristotelian-Ptolemaic-Avicennian natural philosophy/sciences. An examination of this attempt reveals the complex relationship of Ashʿarite occasionalism with medieval natural philosophy and sciences.

Chapter 9 examines Mullā Ṣadrā's account of causality and freedom. It is argued that Ṣadrā's rich metaphysical treatment of the concept of existence establishes causal efficacy and freedom of entities through the expansion of, and participation in, existence. The chapter also includes a discussion of the significance of the concept of essence in Ṣadrā's metaphysics and how this concept is central to his notion of freedom in the created order.

Chapter 10 focuses on a contemporary approach to causality. Here, I offer a detailed survey of Said Nursi's account of causality. Nursi's neo-occasionalism makes original contributions to Ashʿarite occasionalist metaphysics of causation while integrating it with Ibn 'Arabī's theory of Divine Self-Disclosure. As such, his theory of causality suggests an interesting meeting point of *kalām* and Sufi metaphysics. He also defends and emphasizes the idea of disproportionality of cause and effect in an unprecedented way in the history of Islamic occasionalism. In this chapter, I will also analyze Nursi's treatment of free will and theodicy.

Chapter 11 steps back from the specifics of this discussion and investigates the strengths and weaknesses of the various proposed theories of causality in the face of certain contemporary philosophical challenges. As a case study, I look at a central issue in contemporary discussions of religion and science: the reconciliation of religious claims about divine causation with scientific explanations that depart from the premise that the world is a causally closed system. Here, I first provide a brief overview of the important controversies in the discussion of religion and science that are relevant to this topic. I then discuss whether Muslim accounts of causality can resolve certain challenges.

The Conclusion includes my analysis of some of the salient features of the occasionalist and participatory accounts of causation. It summarizes both the continuities and discontinuities identified in the preceding chapters. It also suggests that the participatory approach to causality presents another strong current in the Islamic intellectual tradition, alongside with the occasionalist tradition, with its distinct characteristics and advantages.

1

Causality in the Early Period

Mu'tazilites and the Birth of Ash'arite Occasionalism

This chapter focuses on early Mu'tazilite and Ash'arite theologians. It examines the birth and development of Ash'arite occasionalism as a response to the Mu'tazilite theological project, which aims to preserve the intelligibility of the world and God and, to this end, is ready to accept the idea of *necessity* in the world and, even, in God. The modus operandi of the Ash'arite theological project in this context remains to preserve the divine will and freedom. This, then, leads to construction of what I call a theology of *possibility*. It is within the larger context of this debate that occasionalist theory of causality emerges as the cornerstone of Ash'arite theology of possibility.

There is a very close relationship between the Ash'arite doctrines of the divine attributes and of causality. This school's understanding of the divine attributes, in particular will, power, and knowledge, and their relationship to God, informs its theory of the divine and creaturely agency and leads to a theory of causality in which the accentuation of the divine will becomes the most distinctive feature. Therefore, I start my investigation by examining early Ash'arite and Mu'tazilite discussions about the relationship of the divine attributes to God. I then show how these discussions led to the emergence of Ash'arite occasionalism. Finally, I explore how the occasionalist perspective provided the basis for Ash'arite convictions on other important cosmological and theological discussions.[1]

[1] Abū al-Ḥasan al-Ash'arī (873–935) was the founder of the Ash'arite school of theology. As a former Mu'tazilite, Ash'arī, as George Makdisi writes, "brings along with him his rationalist weapons and places them in the service of traditionalism." His followers then

1.1 THE ISSUE OF THE DIVINE ATTRIBUTES

What is the nature of the relationship between God and the world? This is the fundamental question for any religion due to its implications for one's individual and communal religious experience. Early Muslim engagement with this question arose out of disputes over the nature of the Qur'an. If the Qur'an is the verbatim word of God, then how can the uncreated word of God become part of the created order? This vexing question has prompted uneasy meditations on the nature of the Qur'an.

Mu'tazilites, who traditionally showed a more rationalistic bent, concluded that the Qur'an was created (*makhlūq*). For them, the Qur'an can be either created or uncreated. If it is uncreated, then it should be coeternal with God. However, this coeternality leads to the problem of "multiplicity of eternals" (*ta'addud al-qudamā'*), which is unacceptable because it undermines the oneness of God (*tawḥīd*), for there cannot be more than one eternal being. Thus, the Qur'an must be created.

A question arises here: If there cannot be an eternal thing alongside God, then what is the status of the divine attributes, which are eternally predicated on God? For Mu'tazilites, the divine attributes cannot be thought of as constituting or supporting the divine essence, which is beyond any type of multiplicity or complementarity. To save God from multiplicity or complementarity with coeternal attributes, Mu'tazilites reduced the attributes to God's absolute and indivisible unity. Therefore, Wāsil ibn 'Aṭā' (d. 748) rejects the predication of the attributes of power (*qudra*), will (*irāda*), knowledge (*'ilm*), and life (*ḥayā*), in order to sidestep the issue of the "multiplicity of eternals." Abū al-Hudhayl al-'Allāf (d. 841 or 849), a later Mu'tazilite, thought that essence and attributes were identical. Mu'ammar ibn 'Abbad al-Sulamī (d. 842) refuted the idea that God has will and knowledge in the ordinary sense in order to preserve unity in God's essence. Similarly, Abū 'Ali al-Jubbā'ī (d. 915) asserted that God possesses knowledge that is identical with God's essence, not subsisting alongside it. In general, Mu'tazilites believed that God's attributes and God's essence are one and the same thing. They expressed this oneness by using such formulas as *'ālim bi-'ilm huwa huwa* (knowing by a knowledge that is Him), *qādir bi-qudra hiya huwa*

"march on as the dominant, largest, school of theology, carrying the banner of orthodoxy, straight through the centuries and down to modern times": George Makdisi, "Ash'arī, the Ash'arites and Islamic Religious History I," *Studia Islamica*, 17 (1962): 39.

(powerful by a power that is Him), *ḥayy bi-ḥayā hiya huwa* (living by a life that is Him), and so on.[2]

Ashʿarite theologians reject the Muʿtazilite position because it allocates reason too much of a role in measuring what is applicable to God and what is not. The Ashʿarite attitude here can be traced to an earlier Hanbalite reaction to Mu'tazilites. For the Hanbalites, one must accept the existence of the attributes in the real sense on the grounds that the Qurʾanic utterances on the nature of divinity must be accepted "without (asking) how" (*bi-lā kayfa*). Goldziher, Wensinck, Halkin, Makdisi, Abrahamov, and Watt all believe that Aḥmad ibn Ḥanbal (780–855) was the first advocate of the principle of "without (asking) how."[3] Both Joseph Schacht and Wesley Williams, however, draw our attention to the fact that this formula never appears in the creedal statements attributed to

[2] Abū al-Ḥasan al-Ashʿarī, *Maqālāt al-Islamiyyīn wa Ikhtilāf al-Muṣallīn*, ed. Helmut Ritter (Wiesbaden: Franz Steiner Verlag, 1963/1382), 165–174, 484, 497; Baghdādī, *al-Farq bayn al-Firaq*, ed. M. Zahid al-Kawthari (Cairo: Maktab Nashr al-Thaqafah al-Islamiyya, 1948), 76; Qāḍī ʿAbduljabbār, *Sharḥ al-Uṣūl al-Khamsa*, ed. Abd al-Karim Uthman (Cairo: Maktabat Wahbah, 1965), 183; Shahrastānī, *al-Milal wa-l-Niḥal*, ed. Muhammad Sayyid Kilani (Cairo: Mustafa al-Babi al-Halabi, 1961), I, 44–46, 49–50; Shahrastānī, *Nihāyat al-Iqdām*, ed. Alfred Guillaume (London: Oxford University Press, 1934), 200–201, 239; Nasafī, *Tabṣirat al-Adilla*, ed. Claude Salame (Damascus: Institut Français de Damas, 1990–1993), I, 189, 200. Ibn al-Murtaẓā adds that Kharajites and Shiʿites also believed in this. See Ibn al-Murtaẓā, *al-Munya wa-l-Amal*, ed. Isamuddīn ibn Muhammad Ali (Alexandria: Dar al-Maʿrifa al-Jamiyya, 1985), 109–112. Cited in Osman Demir, *Kelamda Nedensellik:* Ilk Dönem Kelamcılarında Tabiat ve İnsan (İstanbul: TC Kültür ve Turizm Bakanlığı, 2015), 42. Shiʿite theology agrees with the Muʿtazilite position in that not only *qidam*, *baqāʾ*, *waḥda*, etc. but also positive qualities such as life, power, will, and knowledge are identical to the divine Self. See, for example, Muzaffar, *Aqāʾid al-Imāmiyya*, translated into Turkish by Abdulbaki Gölpınarlı (İstanbul: Zaman Yayınları, 1978), 28–30. Also in Fārābī, *al-Madīna al-Fāḍila*, ed. Albert Nasri Nadir (Beirut: Dar al-Mashriq, 1985), 47–48. For a good modern introduction to this debate, see Nader al-Bizri, "God: Essence and Attributes," in *The Cambridge Companion to Classical Islamic Theology*, ed. Tim Winter (Cambridge, UK: Cambridge University Press, 2008), 121–140; Demir, *Kelamda Nedensellik*, 39–41.

[3] Ignaz Goldziher, *The Zahiris: Their Doctrine and Their History*, trans. Wolfgang Behn (Leiden: E. J. Brill, 1971), 125; A. J. Wensinck, *The Muslim Creed* (1932; repr., New Delhi: Oriental Books Reprint Corporation, 1979), 86; A. S. Halkin, "The Hashwiyya," *Journal of the American Oriental Society*, 54 (1934): 15; George Makdisi, *Ibn ʿAqil: Religion and Culture in Classical Islam* (Edinburgh: Edinburgh University Press, 1997), 103, 108; Binyamin Abrahamov, "The *Bi-lā kayfa* Doctrine and Its Foundations in Islamic Theology," *Arabica*, 42 (1995): 366; W. Montgomery Watt, "Some Muslim Discussions of Anthropomorphism," in his *Early Islam* (Edinburgh: Edinburgh University Press, 1990), 88; W. Montgomery Watt, *Islamic Creeds: A Selection* (Edinburgh: Edinburgh University Press, 1994), 16; R. M. Frank, "Elements in the Development of the Teaching of Al-Ashʿari," *Le Museon*, 104 (1991): 155 ff.

Ibn Ḥanbal.[4] Regardless of whether this formula can be attributed to Ibn Ḥanbal, *bi-lā kayfa* became a tool for the Hanbalites to repudiate questions on the nature of the Qur'an and the figurative interpretation of Qur'anic anthropomorphism (*ta'wīl*). For the Hanbalites, the anthropomorphic verses must be taken literally, and the Qur'an must be accepted as uncreated, "without asking how."

Ash'arites differ from the Hanbalite position in that, while acknowledging the limits of rational inquiry, they still proceed to elucidate the relationship of the divine attributes and God. Ash'arites argue against the Mu'tazilite theological position on the createdness of the Qur'an and concede that, although the linguistic structure – with its grammar, letters, and logic – of the Qur'anic revelation is created, that does not entail that the Qur'an itself is created. The divine speech in and of itself is uncreated, but the divine speech as expressed in human language is created. It may thus be said that the Qur'an is created from one perspective and uncreated from another. According to Ash'arites, then, in the Qur'an, the finite and the infinite entangle in a way that defies human cognition.

When Ash'arites extend this logic to the dispute over other attributes, they conclude that the divine attributes are neither identical to nor separate from the divine essence. They are not marked by otherness (*ghayriyya*) or nonexistence.[5] Thus, later Ash'arite theologians, such as Abū Bakr Muḥammad al-Bāqillānī (940–1013) and 'Abd al-Malik al-Juwaynī (1028–1085), assert that these attributes are modes or states that can be categorized neither as created (*ḥādith*) nor as eternal, self-subsisting realities (*qadīm*). Nor can they be qualified with existence or nonexistence.

This understanding of the attributes is sometimes called the Ash'arite theory of *aḥwāl*. The foremost proponents of this theory among Ash'arites appear to have been Bāqillānī and Juwaynī, who claim that there can be certain metaphysical entities that depend on their substrates but that

[4] Joseph Schacht, "New Sources for the History of Muhammadan Theology," *Studia Islamica*, 1 (1953): 34. See also Joseph Schacht, "Theology and Law in Islam," in *Theology and Law in Islam*, ed. G. E. von Grunebaum (Wiesbaden: Otto Harrassowitz, 1971), 11. Wesley Williams, "Aspects of the Creed of Imam Ahmad ibn Hanbal: A Study of Anthropomorphism in Early Islamic Discourse," *International Journal of Middle East Studies*, 34 (2002): 448–449.

[5] Ash'arī, *Kitāb al-Luma'*, ed. Hammuda Ghuraba (Cairo: Mattba'at Misr Sharikah Musahimah Misriyah, 1955), 28–31. The other important Sunni traditional theological school, Maturidism, also concedes this point. Māturīdī asserts that the divine attributes are neither Him nor other than Him and they are coeternal with God (*mawṣūf bi-jamī' ṣifātihi fi-l-azal*). See Abū Manṣūr al-Māturīdī, *Sharḥ al-Fiqh al-Akbar* (Hyderabad: Dairat al-Ma'arif al-Uthmaniyya, 1946), 18–19.

cannot be identified with their substrates. These entities can be categorized as neither existent nor nonexistent. The relationship of the divine attributes to the divine essence appears to be imagined in a similar way by Ashʿarites. The divine attributes cannot exist alongside the divine essence as independent entities; such a condition would violate the divine unity. Nor can they be identified with the divine essence, as Muʿtazilites argue. So, the divine attributes depend on the divine essence for their existence, but still can be imagined as metaphysically distinct entities.[6] God is preeternally qualified with the attributes predicated on God in the Qurʾan and in the prophetic traditions, for the reverse would entail deficiency on God's part.[7]

To conclude, Muʿtazilite and Ashʿarite theologians differ in how they perceive the relationship between the divine essence and attributes. Muʿtazilites reject the notion that God's attributes can be differentiated from the divine essence. Ashʿarites hold that the divine attributes have a distinct status from the divine essence, even as they are dependent on it. Hence, in contrast to Muʿtazilites, who say that "knowing by a knowledge that is Him" or "powerful by a power that is Him," Ashʿarites would say, "God has a knowledge by which He knows," or "God has a power by which He is powerful."

Now, how might these conclusions influence Ashʿarite thinking about causality? It will be argued that the idea of the separability of the divine attributes from the divine essence leads to a distinct view of divine action and causality in the world. The moment one accepts, as Ashʿarites do, that the divine attributes are not identical with the divine essence, the attributes become the means through which God relates to the created order. This is why Ashʿarites incorporate the divine attributes, especially

[6] Bāqillānī, *Kitāb al-Tamhīd*, ed. Imaduddin Ahmad Haydar (Beirut: Muassasa al-Kutub al-Thakafiyya, 1987/1407), 228–229. Juwaynī, *Kitāb al-Irshād*, ed. Asad Tamimi (Beirut: Muassasa al-Kutub al-Thakafiyya, 1985/1405), 92–94, 629. For more on the theory of *aḥwāl*, see Richard M. Frank, "al-Aḥkām in Classical Ashʿarite Teaching," in *De Zenon d'Élée à Poincaré. Recueil d'études en hommage à Roshdi Rashed*, ed. R. Morelon and A. Hasnawi (Louvain: Éditions Peeters, 2004), 771, n. 48; Richard M. Frank, *Beings and their Attributes: The Teaching of the Basrian School of the Muʿtazila in the Classical Period* (Albany, NY: State University of New York Press, 1978); Richard M. Frank, "The Ashʿarite Ontology I: Primary Entities," *Arabic Sciences and Philosophy*, 9 (1999): 163–231; Ahmed Alami, *L'ontologie modale: Étude de la théorie des modes d'Abū Hāshim al-Jubbāʾī* (Paris: Vrin, 2001). For application of the theory in the construction of Ashʿarite atomistic cosmology, see Fedor Benevich, "The Classical Ashʿarite Theory of *Aḥwāl*: Juwaynī and His Opponents," *Journal of Islamic Studies*, 2.2 (2016): 136–175.

[7] Ashʿarī, *al-Lumaʿ*, 24–6.

the divine knowledge, will, and power, into their accounts of divine creative action.[8]

Thus, the divine knowledge is the most comprehensive of God's attributes.[9] It relates to everything that is necessary, possible, and impossible. However, by itself, the divine knowledge is not enough to explain the act of creation. God knows everything but does not create everything that He knows. Some possibilities are created and some are not. It is here that one needs another attribute to differentiate between the possibilities that are created and those that are not created. This additional attribute is the divine will. The function of the divine will is to give preponderance (*takhṣīṣ* or *tarjīh*) to some possibilities. This explains why some "knowns" are created and some are not. The divine will, however, cannot give existence. This is the function of the divine power, which brings possibilities into existence that are known by the divine knowledge and willed by the divine will.[10] In this sense, the divine power is closest of all attributes to the created order. As Ash'arī puts it, "God creates by His power, directs them by His wish, compels them by His strength."[11] The God of Ash'arites acts in the world through these attributes. The divine knowledge knows all possibilities and impossibilities, the divine will gives preponderance to some possibilities, and the divine power creates these "willed" possibilities. These three attributes form the foundation of Ash'arite causal theory.

What is interesting here is that there really is not much difference between Ash'arite and Mu'tazilite positions in terms of the attributes of the divine knowledge and the divine power. Both positions hold that the divine knowledge is all comprehensive. The order and design in the world proves that the divine knowledge is manifested in all entities. God knows and creates everything with His knowledge. God knows all causes and the

8 Bāqillānī, *al-Tamhīd*, 53–56.

9 Ash'arī, *al-Ibāna 'an Uṣūl al-Diyāna*, ed. Abbas Sabbagh (Beirut: Dar al-Nafaais, 1994/1414), 107–111; Juwaynī, *Luma' al-Adilla*, ed. Fawqiya Husayn Mahmud (Cairo: al-Dar al-Misriyya, 1965/1385), 82. Maturidites agree with Ash'arites on this issue. See Māturīdī, *Kitāb al-Tawḥīd*, ed. Bekir Topaloğlu and Muhammad Aruci (ISAM, 2003), 71–72.

10 Ash'arī, *al-Luma'*, 18; Juwaynī, *al-'Aqīda al-Niẓāmiyya*, ed. Muhammad Zubaidi (Beirut: Dar Sabil al-Rashad, 2003/1424), 144; Juwaynī, *al-Irshād*, 62–63; Shahrastānī, *Nihāyat al-Iqdām*, 239.

11 Translated in Ash'arī, *The Elucidation from Islam's Foundation* (*Kitāb al-Ibāna 'an Uṣūl al-Diyāna*), trans. Walter C. Klein. American Oriental Series, vol. 19 (New York: Kraus Reprint Corporation, 1967), 43.

effects they will produce. Thus, the harmony and beauty of the natural order proves the divine knowledge.[12]

Nor is there much difference in terms of the attribute of the divine power. Both schools hold that God is all-powerful over all possibilities and has power over rest, colors, life, death, health, sickness, and all other accidents.[13] It is true that some Ashʿarite theologians sometimes criticize Muʿtazilites for arguing that God does not exert power over such impossibilities (*muḥāl*) as creating motion and rest at once in the same object.[14] However, the same idea can be found among major Ashʿarite theologians as well. Bāqillānī, for example, asserts that although God has power over all possibilities (*mumkināt*), logical contradictions are beyond the domain of possibilities.[15] Similarly, Juwaynī argues that God is powerful over possibilities but logical contradictions are not objects of power (*maqdūrāt*), such as creation of a thing which is neither accident nor substance.[16] Later, Ghazālī asserts that "the impossible is not within the power [of being enacted]. The impossible consists in affirming a thing conjointly with denying it, affirming the more specific while denying the more general, or affirming two things while negating one [of them]. What does not reduce to this is not impossible, and what is not impossible is within [divine] power."[17] That is to say, the divine omnipotence is limited by the law of contradiction. God cannot make yes and no true at the same

[12] For Ashʿarite and Muʿtazilite positions on this attribute, see Ashʿarī, *al-Lumaʿ*, 24; Juwaynī, *al-Irshād*, 33; Qāḍī ʿAbduljabbār, *al-Mughnī*, V, 219–228; Shahrastānī, *Nihāyat al-Iqdām*, 68–69; Baghdādī, *Uṣūl al-Dīn* (Istanbul: Dar al-Funun Ilahiyat Fakültesi, 1928), 5.

[13] Ashʿarī, *Maqālāt*, 199.

[14] Ibn Ḥazm, *al-Faṣl fi-l-Milal wa-l-Ahwāʾ wa-l-Niḥal*, ed. Ibrahim Nasr and Abdurrahman Umayra (Riyadh-Jeddah, 1982/1402), IV, 192–193; Shahrastānī, *al-Milal*, I, 54.

[15] Bāqillānī, *Kitāb al-Bayān*, ed. Richard McCarthy (Beirut: al-Maktabat al-Sharqiyya, 1958), 10–12.

[16] Juwaynī, *al-Shāmil fi Uṣūl al-Dīn*, ed. A. S. al-Nashshar, Faysal Budayr Awn, and Suhayr Muhammad Mukhtar (Alexandria: Manshaʾat al-Maʿarif, 1969), 141, 154. For a good analysis of Juwaynī's account, see Mehmet Dag, *Cuveyni'nin Alem ve Allah Görüşü*, Ph. D. thesis (Ankara, 1976), 143–144.

[17] Ghazālī, *The Incoherence of the Philosophers* (*Tahāfut al-Falāsifa*), a Parallel English–Arabic Text. ed. and trans. M. E. Marmura (Provo, UT: Brigham Young University Press, 1997), 179. See also "It is the cardinal principle of omnipotence that it stands in relation with all objects of power. By the objects of power, I mean all *possible* things" (Ghazālī, *al-Iqtiṣād fi-l-ʿItiqād*, ed. Ibrahim Cubukcu and Huseyin Atay (Ankara: A. U. Ilahiyat Fakultesi Yayinlari, 1962), 93). Moreover, the concept of a "perfect world" is a logical absurdity. Thus, Ghazālī's famous uttering, "there is nothing in possibility anything more wonderful than what is (*laysa fi-l-imkān abdā min mā kāna*)." See, for example, *Iḥyāʾ ʿUlūm al-Dīn* (Cairo, 1916), 4:223 lines 6–7; and *Kitāb al-Arbaʿīn* (Cairo, 1916), 270.

time, nor can He create a second God. These propositions are logical absurdities.

There is, however, a persistent tension concerning the attribute of the divine will. The questions of the divine knowledge and the divine power thus appear to be easily resolved, but the issue of the divine will is less straightforward. Indeed, what is really at stake between the Ash'arite and Mu'tazilite schools is the issue of the divine will and, thus, divine freedom. Discussions on this attribute and its implications appear to have started in the eighth century and focused on the moral perfection of God. Mu'tazilite theologians such as Qāḍī 'Abduljabbār argue that it is necessary for God to do the optimum (*aṣlāḥ*) to be morally perfect. God does not and cannot choose to be evil or ugly (*qabīḥ*). To preserve justice (*'adl*), God necessarily chooses and relates to good (*ḥusn*).[18] This approach, for Mu'tazilites, preserves the divine intelligibility. For Ash'arites, however, it undermines divine will and freedom. In their view, one should not search for a cause, purpose, or even wisdom in God's acts. God is absolutely free, and does as He wishes. Moreover, the Qur'an talks about divine will extensively and states that everything happens in accordance with God's will and that God does as He wishes (*fa'ālun limā yurīd*).[19] From another perspective, God does not owe anything to the created order and hence cannot be held responsible toward anything or anyone. Any type of moral necessity implies limits on the divine will, freedom, and sovereignty.[20]

18 Qāḍī 'Abduljabbār, *al-Mughnī*, IV, 313 and V, 177; Qāḍī 'Abduljabbār, *Sharḥ*, 131–132, 301, 510–512; Shahrastānī, *Nihāyat al-Iqdām*, 397–398.

19 Qur'an 17/19, 18/29, 36/82, 33/17, 2/253, 13/11, 33/17, 6/125. The Qur'an, however, also appears to emphasize justice and wisdom as a basis of the conditionality of divine acts. See, for example, 7/178, 20/81–82, 14/7. For discussions on these and similar verses, see, for example, Ibn Fūrak, *Mujarrad*, ed. Daniel Gimaret (Beirut: Dar al-Mashriq, 1987), 71–73. Also see Ash'arī, *Maqālāt*, 515; Māturīdī, *Kitāb al-Tawḥīd*, 70–71; Juwaynī, *al-Irshād*, 63.

20 Ash'arī, *al-Luma'*, 37; Bāqillānī, *al-Inṣāf*, ed. Imaduddin Ahmad Haydar (Beirut: Alam al-Kutub, 1986/1407), 52–55; Juwaynī, *al-'Aqīda al-Niẓāmiyya*, 175; Ibn Fūrak, *Mujarrad*, 70; Shahrastānī, *Nihāyat al-Iqdām*, 397–398. 'Abd al-Raḥīm ibn Muḥammad al-Khayyāṭ (d. 913/300), argues that Naẓẓām's and other Mu'tazilite theologians' views on the divine necessity and natures do not nullify the divine perfection and freedom in *Kitāb al-Intiṣār wa-l-Rad 'alā Ibn al-Rāwandī al-Mulḥid*, ed. H. S. Nyberg and A. Nader (Beirut: al-Matbaa al-Katolikiyya, 1957), 39; Cf. Osman Demir, *Kelamda Nedensellik*, 50. For more recent evaluations of this issue, see, for example, H. M. Alousi, *The Problem of Creation in Islamic Thought* (Cambridge: The National Printing, 1968), 228–230; Robert Brunschvig, "Mu'tazilisme et optimum," *Studia Islamica* 39 (1974): 5–23; Richard M. Frank, "Reason and Revealed Law: A Sample of Parallels and Divergences in Kalam and Falsafa," in *Recherches d'Islamologie. Recuil d'articles offert a Georges C. Anawati et Louis Gardet par leurs*

Indeed, the big question is whether God acts volitionally (*fāʿil al-mukhtār*) or necessarily (*fāʿil al-matbūʿ*).[21] Muʿtazilite theologians are open to the idea that God sometimes acts "necessarily." For Ashʿarites, this is unacceptable, for it limits the divine will and freedom, which is not bound by the judgements of human intellect.[22] The issues of the divine will and freedom inform Ashʿarite accounts on almost all issues from natural philosophy to prophetology and eschatology, as will be discussed more extensively later in this and following chapters. Furthermore, it is this attribute that has become the distinctive feature of the Ashʿarite theory of causality.

1.2 ASHʿARITE OCCASIONALISM

Muʿtazilite theologians – with the possible notable exception of Jubbāʾī – believe in a necessary relationship between cause and effect.[23] When cotton and fire are brought together, a combustion necessarily occurs. For every object has a "nature" (*ṭabʿ*) and necessarily acts in accordance with it. When a stone is cast into the sky, it necessarily falls back down.[24] The concept of nature/s (*ṭabīʿa, ṭabʿ, ṭibāʿ*) is used by many Muʿtazilite theologians. For Ibrāhīm ibn Sayyār al-Naẓẓām (775–845), God places natures in entities, which then act in accordance with their nature without being determined by it. Abū ʿUthman al-Jāḥiẓ (d. 869) agrees that things such as fire and water have specific natures that do not change.[25] In his "Book of Animals" (*Kitāb al-Ḥayawān*), Jāḥiẓ argues that animate and inanimate entities have intrinsic qualities, which he calls "nature" (*ṭabīʿa*). Although Jāḥiẓ accepts nature as a necessitating principle, he still holds that humans have free will not dictated by their nature. Other

collegues et amis (Louvain: Peeters, 1977), 124ff; Daniel Gimaret, *La doctrine d'al-Ashʿarī* (Paris: Les Editions du Cerf, 1990), 433–435.

21 Alousi, *The Problem of Creation*, 225, 232.

22 There are reconciliatory attempts as well. Maturidites, for example, diverges from Ashʿarite school on this issue. God's acts do not *have* to be full of wisdom, but they are. God is not absurd and creates things in a just and wise fashion. Wisdom (*ḥikma*) does not imply any type of necessity or need. This formulation, however, comes quite close to the Muʿtazilite doctrine of the optimum. The divine justice, wisdom, and generosity imply that God always acts in a wise, just, and generous manner. There is no necessity in divine acts but there is also no absurdity. As the Qurʾan puts it, "we did not create the heaven and earth and between them in play," 21:16. Māturīdī, *Kitāb al-Tawḥīd*, 151–152.

23 Ashʿarī, *Maqālāt*, 412; Juwaynī, *al-Shāmil*, 506; Ashʿarī, *Maqālāt*, 412–413.

24 Ashʿarī, *Maqālāt*, 314.

25 Baghdādī, *Uṣūl al-Dīn*, 336; Shahrastānī, *al-Milal*, I, 75; Khayyāṭ, *al-Intiṣār*, 70.

entities act necessarily in accordance with their natures.[26] Barley will never grow from a wheat seed, because wheat has a specific nature that prevents it from becoming barley. A heavy object cannot levitate in the air without any support. God does not create things in contradiction to their natures or without any cause-reason. To say the opposite is to defend absurdity in the divine acts. Nature and causality is then the principle of intelligibility.

Sometimes the concept of *maʿnā* is used in place of nature. It is mostly used in the thought of Muʿammar ibn ʿAbbād al-Sulamī (d. 835). As Richard M. Frank glosses it, the term *maʿnā* means an "intrinsic causal determinant." These intrinsic causal determinants make a thing what it is. They (*maʿānī*) are the "determinants of the thing's being-so." If one of two bodies is in motion and the other is at rest, this is due to their meaning.[27] In this sense, it is equivalent of the concept of nature or cause. Entities act under the influence of their meanings, causal determinants, or natures. Khayyāṭ writes concerning Muʿammar that "when he observed two bodies at rest, the one next to the other, and observed that one had moved and not the other Muʿammar asserted that the former must have some causal determinant (*maʿnā*) that came to inhere in it and not the latter."[28]

Other Muʿtazilite theories of physical action are also based on the conviction that entities have necessitating natures. Naẓẓām, for example, proposes that things manifest their nature in their life-process by moving

[26] Jāḥiẓ, *Kitāb al-Ḥayawān*, ed. Abdussalam Muhammad Harun (Beirut: Dar Ihya al-Turasi al-Arabi, 1969), I, 149; III, 372, 375; V, 60, 89–90. Cf. Osman Demir, *Kelamda Nedensellik*, 112.

[27] Richard M. Frank. "*Al-Maʿnā*: Some Reflections on the Technical Meanings of the Term in the Kalam and Its Use in the Physics of Muʿammar," *Journal of the American Oriental Society*, 87.3 (Jul.–Sep. 1967): 250, 253. In this article Frank attempts to describe the technical significance of the term *maʿnā* for Muʿammar and concludes that "the causal determinants (*maʿānī*) exist as actually determinant of the effect." In this sense, there is a necessary relationship between *maʿānī* and effects – see p. 255. See also Harry Austryn Wolfson, *The Philosophy of Kalam* (Cambridge, MA: Harvard University Press, 1976), 733–739 and "Muʿammar's Theory of *Maʿnā*," in *Arabic and Islamic Studies in the Honor of Hamilton A.R. Gibb*, ed. George Makdisi (Leiden: 1965), 673–688.

[28] Khayyāṭ, *al-Intiṣār*, 46. Ashʿarī similarly writes that for Muʿammar when a body moves it does so "on account of causal determinant (*maʿnā*) without which it would have no more reason to be moved." *Maqālāt*, 372. Both passages were translated in Richard M. Frank, "*Al-Maʿnā*: Some Reflections on the Technical Meanings of the Term," 253–254.

from potentiality to actuality.[29] This view is also known as the theory of latency (*kumūn*), and this process of actualization of potentialities is sometimes called manifestation or externalization (*ẓuhūr*).[30] This Muʿtazilite theory starts from the idea of nature and explains creation as the gradual unfolding of these natures. The theory also suggests that there is a certain intelligibility of causal relations. Understanding nature renders intelligible what comes out of it.[31]

Despite this strong tendency among Muʿtazilites, Ashʿarites reject the idea of natures due to its necessitarian implications. Ibn Fūrak writes that Ashʿarī had a book called *al-Idrāq* in which he argues that God can prevent fire from appearing even if we bring fire and cotton together. It is not their natures but God who causes burning.[32] Bāqillānī presents one the clearest expression of this theory when he criticizes Muʿtazilites for being "people of nature" (*ahl al-ṭibaʿ*).

> People argue that they know that there is a *necessary* relationship between fire and burning or drinking (alcohol) and drunkenness. This, however, is great ignorance. For all we observe here is that when someone drinks alcohol or an object is brought near fire, there will be some changes. That person will be drunk and that object will burn. However, we do not observe who exactly is the agent here. This problem can be understood through meticulous research and careful thinking. We are of the opinion that this is the act of an Eternal Being . . . Some also argue that it cannot be known whether this relationship between drinking and drunkenness or fire and burning is due to the *natures* of entities or to an external agent.[33]

Or, as Ibn Fūrāk asserts, God creates "without a reason (*sabab*) that makes it necessary or a cause (*ʿilla*) that generates it."[34]

The rejection of natures invites certain questions. If regularity in the world is not caused by the nature of entities, then how do we explain it? Here, Muslim occasionalists introduce the notion of "habit" (*ʿāda*). The notion describes divine acts that occur consistently and are repeated regularly. According to the theory of habit, God acts on freely chosen,

[29] Jāḥiẓ, *Kitāb al-Ḥayawān*, V, 1–13, 15, 16, 18, 21–23; Baghdādī, *al-Farq*, 86–87 Cf. Osman Demir, *Kelamda Nedensellik*, 165–169.

[30] Khayyāṭ, *al-Intiṣār*, 44.

[31] See, for example, Qāḍī ʿAbduljabbār, *al-Muḥīṭ bi-l-Taklīf*, ed. Umar Sayyid Azmi and Ahmad Fu'ad Ahwani (Cairo: al-Sharika al-Misriyya, n.d.), 352, 389–391, 395; Qāḍī ʿAbdaljabbār, *al-Mughnī*, IX, 161.

[32] Ibn Fūrak, *Mujarrad*, 271. As we will see in Chapter 3, Ghazālī borrows this example.

[33] Bāqillānī, *al-Tamhīd*, 62. Emphasis mine.

[34] Ibn Fūrak, *Mujarrad*, 131, 7–8. Also cited in Frank Griffel, *Al-Ghazālī's Philosophical Theology: An Introduction to the Study of his Life and Thought* (New York: Oxford University Press, 2009), 127.

self-imposed habitual paths.[35] The regularity and predictability of natural phenomena are due to the habits of God, not to the natures of things. The concept of habit allows Ash'arite theologians to affirm the regularity of the world.

God, however, is not bound even by these self-imposed habits. This would be contrary to God's absolute freedom. In a world where the notion of necessity is somehow applicable to God, the divine freedom is undermined. Therefore, in some cases, the habits of God could change.[36] As Ibn Fūrak explains, "God creates satiety after eating and drinking. And He creates thirst and hunger in the absence of food and drink ... However, if He wishes, he could do it the other way. This would be a nullification of the habits (*naqḍ al-'āda*)."[37] The same logic applies to mental causation. Ash'arītes do not see a necessary relationship between contemplation (*naẓar*) and knowledge (*'ilm*). God can create knowledge without contemplation. The relationship is one of proximity. God could also choose not to create knowledge despite the existence of contemplation. Contemplation does not necessarily generate (*tawlīd*) knowledge. Thus, cognitive causal relations are also possible. God sustains this relationship due to His habit.[38] Everything – except some logical impossibilities – is possible with God's power.

The cause and effect relationship is thus one of possibility and not of necessity. Then, to explain the intrinsically *possible* nature of causal processes, Ash'arite occasionalism introduces some key concepts, such as conjunction (*iqtirān*) and proximity (*mujāwara*). For Bāqillāni, for example, cause and effect are coupled and happen regularly in close proximity. This creates a certain disposition in mind that they will always

[35] Ibn Fūrak, *Mujarrad*, 131–132. The Qur'anic verses, "there is no change in God's creation" (30:30) or "there is no change in God's words" (10:64) are usually understood to be alluding to this.

[36] Ibid., 131–134, 176–177, 272; Bāqillānī, *al-Bayān*, 50; Juwaynī, *al-Irshād*, 61; Juwaynī, *al-Shāmil*, 114; Qāḍī 'Abduljabbār, *al-Mughnī*, XV, 202–3. See also Gimaret, *La doctrine d'al-Ash'ari*, 459–463; and Mohammad A. al-Jabrī, *The Formation of Arab Reason*, trans. Centre for Arab Unity Studies (Hamra: The Centre for Arab Unity Studies, 2011), 144–146.

[37] Ibn Fūrak, *Mujarrad*, 134.

[38] See for example, Ibn Fūrak, *Mujarrad*, 133; Juwaynī, *al-Irshād*, 27–28, Juwaynī, *al-Shāmil*, 110–115. Later Naṣīr al-Dīn Ṭūsī also writes that Ash'arī and his followers propose a possible and habit-based relationship in mental events. God creates a habitual relation between thinking and knowledge. However, He may also not create it. Ṭūsī, *Talkhīṣ al-Muḥaṣṣal*, ed. Abdullah Nurani (Muassasa-i Motalaat-i İslami Daneshgah-i McGill Şu'ba-i Tahran, 1980), 60.

do so.[39] Yet, this proximity does not imply necessity. There is only conjunction without necessary relation. Any type of necessity would undermine the divine will. For Juwaynī as well, the relationship between consecutive causal events must be perceived in terms of proximity and not of necessity. God creates cause and effect in close vicinity. Coupling cause and effect together is, again, a divine habit.[40]

Hence, the concepts of conjunction and proximity ground the idea that despite observed regularities in the world, causal relations are characterized by possibility rather than necessity. The natural processes are law-like but not strictly law governed. The intrinsic nature of the world-process is based on the notion of possibility. The regularity of natural processes is not necessary but only possible. Thus, such processes can be nullified. It is possible that a stone can levitate in the air, seeing can occur without light, satiety without food, burning without fire when God suspends his His habits.[41]

Prophetic miracles that violate the laws of nature are, in fact, manifestations of the possible nature of causal relations. It is possible that the divine habit is nullified to verify a prophet in a similar fashion to a king's unusual gesture to verify the authenticity of his messengers. As Ibn Maymūn (Maimonides) writes, "a king's habit is to ride a horse through the market place . . . but it is *possible* that he walks through."[42] This view of miracles differs from Muʿtazilite theory, which suggests a necessary relationship based on the notion of nature. At this juncture, Qāḍī ʿAbduljabbār (935–1025) raises an important objection to this view of miracles from the perspective of moral value and intelligibility of the divine actions. He accepts that a miracle can be perceived as a nullification of the divine habits. However, for a miracle to be a proof affirming the prophecy of a person, it needs to be created by a "just" and intelligible God. If, as Ashʿarite theologians argue, one accepts that God's will cannot be bound by the judgements of human intelligence and moral necessities, then how can one claim that these nullifications of habits, are, in fact, affirming a prophetic claim? If there are no moral criteria applicable to the divine actions, how can one attribute moral-teleological value to a miracle? It is inconsistent for Ashʿarites to present a miracle as a

39 Bāqillānī, *al-Bayān*, 50.

40 Juwaynī, *al-ʿAqīda al-Niẓāmiyya*, 219; Juwaynī, *al-Irshād*, 61.

41 Ibn Fūrak, *Mujarrad*, 133–134. For Bāqillānī, God never breaks His habits, accept for the support and safety of His messengers. See *al-Bayān*, 52–55.

42 Ibn Maymūn (Maimonides), *The Guide for the Perplexed* (Dalālat al-Ḥāʾirīn), trans. M. Friedlander, 2nd ed. (Skokie, IL: Varda Books, 2002), 128. Translation modified.

proof of something (e.g. prophethood) while removing intelligibility from divine actions.[43]

To conclude, Mu'tazilite theologians use such concepts as *ṭabī'a*, *tawlīd*, *i'timād*, *iḍtirār*, and *kumūn-ẓuhur* to suggest a theology and cosmology based on necessity and, thus, *intelligibility*. Ash'arites, due to the fundemental importance of the divine will and freedom for their theology, offer concepts like *imkān*, *jawāz*, *iqtirān*, *mujāwarat*, or *'āda* in a way that the notion of *possibility* becomes the cornerstone of theology and cosmology. The rejection of the concept of natures and necessity leads to a world view in which the modus operandi is the idea of *possibility* (*imkān* or *tajwīz*). The world is now an interplay of possible events. Ash'arite theory then proceeds to frame every important theological discussion in light of the notion of possibility.

1.3 THE DIVINE WILL, ATOMISM, AND COSMOLOGY

The idea of indivisible parts (*al-juz' alladhī lā yatajazza'* or *al-juz' alladhī lā yataqassam*) or atoms was first proposed by early Mu'tazilites. Atomistic concepts such as *jawhar al-wāhid*, *al-juz' alladhī lā yataqassam*, *al-juz' al-wāhid* appear quite early during the discussion of the divine attributes.[44]

Hudhayl argues that created beings must have limits and be composed of parts as opposed to an eternal and uncreated being. He extrapolates the existence of atoms from this idea. These atoms must be limited in number. If the divine attributes, such as knowledge,

[43] Qāḍī 'Abduljabbār, *Sharḥ*, 571. It must also be said that the idea of nature was not defended by Mu'tazilite theologians alone. Ibn Ḥazm also accepts natures and, thus, a necessary relationship in causality. He criticizes Ash'arite theologians for rejecting natures. Ibn Ḥazm holds that the concept of habit cannot explain regularity of natural processes in the world, for habit connotes a character trait that can be broken, but in nature there are no such breaks. Although Ibn Ḥazm argues for necessary relation in the world, he also emphasizes that God is beyond all causality and created the world without a cause (*'illa*). *al-Taqrīb li-Ḥadd al-Mantiq*, ed. Ihsan Abbas (Beirut: Dar al-Maktaba al-Hayat, 1959), 169. The opposite would make God obliged (*muḍtār*), a quality that goes against divine freedom and perfection. Ibn Ḥazm, *'Ilm al-Kalām*, ed. Ahmad Hijazi (Cairo: al-Maktaba al-Thakafiyya, 1989), 22. Cf., Osman Demir, *Kelamda Nedensellik*, 29. Interestingly, the founder of the other major Sunnite school of theology, Māturīdī, accepts the idea of natures. Māturīdī, however, appears to reject a necessary relationship between natures and acts. Things have natures but they do not have to act in accordance with their nature: *Kitāb al-Tawḥīd*, 354–355.

[44] Ash'arī, *Maqālāt*, 59, 568.

encompass everything, then the world should be limited.[45] Something infinite cannot be encompassed. Hence, the number of atoms must be finite for the world to be finite. Similarly, Ashʿarī thinks the number of atoms is not infinite. He concedes that such Qurʾanic verses as "and everything has been numbered by us" (36:12) suggest that the universe is composed of a limited number of discrete atoms and emptiness in which they move.[46] These atoms are not composed of parts, "nor is it possible to imagine their division."[47]

Later Ashʿarite theologians also offered more rational arguments to support this claim. One of them runs according to the following logic. The different sizes of objects are possible if entities are composed of indivisible substances (*jawhar al-fard*). If a body (*jism*) could be divided infinitely, then an ant's size should be equal to an elephant's size, for both ant and elephant would have an infinite number of parts. If both have an infinite number of parts, on what basis can they have different sizes? If both can contain an infinite number of parts, then their sizes should be equal. But this is obviously not true; an elephant is larger than an ant. Hence, objects must be composed of a limited number of indivisible parts.[48]

Almost all Ashʿarites agree that atoms are homogeneous (*mutajānis/mutamāthil*). For instance, Juwaynī writes:

> Atoms/substances *(jawāhir)*, in the view of the true believers [i.e. the Ashʿarites] *(ahl al-ḥaqq)* are homogeneous. All the Muʿtazilites [also] held this position. Naẓẓām disagreed with it, for he does not consider substances to be similar unless their accidents are similar.[49]

If these atoms are homogeneous, then, what differentiates atoms and entities from each other? The classical Ashʿarite response resorts to the concept of accidents (*aʿrāḍ*) to answer this question. The world is

[45] Alousi, *The Problem of Creation*, 273–277.

[46] Ashʿarī, "A Vindication of the Science of Kalam (*Risāla fī Istiḥsān al-Khawḍ fī ʿIlm al-Kalām*)," in *The Theology of Ashʿari*, ed. Richard J. McCarthy (Beirut: Imprimerie Catholique, 1953), 127; Ibn Fūrak, *Mujarrad*, 202–204, 208. A good summary of early discussions around the concept of atoms can be found in M. Şemsettin Günaltay, *Kelam Atomculuğu ve Kaynağı Sorunu*, ed. and noted by Irfan Bayın (Ankara: Fecr, 2008).

[47] Ibn Fūrak, *Mujarrad*, 202. Cited in Alnoor Dhanani, *The Physical Theory of Kalām: Atoms, Space, and Void in Basrian Muʿtazilī Cosmology* (Leiden: Brill, 1994), 136 fn. 126. See also *Mujarrad*, 203–204.

[48] For different versions of this argument please see Bāqillānī, *al-Tamhīd*, 37; Baghdādī, *Uṣūl al-Dīn*, 36; Juwaynī, *al-Shāmil*, 146; Ibn Ḥazm, *al-Faṣl*, V, 96.

[49] Juwaynī, *al-Shāmil*, 153–154. Cf. Dhanani, *The Physical Theory of Kalām*, 118, fn. 67. Also in Ibn Maymūn (Maimonides), *Dalālat al-Ḥāʾirīn*, 120.

composed of not only atoms and but also accidents.[50] Bodies are different from each other due to accidents that inhere in these homogenous atoms.[51] The atoms in themselves are homogeneous, "perfectly alike" and do not have any differentiating qualities. For if they did, they would have distinct "natures" necessitating their behavior.[52] This, however, must be rejected due to its necessitarian implications, as discussed earlier in this chapter. Accidents inhering in these atoms, therefore, are assigned solely by God's differentiating will. Atoms cannot have any feedback or any demand in this system because they do not have any intrinsic nature. Atoms are neutral loci of the divine activity. The differentiation of homogenous atoms occurs due solely to the divine will, which can differentiate without a reason. So, beings composed of homogeneous atoms have their differentiating properties due to accidents assigned purely by the divine will.

A similar accentuation of the divine will can be seen in the idea of the vacuum (*al-khalāʾ*) between atoms.[53] Formations and deformations of entities occur due to the activities of atoms. Atoms form bodies by coming together or by being side by side. But they do not interpenetrate (*tadākhul*) or encompass each other.[54] The reason for the rejection of interpenetration seems to be that atoms need to be in a state of proximity without directly interacting with each other, as the idea of interpenetration implies. As discussed above, the notion of proximity (*mujāwara*) is fundamental to the Ashʿarite theology of possibility to establish the idea that cause and effect are created side by side and occur together, but they are not inseparably attached to each other. If the relationship between atoms is one of proximity but not of interpenetration, then they can be separated. Thus, their causal relationship is to be thought of in terms of possibility, not of necessity. It is God who creates the relationship between cause and effect at the level of atoms.

50 Bāqillānī, *al-Tamhīd*, 37–38; Bāqillānī, *al-Inṣāf*, 27; Juwaynī, *al-Irshād*, 39; Juwaynī, *al-Shāmil*, 142; Juwaynī, *al-ʿAqīda al-Niẓāmiyya*, 129; Juwaynī, *al-Lumaʿ al-Adilla*, 77; Baghdādī, *al-Farq*, 197; Pazdawī, *Uṣūl al-Dīn*, ed. Hans Peter Lins (Cairo: Dar Ihya al-Kutub al-Arabiyya, 1963), 11; Ibn Maymūn (Maimonides), *Dalālat al-Ḥāʾirīn*, 120–121. Also see Richard M. Frank, "Bodies and Atoms: The Ashʿarite Analysis" in *Islamic Theology and Philosophy: Studies in Honor of George F. Hourani* (Albany, NY: State University of New York Press, 1984), 39–63.

51 Baghdādī, *Uṣūl al-Dīn*, 35; Juwaynī, *al-Shāmil*, 150, 167; Juwaynī, *al-Irshād*, 17.

52 Ibn Maymūn (Maimonides), *Dalālat al-Ḥāʾirīn*, 127, 129; Tahānawī, *Kashshāf*, II, 1302.

53 See, for example, Juwaynī, *al-Shāmil*, 508–509. Ibn Ḥazm rejects the idea of vacuum. Ibn Ḥazm, *al-Faṣl*, V, 70. Cf. Dhanani, *The Physical Theory of Kalam*, 6–14.

54 Juwaynī, *al-Shāmil*, 160–162.

This mode of thinking is also extended to the macrocosmic level. Juwaynī, for example, holds that celestial bodies, like planets and stars, could be in different places than they are now or could have different sizes than they have now. There has to be a preponderer and an assigner (*mukhaṣṣiṣ* or *murajjiḥ*) who wills and determines the location, size, and all the other properties of those celestial bodies.[55]

This atomistic cosmology thus makes the divine will the sole determining factor in both terrestrial and celestial domains. All entities and occurrings are results of God's will.[56] There is a need for a 'preponderer' at all levels. Homogeneous atoms can only be assigned different accidents through the uncaused act of the divine will. Their causal relationship is not necessary but possible. The observed differences in the created order, then, show the all-permeating and differentiating effect of the divine will.

1.4 CONSTANT RE-CREATION

In accordance with their theology of possibility, Ashʿarites also lean toward the idea of the constant re-creation of the world in order to keep the moments of the cosmic history discrete. The constant re-creation of the world anew at each moment negates the need for a causal glue between two consecutive events. The Ashʿarite world continuously pulsates between existence and nonexistence. The only thing that connects past, present, and future is the divine will and power. The relationship between two consecutive moments is, therefore, not necessary but possible.

Ḍirār ibn ʿAmr (d. 796) appears to have been the first Muslim thinker to assert the constant re-creation of the world based on the idea that accidents cannot subsist for two moments. Ḍirār holds that things are bundles of accidents.[57] There is no substance on which accidents inhere. If there is nothing but accidents, and if accidents cannot subsist by themselves for two consecutive moments, then the world must be created anew at each moment. The idea that "accidents do not subsist for two

[55] Shahrastānī, *Nihāyat al-Iqdām*, 13, 239–240; also see Juwaynī, *al-Irshād*, 63–65.

[56] Ashʿarī, *al-Lumaʿ*, 47; Ibn Furak, *Mujarrad*, 69–70; Bāqillānī, *al-Tamhīd*, 47–48; Bāqillānī, *al-Inṣāf*, 55; Juwaynī, *al-ʿAqīda al-Niẓāmiyya*, 175; Juwaynī, *al-Irshād*, 29; Baghdādī, *Uṣūl al-Dīn*, 102; Shahrastānī, *Nihayat al-Iqdām*, 249.

[57] Majid Fakhry, *Islamic Occasionalism* (London: George Allen & Unwin Ltd, 1958), 33; Dhanani, *The Physical Theory of Kalam*, 5.

consecutive moments" was accepted by most Mu'tazilites, with some notable exceptions such as Hishām ibn Ḥakem (d. 795) and Jāḥiẓ.[58]

Ash'arite theologians find the idea that "accidents do not subsist for two moments" quite useful for supporting their will-based cosmology. Ash'arite atoms do not subsist by themselves and are continuously created in time. God assigns the accident of "subsistence" (*baqā'*) to atoms to continue their existence. The divine command "continue to exist!" assigns the accident of duration and continuity to atoms. Both atoms and the accidents inhering in them are constantly re-created at each moment by the divine will and power.[59]

This idea also allows Ash'arites to assert that there is no necessitating essence in the world, and that there is also nothing unchanging.[60] Accidents are continuously created anew. Since substances cannot exist without accidents, annihilation of accidents implies annihilation of substances. God creates accidents and atoms similarly due to His habit, and thus there is also a continuity. In this case the world continuously requires an outside Sustainer.[61]

This also means that not only space but also time is atomized and consists of temporal fragments and vacuums. As dividing the space into discrete parts leads to atomism, dividing time into indivisible leaps leads to "atomism of time." The idea that time is not an uninterrupted process but is a multiplicity of discrete parts (*waqt*) or smaller leaps (*ṭafra*) appears to have first been suggested by Naẓẓām. For Naẓẓām, an object can go from point A to C without visiting point B.[62] These leaps are so

58 Sholomo Pines, *Mazhab al-Zarra*, trans. Muhammad Hadi Abu Rida (Cairo: Maktabat al-Nahdat al-Islamiyya, 1946), 27.

59 Ash'arī, *Maqālāt*, 359–360; Ibn Fūrak, *Mujarrad*, 205, 208, 237, 257; Bāqillānī, *al-Tamhīd*, 38–39; Juwaynī, *al-Irshād*, 41; Pazdawī, *Uṣūl al-Dīn*, 12. Also see D. Perler and U. Rudolph, *Occasionalismus: Theorien der Kausalität im arabisch-islamischen und im europäischen Denken* (Göttingen: Vandenhoeck & Ruprecht, 2000), 28–62; Gimaret, *La doctrine d'al-Ash'ari*, 43–130.

60 Muhammad Iqbal uses this aspect of Ash'arite atomism to create a dynamic view of the world and, thus, to encourage the notion of "change" in religious thought. Muhammad Iqbal, *The Reconstruction of Religious Thought* (Stanford, CA: Stanford University Press, 2013), 70–75.

61 In fact, the Qur'an uses the term *a'rāḍ* in a quite similar way. The term usually refers to transient commodities of this world. See, for example, 4/94, 7/169, 8/67, 24/33.

62 For Naẓẓām's views on this see Ash'arī, *Maqālāt*, 321; Juwaynī, *al-Shāmil*, 145; Shahrastānī, *al-Milal*, I, 56; Ibn Mattawayh, *al-Tadhkira fī Aḥkām al-Jawāhir wa-l-A'rāḍ*, ed. Daniel Gimaret (Cairo: al-Ma'had al-'Ilm al-Faransi, 2009), I, 94–100. Also see Dhanani, *The Physical Theory of Kalām*, 38–47; and Richard M. Frank, *The Metaphysics of Created Being According to Abū al-Hudhayl Al-'Allāf* (Istanbul: Netherlands Historische-Archeologisch Instituut, 1966); and Josef van Ess, *Theologie*

small and so fast that they create an illusion of continuity and flow. Time does not stand beyond the scope of the continuous creative act, and hence both temporal and spatial atoms are continuously created.

As should be clear by now, there is no causal glue between consecutive events in the world of the Muslim occasionalists. This world pulsates unceasingly between existence and nonexistence. As a stone moves in the air, its atoms and accidents are re-created anew at each moment in different locations. The fact that this motion can be studied in light of mathematical formulae does not imply necessity, though it suggests that God creates in a predictable manner. If both time and space are continuously re-created, one need not posit a necessary causal connection between two consecutive events. As such, the notion of possibility runs through time and motion.

1.5 ACQUISITION (*KASB*)

The same accentuation of the divine will shapes the Ashʿarite theory of human agency. The theory of acquisition limits the role of human power to acquisition of an act created by God. God's will and power relate to all objects (*maqdūrāt* and *murādāt*), and *kasb* becomes an occasion for the divine creative act. However, human will and power are still under the control of the divine will and power.

This theory is developed in the context of other competing theories. We already examined how one of the things Muʿtazilite theology aims to establish in the cosmic order is the divine intelligibility. Muʿtazilites seek a similar logic in divine reward and punishment. The servant of God is the creator of his own acts. God does not create people as believers or infidels. Man chooses to be one of those.[63] In this rejection, one sees that Muʿtazilite doctrine aims to distance the evil and ugly (*qabīḥ*) from God. God does not do anything evil or ugly. Hence, evil must be attributed to man, which in turn makes man the creator of his own (evil) acts.[64] Responsibility is possible only through humans' creative power. Otherwise we would have to accept that God punishes without giving any

und Gesellschaft im 2. und 3. Jahrhundert Hidschra. Eine Geschichte des religiosen Denkens im fruhen Islam, 6 vols (Berlin: Walter de Gruyter, 1991–1997), 3:224–229, 309–335.

[63] Ashʿarī, *Maqālāt*, 190; Shahrastānī, *al-Milal*, I, 55; Baghdādī, *Uṣūl al-Dīn*, 146; Qāḍī ʿAbduljabbār, *al-Mukhtaṣar fī Uṣūl al-Dīn* (Cairo: Dar al-Hilal, 1971), 197, 210.

[64] Qāḍī ʿAbduljabbār, *Sharḥ*, 131–132, 510–512; *al-Mukhtaṣar*, 203.

meaningful power to his servants.[65] Therefore, man must have causal power. This causal power is called *istiṭā'a*, or *qudra*.[66] Humans are the causes of their own acts, although it is God who gives this causal power to man. After bestowing this power to human individuals, God leaves them alone with their freedom. It is in this sense that humans are the creators of their own acts.[67] This view is sometimes called authorization (*tafwīḍ*) by Mu'tazilite theologians.

Ash'arites reject this view. From a theological perspective, attributing a creative power to man is a sort of idolatry (*shirk*). Moreover, a servant cannot be the creator of his acts, because his knowledge does not relate to every moment and detail of the act. He cannot be the cause of that which he does not know. The act of eating, for example, cannot really be attributed to the servant, for the servant does not really know or control how their body digests food.[68] Despite this criticism, Ash'arite theologians do accept a type of power on the part of the servant. This, however, is an acquisitive power and not a creative one. The difference here is that for Mu'tazilites this power is causally efficacious and creative, whereas for Ash'arites, it can only acquire what is already created.[69] All in all, Ash'arites replaced Mu'tazilites' notion of *istiṭā'a* with *iktisāb*.

From where does the concept of acquisition emerge? Abū Hanifa appears to be the first one to use the term *kasb*. It is God who creates good and evil, but human will has a role to play. The acquisitive power is the basis of human responsibility. We are therefore not totally determined (*jabr*).[70] Ḍirār also talked about acquisition before the Ash'arites did. According to Ḍirār, the same act is simultaneously created by God and

[65] Qāḍī 'Abduljabbār, *Sharḥ*, 778. [66] Ash'arī, *Maqālāt*, 230–231.

[67] Qāḍī 'Abduljabbār, *al-Mughnī*, VII, 162; Qāḍī 'Abduljabbār, *Sharḥ*, 390–394.

[68] As far as I am aware, this argument has no precedent and belongs to Ash'arites. The emergence of the argument can be attributed to their overall attempt to reject the idea of necessity and to describe all causal relations in terms of possibility and proximity. For different versions of this argument, see Bāqillānī, *al-Inṣāf*, 205; Juwaynī, *al-Irshād*, 174, Juwaynī, *al-'Aqīda al-Niẓāmiyya*, 191; Ghazālī, *al-Iqtisād*, 87–88. It is interesting to note that Western occasionalists also used this argument. Arnold Geulincx, for example, writes that "You are not the cause of that which you do not know how to bring about." *Arnoldi Geulincx antverpiensis Opera philosophica*, ed. J. P. N. Land, vol. 2 (The Hague: Martinum Nijhoff, 1893), 2:150–151. Also see D. Gimaret, *Théories de l'acte humain en théologie musulmane* (Paris: J. Vrin, 1980), 79–170.

[69] See, for example, Juwaynī, *al-'Aqīda al-Niẓāmiyya*, 189.

[70] Abū Hanīfa, *al-Fiqh al-Akbar*, 72–73; Abū Hanifa, *al-Fiqh al-Absat*, 46–48, 60. Both *al-Fiqh al-Akbar* and *al-Fiqh al-Absaṭ* are in *İmamı Azamın Beş Eseri*, trans. Mustafa Öz (Istanbul: Marmara Universitesi Ilahiyat Fakultesi Vakfi, 1992).

acquired by the servant.[71] In the Ashʿarite formulation, God creates acts and the servant acquires them. The uncreated power of God is the real agent. Man's created (*ḥādith*) power has only a role in acquiring the created act.[72] Accordingly, Bāqillānī defines acquisition as "the influence (*taṣarruf*) the servant has on his own will."[73] Juwaynī agrees in that the servant's acquisition has no creative power and is only an occasion for the divine creative act. In accordance with Ashʿarite occasionalism, he reduces human agency to an occasion with no creative power.[74] Juwaynī also presents an argument that would be taken up by later Ashʿarites. He contends that the moment we accept that the created power of the servant is causally efficacious, God's absolute creative power is undermined. It is also impossible to accept that the same act is caused by both the uncreated (*qadīm*) and created power, for that would entail the acceptance of two creators, which is a form of association (*shirk*). The servant's power is created. If we accept a real causal efficacy in the created power, then the created and uncreated power will have to meet on the same object. This implies that there are two creators of one event. Although the created power effects the act, this cannot be called creation. The act cannot be a result of both created and uncreated power. One act cannot come from two agents. Two does not become one.[75]

71 Ashʿarī, *Maqālāt*, 383, 407–408; Qāḍī ʿAbduljabbār, *al-Muḥīṭ*, 408. Qāḍī ʿAbduljabbār provides a short summary of different positions on the idea of acquisition in *al-Muḥīṭ*, 407–409. Also see Ibn Ḥazm, *al-Faṣl*, IV, 192.

72 Ashʿarī, *al-Lumaʿ*, 72; Ibn Fūrak, *Mujarrad*, 91–92; Ibn Maymūn (Maimonides), *Dalālat al-Ḥāʾirīn*, 125–126.

73 Bāqillānī, *al-Tamhīd*, 346–347. His proof for this acquisitive power is our experiential awareness of freedom and our ability to discern when we are or are not free. *al-Tamhīd*, 323–324.

74 Juwaynī, *al-ʿAqīda al-Niẓāmiyya*, 188–194.

75 Ibid., 188–189; also see Juwaynī, *al-Irshād*, 188–189. It must be mentioned that the other major Sunni school, the Maturidites, offer a different perspective here. The same act can be attributed to both God and man from different perspectives. In this sense, two *can* become one. God is the owner of the act as much as this is a question of creation; the servant owns it as much as this is a question of acquisition. From the perspective of the servant, it is called acquisition (*kasb*), while from the perspective of the divine, it is called creation (*khalq*). They attribute the act to God and the servant simultaneously in the real sense. In this sense, human individuals are free, capable, and responsible, although that God is the creator of everything. They must be free because God is just. Any judgement without freedom and capacity to choose is ugly (*qabīḥ*) and against wisdom (*ḥikma*). Furthermore, God's preknowledge does not contradict the servant's freedom. See, for example, Sabūnī's summary of Maturidite position on this in *al-Bidāya fī Uṣūl al-Dīn* (Maturidiyye Akaidi), (Turkish translation) trans. Bekir Topaloğlu (Istanbul: Diyanet İşleri Başkanlığı Yayınları, n.d.), 139–142, 145–147, 149, 160–161. There is also an interesting argument for human freedom in Maturidite theologians' writings. Our

Recall also that one of the principles of Ash'arite cosmology is that "accidents do not subsist for two moments." Now, the Ash'arite tradition describes the acquisitive power as an accident. If *kasb* is an accident, then, like other accidents, it does not have subsistence. This acquisitive power is to be re-created anew at each moment. If this is the case, there cannot be a causal relation between the created power and act in the real sense. Hence the relationship between the created power and act is one of possibility, conjunction, and proximity.[76] Or as Ibn Maymūn writes, in the instance of writing, man's will to move the pen and the motion of the pen are "only related to each other as regards the time of their coexistence, and have no other relation to each other."[77]

Here, again, the Ash'arite theology of possibility rejects any necessitarian relationship between the acquisitive power and human acts by detaching the former from the latter. Their relationship is one of proximity (*mujāwara*) rather than necessity. God habitually creates an act after the servant's tendency toward that act. The servant does not have a causal efficacy other than this disposition toward an act. Human will is an occasion for the divine creative act. Although there is no necessary relationship between human will and created act, God habitually creates an act in accordance with the tendencies of human will. This is how a human will acquires some acts and not others.

However, despite the Ash'arites' efforts to ground human agency while at the same time not attributing to it any causal efficacy, it is not clear whether this acquisitive power is truly free. Ash'arī himself appears to suggest that even this acquisitive power is under the control of the divine will and power. As he writes, "God creates acquisition for his servants and *he is also powerful over their acquisition*";[78] and, "there cannot be, under the authority of God, any acquisition that God does not will."[79] These passages imply that acquisition is not an uncaused cause. It remains caused by God. This is probably why Shahrastānī asserts that Ash'arite theologians fall into determinism when they assert that the servant's acquisitive power is also caused by God. If human will is not an uncaused

freedom is evident to us. We are precognitively aware of our freedom. It thus requires no proof. See, for example, Māturīdī, *Kitāb al-Tawḥīd*, 358–359 and Sabūnī, *al-Bidāya fī Uṣūl al-Dīn*, 151.

[76] Juwaynī, *al-Irshād*, 196–198.

[77] Ibn Maymūn (Maimonides), *Dalālat al-Ḥā'irīn*, 125.

[78] Ash'arī, *Maqālāt*, 552. See also Ash'arī, *al-Ibāna*, 37.

[79] Translated in Ash'arī, *The Elucidation from Islam's Foundation* (*Kitāb al-Ibāna*), 103.

cause of itself, then it is not free.[80] As such, Ashʿarite occasionalism, while aiming to introduce the divine causality to all levels of existence and to make the immensity of God concretely present in the world, appears to render human will subservient to the will of God.

1.6 CONCLUSION

This chapter has outlined two major theological tendencies. The modus operandi of the Muʿtazilite theological project is to construct a worldview in which God and the world remain intelligible to humans. To preserve the intelligibility of the world and the divine acts, Muʿtazilites are ready to accept the idea of necessity in the world and even in God. The guiding principle of Ashʿarite theological project, however, is to accentuate the divine will and freedom. This leads to construction of a theology of possibility. All of the major Ashʿarite positions, from cosmology to ethics, can be traced back to this concern to accentuate the divine will, even at the expense of losing the intelligibility of the world, morality, and the divine acts. The centrality of the divine will and freedom renders the concept of possibility fundamental for Ashʿarite theology.

It is within the larger context of this debate that occasionalism emerges as the backbone of the Ashʿarite theology of possibility. Concepts such as habit (*ʿāda*), conjunction (*iqtirān*), proximity (*mujāwara*), and preponderance (*tarjīh*) provide the grounds to reject any necessary relationship between cause and effect. The connection between cause and effect is no more than a constant conjunction. Cause and effect are habitually conjoined by God. The connection in causal relations is one of possibility and hence it can be nullified, as in the case of a miracle. Atoms are homogenous and do not have innate natures. Accidents are assigned to atoms as a result of the divine preponderance without any necessitating reason. That is to say the connection between substance and accidents is also one of possibility. Both atoms and accidents are re-created anew at each moment. Hence, both space and time are atomized to remove causal glue

[80] Shahrastānī, *al-Milal*, I, 98-9; Shahrastānī, *Nihāyat al-Iqdām*, 78–79. Ibn Maymūn (Maimonides) agrees with Shahrastānī: "The Ashʿarites were therefore compelled to assume that motion and rest of living beings are predestined, and that it is not in the power of man to do a certain thing or to leave it undone." *The Guide for the Perplexed*, 284. The fundamental criticism of Ibn Maymūn here is that Ashʿarite attempts to reconcile human acquisition and the divine creation can "exist only in words, not in thought, much less in reality," 69.

from the world-process. Thus, the relationship between two consecutive moments of the cosmic history is also one of possibility. The human acquisitive power (*kasb*) has no creative role and is only an occasion for the divine creative act. Therefore, the relationship between the acquisition and acts is also one of possibility. As such, the notion of possibility runs through the whole cosmos, rendering the divine will the sovereign principle of all existence.

2

Toward a Synthesis of Aristotelian and Neoplatonic Understandings of Causality

The Case of Ibn Sīnā

This chapter examines Ibn Sīnā's account of causality and freedom through an analysis of his concepts of existence (*wujūd*) and essence (*māhiyya*).[1] It will be argued that these concepts allow Ibn Sīnā to make a distinction between metaphysical and physical causality and, then, to locate physical causality within the larger context of metaphysical causality. As such, he offers an integration of Aristotelian and Neoplatonic theories of causality. The result is a participatory theory of causality with strong Aristotelian elements that affirms freedom both in the created order and in the First.[2]

[1] Some passages in this chapter also appeared in Ozgur Koca, "Revisiting the Concepts of Necessity and Freedom in Ibn Sīnā (Avicenna) (c. 980–1037)," *Sophia*, 2019, https://doi.org/10.1007/s11841-019-0706-9. Reprinted by permission from Springer/Sophia.

[2] My examination in Chapter 1 indicates that there is a persisting tension between Ashʿarite theories, which accentuate the divine will-freedom, and Muʿtazilite theories, which emphasize the divine necessity-intelligibility. This dichotomy between the divine will-freedom and the divine intelligibility-necessity exists because both schools insist that the notions of necessity and freedom are mutually exclusive, both in God and the natural order. Ibn Sīnā's relationship to the preceding theological discussions is not clear. However, in my view, he aims to show that the notions of necessity and freedom can be reconciled in a larger metaphysical framework. In fact, Michael Marmura suggests that Ibn Sīnā develops his ideas with an eye toward both Ashʿarite and Muʿtazilite theology. See Michael E. Marmura, "The Metaphysics of Efficient Causality in Avicenna," in *Islamic Theology and Philosophy* (Albany, NY: State University of New York Press, 1984), 185–188. Also see Michael E. Marmura, "Avicenna and the *Kalam*," *Zeitschriftfür Geschichte der Arabisch-Islamischen Wissenschaften*, 6 (1990): 172–206. Jean Jolivet also suggests that *kalām* debates rather than Greek thought was the primary intellectual context for Ibn Sīnā. See "Aux origines de l'ontologie d'Ibn Sīnā," in *Etudes sur Avicenne*, ed. J. Jolivet and R. Rashed (Paris, 1984), 19–28. Robert Wisnovsky

Before I introduce my interpretation of Ibn Sīnā's account, it must be noted that his views on causality and, thus, necessity and freedom, have been examined by many scholars. These scholars have reached differing conclusions as to whether Ibn Sīnā embraces a causal determinism or affirms freedom in the created order and in God. Goichon, for example, states that Ibn Sīnā's metaphysics leaves no place for contingency and thus freedom.[3] For Gardet, Ibn Sīnā's notion of "necessary emanation" implies causal necessitarianism and thus leaves no place for true freedom.[4] Hourani argues that Ibn Sīnā's notion of predestination implies strict determinism in light of his notion of necessary emanation and concludes that he does not abandon Neoplatonic necessitarianism even at the expense of weakening his account of the divine justice.[5] Yahya Michot also argues for the absolute determinism of Ibn Sīnā.[6] Richard M. Frank agrees with these scholars and holds that for Ibn Sīnā, everything is determined.[7] Marmura contends that for Ibn Sīnā, "God necessitates the world's existence. Since God, the necessitating cause, is eternal and changeless, the world, the necessitated effect, is eternal. Cause and effect co-exist, God's priority to the world is non-temporal."[8] The necessary emanation also imposes necessity on all causal relations. Ibn Sīnā's universe is a necessitarian one, not only as it pertains to its origination by

supports this idea and provides a detailed discussion on how Ibn Sīnā's distinction between essence and existence might have been inspired by previous *kalām* discussions. See "Notes on Avicenna's Concept of Thingness,"*Arabic Sciences and Philosophy*, 10 (2000): 181–221. Wisnovsky also states that "the debt Avicenna owes to *kalām* discussion of things and existents seems self-evident, given the similarity of his position to tht of the Ashʿarites and Maturidites." Robert Wisnovsky, *Avicenna's Metaphysics in Context* (New York: Cornell University Press, 2013), 153. Wisnovsky also mentions that Ibn Sīnā studied *kalām* as a youngster. *Avicenna's Metaphysics in Context*, 17.

3 A. M. Goichon, *La distinction de l'essence et de l'existence d'après Avicenne* (Paris: Desclée de Brouwer, 1937), 162–163.

4 L. Gardet, "La pensé religieuse d'Avicenne' (Ibn Sīnā)," in *Études de Philosophie Médiévale*, 41 (Paris: Vrin, 1951), 45–46.

5 G. F. Hourani, "Ibn Sīnā's 'Essay on the Secret of Destiny," *Bulletin of the School of Oriental and African Studies*, 2.1 (1966): 25–48.

6 J. [Yahya] Michot, *La destinée de l'homme selon Avicenne* (Louvain: Peeters, 1986), 61–64.

7 Richard M. Frank, *Creation and the Cosmic System: Ghazālī and Avicenna* (Heidelberg: Carl Winter Universitatsverlag, 1992), 23–24.

8 Marmura, "The Metaphysics of Efficient Causality in Avicenna," 175. For similar necessitarian readings of Ibn Sīnā, see Frank, *Creation and the Cosmic System*, 22–25. Kogan argues that Ibn Rushd also thinks Ibn Sīnā is a necessitarian. For his discussion, please see Barry S. Kogan, *Averroes and the Metaphysics of Causation* (Albany: State University of New York Press, 1985), 17–70.

the First but also during its continuation. Griffel agrees with these scholars and posits that for Ibn Sīnā "there can be only one true explanation of any given phenomenon in the world. True human knowledge describes the necessary and only way the world is constructed."[9] More recently, Belo has rejected the idea that Ibn Sīnā ascribes any liberating, active role to "matter" and holds that Ibn Sīnā is "strictly determinist."[10] For Richardson, Ibn Sīnā's modal distinction indicates that within his system all existence is necessary,[11] and that God cannot act otherwise than He does.[12]

No doubt, there are passages in Ibn Sīnā's large corpus that permit a necessitarian reading. Ibn Sīnā himself directly suggests that "God cannot act otherwise than He does." He also expresses explicitly that causal relations are based on the principle of necessity. He writes, for example, that "with the existence of the cause, the existence of every effect is necessary; and the existence of its cause necessitates the existence of its cause."[13] An effect comes into being because it is necessitated by its cause (*wajaba ʿanhu*). Things are possible in themselves, but they are necessary in relation to their causes. Moreover, Ibn Sīnā makes causality one of the central departure points of his thought and understands metaphysics as "knowledge of the first thing in existence, namely the First Cause (*al-ʿilla al-awwal*)."[14] In *Dānesh Nāma-i ʿAlāʾī*, Ibn Sīnā states:

> You know that things do not occur without being necessary. There is a cause for everything, but not all causes are known to us ... if we would have known all causes, we would have had certainty about it. Every existent has its origin in the Necessary Existent, and its procession from the Necessary Existent is necessary.[15]

[9] Frank Griffel, *Al-Ghazālī's Philosophical Theology: An Introduction to the Study of his Life and Thought* (New York: Oxford University Press, 2009), 177.

[10] Catarina Belo, *Chance and Determinism in Avicenna and Averroes* (Boston, MA: Brill, 2007), 53. See in particular chapter 3 and the conclusion.

[11] Kara Richardson, "Avicenna's Conception of the Efficient Cause," *British Journal for the History of Philosophy*, 21.2 (2013): 228.

[12] Kara Richardson, "Causation in Arabic and Islamic Thought," *The Stanford Encyclopedia of Philosophy* (Winter 2015 Edition), ed. Edward N. Zalta: https://plato.stanford.edu/archives/win2015/entries/arabic-islamic-causation/.

[13] Ibn Sīnā, *al-Shifāʾ al-Ilāhiyyāt (The Metaphysics of The Healing: A Parallel English-Arabic Text)*. Edited and translated by Michael E. Marmura (Provo, UT: Brigham Young University Press, 2005), 27.

[14] Ibid., 11.

[15] Ibn Sīnā, *Dānesh Nāma-i ʿAlāʾī*, MS Nuruosmaniye Library, No. 2258/2682, 60a. Translation is mine.

Furthermore,

> This compound and these parts are all, in themselves, possible in existence and they *necessarily have a cause that necessitates their existence.*[16]
>
> What proceeds from the Necessary existent is necessary.[17]
>
> Since nothing other than He is a necessary existent, He is *the principle of the necessitation* of the existence of everything, necessitating each thing either in a primary manner (*awwaliyyan*) or through an intermediary (*bi-wāsiṭa*).[18]

Despite these and similar statements and the prevailing opinion regarding Ibn Sīnā's necessitarianism, there are also scholars who read Ibn Sīnā as affirming freedom both in God and in the created order. Ṭūsī offers one such reading in his commentary on Ibn Sīnā's Pointers and Reminders (*al-Ishārāt wa-l-Tanbīhāt*). Ṭūsī rejects Ghazālī's and Rāzī's necessitarian readings and endorses the opinion that Ibn Sīnā's God creates by choice.[19]

One can see a similar tendency in more recent scholarship. For example, Ivry argues that for Ibn Sīnā, matter is "governed by God but not totally overwhelmed by Him" and hence "preserves its own semi-autonomous being." This is the basis of freedom in Ibn Sīnā's system: it provides a "full rationale for the presence of evil." There is evil because of matter's "instability" and semi-autonomous quality.[20] Matter is the "source of change and privation/evil, unknowable in itself and hence unpredictable in its relation to form."[21] Ivry adds that the existence of moral injunctions and encouragements in Ibn Sīnā's writings presupposes the efficacy of human will and supports this indeterministic reading.

Janssens contends that according to Ibn Sīnā, "man has some freedom" as it pertains to moral choice and intellectual development.[22] Rashed argues for freedom in Ibn Sīnā's system by starting from certain irregularities in movements of the celestial spheres. The unpredictability of celestial motion indicates the possibility of freedom.[23] Goodman believes that the idea of necessary emanation does not require that natural

[16] Ibn Sīnā, *al-Shifāʾ al-Ilāhiyyāt*, 48. Emphasis mine. [17] Ibid., 302.

[18] Ibid., 273. Emphasis mine.

[19] Ibn Sīnā, *Pointers and Reminders (al-Ishārāt wa-l-Tanbīhāt) with Naṣīr al-Dīn Ṭūsī's Commentary*, ed. S. Dunya (Cairo: 1957–1960), V. 3.

[20] A. Ivry, "*Destiny Revisited: Avicenna's Concept of Determinism*," in *Islamic Theology and Philosophy*, ed. Michael E. Marmura (Albany: State University of New York Press, 1984), 163–164.

[21] Ibid., 167.

[22] J. Janssens, "The Problem of Human Freedom in Ibn Sīnā," in *Actes del Simposi Internacional de Filosofia de l'Edat Mitjana* (Vic-Girona, 1996), 117.

[23] M. Rashed, "Théodicée et approximation: Avicenne," *Arabic Sciences and Philosophy*, 10 (2000): 227, 229, 232.

processes also be necessary.[24] Ruffus and McGinnis hold that although Ibn Sīnā allows "human freedom in principle," this freedom "is only truly exercised rarely and then only by prophets, sages and philosophers."[25]

This chapter aims to contribute a new perspective to this discussion. It will be argued that Ibn Sīnā offers a participatory account of causality that affirms both creaturely and divine freedom based on the two fundamental concepts of his metaphysics: existence and essence.

2.1 EXISTENCE AND ESSENCE

What exactly is existence? Ibn Sīnā's definition is based on his distinction between essence (*māhiyya*) and existence (*wujūd*).[26] Existence is common to all categories. "There is nothing more general than existence."[27] What differentiates entities is their essence. "Each thing has a reality proper to it (*ḥaqīqa khāṣṣa*), namely its essence," and "definition is nothing other than the essence of the thing defined."[28] After establishing the universality of existence, Ibn Sīnā famously distinguishes among three modes of existence: necessary, contingent, and impossible. The Necessary Existent "is an existent whose nonexistence entails impossibility (*muḥāl*)."[29]

[24] L. E. Goodman, *Avicenna* (London: Routledge, 1992), 81.

[25] Anthony Ruffus and Jon McGinnis, "Willful Understanding: Avicenna's Philosophy of Action and Theory of the Will," *Archiv für Geschichte der Philosophie*, 97.2 (2015): 171. See also Étienne Gilson, "Avicenne et les Origines de la Notion de Cause Efficiente," *Atti Del XII Congresso Internazionale di Filosofia*, 9 (1958): 121–130; Étienne Gilson, "Notes pour l'histoire de la cause efficiente," *Archives d'Histoire doctinrale et littéraire du Moyen Age*, 37 (1962): 7–31; Taneli Kukkonen, "Creation and Causation," in *The Cambridge History of Medieval Philosophy*, ed. R. Pasnau and C. Van Dyke (Cambridge, UK: Cambridge University Press, 2010), 232–246; Robert Wisnovsky, "Final and Efficient Causality in Avicenna's Cosmology and Theology," *Quaestio*, 2 (2002): 97–124; Amos Bertolacci, "The Doctrine of Material and Formal Causality in the 'Ilāhiyyāt' of Avicenna's 'Kitāb al-Shifā'’," *Quaestio*, 2 (2002): 125–154.

[26] One can find similar distinctions made by both Plato (*Phaedo* 74a, *Republic* 509b, *Timaeus* 50c) and Aristotle (*Posterior Analytics* 92 b–93a and *Metaphysics* 1003–1004). Ibn Sīnā, however, makes this distinction his starting point.

[27] Ibn Sīnā, *al-Shifā' al-Ilāhiyyāt*, 10. See also "Just as the existence and the one are among the things common to the categories." Ibid., 186. In other words, 'existence' is what the scholastics called a transcendental notion. On this idea, see T. Koutzarova, *Das Transzendentale bei Ibn Sīnā* (Leiden: Brill, 2009).

[28] Ibn Sīnā, *al-Shifā' al-Ilāhiyyāt*, 180. He follows the Aristotelian account of definition here. Definition is "an account which signifies what it is to be for something" (*logos ho to ti ên einai sêmainei*) or, to use another expression, "the what-it-is-to-be" (*to ti ên einai*) of an entity.

[29] Ibid., 262.

The Necessary Existent cannot not be. The contingent existent (*mumkin al-wujūd*) is "an existent whose existence does not entail impossibility." The Necessary Existent is its own cause; it is due to itself (*wājib al-wujūd bi-dhātihī*). The contingent existent is necessary too; otherwise it would not exist. But the necessity of the contingent existent is due to something other than itself (*wājib al-wujūd bi-ghairihī*).[30] A contingent existent is contingent because it is caused to exist by something other than itself – the Necessary Existent. There is also a third category, the impossible existent (*mumtaniʾ al-wujūd*), whose existence entails impossibility, such as a second necessary existent.[31]

Key to our discussion is Ibn Sīnā's definition of the First as *pure existence*.

He is pure existence (*mujarrad al-wujūd*) with the condition of negating privation (*ʿadam*) and all other descriptions of Him. Moreover, the rest of the things possessing essences are possible, coming into existence through Him. The meaning of my statement "He is pure existence" suggests the condition of negating all other additional attributes of Him.[32]

Other entities are compositions of existence and essence. The First is pure existence without essence. For, "the Necessary Existent cannot be of a characterization that entails composition so that there would be some essence."[33] Everything that has an essence is composed, and everything

[30] Ibid., 263.

[31] Ibn Sīnā's argument that there must be a "necessary existent" that subsists through itself and explains its own existence was repeatedly used as proof for the existence of God by Muslim, Jewish, and Christian philosophers. See for example, H. A. Davidson, *Proofs for Eternity, Creation, and the Existence of God in Medieval Islamic and Jewish Philosophy* (Oxford: Oxford University Press, 1987); T. A. Druart, "Ibn Sina (Avicenna) and Duns Scotus," in *John Duns Scotus, Philosopher: Proceedings of The Quadruple Congress on John Duns Scotus*, ed. M. B. Ingham and O. Bychkov (Munster: Aschendorff, 2010), 13–27. As Peter Adamson points out, Ibn Sīnā is also aware that identifying the necessary existent with God needs further evidence. The proof shows why there must be a necessary existent without showing why we should identify this existent with God. As discussed in the following pages, however, Ibn Sīnā's proof that there must be a necessary existent is in fact the first step of a long chain of arguments, which would finally yield a unique, intellective, all-knowing, generous, good, powerful God. Peter Adamson, "From Necessary Existent to God," in *Interpreting Avicenna: Critical Essays*, ed. Peter Adamson (Cambridge, UK: Cambridge University Press, 2013), 170–189.

[32] Ibid., 276.

[33] Ibid., 274. This passage seems relevant to the discussion on the primacy of existence or essence in Ibn Sīnā. The passage actually suggests that existence precedes essence. For more on this discussion, see Robert Wisnovsky's essay, "Avicenna and the Avicennian Tradition," in *The Cambridge Companion to Arabic Philosophy*, ed. Peter Adamson and Richard C. Taylor (Cambridge, UK: Cambridge University Press, 2005). For a lucid study

that is composed is an effect, not a self-subsistent uncaused cause. Every composition needs its own parts as well as a composer to come into existence. In this case, the First would need something else to be what it is, which is absurd. The First would be an effect, not the absolutely self-subsistent cause of all existents. Therefore, "the *primary attribute* of the Necessary Existent consists in His being an existent."[34]

Then, Ibn Sīnā traces all of the divine attributes back to the pure existence of the Necessary Existent. There can be no potentiality in the First. It is therefore *pure actuality*. "He is one because He is perfect in existence and nothing in Him awaits completion."[35] There is no potentiality in the First. The First principle should thus be pure and undifferentiated actuality.[36]

God is *pure good*, for He is pure and actual existence, which is free from essences and potentialities. Essences or potentialities imply delimitation of pure existence, and hence imperfection. Anything other than pure existence has its share from nonexistence, which is the cause of evil. God is free from the possibility of nonexistence. Thus, "what in reality is desired is existence. Existence is thus a *pure good* (*khayr mahḍ*) and pure perfection."[37] Entities other than God "bear the possibility of nonexistence; and that which bears the possibility of nonexistence is not in all respects devoid of evil and deficiency."[38] The Necessary Existent is also good in moral terms. It shares His existence with other essences, since "good is also said of that which *bestows* perfections of things and their good qualities. So, it has become evident that the Necessary Existent must

on the connection between God's existence and the divine attributes, see Peter Adamson, "From the Necessary Existent to God," in *Interpreting Avicenna*, ed. Peter Adamson (Cambridge, UK: Cambridge University Press, 2013). For T. Izutsu's discussion of Ibn Sīnā's take on this issue, see T. Izutsu, *A Comparative Study of the Key Philosophical Concepts in Sufism and Taoism* (Tokyo: Keio University; 2nd ed., *Sufism and Taoism*, Los Angeles: University of California Press, 1983 [1966]), 3–5. For an examination of Suhrawardī's position on this discussion, see Sajjad H. Rizvi, "Roots of an Aporia in Later Islamic Philosophy: The Existence-Essence Distinction in the Philosophies of Avicenna and Suhrawardī," *Studia Iranica*, 29 (2000): 61–108; and Sajjad H. Rizvi, "An Islamic Subversion of the Existence-Essence Distinction? Suhrawardī's Visionary Hierarchy of Lights," *Asian Philosophy*, 9.3 (1999): 219–227. For precedents for this distinction in Fārābī, see N. Rescher, "Al-Fārābī on the Question: Is Existence a Predicate?" in *Studies in the History of Arabic Logic* (Pittsburgh, PA: University of Pittsburgh Press, 1963), 39–42; for an overview of the discussion, see N. Rescher, "The Concept of Existence in Arabic Logic and Philosophy," in *Studies in Arabic Philosophy* (Pittsburgh, PA: University of Pittsburgh Press, 1966), 69–80.

34 Ibn Sīnā, *al-Shifāʾ al-Ilāhiyyāt*, 296. Emphasis mine. 35 Ibid., 299. 36 Ibid., 292.

37 Ibn Sīnā, *al-Shifāʾ al-Ilāhiyyāt*, 283. 38 Ibid., 284.

in Himself be the furnisher of all existence and every perfection of existence."[39] The First bestows perfection to something other than Himself, because He is good and generous.

After equating existence with pure good he also asserts that existence is also *pure intellect*:

> The Necessary Existent is *pure intellect* (*'aql mahḍ*) because He is an essence disassociated from matter in every respect. You have known that the cause that prevents a thing from being apprehended intellectually is matter and its attachment, not existence ... Hence, that which is free from matter and its attachments realized through existence separate from matter is an intelligible for itself. Its essence is, hence, at once *intellect, intellectual apprehender, and intelligible*.[40]

As pure intellect, the Necessary Existent knows everything, through knowing Himself as the principle of every other existent. God "intellectually apprehends Himself and apprehends that He is principle of every existent; He apprehends the principles of the existents proceeded from Him and what is generated by them."[41] The intellectual apprehension of possible entities does not negate the purity of existence because "He intellectually apprehends things all at once without being rendered by them multiple in His substance, or their becoming."[42]

Ibn Sīnā continues to trace other divine attributes back to the existence of the Necessary Existent. It is one (*wāḥid*) and undifferentiated (*lā yanqasim*); It has no companions nor any quantitative or categorical divisions.[43] It is the "First" (*al-awwal*), for nothing precedes Its existence. The First is the "principle," for the existence of what is other than the First is from the First. The First is "substance," for It does not inhere in anything other than Itself. The First is "preeternal," for Its nonexistence is unintelligible and impossible. The First is "everlasting," as negation of the existence of It, the Necessary Existent, is unintelligible. The First is

[39] Ibid.

[40] Ibid., 284–285. Emphasis mine. See also "this is because inasmuch as its haecceity (*huwiyya*) is denuded (from Matter) it is intellect (*'aql*) ... inasmuch as it is denuded (of matter) it is intelligible (*ma'qūl*) ... and in as much as it is denuded (of matter) it is intellector (*'āqil*)" ibid., 285; and: "intellectual apprehender" requires something which is "intellectually apprehended" ibid. For modern studies of Ibn Sīnā's epistemology, see Micheal E. Marmura, "Some Aspects of Avicenna's Theory of God's Knowledge of Particulars," *Journal of the American Oriental Society*, 83 (1962): 299–312. Michael E. Marmura "Divine Omniscience and Future Contingents in Al-Farabi and Avicenna," in *Divine Omniscience and Omnipotence in Medieval Philosophy: Islamic, Jewish and Christian Perspectives*, ed. Tamar Rudavsky (Dordrecht: D. Reidel, 1984), 81–94.

[41] Ibn Sīnā, *al-Shifā' al-Ilāhiyyāt*, 288, translation modified.

[42] Ibid., 291.

[43] Ibid., 299.

"creator," for everything necessarily emanates from It. The First is "powerful" (*qādir*), as all things emanate from It, and all things are actualized with this emanation. The First is "willer" (*murīd*), for It knows what emanates from It, and It is not averse to the emanation of the cosmos and its content from it. The First is "life," for It knows, acts, and wills. Living is the one who is "apprehender and enactor." The First is "generous," for the whole emanates from It, not for any purpose that reverts to It. It is completely independent of the world; the world is completely dependent upon It. The First is "love," for every perfection that is possible is in It. It is the utmost perfection and It apprehends Its perfection. This perfection is the cause of love. It is pure beauty and splendor (*jamāl wa-bahā al-mahḍ*).[44] Moreover, Ibn Sīnā bases his apophatic theology on the premise that the First is pure existence. If the First is pure existence and has no essence, it follows that It has no genus (*jins*), no definition (*ḥadd*), no demonstration (*burhān*), no quantity (*kam*), no quality (*kayf*), no place (*ayn*), no partner (*sharīk*), no contrary (*ḍidd*).[45]

It is important to understand what existence means for Ibn Sīnā to grasp how he uses it to construct his theory of causality. In contrast to Ashʿarite theory of the divine attributes, he constructs the relationship between God and the world through the notion of existence and establishes that all of the divine attributes are ultimately drawn from the First's pure, undifferentiated, and actual existence. The "bestowal of existence" upon essences becomes the metaphysical basis for all causal activity. We will examine this relationship in the following section.

2.2 METAPHYSICAL AND PHYSICAL CAUSALITY

It will be argued that Ibn Sīnā identifies two distinct categories of causality: physical and metaphysical. God is not only the cause of the "motion and rest" of entities but also the immediate cause of their very existence. And it is this distinction between physical and metaphysical causality that allows Ibn Sīnā to frame Aristotelian and Neoplatonic conceptions of causality as complementary and not contradictory.

Ibn Sīnā divides theoretical knowledge into three categories: the natural (*al-ṭabīʿiyya*), the mathematical (*al-riyāziyya*), and the divine (*al-ilāhiyya*).

[44] For Ibn Sīnā's discussion on the relationship between the concept of existence and the divine attributes, see Ibn Sīnā, *al-Shifāʾ al-Ilāhiyyāt*, 291–298. Also see Ibn Sīnā, *Kitāb al-Najāt*, ed. Majid Fakhry (Beirut: Dar al-Afaq al-Jadida, 1985), 263–265.

[45] Ibn Sīnā, *al-Shifāʾ al-Ilāhiyyāt*, 299.

He then defines the subject matter of the natural knowledge as bodies with respect to their being "in motion and at rest" (*al-ḥaraka wa-l-sukūn*). As he writes:

The subject matter of natural sciences was body, not by way of its being an existent (*mawjūd*), nor by way of its being a substance (*jawhar*), nor by way of being composed of two principles (*hayūlā wa-l-ṣūra*), but by way of its being subject to *motion and rest*.[46]

The subject matter of mathematics is quantity abstracted from matter or quantity, as much as it is quantity. It also examines the states and relations of quantity.[47] The subject matter of metaphysics, however, is being *qua* being, or being without qualification:

The existent inasmuch as it is an existent (*al-mawjūd bimā huwa mawjūd*) is something common to all these things and therefore it must be made the subject matter of this art (of metaphysics).[48]

This science (metaphysics) will also investigate the First Cause, from which emanates *every caused existent inasmuch as it is a caused existent, not only inasmuch as it is an existent in motion or quantified*.[49]

The difference in the subject matter suggests that the question of causality can be evaluated by starting from the particular question that each science can ask. From the perspective of physical-natural sciences, one's understanding of causality is formulated from the perspective of *motion and rest*. From the perspective of metaphysics, however, the question of causality must be formulated in terms of *existence*. As a metaphysician, Ibn Sīnā holds that God is not only the first mover or the first principle of emanation but also the "giver of existence." It is here one sees two distinct formulations of causality emerging. Metaphysical causality constructs a more intimate and immediate relation between God and the world than does physical causality. One of the best expressions of dual causality can be found in the following passage.

Causes as you heard consist of form (*ṣūra*), element (*ʿunṣur*), agent (*fāʿil*), and purpose (*ghāya*). By the formal cause, we mean the cause which is part of subsistence of the thing and in terms of which the thing is what it is in actuality. By the elemental cause [we mean] the cause that is part of the subsistence of the thing, through which the thing is what it is in potency and in which the

[46] Ibid., 7. [47] Ibid., 2.

[48] Ibid., 9. See also "The primary subject matter is the existent inasmuch as it is an existent; and the things sought after are those that accompany (the existent), inasmuch as it is an existent, unconditionally," ibid., 10.

[49] Ibid., 11. Emphasis mine.

potentiality of existence resides. By agent [we mean] the cause which bestows an existence that is other than itself... This is because the metaphysical philosophers (*al-falāsifa al-ilahiyyīn*) do not mean by "agent" only the principle of motion, as the naturalist means, but *the principle (mabda') and giver (mufīd) of existence*, as in the case of God with respect to the world. As for the natural efficient cause, it does not bestow any existence other than motion in one of the forms of motion. By "purpose" we mean the cause for whose sake the existence of something different from it is realized.[50]

Ibn Sīnā accepts that the doctrine of the four causes is a necessary tool for any attempt to know the world around us. These four (material, formal, efficient, and final) causes can be used to give an answer to any why-question.[51] Why, then, does he introduce a new perspective on causality? In my view, it is because Aristotle's account is specific to the study of the physical world and does not deal with the metaphysical basis of causality. Ibn Sīnā's aim here is to preserve Aristotelian understanding of causality in the domain of natural world but also to establish the idea of metaphysical causality. Ibn Sīnā thus contextualizes Aristotelian doctrine of physical causality within the larger context of metaphysical causality.

What exactly is metaphysical causality? In many passages, God is defined as the "giver of existence." Ibn Sīnā repeatedly suggests that "the Agent *bestows from itself an existence* upon another thing, which this latter did not possess."[52] He also states that "the rank of completion (belongs) to the First Intellect. For every other thing that comes about from it is from *the existence emanating from the First.*"[53] Ibn Sīnā's distinction between existence and essence also implies that the notion of essence does not exhaust the reality of all things. An entity is more than its essence. Existence and essence together constitute the totality of an entity.[54] If this is so, for an

[50] Ibid., 194–195.

[51] A brief introduction the basic tenets of Aristotle's theory of causality is provided in the Introduction. See also *The Complete Works of Aristotle*, ed. Jonathan Barnes, 2 vols (Princeton, NJ: Princeton University Press, 1984), *Physics*, II. 3; *Metaphysics*, V. 2.

[52] Ibn Sīnā, *al-Shifā' al-Ilāhiyyāt*, 196. Emphasis mine.

[53] Ibid., 145. Emphasis mine.

[54] This is also evident on his account of definition. There is more to an entity than its definition. Thus, "the definition is other than the thing defined," ibid., 185. This also suggests that Ibn Sīnā understands the problems of the Aristotelian take on the concept of definition, despite criticisms on this point from the founder of the Illuminationist School, Suhrawardī. Suhrawardī says, for instance, that "it is clear that it is impossible for a human being to construct an essential definition in the way the Peripatetics require – a difficulty which even their master [Aristotle] admits." Suhrawardī, *The Philosophy of Illumination: A New Critical Edition of the Text of Hikmat al-Ishraq*, with English trans., notes, commentary, and intro. J. Walbridge and H. Ziai (Provo, UT: Brigham Young University Press, 1999), 11. 5–9.

entity to exist and continue to exist, it must be given existence by the "giver of existence," the First. Without existence, an entity is just an essence or a possibility or a pure definition. The First is pure existence; everything else is a blend of existence and essence. Existence, then, "occurs to essences."

It is impossible that the essence would have an existence prior to its existence. It remains that the existence it has is due to a cause. Hence, everything that has an essence is caused ... The rest of the things other than the Necessary Existent has essences. And it is these essences that in themselves are possible in existence, existence *occurring to them* externally.[55]

The First does not need a cause, for "the First has no essence other than His individual existence."[56] Something that has an essence must have a cause to be existentiated. This existentiating cause is the First, the pure existence, for which "there is no essence other than its being the Necessary Existent, which is (Its) thatness (*al-inniyya*)."[57] There is thus a very close relationship between the concepts of existence and causality.

The First, hence, possesses no essence. Those things possessing essences have existence emanate on them from Him. He is pure existence (*mujarrad al-wujūd*) with the condition of negating privation (*ʿadam*) and all other descriptions of Him. Moreover, the rest of the things possessing essences are possible, coming into existence through Him.[58]

... the Necessary Existent is above perfection because not only does He have the existence that belongs only to Him, but every other existence is also an overflow (*fāiʾḍun ʿanhu*) of His existence.[59]

Moreover, Ibn Sīnā asserts the same idea by using the concepts of potentiality and actuality. The First has no essence and therefore no potency. The First is pure actuality. An essence is pure potentiality. If it is given existence, it becomes an actualized potentiality. Things with essences receive their existence from the First, which actualizes them. As he puts it:

You have thus learned that, in reality, act is prior to potency and moreover, that it is prior in terms of nobility and perfection ... There must be some other thing through which the potential becomes actual. Otherwise, there will be no act at all, since potentiality by itself is insufficient to become an act but requires that which would change it from potentiality to actuality.[60]

55 Ibn Sīnā, *al-Shifāʾ al-Ilāhiyyāt*, 276. Emphasis mine.

56 Ibid., 274.

57 Ibid., 276. This latter statement grounds his demonstration of the First. "There is no demonstration for Him. He is the demonstration of all things; indeed, there are for Him only clear evidential proofs," 282.

58 Ibid., 276.

59 Ibid., 283.

60 Ibid., 143. Also see "Potency needs to be actualized by something existing in act at the time of the thing's being in potency," ibid., 141; "Act is prior to potency in perfection and

The First is the "uncaused cause," for it is pure existence. Everything else needs to be caused, for they have essences, definitions, compositions. Anything with an essence must be caused. As Ibn Sīnā explains, "everything with the exception of the One who in essence is one and the existent acquires existence from another, becoming through it an existent, being in itself a nonexistent. This is the meaning of a thing's being created – that is, *attaining existence* from another."[61]

So, metaphysical causality is to be understood in light of the notion of existence. The act of bestowal of existence existentiates essences and actualizes possibilities. As such, it is the metaphysical basis of all motion and rest in the world. Existence, as an all-encompassing notion, provides a larger framework in which physical activities occur. Existence is the basis for all causality.[62]

2.3 EXISTENCE AND FREEDOM

We can now turn to Ibn Sīnā's establishment of freedom in the created order in accordance with this understanding of causality. The question of

purpose. For potentiality is a deficiency, while actuality is a perfection. The good in all things is in conjunction with being actual," ibid., 142.

61 Ibid., 272. Emphasis mine.

62 This is a novel approach to the question of causality. Muʿtazilites and Ashʿarites certainly had not formulated a similar doctrine. However, it is possible to find the idea of "giving of existence" in accordance with the essences in the thought of both Kindī and Fārābī. Kindī, for instance, writes that "emanation of unity from the One gives existence to all sensible existents. When It bestowed his existence to every existent they were existentiated." Yāʿqūb ibn al-Isḥāq al-Kindī, *Rasāʾil al-Kindī al-Falsafiyya*, ed. M. A. H. Abu Riadah (Cairo: Dar al-Fikr al-Arabi, 1950), 89. The same idea can also be found in Fārābī. In *al-Madīna*, for example, Fārābī writes that "each existent receives from the First its share of existence, in accordance with its rank," Fārābī, *al-Madīna*, 97; and, "every existent gets its allotted share and rank of existence from it … followed by more and more deficient existents until the final stage of being is reached beyond which no existence whatsoever is possible," ibid., 95. What is different about Ibn Sīnā's system is that this idea becomes the basis for metaphysical causality. This allows Ibn Sīnā to establish a more intimate relationship between divine and physical causality in comparison to Kindī and Fārābī. Kindī also makes a distinction between near and distant cause (*ʿilla qaribatun and ʿilla bi-tawaṣṣūt*). Kindī, *Rasāʾil al-Kindī*, 274. According to this distinction, the First is the distant cause of all effects. Kindī uses an analogy of the archer and arrow to explain his distinction. When arrow hits a target, the archer is the real but distant cause. The arrow is a secondary (*bi-l-majāz*) but also immediate cause, ibid., 314. What is different in Kindī's and Ibn Sīnā's accounts here is that the latter proposes a more intimate relation between the First and created order through the idea of metaphysical causality.

freedom in Ibn Sīnā's system can be approached from the perspectives of the concepts of existence (*wujūd*) and essence (*māhiyya*), as he understands them.

From the perspective of existence, the following can be observed. The above examination suggests that God, from the perspective of metaphysical causality, is the giver of existence to essences, or the giver of actuality to potentialities. The First existentiates essences by giving, bestowing, and sharing Its existence. In sharing Its existence with other essences, existence also becomes qualified in the "particularity of their existence."

All that is necessary to an existent is [its] truth because the truth (*ḥaqq*) of each thing is the particularity (*khuṣūṣiyya*) of its existence that is established for it. Hence, there is nothing "truer" than the Necessary Existent.[63]

The absolute and pure existence becomes individuated, particularized, and delimited in the essences of entities. Recall also that every attribute – such as intellect, power, and will – is reduced to the aspects of pure existence. In light of these conclusions, it is possible to argue that if the First is the giver of existence and if existence is the root of all divine attributes, then in sharing its existence with entities, the First also shares the qualities that are entailed by existence, including will, intellect, and freedom. To give existence is to give intellect, will, and, thus, freedom. As such, entities participate in the divine freedom by receiving their share from the "gift" of existence.[64]

But does this not give rise to the idea that everything that has existence also has will and freedom, including rocks and minerals? In a way, it does. However, entities have their share from the First's existence in accordance with their right or capacity. An entity receives "what it itself deserves (*bi-istiḥqāqi nafsihi*),"[65] and "it is not the case that whenever the agent [the

[63] Ibid., 284.

[64] The assumption here is that The First is free in Ibn Sīnā's philosophy. It can be argued that Ibn Sīnā does not see a contradiction between freedom and necessity in the First. The emanation of the world from the First out of "necessity" may also be described as a "voluntary" act. For, this necessity comes solely from the ontological, moral, and intellectual perfection of God. This is not a necessity imposed by another entity, or an external principle, or a desire to realize an unrealized potentiality. If there is necessity, this is a moral and intellectual necessity, not a mechanical necessity, as appears to be suggested by Ghazālī. For an extensive discussion on this issue, please see Ozgur Koca "Revisiting the Concepts of Necessity and Freedom in Ibn Sīnā (Avicenna) (c. 980-1037)" Sophia, 2019, https://doi.org/10.1007/s11841-019-CO0706-9.

[65] Ibn Sīnā, *al-Shifā' al-Ilāhiyyāt*, 273.

First] bestows existence, it bestows an existence like itself."[66] Furthermore, "this light which is in the sun and this light originating from it should not, in this, be equal … However, [the two instances of light] would be one species for those who perceive the difference in deficiency (*naqṣ*) and excess (*ishtidād*)."[67]

These passages suggest a gradational ontology in which rocks and minerals have their share of existence but not in the same way or with the same intensity as humans. Their essences delimit participation in the divine existence. This allows, in my view, a gradational view of freedom in entities due to the gradational participation of entities in existence. As such, from the perspective of Ibn Sīnā's metaphysical causality, freedom is intrinsic in the created order in differing degrees due to entities' particular shares of God's existence.[68]

Also recall that in the First, the pure intellect and the pure existence are one and the same thing. It must therefore be the case that this "gift" of existence is the basis of intellect in the created order. To give existence in accordance with essences is to give intellect in accordance with essences. If this is true, then existence is the basis of intellect and, hence, intellectual volition.[69] If intellectual volition is the basis of the divine freedom, then human individuals must have their share of this freedom to the extent allowed by their essences and capacities.

2.4 ESSENCE AND FREEDOM

There is also the concept of essence (*māhiyya*). The role of essence in Ibn Sīnā's system is compatible with the freedom of entities. We have already seen that in this system, "everything that has an essence is caused." Questions arise here. Where do essences come from? What causes them to be what they are? Are they determined by God? Or are they uncaused

[66] Ibid., 205. See also "Hence, that which bestows a thing's existence inasmuch as it is existence has the greater claim to existence than the thing," ibid., 207.

[67] Ibid., 208.

[68] This interpretation is supported by Rashed's argument mentioned above that the irregularity and unpredictability of certain movements of the celestial spheres affirms freedom and contingency in the created order. Rashed, "Théodicée et approximation: Avicenne," 227, 229, 232.

[69] What is interesting here is that Ibn Sīnā uses similar terms to describe the divine and human intellect. For example, he writes that "the human soul conceptualizes itself … [it] makes itself an intellect, something that intellects and something that is intellected." Ibn Sīnā, *Avicenna's De anima*, ed. F. Rahman (London: 1959), V.6 [239]. That is to say, the intellect is the basis of contemplation, self-awareness, and thus approaching the "thought thinking itself" and becoming God-like (*ta'alluh*), ibid., X.4 [7].

objects of the First's knowledge? Many passages appear to indicate that essences are not determined by the First. The First knows them as It knows Its own nature and gives them existence. But It does not determine the essences to be what they are.

> Whatever is a possible existent is always considered in itself a possible existent; but it may happen that its existence becomes necessary through another . . . That whose existence is always necessitated by another is also not simple (*basītun*) in its true nature. This is because what belongs to it [when] considered in itself is other than what belongs to it from another. It attains its haecceity (*huwiyya*) in existence from both together.[70]

An entity is not "simple" in its true nature in the way the First is. A possible being's haecceity has necessarily two aspects, essence and existence. It has already been made clear that existence comes from the First. Essence is "what belongs to it in itself," and existence is "what belongs to it from another." When the two come together, the entity attains its haecceity. Thus, in any relationship between the Necessary Existent and a possible being, both sides have a role to play. Essences belong to the possible being, while existence can only be given by God. Recall Ibn Sīnā's statement, cited above, that "all that is necessary to an existent is [its] truth because the truth of each thing is the particularity of its existence that is established for it. Hence, there is nothing 'truer' than the Necessary Existent."

How can the concept of essence be the basis of freedom? In Ibn Sīnā's understanding of metaphysical causality, God is the giver of existence to essences, or the giver of actuality to potentialities. Nowhere, as far as I am aware, does Ibn Sīnā present God as causing essences or potentialities to be what they are. His writings only suggest that existentiation of essences occurs in accordance with their right or capacity (*istiḥqāq*) and "what they deserve."[71] But this right or capacity is not determined by God.

If this is true, then essences can be understood as uncaused objects of the divine knowledge. They are uncaused insofar as they are essences. It is here they can be seen as free to be what they are. Without God's existentiation, essences are mere possibilities, yet their whatness fashions their relationship with the Necessary Existent. The gift of existence is not given arbitrarily. Essences have a certain priority before the existentiating act of the First. And this priority is the basis of their freedom. In this sense, often-used concepts such as essence, potentiality, capacity, or right (*ḥaqq*) in Ibn Sīnā's writings can be read as principles of the freedom of entities.

[70] Ibn Sīnā, *al-Shifāʾ al-Ilāhiyyāt*, 38. [71] Ibid., 273.

In addition, according to Ibn Sīnā's emanationism, what proceeds from the One can only be one. Existence, which proceeds from the One as an undifferentiated and absolute unity, becomes delimited by essences. One thing becomes many in accordance with the essences of entities.

Thus, the multiplicity of the recipient becomes a cause for the multiplicity of the act of a principle that is one in essence ... For, if the cause of multiplicity is not in the agent, it must necessarily be in the recipient.[72]

I mean this light which is in the sun and this light originating from it should not, in this, be equal ... However, [the two instances of light] would be one species for those who perceive the difference in deficiency (*naqṣ*) and excess (*ishtidād*) to be a difference in terms of accidentals and individual intentions (*tashakhkhuṣāt*).[73]

One thing becomes many due to specificities of the recipient, as uncolored light becomes colored when it is reflected by an object. The object, in a way, delimits what is undelimited. The light is differentiated in terms of "deficiency and excess." The essence then individualizes the light of existence. Still, this does not tell us where the essences come from in the first place. Again,

They [the Philosophers] transferred the "potency" (*quwwa*) to mean "possibility" (*imkān*). Then they named the thing whose existence is within the bound of possibility "an existent in potency" (*al-imkān mawjūdan bi-l-quwwa*). And they named the possibility of a thing's receptivity [to be acted upon], and be affected, "potency to be acted upon" (*quwwa infiʿāliyya*). Then they termed the completion of this potency an act, even though this is not action but the reception of action, such as being moved, acquiring configuration, and the like ... and by act they meant the realization of existence (*ḥuṣūl al-wujūd*) ... this then is potency that is receptive to action. Perhaps they have said "potency" because of the excellence and intensity of this "receptivity" (*infiʿāliyya*).[74]

In this passage, Ibn Sīnā draws the reader's attention to the concepts of potency (*imkān*) and receptivity (*infiʿāliyya*). From the perspective of his metaphysical causality, an act means "realization of existence." This act realizes a potential in accordance with what it is. Again, the concept of *imkān* here implies freedom, for an act realizes potency but does not impose it.

With every originated thing, before its origination, it is in itself (such) that it is possible for it to exist or impossible for it to exist. That whose existence is impossible does not exist. That *whose existence is possible is preceded by the possibility of its existence* and the fact that it is possible for existence.[75]

[72] Ibid., 333–334. [73] Ibid., 208. [74] Ibid., 131. [75] Ibid., 140. Emphasis mine.

Here we also read that an existent being is preceded by "the possibility of its existence." God knows these preexisting essences, or potentialities: "The First through his own essence knows all things; that is because He is the principle of all things."[76] The First is a "knower," since whatever emanates from It is known to It. In a way, the First's knowledge of Itself is the cause of emanation of all things from It. The knowledge of the created order in the First's essence is the cause for the emanation of the created order. That is to say, the act of intellection and the act of creation are one and the same thing.

Again, despite all these statements, Ibn Sīnā does not indicate any "cause" for the emergence of these essences as they are in the divine knowledge. God does not determine them but only knows them. These essences are *uncaused* objects of God's knowledge. There is no cause for an entity to be the kind of entity it is in God's knowledge, although God is the cause of a possible being's existence as more than a mere possibility. In other words, the knowledge follows the known. Second, the idea of preexistence of essences or potentialities before their existentiation or actualization implies that every causal relation occurs in accordance with these possibilities in the divine knowledge and not haphazardly. Thus, Ibn Sīnā writes: "Other than the First everything's existence comes about, after not having existed, in accordance with its right or capacity (*istiḥqāq*), what it itself deserves."[77]

Recall that the First's self-knowledge implies knowledge of essences. The First knows an infinite number of objects, but this knowledge does not violate the divine simplicity. It can thus be argued that essences are coeternal with the divine Self as objects of the divine knowledge. Positing coeternity does not undermine the divine oneness so long as their existence – not essence – is causally dependent on God. If essences are eternal objects of the divine knowledge, they in a certain way must be uncaused, as much as they are essences. An eternal thing does not need a first cause and can be considered the uncaused cause of itself. However, they still depend on God for their existentiaton.

The agent is, in a way, a cause of the end; how could it not be so, when the agent is what makes the end occur as an existent? The end is, in a way, the cause of the agent; how could it not be so, when the agent acts only on account of it; otherwise, why would it be acting? For the end sets the agent in motion toward being an agent ... Exercise is the efficient cause of health, and the health is the final cause of exercise ... *The agent is not a cause of the end's becoming an end, nor of the end's essence itself (wa-lā li-māhiyyati al-ghāyati fī nafsihā); rather it is a cause of the*

[76] Ibid., 290. [77] Ibn Sīnā, *al-Shifāʾ al-Ilāhiyyāt*, 273. Translation modified.

> *existence of the essence in concrete reality*. The difference between essence and existence is as you already know. The end is a cause of the agent's being an agent, for it is the cause of the agent's being a cause, whereas the agent is not a cause of the end in terms of the end's being a cause. This will be made clear in First Philosophy.[78]

Thus, the First does not impose essences, but It bestows the gift of existence on essences. Hence, as it pertains to essences, entities have freedom to be what they are; and, as it pertains to existence, essences are dependent on the First's existentiating act to be actualized into what they are. There is then a priority of essence to the existentiating act of the First. It is this priority that implies freedom. As Ṭūsī writes:

> The essence of the end and its (being an) intentional object – I mean its being some particular thing or another – is different from its existence. The final cause's causality (*illiyatuhā*) consists in the fact that it *makes the agent actual* and is thus a cause of the agency of the agent. *The agent is a cause of the fact that essence becomes an existent. Thus, the essence of the end is a cause of the cause of its existence not in an absolute sense, but in a certain respect, so no circularity need be implied by this.*[79]

To conclude, essences are uncaused and eternal objects of the divine knowledge. They are the causes of delimitation of pure existence and, hence, differentiation. Entities are given existence in accordance with their essences. But this is not to suggest that God determines essences to be what they are in the divine knowledge and subsequently in the phenomenal domain. God knows and existentiates essences in accordance with His knowledge but does not determine what those essences are. In other words, entities cannot be the cause of their own existence, which they have to receive from the Necessary Existent, but they can cause their own essences. If we define freedom as an entity's capacity to be the uncaused cause of itself, then concepts such as essence (*māhiyya*), potentiality (*imkān*), and capacity (*istihqāq*) can be taken as the principles of freedom in Ibn Sīnā's system.

2.5 CONCLUSION

Ibn Sīnā approaches the question of causality from two perspectives. On the one hand, causality can be understood from the perspective of the

78 Ibn Sīnā, *Kitāb al-Shifā'/Ṭabīʿiyyāt* (1): *al-Samāʿ al-Ṭabīʿī*, ed S. Zāyid (Cairo, 1983), 1.11, 53, 4–12. Cited in Wisnovsky, *Avicenna's Metaphysics in Context*, 177–178. Emphasis mine.

79 Ṭūsī, *Sharḥ al-Ishārāt*, 193, 31–194, 6. Cited in Wisnovsky, *Avicenna's Metaphysics in Context*, 171. Emphasis mine.

"motion and rest" of physical objects. On the other hand, it can be approached from the perspective of existence. This is because God is not only the principle of motion and rest but also the principle and giver of existence. In his definition of physical causality, Ibn Sīnā agrees with Aristotle. In his definition of metaphysical causality, he constructs a relationship between God and the world based on the concept of existence. His account of existence indicates that the act of bestowal of existence is in fact the basis of physical activity. As such, Ibn Sīnā understands physical causality within the larger context of metaphysical causality.

Ibn Sīnā establishes creaturely freedom by starting from the two fundamental concepts of his metaphysics, existence and essence. Existence is the ground of all divine attributes. It implies and necessitates them. Entities receive existence from God to the extent allowed by their essences. As such, they participate in the divine existence. This participation in existence is the basis of creaturely freedom, for to participate in existence is to participate in the divine attributes, including consciousness and freedom, to the extent allowed by essences. The concept of essence provides another perspective, for essences are described as *uncaused* objects of the divine knowledge. Thus, essences can be considered as the principles of creaturely freedom. God knows and existentiates essences but does not cause them to be what they are in the divine knowledge.

As will be discussed in the following chapters, Ibn Sīnā's conceptualization of existence and essence provides a general philosophical framework for understanding causality and freedom.[80] There appears to be consensus among Suhrawardī, Ibn ʿArabī, Qūnawī, Qayṣarī, and Mullā Ṣadrā that the distinction between existence and essence and the description of God as pure existence has profound implications for divine and creaturely causality and freedom. Ibn Sīnā's writings also provoke a series of occasionalist responses, to be examined in Chapter 3.

[80] For more on Ibn Sīnā's influence on the later Islamic philosophical tradition, see Robert Wisnovsky, "Avicenna's Islamic Reception," in *Interpreting Avicenna: Critical Essays*, ed. Peter Adamson (Cambridge, UK: Cambridge University Press, 2013), 190–213. For his reception in Jewish and Christian-Latin Medieval traditions, see Gad Freudenthal and Mauro Zonta, "The Reception of Avicenna in Jewish Cultures, East–West," in ibid., 214–241; and Amos Bertolacci, "The Reception of Avicenna in Latin Medieval Culture," in ibid., 242–269.

3

Occasionalism in the Middle Period

Ghazālī's and Rāzī's Responses to Ibn Sīnā

Ibn Sīnā's philosophy presents certain theological and cosmological challenges to the occasionalist worldview. First, it removes the distinction between *wujūd* and the divine attributes and claims that all of the divine attributes are concealed and necessitated by *wujūd*. As discussed in the Chapter 1, the separation of the divine attributes from the divine essence and the subsequent accentuation of the divine will is the theological basis for the occasionalist understanding of the divine action and causality. Ibn Sīnā's decentralization of the divine will in his account of causality was seen by some as imposing necessity upon God and the world and thus erroneously implying some constraint on the divine will. Ashʿarite theology, which emphasizes the divine will and freedom, finds this conception problematic. Second, Ibn Sīnā's strong defense of hylomorphism and his attack on atomism further challenge the fundamental elements of the occasionalist worldview, including the concept of the constant re-creation of the world and the denial of necessary relation between subsequent causal events.

This chapter focuses on two responses to Ibn Sīnā's theological and cosmological challenges to occasionalism by two later thinkers in that tradition: Ghazālī and Rāzī. Ghazālī was more interested in responding to Ibn Sīnā's theological challenges.[1] What makes Ghazālī important for our discussion is not the formulation of occasionalist theory of causality,

[1] For Ghazālī's bibliography, see R. J. MacCarthy's "Annotated Bibliography," in *Freedom and Fulfillment: An Annotated Translation of Al-Ghazālī's al-Munqidh min al-Dalal and Other Relevant Works of al-Ghazālī* (Boston, MA: Twayne Publishers, 1980), 383–392; K. Nakamura, "A Bibliography on Imam al-Ghazālī," *Orient*, 13 (1977): 119–134.

which had already been introduced and elaborated by earlier Ash'arite theologians as examined in Chapter 1. He is important for his rigorous attempt to put Ash'arite occasionalism in conversation with Ibn Sīnā's synthesis of Aristotelian and Neoplatonic ideas about causality. He is also important for introducing novel applications of older ideas, such as his use of the concept of "preponderance without reason" to explain the creation of the world from nothing without implying a change in the nature of God. Ghazālī's novel applications in turn influenced later occasionalists such as Jurjānī and Nursi, as will be discussed in the following chapters.

Ghazālī was less interested in responding to Ibn Sīnā's arguments against Ash'arite atomism, and it is here that Rāzī becomes relevant to our discussion.[2] Rāzī advances a series of arguments in to defend *kalām* atomism. Rāzī's atomistic response to Ibn Sīnā's hylomorphism was a major development in the history of occasionalism and was well known and widely used by later generations of Muslim scholars. It will also be argued that Rāzī's awareness that Euclidian geometry can be used both *for* and *against* atomism with equal power led to a novel, pragmatic view of the dominant scientific models of his time. This new view held that although such models were practical and useful descriptions of nature, they cannot impose philosophical or theological commitments, since they are open to multiple philosophical and theological interpretations. This point was taken up and developed by later occasionalists such as Jurjānī, as will be discussed in this chapter.

3.1 GHAZĀLĪ AND THE DIVINE WILL

There is disagreement among modern scholars over whether Ghazālī was truly an occasionalist. In the view of A. J. Wensinck, Ghazālī regards God as the only agent in the world, even though he does not refrain from using the term "causality" as a heuristic device – a concept for thinking about

[2] For a concise account of Rāzī's life and works, see G. C. Anawati, "Fakhr al-Din al-Razi," in *Encyclopedia of Islam* 2, 2010, https://referenceworks.brillonline.com/entries/encyclopaedia-of-islam-2/fakhr-al-din-al-razi; Muhammad Salih al-Zarkān, *Fakhr al-Dīn al-Rāzī wa-Arā'uhu al-Kalāmiyyah wa-l-Falsafiyyah* (Beirut: Dar al-Fikr, 1963), 8–36; Tony Street, "Concerning the Life and Works of Fakhr al-Din al-Razi," in *Islam: Essays on Scripture, Thought and Society, a Festschrift in honour of Anthony H. Johns* (Leiden: Brill, 1997), 135–146.

natural phenomena that does not exist *in concreto*.[3] Majid Fakhyr claims that while Ghazālī rejects ontological causal necessity, he accepts logical necessity.[4] Goodman argues that Ghazālī does not deny causality. Ghazālī does not consider man only in terms of his passivity, as is suggested by occasionalist readings of his philosophy. Ghazālī also does not subscribe to Ashʿarite cosmology; he adopts Aristotelian and Avicennian hylomorphism and holds that God acts through man and nature, not despite them.[5] H. A. Wolfson joins Wensinck and contends that Ghazālī does not accept causality, despite the terminology of certain passages of his writings.[6]

W. J. Courtenay has argued that Ghazālī's conception of causality must be understood in light of his attempt to outline a natural order in which miracles are possible. To this end, Ghazālī offers both occasionalist and rationalist theories of causality. His main purpose is to refute Islamic philosophers rather than to present a positive theory of causality. He aims to eliminate the concepts of necessity and demonstrability from accounts of the natural order and instead underscore "contingency and dependability."[7]

Ilai Alon holds that Ghazālī attempts to reconcile two seemingly opposing views on causality, namely the "philosophical-necessitarian" and "kalamic-occasionalist" views on causality. Hence, Ghazālī cannot be said to be following traditional Ashʿarite occasionalism. This attempt fits Ghazālī's general tendency to reconcile opposing views, such as Sufism and "orthodoxy."[8] For Marmura, Ghazālī denies not only causal necessity between subsequent events but also any type of intermediation, whether angelic or anthropic, between God and the world.[9]

Abrahamov focuses on Ghazālī's non-philosophical writings and argues that Ghazālī combines divine causality with secondary causality.

3 A. J. Wensinck, *La Pensee de Ghazālī* (Paris: Libr. d'Amérique et d'Orient A. Maisonneuve, 1950), 60.

4 Majid Fakhry, *Islamic Occasionalism* (London: Allen & Unwin, 1958), 60.

5 L. E. Goodman, "Did Ghazālī Deny Causality?" *Studia Islamica*, 47 (1978): 83–120.

6 H. A. Wolfson, *The Philosophy of the Kalam*, 548–551.

7 W. J. Courtenay, "The Critique on Natural Causality in the Mutakallimun and Nominalism," *The Harvard Theological Review*, 66.1 (1973): 93–94.

8 Ilai Alon, "Ghazālī on Causality," *Journal of American Oriental Society*, 100.4 (1980): 397.

9 Michael E. Marmura, "Ghazālī's Second Causal Theory in the 17th Discussion of his *Tahafut*," in *Islamic Philosophy and Mysticism*, ed. Parviz Morewedge (New York, 1981), 85–112; also see M. E. Marmura, "Ghazālī on Bodily Resurrection and Causality in *Tahafut* and the *Iqtisad*," *Aligarh Journal of Islamic Thought*, 1 (1989): 46–75.

God creates both cause and effect and maintains their relation, but cause and effect also have inherent natures – a fact that renders causality relatively necessary.[10] Nazif Muhtaroglu argues that Ghazālī was a thoroughgoing occasionalist.[11] Blake Dutton pursues a fairly traditional occasionalist reading of Ghazālī by starting from his analysis of the concept of possibility.[12] Frank Griffel believes that Ghazālī "remains uncommitted" between occasionalism and secondary causality. For Ghazālī, human inquiry into nature and revelation cannot settle the dispute between the two options, and so occasionalism cannot be completely disregarded.[13]

I agree with Frank Griffel's observation that Ghazālī holds that because human investigation of nature and revelation cannot settle the dispute between occasionalist and necessitarian understandings of causality, both positions are tenable options. However, as I will argue, for Ghazālī, these two positions are not equally tenable. Occasionalism appears to be the more probable option. For, Ghazālī's arguments in the *Tahāfut* and in his other writings are in accordance with the general tendencies of earlier Ashʿarite theology of possibility examined in Chapter 1. He resorts to the same analogies proposed by the earlier Ashʿarites. His response to Ibn Sīnā is based on the Ashʿarite occasionalist notion of "preponderance without reason." Throughout the *Tahāfut*, his main intention is to preserve the centrality of the divine will among the divine attributes. These and similar continuities suggest that Ghazālī's response to Ibn Sīnā in the *Tahāfut* is rooted in Ashʿarite theology of possibility. Accordingly, I believe, Ghazālī sees the occasionalist account of causality as the more probable – if not fully provable – one.

Now, as considered in Chapter 1, Ashʿarite theory understands the divine agency in light of three fundamental attributes: knowledge, will, and power. Then it proceeds to centralize the divine will. In accordance with the general Ashʿarite tendency, Ghazālī's theory of divine agency also follows from a desire to preserve a robust understanding of the divine

[10] B. Abrahamov, "Ghazālī's Theory of Causality," *Studia Islamica*, 67 (1988): 75–89.

[11] Nazif Muhtaroglu, *Islamic and Cartesian Roots of Occasionalism* (Ph.D. dissertation, University of Kentucky, 2012).

[12] Blake D. Dutton, *Medieval Philosophy and Theology*, 10 (2001): 23–46.

[13] Frank Griffel, *Al-Ghazālī's Philosophical Theology: An Introduction to the Study of his Life and Thought* (New York: Oxford University Press, 2009), 176. Also see George E Hourani, "The Dialogue between Ghazālī and the Philosophers on the Origin of the World," *The Muslim World*, 48 (1958): 183–191; Eric Ormsby, *The Makers of the Muslim World: Ghazālī* (Oxford: One World, 2007), 80–82; Simon Van den Bergh, *Averroes' Tahafut al-Tahafut* (The Incoherence of the Incoherence): Notes (London: Messrs. Luzac and Company, Ltd, 1954), II, 184, note on 1.329.5.

will (*irāda*) and freedom. Almost all of his arguments against Ibn Sīnā in his *Tahāfut* can be traced back to this fundamental concern. For him, when the Philosophers defend the preeternity of the world, the necessary emanation of the world from the First, and necessity in causality they lose the divine will and freedom. Furthermore, once the divine will is compromised, other of the divine attributes such as knowledge, life, seeing, or hearing are also compromised. When the Philosophers argue that the First is pure existence they again compromise the divine attributes of will, power, and knowledge. Ghazālī's defense of the theory of preponderance without reason (*tarjīh bi-lā murajjīh*) as the intrinsic feature of the divine will is also based on the same motivation to preserve divine freedom. Let us examine this more closely.

In the first discussion of the *Tahāfut*, Ghazālī argues against the doctrine of the preeternity of the world. The Philosophers argue that the world must be preeternal because it is impossible for a temporal being to proceed from an eternal being. This raises the so-called particularization problem. Such an act would imply a change in the essence of the eternal being by way of power, will, nature, and time. A change in the state of the Eternal is impossible, since such a change would mean that the Eternal previously had some unrealized potential and was thus imperfect until it realized that potential. The world therefore must have existed eternally together with its cause.[14] For Ghazālī, the necessitarian implications of this doctrine compromise the divine will and thus render the doctrine invalid. To say that the world necessarily emanates from the First Principle is to say that the world is not willed, but rather necessitated by the nature of the First. The Philosophers' God does not act voluntarily but out of necessity.[15] Therefore, their God is not the "God of the Qur'an."[16] Ghazālī concludes that nothing proves the existence of the divine attribute of will except the temporal creation of the world.[17] The world then must have been created *ex nihilo* and in time through the act of the divine will.

[14] Ghazālī, *The Incoherence of the Philosophers* (*Tahāfut al-Falāsifa*), a Parallel English–Arabic Text, ed. and trans. M. E. Marmura (Provo, UT: Brigham Young University Press, 1997), 30–33.

[15] Ghazālī, *Tahāfut*, 161, 172. [16] Ibid., 169.

[17] Ibid., 131–134. Elsewhere Ghazālī gives a definition of the divine attribute of power and how it functions together with two other divine attributes: will and knowledge. He writes that "Power is equivalent to the intention by which a thing comes into existence according to a determinate plan of will and knowledge, and inconformity with both of them." Ghazālī, *al-Maqsad al-Asnā fī Sharḥ al-Maʿānī Asmāʾ Allāh al-Ḥusnā* (The Ninety-Nine Beautiful Names of God), trans. David B. Burrel and Nazer Daher (Cambridge, UK: The Islamic Texts Society, 1992), 131.

What about the Philosophers' concern that projecting a change in God is repugnant because it implies a move from potentiality to actuality in the First which is already perfect and thus can have no potentiality waiting to be actualized? Ghazālī refutes this point by arguing that the divine will could bring about a temporal event without necessitating a change from potentiality to actuality. It is possible that the divine will chooses without preference, without any objective. Will is an attribute whose function is to differentiate one similar or identical thing from another, even if there is no reason to give preponderance (*tarjīh bi-lā murajjīh*). If we are standing in front of two *equal* dates, at an equal distance, hungry and being forced to choose only one of them, we would inevitably take one of them without preference, with the help of the attribute of will, whose function it is to "differentiate one thing from its similar" where there is no reason to differentiate.[18] This understanding enables Ghazālī to preserve the divine will and connect it with the temporal creation without implying change in the First.[19]

Furthermore, if the divine will is compromised, Ghazālī concludes, then we also necessarily compromise the divine knowledge. This is because, for something to be willed, it must be known by the willer. If the world is not willed but necessitated, then the Philosophers' account of the world does not require the attribute of the divine knowledge. They fail to provide a proof for the knowledge of God.[20] For example, the Philosophers argue that God knows through a universal knowledge that does not change. This knowledge embraces the past, the present, and the future as one eternal moment. There cannot be change in God's knowledge, since such a change would contradict God's perfection. If the known object changes, knowledge changes; and if knowledge changes, the knower changes. God knows temporal events, such as an eclipse, as unaffected by time and space. However, for Ghazālī, this conception of divine knowledge leads to dire conclusions. Once we separate God's knowledge from spatio-temporality, it follows that God does not know man in his particularity but only as a species and that God knows all the attributes of the human species but is unable to distinguish one man from another. From this, repugnancies necessarily ensue: God in this case would not know individuals such as the Prophet Muhammad.[21]

[18] Ghazālī, *Tahāfut*, 23–24.

[19] As will be discussed in Chapter 4, Ibn Rushd argues that this conclusion comes at a heavy price, for it implies that the First acts without an objective, purpose, or cause.

[20] Ibid., 125–128.

[21] Ghazālī, *Tahāfut*, 140.

Ghazālī then takes this argument a step further, positing that when we lose the divine will we also lose the attribute of life. Namely, that from the divine will one infers the divine knowledge and from the divine will and knowledge, one infers the divine life.[22] Therefore, a God without will is a God without knowledge and life. Such a God would resemble an inanimate being or even "a dead person" who does not know or will what proceeds from him. Then, when the Philosophers' doctrine negates the divine will and freedom it also negates other essential divine attributes such as knowledge, life, hearing, and seeing.[23]

Again, Ghazālī's criticism here stems from the general Ashʿarite tendency to centralize the divine will. Moreover, harking back to the Ashʿarite account of the relationship of God and the divine attributes, Ghazālī argues that the Philosophers' doctrine of the simplicity of the First compromises the divine attributes. He further claims that the Philosophers' attempt to "reduce the divine attributes to essence" leads to "the denial (*nafy*) of attributes."[24] Recall that it was argued in Chapter 1 that the idea of the separability of the divine attributes from the divine essence is fundamental for the Ashʿarite view of the divine action and causality in the world. If these attributes are not identical with the divine essence, then they can be perceived as the means through which God relates to world. To defend Ashʿarite doctrine, Ghazālī contends that the separability of attributes from God's essence is not impossible – as the Philosophers argue. It is possible for the attributes to be in the divine essence as coeternal concomitants. Furthermore, plurality and quiddity in the Necessary Existent is not impossible.[25] The First, simply, is "an eternal being having eternal attributes." And "there is neither a cause for His essence nor for His attributes, nor for the subsistence of His attributes in His essence."[26] To say that God is perfect and self-subsistent is to say that God has coeternal attributes of perfection. For, "the attributes of perfection do not separate from the essence of the Perfect." To deny the attributes "through which the divinity is perfected" is like saying "the Perfect is the one who does not need perfection."[27] Therefore, the multiplicity of the attributes subsisting in the essence of God does not negate the perfection and self-subsistence of the Necessary Existent, as the Philosophers argue. On the contrary, they are necessary concomitants of divine perfection.[28]

[22] Ibid., 107, 131–132. [23] Ibid., 130, 132. [24] Ibid., 96. [25] Ibid., 97, 116.
[26] Ibid., 101. [27] Ibid., 100. [28] Also see ibid., 116–119.

For Ghazālī, then, these theories suggested by the Philosophers compromise the divine attributes, especially the divine will, and undermine the divine agency. The "agent" – in order to be an agent in the proper meaning of the word – should be "a knower, a willer, and a chooser." Since the Philosophers assert that the world necessarily proceeds from the First, they do not need the divine will. Nor do they require the divine knowledge, which for Ghazālī is meaningless without the divine will. To be able to will something, one must know it. If there is no will, there is no need for knowledge. According to the system of the Philosophers, God is not really an "agent."[29] Moreover, the term "act" indicates a temporal occurrence that is willed. If the Philosophers agree that the world is eternal, then it cannot really be an "act" of the First, since an eternal being does not need an originator agent. The only thing they can say is that God precedes the first emanated being. Thus, for the Philosophers, the terms "agent" and "act" are devoid of their real meaning (as Ghazālī understands them), implying only God's *essential* priority to the world. If they use the term "agent," it is only to endear themselves to the larger public (*tatajammalūn*).[30]

It is clear that Ghazālī's criticism of the Philosophers' theory of "agency" follows from the Ashʿarite definition of the divine agency, which is formulated around the divine attributes of will, power, and knowledge. In *al-Iqtisād*, Ghazālī also writes: "The agent, however, is not called an agent and a maker by simply being a cause, but by being a cause in a special respect, namely, by way of will and choice. So, if one were to say that the wall is not an agent; the stone is not an agent; the inanimate is not an agent ... this would not be denied, and the statement would not be false."[31] Clearly, the divine will appears to be more central than the other attributes in Ghazālī's construction of the divine agency. His concern for other divine attributes such as knowledge, hearing, seeing, and life is closely related to his understanding of this central attribute.

It is in this context that Ghazālī endorses the Ashʿarite occasionalist theory of causality and offers one of the clearest expressions of Ashʿarite occasionalism: "The connection between what is habitually believed to be a cause and what is habitually believed to be an effect is not *necessary*

[29] Ghazālī, *Tahāfut*, 56–57. [30] Ibid., 64.

[31] Ghazālī, *al-Iqtiṣād fi-l-Iʿtiqād* (Moderation in Belief), trans. Michael E. Marmura in *Ghazālī's Chapter on Divine Power in the Iqtiṣād*" *Arabic Sciences and Philosophy*, 4 (1994), 296.

according to us."[32] Connection between cause and effect "is due to God's decree, Who creates them *side by side*, not to its being necessary in itself, incapable of separation."[33] Observation shows only concomitance – not any necessary connection between cause and effect. Ghazālī reiterates these ideas in his later writings. For example, in the 31st book of *Iḥyā'*, he writes that God creates both cause and effect and that He does so in an orderly manner. One of the verses most frequently quoted by Ghazālī to support this view is the following: "You will not find any change in God's habit" (Qur'an 33:62 and 48:23).[34] Ghazālī then echoes these views in the *Iqtiṣād*:

> You have known from the sum of this that all temporal events, their substances and accidents; those occurring in the entities of the animate and the inanimate come about through the power of God, exalted be He. He alone holds the sole prerogative of inventing them. No created thing comes about through another [created thing]. Rather, all come about through [divine] power.[35]

God can create an effect without its habitual cause, such as satiety without drinking. Cotton can transform into ashes without contact with fire. Constant conjunction of cause and effect does not prove a necessary connection. One can say effect exists *with* cause, but one cannot say effect exists *by* cause.[36] "All the acts of His servants are His creation, connected with His power."[37] Moreover, "all temporal events, their substances and accidents, those occurring in the entities of the animate and the inanimate, come about through the power of God, exalted be He. He alone holds the sole prerogative of inventing them. *No created thing comes about through another* [created thing]. Rather, all come about through [divine] power."[38] Observation cannot locate any necessitating connection between cause and effect. All we observe is constant conjunction. If a person who is "blind from birth and has a film on his eyes and who has never heard from people the difference between night and day were to have the film cleared from his eyes in daytime," he would believe that "the opening of his sight is the cause of the apprehension of the forms of

32 Ghazālī, *Tahāfut*, 166. Emphasis mine.
33 Ibid. Emphasis mine.
34 Ghazālī, *Iḥyā' 'Ulūm al-Dīn*, 16 parts (Cairo: Lajnat Nashr al-Thaqafa al-Islamiyya). Reprint Beirut: Dar al-Kitab al-Arabi, n.d. [*c.*1990], 1937–1938.
35 Ghazālī, *Iqtiṣād*, 314–315.
36 Ghazālī, *Tahāfut*, 168.
37 Ghazālī, *al-Maqṣad*, 21.
38 Ghazālī, *Iqtiṣād*, 314–315. Emphasis mine. See also Michael E. Marmura "Ghazālian Causes and Intermediaries," *Journal of the American Oriental Society* 115 (1995): 94; Edward Omar Moad, "Ghazālī on Power, Causation, and Acquisition," *Philosophy East West*, 57.1 (2007): 1–13.

the colors." But when the sun sets and the atmosphere becomes dark, he would then know that "it is the sunlight that is the cause for the imprinting of the colors in his sight."[39]

To conclude, Ghazālī's main concern in responding to Ibn Sīnā is to preserve the Ashʿarite conception of the divine agency, which emphasizes the divine will and freedom. Ghazālī's rejection of the preeternity of the world, the idea of necessary emanation, the simplicity of the First, and his defense of the concept of "preference without reason" (*tarjīh bi-lā murajjīh*), the plurality and quiddity in the First are based on this concern to preserve the divine will. As a result of his general tendency to emphasize the divine will, he appears to endorse the occasionalist conclusion that there is no necessary relation between cause and effect.

3.2 RĀZĪ AND ATOMISM

Ibn Sīnā also attacks atomism, a fundamental concept in Ashʿarite cosmology and theology. Ghazālī appears largely uninterested in this aspect Ibn Sina's thought. There are very few references to atomism in Ghazālī's writings. One of the few can be found in the *Tahāfut*, where he merely writes, "the discussion of the atom is linked with geometrical matters whose solution will lengthen the discussion."[40] Rāzī, however, takes up the challenge and discusses atomism, as well as Ibn Sīnā's hylomorphism, in many extant works. It will be argued that Rāzī's reformulation of Ashʿarite atomism was a novel development in the history of occasionalism. In contrast to Ghazālī, Rāzī is keenly aware of Ibn Sīnā's criticism of atomism and offers a series of arguments to counter his challenges.

Below, I first provide an overview of the occasionalist elements in Rāzī's theology. I then examine both Ibn Sīnā's arguments *against* atomism and Rāzī's arguments *for* atomism. Finally, I comment on Rāzī's responses and argue that his writings reflect a highly pragmatic philosophy of science.

3.3 RĀZĪ AS AN OCCASIONALIST

As with previous Ashʿarites, Rāzī holds that created beings lack causal efficacy. He writes that it is "invalid to claim for the existence of an

[39] Ghazālī, *Tahāfut*, 168. [40] Ibid., 191.

effective agent other than God."[41] The relationship between cause and effect is not one of necessity. It is, however, consistent and predictable. God creates both cause and effect and relates them to each other on a self-imposed habitual pattern. This habituality guarantees predictability.

Accordingly, Rāzī rejects the notion of nature as a causally efficacious principle. For him, if nature refers to the essence of a thing, "the principle of its motion and rest,"[42] then it must be rejected, for it supports the idea of necessity in causality, which contradicts divine freedom and sovereignty. Moreover, for Rāzī, "this nature is itself is in need of a creator and an originator (*mūjid*)."[43] A necessary relationship between natures and causal events cannot be established. This view takes away causal efficacy from the secondary causality. In the Qur'anic verse "And He (Who) has caused water to pour down from the sky, thereby producing fruits as food for you" (2:22), neither water nor the earth are causally efficacious. God creates the fruits without needing the causality of water and earth. What then is the function of secondary causality and intermediaries? For Rāzī, intermediaries exist for ethical and epistemological reasons, not as causes, as transmitters of divine causal influence from God to the created order. It is us who impose causal efficacy upon secondary causality due to the regularity of phenomenal processes. This regularity creates the illusion of necessity.[44] In fact, causality is a "veil." The reason that God creates behind the veil of causes is to preserve the nature of the world as a "test." Creation without the seeming existence of causes would render unbelief impossible. Therefore, "were it not for the causes the doubter would not have doubted!" (*law lā al-asbābu lamā irtāba murtābun*).[45]

Rāzī also follows Ash'arite tradition on the issue of the divine attributes, holding that they are neither separate from nor identical to the divine essence. In the *Muḥaṣṣal*, for example, he writes that "God has knowledge with his knowledge, power with his power, and life with his

[41] Cited in Zarkān, *Fakhr al-Dīn al-Rāzī*, 356.

[42] Fakhr al-Dīn al-Rāzī, *al-Mabāḥith al-Mashriqiyyah*, ed. Muhammad al-Mu'tasim biLlah al-Baghdadi, 2 vols (Beirut: Dar al-Kitab al-Arabi, 1990), 1: 645

[43] Fakhr al-Dīn al-Rāzī, *al-Tafsīr al-Kabīr*, 32 vols (Beirut: Dar Ihya al-Turath al-Arabi, 1996), 8 (23), 268. Cited in Adi Setia, "Fakhr al-Dīn al-Rāzī on Physics and the Nature of the Physical World: A Preliminary Survey," *Islam & Science*, 2.2 (2004): 167.

[44] Setia, "Fakhr al-Dīn al-Rāzī on Physics and the Nature of the Physical World: A Preliminary Survey," 166

[45] Rāzī, *al-Tafsīr al-Kabīr*, 1 (2), 343.

life."[46] Now, as discussed in Chapter 1, this theory constructs the relationship between God and the world through the divine attributes and subsequently presents a particular understanding of divine action that emphasizes the divine will. Rāzī's appropriation of this line of thinking is evident in many passages, especially those concerning the issue of preponderance (*tarjīh*):

God's works needs a preponderer. The attribute of power is not a preponderer, for its function is to create objects toward which it has the same relationships. The *preponderer* cannot be knowledge, for knowledge follows the known and does not necessitate the known, for regression is impossible. It is understood that none of the attributes but *the divine will* can differentiate.[47]

Here, Rāzī draws on the idea of "preponderance without reason" as formulated by Ghazālī. God creates the world and differentiates things without having a purpose. As is the case in Ghazālī's example of the two dates, differentiation occurs between equal options as a result of the intrinsic quality and ability of the divine will, which can differentiate without reason. For "the divine will is exalted (*munazzah*) from having aims. In fact, to create an object in a specific time is necessitated (*wājib*) by the essence of will."[48] The issue of preponderance is also understood in a cosmological and spiritual sense:

The bodies of the world are homogenous (*mutasāwiya*) with respect to their essential corporeality (*māhiyyat al-jismiyya*), whereas they are different (*mukhtalifa*) with respect to their characteristics, which are their colors, places, and modes of being. It is impossible that each body's specificity (*ikhtiṣāṣ*) with regard to a particular characteristic is due to its corporeality per se, or to the concomitants of corporeality, or else the bodies would all be homogenous. Thus, it is necessary that this specificity be due to the specifying act of a specifier (*mukhaṣṣiṣ*) and the organization of an organizer (*tadbīr mudabbir*) ... Once you realize this, it will be manifest that each one of the particles of the heavens and the earth is a truthful witness to and an articulate informer of the existence of the powerful, wise, and omniscient God.[49]

In a similar vein, Rāzī argues that the Qur'anic verses affirming human volition and accountability are to be read in the context of other verses that affirm the robust understanding of divine agency in the world,

[46] Fakhr al-Dīn al-Rāzī, *Muḥaṣṣal Afkār al-Mutaqaddimīn wa-l-Muta'akhkhirīn*, ed. Abd al-Rauf Said (Cairo: Maktabat al-Kulliyat al-Azhariyya, n.d.), 180.

[47] Rāzī, *Muḥaṣṣal*, 169. Emphasis mine. [48] Ibid., 170.

[49] Rāzī, *al-Tafsīr al-Kabīr*, 1 (1): 26. Cited in Setia, "Fakhr al-Dīn al-Rāzī on Physics and the Nature of the Physical World: A Preliminary Survey," 179. Translation was modified.

such as "everything happens with the divine decree"; "He is the creator of everything"; "God creates you and what you do"; and "God does as he wishes."[50] To solve the apparent contradiction here between these verses and the verses affirming human volition, he employs the theory of acquisition, like other Ashʿarites. "Although we reject that man is the creator of his own deeds, we affirm that he does and acquires them." In other words, "man leans toward submission and God creates it; or man leans toward transgression and God creates it. According to this principle, although man is not the originator of the act, he become like the originator."[51] This tendency suffices to render human beings responsible for their actions without holding them to be the creators of their actions. And it is on this possibility that the Qurʾan's commandments are based.[52] Moreover, the concept of the divine habit is also introduced to establish a consistent link between acquisition and creation of acts. The constant conjunction of acquisition and creation is a habit of God.

Again, following previous occasionalists, Rāzī describes miracles as breaks in the divine habitual creation.[53] God creates them to affirm "the truthfulness of his messengers." As such, miracles also show humans' inability to go beyond habitual boundaries without divine support. He thus writes:

> If a man, in the presence of a king, declares that he is a messenger of the king and asks the king to stand up, and if the king stands up, then people in the presence of the king would believe in the truthfulness of the messenger.[54]

Rāzī also borrows some arguments from earlier occasionalists. For example, he argues that to be the creator of an act or the causer of an effect, one should know everything about the act or the effect. To truly cause an arm to move, one would need to know and manage every single process and detail that leads to the motion of the arm – which humans do not. Thus,

> If man is the creator of his acts then he should have known them in all details (*bi-tafāṣīlihā*). For, if we accept that one can create without knowing, then all the proofs of the divine knowledge also collapse. For the universal end does not suffice for the occurrence of the particular ends ... Thus, it is necessary that there needs to be a specifying knowledge conditioning and creating the particular aims. So,

50 Rāzī, *Muḥaṣṣal*, 198. 51 Ibid. 52 Ibid., 199. 53 Ibid., 207.
54 Ibid., 208. Also see 215.

one who creates his own acts should know these acts in all details, which is evidently not the case.[55]

Rāzī can safely be located in the occasionalist tradition. He denies the causal efficacy of created beings, rejects the concept of natures, affirms the concept of "preponderance without reason" to explain differentiation of homogeneous bodies, accepts the theory of acquisition, uses the concept of habit to explain the regularity in the world, and sees miracles as possible breaks in the patterns of the divine habit.

3.4 RĀZĪ AND ATOMISM AFTER IBN SĪNĀ

Rāzī thus largely accepts the fundamental convictions of Ashʿarite theology without modification. We find Rāzī's novel contribution to the occasionalist tradition is his enrichment of the atomistic theory, following Ibn Sīnā's strong criticism of it. He constructs novel arguments through an exploration of Euclidian geometry and sensual experience of time, space, and motion. In this regard, it is possible to speak of a post-Avicennian atomism. Before examining Rāzī's arguments for atomism, however, we must first consider Ibn Sīnā's arguments against atomism.

3.4.1 *Ibn Sīnā's Arguments against Atomism*

In Book Three of the *Physics of the Shifā'*, Ibn Sīnā constructs several arguments to refute Ashʿarite atomism.[56] In these arguments, Ibn Sīnā attacks the atomists' contentions that atoms are physically and conceptually indivisible, that they are not bodies, and that they exist and move in the void.

[55] Ibid., 190. For different versions of this argument before Rāzī, see, for example, Bāqillānī, *al-Inṣāf*, 205; Juwaynī, *al-Kitāb al-Irshād*, 174. Maturidite theologians also use the same argument. See, for instance, Nasafī, *Tabṣirat al-Adilla*, 613–618. The argument also exists in more recent occasionalist thought, as we will see in Nursī, *Mesnevī, RNK*, 2: 1347.

[56] A good summary of Ibn Sīnā's arguments can also be found in Alnoor Dhanani, "The Impact of Ibn Sina's Critique of Atomism on Subsequent Kalam Discussions of Atomism," *Arabic Sciences and Philosophy*, 25 (2015): 79–104 and Adi Setia, "Atomism Versus Hylomorphism in the *Kalām* of al-Fakhr al-Din al-Rāzī," *Islam & Science*, 4.2 (2006): 113–140. For an interesting modern critique of Ibn Sīnā's arguments, see F. A. Shamsi, "Ibn Sina's Arguments against Atomicity of Space," *Islamic Studies*, 23.2 (Summer 1984): 83–102.

1 **Arguments from Euclidian Geometry:** Ibn Sīnā posits that if there are atoms occupying space (*mutaḥayyiz*) that cannot be divided conceptually or physically, as *kalām* atomism claims, then it would be impossible to have such commonplace geometrical shapes as circles and diagonals. Imagine a right-angled triangle with two equal sides. If each equal side has four atoms then, given the Pythagorean Theorem, $A^2 + B^2 = C^2$, the length of the hypotenuse should be about 5.65 atoms. This implies that the length of the hypotenuse falls below the unit of an atom: we would need 5 whole atoms and 65 percent of a sixth atom. The atomists cannot allow units smaller than atoms without contradicting their claim regarding the indivisibility of atoms and, thus, without giving up the whole theory. If they argue that "vision errs with respect to the circle and right-angled triangle, and that these figures are serrated" (*ashkāl muḍarassa*), then they cannot account for any geometrical shape which has circular or diagonal lines. Now, if one needs to choose between the Pythagorean Theorem, which is one of the most axiomatic principles of mathematics, and a physical theory based on certain dubious thought experiments, one should obviously choose the former.

2 **Argument from Physical Experience:** Imagine there is a sheet of a single layer of atoms between an observer and the sun. If atoms are indivisible and have no dimensions or sides, then the sun must simultaneously illuminate both sides of the atoms. In this case one cannot distinguish one side from the other. There is no reason to believe that there is a sheet of atoms between the observer and the sun. But there is a sheet of atoms. And if one posits that there is a sheet of atoms, then it necessarily follows that atoms have a sun-side and an observer-side.[57] This implies that atoms have dimensions and sides and are therefore divisible, which disproves the basic claim of atomism.

3 **Argument from the Void:** Ashʿarite atomism claims that the world is composed of atoms and the void in which they move. Ibn Sīnā attacks the concept of the void. He argues that the void is not intelligible and is therefore an empty concept. In other words, if the void is absolutely nothing with no positive quality at all, then how can one claim that it actually exists? If the void is tantamount to "nothing," then it does not exist. If it does not exist, then atomists would have to agree with Aristotle and Ibn Sīnā, who claim that there is no void. If the void is something, then it should have some positive quality. Ashʿarite theology actually

[57] Ibn Sīnā, *The Physics of the Healing*, trans. J. McGinnis (Provo, UT: Brigham Young University Press, 2009), 2, 284.

attributes a positive quality to the void when it talks about a greater or lesser distance between atoms. In the Ashʿarite view, a void can be greater or lesser, and being greater or lesser is a quality that pertains to the void. In this case, we would have to imagine the void as a "substance" possessing accidental qualities. However, according to Ashʿarites, we are not allowed to say that the void is a substance. If it is not a substance, then how can it have accidental qualities? If it is a substance, then how it is different from "atoms," which are the substances posited by Ashʿarites? This is an evident contradiction.[58]

4 **Arguments from Conceptual Divisibility:** First, imagine three atoms (x, y, z) in a row. If y is between x and z, then it must exist in a distinct relationship to each of them: y is in contact with x and z with different "sides" of itself. Otherwise it is impossible to speak of "in-betweenness." And if y can be in contact with x and z with different "sides" of itself, then one must conclude that it has sides and is conceptually divisible.[59]

Second, a gnomon on a sunny day produces shadows on the ground. When the sun moves in the sky the distance of an atom, the shadow also moves. The distance that the shadow moves will have a fractional value. This entails that there can be a size smaller than the size of an atom, and hence that atoms are conceptually divisible.

Third, consider two atoms separated by the void. Consider also that the void between them is the size of an atom. When these atoms are pushed toward each other they will move toward the empty space and meet somewhere in the middle. The distance they move will necessarily be less than the size of an atom. This implies that one can at least conceive of sizes smaller than an atom. Hence, atoms are conceptually divisible.[60]

Four, consider an atom a on top of two adjacent atoms, b and c. Atom a can either be on top of b or c, or on top of both b and c. Therefore, the moment an atomist theologian accepts that the atom a can simultaneously touch both b and c, he is conceptually dividing the atom. This is a clear contradiction.

In this and similar arguments, Ibn Sīnā repeats the same idea. If one envisages sides or edges, one then has to accept that atoms can conceptually be divided, even though we may not be able to divide them in actuality.[61]

5 **Arguments from Motion:** First, recall that Ashʿarite atomism describes motion in terms of spatio-temporal "jumps." An arrow, during

[58] Ibn Sīnā, *The Physics*, 2, 8. [59] Ibid., 2, 282–284. [60] Ibid., 2, 299–300.
[61] Ibid., 2, 291–292.

its motion, is recreated anew in subsequent locations, creating the illusion of continuous motion. For Ibn Sīnā, this leads to a conundrum regarding the variation in velocity of objects. If speed is determined by the number of interspersed rests, then the sun and a galloping horse moving simultaneously will have different numbers of interspersed rests. The horse will have many more rests than the sun, which account for its relative slowness. But this presents a difficulty, because they move simultaneously. In this case, we would have to imagine a different re-creation frequency for each object moving at different speeds. The world, then, is re-created anew at a different frequency for each object.[62] For Ibn Sīnā, the problem here appears to be that Ashʿarite atomism posits only one re-creation frequency when it argues that the world is re-created anew at each moment and, therefore, cannot account for this difficulty.

3.4.2 *Rāzī's Arguments for Atomism*

1 **Arguments from Space and Motion:** If space is infinitely divisible, then to arrive at point b by starting from point a would be impossible: in order to cover the distance between the two points, one first needs to arrive at the halfway point between a and b, and then the halfway point at the middle of the remaining half, and so on. A person reaches the points $1/2$, $3/4$, and $7/8$, on the way to his goal and gets infinitely close to but never arrives at $1/1$.[63] If the number of parts between the two distances is infinite, as implied by the concept of infinite divisibility defended by Ibn Sīnā, then one would have to cover an infinite number of parts to journey from one

[62] Ibid., 2, 196–197. For the *kalām* discussion, see Dhanani, "Problems in kalām physics," *Bulletin of the Royal Institute of Interfaith Studies*, 4 (2002): 73–96.

[63] Rāzī reiterates this argument in a number of places. See, for example, Rāzī, *Muḥaṣṣal*, 115–117. This is obviously a reformulation of Zeno's paradox of the Stadium, in which the runner reaches an infinite number of points on his way. For Aristotle's reconstruction of the paradox, see *Physics* 6.9, 239b 11–13. Similarly, in another paradox, Achilles cannot catch the tortoise despite the difference in their speeds, for the distance between the two is infinitely divisible. *Physics* 6.8, 239b 14–16. It is interesting to see how both Ibn Sīnā and Rāzī use Zeno's paradoxes to argue for the continuous and the discrete models of the universe. For the relevance of Zeno's paradoxes to the debate on the continuous or discrete nature of the physical world, see M. J. White, *The Continuous and the Discrete: Ancient Physical Theories from a Contemporary Perspective* (Oxford: Clarendon Press, 1992). Adolf Grünbaum, *Modern Science and Zeno's Paradoxes* (Middletown, CT: Wesleyan University Press, 1967). Michael Dummett, "Is Time a Continuum of Instants?" in *Philosophy* (Cambridge, UK: Cambridge University Press, 2000), 497–515; Wesley C. Salmon, ed., *Zeno's Paradoxes* (Indianapolis and New York: The Bobbs-Merrill Company, Inc., 1970; repr. 2001).

point to another. It would take an infinite amount of time to journey from one point to another. This would make motion itself impossible, which is evidently absurd. Hence, there has to be a finite number of points between a and b, as is suggested in Ashʿarite atomism.[64]

2 **Argument from Time:** If time is infinitely divisible then the how can one talk about the passage of time? The continuity of time implies that the "now" is continuous with nonexisting past and nonexisting future. The past, however, has passed and it is nonexistent. Similarly, the future has not happened yet, it is also nonexistent. Thus, the past and the future cannot be continuous with the now, for they are nonexistent. The now, therefore, should stand as an independent unit. It follows that the time is constituted from successive detached units, temporal atoms, and, hence, must be discrete (*munfaṣil*).[65]

3 **Argument from Bodies:** Consider a mustard seed and a mountain. If each of them is infinitely divisible, then there is no reason to claim that the mountain has more parts than the mustard seed. In this case one cannot compare their sizes, which is an evidently absurd conclusion. Hence, the mountain and the mustard seed must be composed of indivisible parts, so that the mountain would have more parts than the mustard seed.[66]

4 **Arguments from the Point:** If point is a real thing, then the point-like definition of the atom by the atomists is true. And the point should be a real thing, since "a line touches another line at a point." If the point is not real, then there is no way to conceive of the "touching" (*mulāqāh*) of any two lines. This is evidently false. Thus, the point does not only exist in the imagination but also "in concrete reality" (*fī-l-aʿyān*).[67] He writes that "there is consensus that the point is an existing thing. For a line touches another line at a point. The act of touching really occurs and is not nonexistent ... And if this point occupies a location, then the reality of the atom is established."[68] It is not clear how Rāzī moves from the geometrical indivisibility of point to the concrete indivisibility of the atom. However, recall that Ibn Sīnā was mainly attacking conceptual indivisibility, not actual indivisibility. So, if Ibn Sīnā aims to establish

64 This is an interesting idea but appears to ignore that the sum of an actually infinite series could be a finite quality. For instance, the sum of 1/2 + 1/4 + 1/8 + ... converges to 1.

65 Rāzī, *Muḥaṣṣal*, 116–117.

66 Rāzī, *al-Maṭālib al-ʿĀliya*, ed. Ahmad Hijazi al-Saqa, 9 vols (Beirut: Dar al-Kitab al-Arabi, 1987), vol. 6, 61. Also see 71–72.

67 Rāzī, *Maṭālib*, vol. 6, 54–55. Rāzī, *Muḥaṣṣal*, 105–106.

68 Rāzī, *Muḥaṣṣal*, 116.

the idea that there can be no indivisible point, Rāzī aims to argue that at least conceptually we should be able to establish the reality of indivisibility as in the case of point. The same objection can be raised against Ibn Sīnā, who also moves from conceptual divisibility to concrete divisibility.

5 **Arguments from the Line:** If the point is further divisible, then we lose not only the concept of the point but also the concept of the line, because the point is the end of a line. "If the point is further divisible, then the line would have two ends. Hence, its end would be one of the parts, which is self-contradictory."[69] Furthermore, if the point is divisible, then an object moving on a line from point a to point b would have multiple departure and arrival points. This would entail that the object would begin to move from multiple locations and end in multiple locations, which is impossible.[70]

Consider two perpendicular lines, one of which moves along the other from its beginning until its end. During its motion, the moving line will have touched with its extremity every point of the line on which it moves. In this case, "moving on something without touching it is inconceivable. This will then entail that it should be said that the line being moved on is generated from entities touched by the extremity of the moving line, but the extremity of the moving line is a point, and [so] that touched by a point is a point [too]. Therefore, the line being moved on must of necessity be composed of points, and this is what is sought."[71]

6 **Arguments from the Circle:** Consider a sphere on a level surface. The point of contact between the sphere and the surface has to be an indivisible point. If not, the sphere would have multiple points of contact, meaning it would have level surfaces or lines and thus not be a true sphere. Thus, the idea of infinite divisibility is evidently false, if the sphere is to remain a sphere.

When the sphere is rolled on a level surface, "the locus of contact leaves a point and the locus of contact (again) obtains a point and there is nothing between these two points."[72] Thus, the sphere must be composed of indivisible points for this motion to be possible. Furthermore, during this motion, a line can be traced by bringing together these points of contact. Now, if a line is a "composition of points," then the sphere

[69] Ibid. [70] Rāzī, *Maṭālib*, vol. 6, 58–59.
[71] Ibid., 6, 52. Translated in Adi Setia, "Atomism Versus Hylomorphism in the *Kalām* of al-Fakhr al-Din al-Rāzī," *Islam & Science*, 4.2 (2006): 133.
[72] Rāzī, *Muḥaṣṣal*, 116. Also in *Maṭālib*, vol. 6, 47.

drawing the line has to be a composition of points. If a line is a composition of points and if a "surface is a composition of points," then a sphere is also a composition of points. In these arguments, Rāzī moves from the dimensionless point, to a one-dimensional line, to a two-dimensional surface, and then to a three-dimensional sphere.[73]

By means of these four proofs, it is thereby established that the locus of contact is something indivisible; and we say [further] that if this is the case, then it is imperative to recognize the existence of the indivisible atom. This is so because when we roll the sphere over the plane in a full circle, there is no doubt that whenever the locus of contact leaves a point, the locus of contact [again] obtains at another point, and there is nothing intervening between these two [successive contact] points. This is because we are speaking about that [second] point at which contact is realized at the very moment when contact ceases at the first [previous] point, and thus, on this supposition, a line is traced through a composition of these [successive contact] points; and if a line is obtained through a composition of points, then likewise a plane is obtained through a composition of lines, and a body through a composition of planes. Therefore, on this supposition, the locus of contact on a circle is something indivisible, and by the drawing together of similar indivisibles, the body is obtained. Such then is what is meant by the indivisible atom.[74]

There is another argument from the circle that Rāzī presents: "the center of a circle aligns with all parts of the circle. For this to happen, the center must be an indivisible point."[75] What exactly does this mean? In light of the preceding arguments, an explanation can be offered here. If the center is further divisible, then the center would not have the same distance from the circumference. The radius of the circle would have unequal lengths. Moreover, if a diameter passing through the circle is drawn, it would have to pass through multiple points and thus would not align with the points composing the circumference. In short, if the idea of the divisibility of the center is accepted, then the whole concept of circle collapses. So, the idea of the divisibility of the center is false, if the circle is to remain a circle.

Notice that Rāzī does not attack Ibn Sīnā's arguments directly. His strategy is to show that the same Euclidian geometry that Ibn Sīnā invokes against atomism can also be used to argue for the atomistic model of the world. If Ibn Sīnā uses Euclidian geometry to argue for the impossibility

[73] Rāzī, *Muḥaṣṣal*, 116. Also in *Maṭālib*, vol. 6, 47–49.
[74] Rāzī, *Maṭālib*, vol. 6, 47–49, Translated in Setia, "Atomism Versus Hylomorphism in the *Kalām* of al-Fakhr al-Dīn al-Rāzī," 132–133.
[75] Rāzī, *Muḥaṣṣal*, 116.

of circles and diagonals in the discrete world of atomists, Rāzī uses Euclidean geometry to argue for the impossibility of points, lines, and circles in the continuous world of hylomorphism. As such, Rāzī's arguments introduce the idea that Euclidian geometry allows both the continuous and discrete worldviews. As with a double-edged sword, it cuts both ways.

3.5 CONCLUSION

Both Ghazālī's and Rāzī's responses to Ibn Sīnā have been very influential in the later occasionalist tradition. Although much of Ghazālī's work relied on earlier occasionalist theories and arguments, his innovative use of the concept of "preponderance without reason" (*tarjīh bi-lā murajjih*) constitutes an important contribution. As discussed in Chapter 1, pre-Ghazālīan occasionalists used this idea to explain how homogenous atoms are differentiated from each other. God differentiates otherwise homogenous atoms from each other by assigning them accidents entirely based on preponderance without reason. This is because homogenous and identical atoms present no reason for differentiation. Ghazālī uses this old idea to bolster the Ashʿarite theological claim of creation from nothing and to reject the preeternity of the world. For the Philosophers, the creation of the world in time and from nothing contradicts the divine perfection, for it implies a change in the First in terms of "having no will to having will" to realize an unrealized potentiality. To solve this problem, Ghazālī argues that for God, creation and noncreation of the world are like two equal dates. God gives preponderance over the existence of the world without this choice causing a change or realizing a hidden potential in God or adding anything to God. Ghazālī's novel application of the idea appears to have inspired later theologians to apply it to a variety of topics. For example, Jurjānī uses it to explain the differentiation of the positions and motion of the celestial objects, and Nursi applies it to the problem of free will. It may be argued that the idea of "preponderance without reason" became a core tenet of the occasionalist worldview after Ghazālī.

In a similar fashion, Rāzī's defense of atomism was well known and widely used by later occasionalists. Rāzī's influence, however, is not limited to this defense. His realization that Euclidian geometry could be used to argue for two contradictory depictions of the physical nature of the world – discrete and continuous – appears to have led to the emergence of a distinct philosophy of science. Rāzī's philosophy of science is marked by skepticism apropos the ability of the scientific theories to tell us the reality of the world in an exhaustive way. The reality of the world is far too complex to be encapsulated in its totality by the dominant scientific models of his time, such as Euclidian geometry, Ptolemaic astronomy, or Aristotelian hylomorphism and physics. This skepticism may explain why Rāzī's writes that "at the end of the day all of these theories are estimations and suppositions."[76]

This skepticism also implies that these theories are not strong enough to determine our theological commitments. Euclidian geometry can be used for the defense of both atomistic and hylomorphic models of the world.[77] These models in turn are used to defend theological and philosophical convictions. If Euclidian geometry can be used to support contradicting theological convictions, then it does not provide a solid grounding for these convictions. This skepticism, however, does not lead to a total rejection of these models, as we already saw in Rāzī's extensive use of Euclidian geometry. For, despite their deficiencies, they are still the best descriptions available and may be practically useful. Thus, Rāzī recommends the use of Euclidian geometry for determining the proper position of the *qiblah*, despite his skepticism regarding its ability to describe exhaustively the world around us.[78]

[76] Rāzī, *Maṭālib*, vol. 6, 214. In another passage, Rāzī discusses the concept of possibility: "We see it possible that a man can be created without a father and mother, rivers can be turned into blood, and the mountains into gold. Then, despite believing in the possibility of these things, we also believe with certainty that they will never happen," *Muḥaṣṣal*, 215. This passage implies that, on the one hand, scientific regularities are taken as principles for understanding the world, and, on the other hand, the world can also present irregularities. This is an attitude that brings together the trust in the regularities as well as a certain skepticism.

[77] This was also noted by Adi Setia in "Atomism Versus Hylomorphism in the Kalām of al-Fakhr al-Dīn al-Rāzī," 126–128.

[78] Zarkān, *Fakhr al-Dīn al-Rāzī*, 434. Also cited in Setia, "Atomism Versus Hylomorphism in the *Kalām* of al-Fakhr al-Dīn al-Rāzī," 127. It must be noted that a similar pragmatic and skeptical attitude toward Aristotelian logic may also be present in the work of Ghazālī. As is well known, Ghazālī claims to adhere to Aristotelian logic, which he attempts to integrate into the larger body of Islamic sciences. However, the occasionalist assumption he appears to accept is that the experience of the consequential relationships in causal relations cannot be said to constitute a valid basis for the idea of necessity therein. In other words, Aristotelian logic starts from the fundamental assumption that necessary causality is the basis of justified premises in demonstrative syllogism. How, then, can Ghazālī accept Aristotelian logic? He is either not aware of the inconsistency here or approaches the issue from a pragmatic point of view and accepts Aristotelian logic, despite his skepticism toward the very basis of it.

Here we see a pragmatist philosophy of science marked by a tendency toward practical use together with philosophical skepticism. Scientific theories are approximate definitions of the world and have practical functionality, even if they should not challenge our theological commitments. The influence of this pragmatic view of science can also be found in the work of other Ashʿarite scholars, such as Jurjānī, as will be discussed in later chapters.

4

The First as Pure Act and Causality

The Case of Ibn Rushd

It is argued in this chapter that Ibn Rushd's theory of causality preserves the Aristotelian understanding of causality within the larger context of a participatory account of causality. Ibn Rushd, like Ibn Sīnā, finds the basis of causal efficacy of entities in their participation in the pure existence-act of the First. The First is pure existence-act, and entities are pure essence-potentialities. Creation is transformation of these essence-potentialities into actualities. The essence-potentialities are existentiated-actualized by the bestowal of the First's pure existence-act. Entities are causally efficacious through their participation in the First's pure act. The most important implication of this understanding of causality is that despite the occasionalist critique that we do not and cannot observe a necessary connection between cause and effect; for Ibn Rushd, the moment one defines existence as pure act, it metaphysically makes more sense to accept causal efficacy of entities, for they participate in the pure existence-act of the First.

There are also Aristotelian elements in Ibn Rushd's theory, which accepts that everything happening in this world has a cause. Even miracles are principally causal events, although their causes might remain unknown. Hence, the core of the Ashʿarite worldview, the idea that certain things happen due to the divine "preponderance without reason," is rejected. As will be argued, Ibn Rushd's conviction that we live in a strictly causal world does not lead to rejection of creaturely freedom. Ibn Rushd secures agency and freedom of entities on the basis of the idea that God is the knower and *actualizer* of essence-potentialities, not the determiner. God knows and actualizes essence-potentialities but does not determine what kind of essence-potentiality an entity has. As such, the concept of essence-potentiality allows creaturely freedom.

There are also differences between Ibn Sīnā and Ibn Rushd that stem from the latter's efforts to address some of Ghazālī's challenges. Ibn Rushd agrees with Ghazālī in that plurality can emanate from the First without emanationist intermediation and solely based on the nature-capacity-form of beings. This view establishes a closer connection between the First's existence-act and the world than Ibn Sīnā's metaphysics allows. As he also acknowledges, Ibn Rushd's modification here brings his account very close to those of Sufi metaphysicians, such as Ibn ʿArabī and Qūnawī, who will be examined in later chapters.

4.1 A CRITIQUE OF ASHʿARITE OCCASIONALISM

Ibn Rushd's rejection of Ashʿarite occasionalism is well known. It will be briefly summarized here before our examination of how Ibn Rushd himself provides a metaphysical justification for the causal efficacy of entities.

4.1.1 *Identity*

Ibn Rushd argues that by accepting occasionalist conclusions, one compromises the individual identity of entities. First, if an entity has no specific nature – which is rejected by Ashʿarites due to its necessitarian conclusions – then "it would not have a special name nor a definition, and all things would be one." Without a nature, an entity would not have "one special act or one special passivity," for "special acts proceed from special natures."[1] Thus, rejection of necessity and natures leads to rejection of the identity of entities, which is absurd.

4.1.2 *Knowledge*

Second, rejection of necessity and natures undermines all attempts to make sense of the world, including that of the Ashʿarites, because if

[1] Ibn Rushd, *Tahāfut al-Tahāfut*, trans. Simon Van den Bergh (London: Messrs. Luzac and Company, Ltd, 1954), 318. Emphasis mine. The problem of losing identity can also be observed in the conclusions of British Empiricism, which has a comparable skepticism toward causal necessity. If all knowledge derives from sensory experience, we lose not only the material world, as in Berkeley, but also our own identities, as in Hume. The "I" becomes merely a series of sensations. As Hume writes, "I never can catch *myself* at any time without a perception, and never can observe anything but the perception." *Treatise of Human Nature*, ed. L. A. Selby-Bigge and P. H. Nidditch (Oxford: Oxford University Press, 1978), 1.4.6.3.

"intelligence is nothing but the perception of things with their causes," then one "who denies causes must deny the intellect." Intellect functions on the logical basis that "knowledge of the effects" can only be rendered possible "through knowledge of their causes." Therefore, "denial of cause implies the denial of *knowledge*, and denial of knowledge implies that nothing in this world can be really known."[2]

Here, Ibn Rushd echoes the classical Aristotelian position. For Aristotle, one can have knowledge of something when one knows its cause, why a thing is what it is, why it is the way it is, and why it cannot be other than it is.[3] In the world of Ashʿarites, however, all one can have is "nothing but *opinion.*" In this case, "neither proof nor definition exist, and that the essential attributes which compose definitions are void. The man who denies the necessity of any item of knowledge must admit that even this, his own affirmation, is not necessary knowledge."[4]

This is not to say that Ibn Rushd completely rejects the idea of opinion, if by "opinion" one means tentative knowledge. He acknowledges that there can be "knowledge which is not necessary."[5] The soul can form "a judgement" or an opinion and "*imagine it to be necessary*, whereas it is not necessary." However, to accept the tentativeness of knowledge, one does not need to be an Ashʿarite. This view of knowledge is also possible within the Philosophers' system. The Philosophers do not deny this. To believe that everything must have a cause does not guarantee that we have access to all causes. Hence, from the perspective of human knowledge, some aspects of world processes may remain tentatively knowable, despite the fact that these processes are actually causal.

4.1.3 *Habit*

In accordance with this view, Ibn Rushd denies that God can have "habits." First, "habit" is an "ambiguous" term. If it is examined, it means "only a hypothetical act." When it is said that "so-and-so has the habit of acting in such-and-such a way," it means "he will act in that way most of the time." Again, this imposes a certain epistemological

[2] Ibn Rushd, *Tahāfut al-Tahāfut*, 319.
[3] *Posterior Analytics* 71 b 9–11; *Physics*, 194 b 17–20; Cf. *Posterior Analytics* 94 a 20.
[4] Ibn Rushd, *Tahāfut al-Tahāfut*, 319. Emphasis mine. [5] Ibid., 320.

distrust. For, "if this were true, everything would be the case only by *supposition*."[6]

> It is, however, *impossible that God should have a habit*, for a habit is a custom that the agent acquires and from which a frequent repetition of his act follows, whereas God says in the Holy Book: "Thou shall not find any alteration in the course of God, and they shall not find any change in the course of God." If they mean a habit in existing things, habit can only exist in the animated; if it exists in something else, it is really a nature, and it is not possible that a thing should have a nature which determined it either necessarily or in most cases. If they mean our habit of forming judgements about things, such a habit is nothing but an act of the soul, which is determined by its nature and through which the intellect becomes intellect.[7]

It is impossible for God to have habits if the term is defined as a "custom that the agent acquires and from which frequent repetition of his act follows." If there is no alteration in the "course of God," the very idea of habit implies acquiring a new course and changing it from time to time. This attributes far more variability to God's actions than the Qur'an suggests.

Accordingly, Ibn Rushd repudiates Ghazālī's argument that Ash'arite occasionalism could provide a basis for certain knowledge about the world. Ghazālī argues that "God has created in us the knowledge that He will not do all these possible things, and we only profess that these things are not necessary, but that they are possible and may or may not happen, and protracted habit time after time fixes their occurrence in our minds according to the past habit in a fixed impression."[8] For Ibn Rushd, this is not a solid grounding for knowledge, because "if God interrupts the habitual course by causing this unusual event to happen, this knowledge of the habitual is at the time of the interruption removed from their hearts, and He no longer creates it."[9] The problem with Ghazālī's argument for Ibn Rushd is that if these habits can be broken, they cannot be the basis for trust in the world's past, present, and future. The very idea of habit, due to its intrinsic arbitrariness, cannot serve as a solid grounding for attempts to understand the world in certain terms. If the Ash'arite view were true, then "there would no longer, even for the twinkling of an eye, be any permanent knowledge of anything, since we suppose such an agent to rule existents like a tyrannical prince who has the highest power, for whom nobody in his dominion can deputize, of *whom no standard or custom is known to which reference might be made*."[10]

[6] Ibid. [7] Ibid. [8] Ibid., 324. [9] Ibid. [10] Ibid., 325. Emphasis mine.

4.1.4 *Miracles*

It must also be added that Ibn Rushd's account of miracles is in accordance with his emphasis on causal necessity. For Ibn Rushd, Ghazālī defends the position that miracles that interrupt the usual course of nature, such as "the changing of the rod into a serpent or the resurrection of the dead or the cleavage of the moon," can occur only because causal relationships are not necessary and God's habit can change.

The Philosophers hold that "the ordinary course of nature is a logical necessity."[11] The Philosophers, then, explain these miracles with "keen insight" for future prediction or "the power of the soul." In a similar way, the soul controls "the bodily faculties," its power could reach such a degree that the natural powers outside a man's body also obey it. Thus, the power of the soul can control "the blasts of the wind or the downpour of rain, or the striking of a thunderbolt or the trembling of the earth, etc."[12] According to Ibn Rushd's reading, Ghazālī accepts these explanations. He "does not deny anything they have mentioned, and that such things happen to prophets." He is "only opposed to their *limiting themselves to this*, and to their denial of the possibility that a stick might change into a serpent, and of the resurrection of the dead and other things."[13]

Ibn Rushd also accepts that "a stick might change into a serpent." He agrees with Ghazālī that these things are not allegorical stories and might really happen. The important difference between the two is that Ibn Rushd insists, in accordance with his emphasis on necessary relation between cause and effect, that everything must have a cause. Ashʿarites' explanation of miracles as breaks in the divine habits, however, "abolishes any perception of the existence of causes and effects."[14] What happens in the case of miracles is not suspension of the course of nature but occurrences of rare yet possible causal networks. Miracles are not "breaks in God's habits" or violations of natural laws but are extraordinary yet causal events. They can emerge as certain rare possibilities hidden in the warp and weft of the cosmic structure. The world remains causal, yet causal possibilities include highly extraordinary events.

4.2 THE FIRST AS PURE ACT AND CAUSALITY

In his criticism of Ashʿarite occasionalism, Ibn Rushd clearly argues that the ideas of causal necessity and natures are required in order to establish

[11] Ibid., 313. [12] Ibid., 314. [13] Ibid. Emphasis mine. [14] Ibid., 324.

the distinct identities of entities, the possibility of human knowledge, and the divine wisdom. Yet it is not clear how Ibn Rushd provides a metaphysical justification for the causal efficacy of entities. One might assume that Ibn Rushd offers strict determinism to oppose Ashʿarite probabilism. However, I believe that this is not the case and contend instead that Ibn Rushd introduces metaphysical justifications for causal efficacy and freedom of entities by moving toward a *participatory* account of causality that is in turn based on an understanding of the First as pure existence-act and on his distinction between existence-actuality and essence-potentiality.

Barry Kogan has already indicated that "causal efficacy is rooted for Ibn Rushd in the very structure of actuality or being."[15] He also writes that "being and actuality are mutually implied by one another. For anything to be or to exist it must be actual. But it must actually be a thing of a specific kind – a fire, a flower, a puzzled philosopher."[16] This is to say, existence implies actuality, and the First as pure existence-act is the basis of causal activity and, hence, causal efficacy.

How does Ibn Rushd go from the description of the First as pure existence-act to causality? Now, he follows the Aristotelian idea that there should be no potency in the First, for the notion that there is something unrealized in the First waiting to be actualized contradicts its perfection. The First must be pure act without any potentiality. Thus, "it is necessary that the process should terminate in an absolutely necessary existent in which there is *no potency at all*, either in its substance, or locally, or in any other forms of movement."[17]

Ibn Rushd also indicates that there is no beginning of the divine pure act, because there is no beginning of the First or any point where the First has potentiality. The First, then, must have always been in a state of pure act. It is from this idea that Ibn Rushd derives the preeternity of the world. If this is true, then the First's act must have given existence to the created order in an eternal fashion. This act must be eternal because it would be an absurdity to hold that there was once no movement. For, in this case, "there would be no way of originating it [movement], since the only thing qualified to originate it would be, contrary to our

[15] Kogan, *Averroes and The Metaphysics of Causation*, 114.

[16] Ibid., 113. Kogan also compares Ghazālī's and Ibn Rushd's definitions of "agent." The agent for Ibn Rushd means God as *wujūd-act*, while for Ghazālī it means God as *agent-willer*, 62–68.

[17] Ibn Rushd, *Tahāfut al-Tahāfut*, 394.

assumption, another movement."[18] This is why "the world has come into being from *an eternal agent having an eternal act*, i.e. *an act without beginning or end*."[19]

This eternal and continuous act of the First can also explained in moral terms. Existence or actualization is "better" for entities that are waiting to be existentiated or actualized. To give existence to a possible being is an act of goodness; it is good "when a thing passes into existence from nonexistence, for it cannot be doubted that existence is better for it than nonexistence. It is in this way that the Primal Will is related to the existing things, for it chooses for them eternally the better of two opposites."[20] The First knows and actualizes potentialities because simply their existentiation-actualization is better than their nonexistence. So, the creation of the world is not due to God's "preponderance without reason" as Ashʿarites would argue but rather is due to the divine goodness.

Ibn Rushd, however, appears to agree with the Ashʿarites that the world is "converted from non-being into being" continuously. The world is in a state of "eternal becoming" due to the First's act.[21] The difference is that Ibn Rushd envisions this conversion as a continuous process from potentiality to actuality. The Ashʿarites, on the other hand, do not really have the concept of potentiality (natures) on which continuous creation is based. For them, God creates the world anew at each moment on the basis of the divine will, which gives "preponderance without reason." Unactualized potentialities do not have any claim on the present creation of the world. In Ibn Rushd's view, though, the creative emanation of existence-act continuously actualizes potentialities (or essences) known by the divine knowledge during the world-process. There is no creation ex nihilo but only creation from existing possibilities. This also suggest that, for Ibn Rushd, the idea of continuous creation of the world can be preserved in the Aristotelian framework without completely detaching the moments of the world and depicting it as a discontinuous and "arbitrary" flow of events.

[18] Ibid., 394.

[19] Ibid., 156. Emphasis mine. The world, however, is not "eternal by itself" and owes its eternity to the First. It is eternal because of "an eternal agent having an eternal act." The world cannot be "truly eternal . . . for what is truly eternal has no cause (*al-qadīm al-ḥaqīqī laysa lahu ʿillatan*)." Ibn Rushd, *Decisive Treatise and Epistle Dedicatory* (*Kitāb Faṣl al-Maqāl* and *Risāla al-Ihdāʾ*), trans. Charles Butterworth (Provo, UT: Brigham Young University, 2008), 15–16 It is also not really created in time, for "what is truly generated is necessarily corruptible (*al-muhdath al-ḥaqīqī fāsid ḍarūratan*)," ibid.

[20] Ibn Rushd, *Tahāfut al-Tahāfut*, 22.

[21] Ibid., 103. See also Ibn Rushd, *Faṣl al-Maqāl*, 15.

As he puts it, "the Philosophers' theory indeed is that the world has an agent, acting from eternity and everlastingly, converting the world eternally from non-being into being."[22] The First acts eternally to realize an infinite number of possibilities at each moment:

> Can there be a greater imperfection than to assume the act of the Eternal as finite and limited, like the act of a temporal product, although a limited act can only be imagined of a limited agent, not of the eternal agent whose existence and action are unlimited? All this, as you see, cannot be unknown to the man who has even the slightest understanding of the rational. And how can it be thought that the present act proceeding from the Eternal cannot be preceded by is another act, and again by another, and so in our thinking infinitely, like the infinite continuation of His existence?[23]
>
> If the meaning of 'eternal' is that it is in everlasting production and that this production has neither beginning nor end, certainly the term 'production' is more truly applied to him who brings about an everlasting production than to him who procures a limited production.[24]

Now, the creative act of the First is without beginning and continuous. There is an eternal move from potentiality to actuality. From this idea, Ibn Rushd derives his definition of agency. An agent is "what causes some other thing to pass from potency to actuality and from nonexistence (*ʿadam*) to existence (*wujūd*)."[25] Creation is "the conversion of a thing from potential into actual existence" and "destruction is the change from the actual into the potential."[26]

For Ibn Rushd, the move from potentiality to actuality is the same as the move from nonexistence to existence. God eternally moves possibilities from potency to actuality or from nonexistence to existence thanks to His being pure actuality. Since the First is pure act and the source of all actuality, it can be said that things are actualized by having their share from the pure actuality of the First. Therefore, the causal efficacy of beings rests on the pure act of the First. As Ibn Rushd states: "The world is an act, or a thing whose existence is consequent upon this [the First's] act."[27]

If this is true, it can be concluded that entities are actualized by *participating* in the First's pure act or pure existence. The causal efficacy of beings is, then, based on their participation in the pure act and existence of the First. In this view, the idea of participation in the First's act posits a very close relationship between entities and the First. How does Ibn Rushd establish this intimate relationship?

[22] Ibn Rushd, *Tahāfut al-Tahāfut*, 103. [23] Ibid., 56. [24] Ibid., 97. [25] Ibid., 150.
[26] Ibid., 78. [27] Ibid., 156.

Ibn Rushd rejects the idea – often attributed to the Philosophers – that the First cannot have any type of plurality and thus that plurality cannot proceed from the One without intermediation of the celestial intellects. For Ibn Rushd this idea is "the fundamental mistake" of Ibn Sīnā and Fārābī; "they made the statement that from the one only one can proceed, and then assumed a plurality in the one which proceeds."[28] As his take on the divine knowledge suggests, Ibn Rushd holds that a type of plurality can be envisaged in the First without violating its absolute unity. This in turn affects his understanding of the relationship between the First and the world. Plurality can come from the First without any need for pluralizing intermediation of the intellects and spheres.

How untrue is this proposition that the one can produce only one, if it is understood in the way Avicenna and Fārābī understand it, and Ghazālī himself in his Niche for Lights, where he accepts their theory of the First Principle.[29]

He says that if a plurality in the first effect is permissible without a cause, because out of the First Cause there does not follow a plurality, one may also suppose a plurality within the First Cause, and there is no need to assume a second cause and a first effect.[30]

He agrees with Ghazālī on this point.

Ghazālī means that, when the Philosophers assume that the First thinks its own essence and knows through this that it is the cause of others, they must conclude that it is not absolutely one. For it has not yet been proved that God must be absolutely one.[31]

In sharp contrast to Ibn Sīnā and Fārābī, Ibn Rushd suggests that if there is plurality in the First, then plurality may proceed from it without emanationist interventions. Ibn Rushd holds that the Philosophers "would have saved themselves from these objections of Ghazālī, and disengaged themselves from these false theories," if they accept that what proceeds from the First is at once *one and many*.

If, however, Ibn Sīnā and these other philosophers had answered that the first effect possesses plurality, and that necessarily any plurality becomes one through a unity which requires that plurality should depend on unity, and that this unity through which plurality becomes one is a simple entity which proceeds from an individual simple "One" [*al-wāḥid*].[32]

There is in the First an infinite plurality together with absolute simplicity and unity. The First knows Itself and knows every potentiality (or essence)

[28] Ibid., 148. [29] Ibid., 146. [30] Ibid., 147. [31] Ibid., 123.
[32] Ibid., 148. Translation modified.

that proceeds from Itself. Since the number of potentialities is infinite, and since It knows them with one single act, there must be infinite plurality in the absolute simplicity of the First. This differs from Ibn Sīnā's account, which locates the initial plurality in the first intellect that thinks of its source and itself.[33]

How exactly then does Ibn Rushd explain the procession of plurality from the First? He harkens back to Aristotle here: "Aristotle, in the twelfth book of his *Metaphysics*, expresses pride in his solution and says that none of his predecessors could say anything about this problem. In the sense in which we have expounded the Aristotelian doctrine, this statement that out of *the one only one can proceed is true, and the statement that out of the one a plurality proceeds is equally true*."[34] How could this be? "From the simple numerically one, only one simple one – not something numerically one in one way, but plural in another – can proceed, and ... its unity is the cause of the existence of plurality."[35]

How can one explain these enigmatic passages? In my view, Ibn Rushd suggests here that what emanates from the One as one (*al-wāḥid*) is "existence," which is given by "the bestower of existence" to other existents in accordance with their essences-potentialities. Due its infinite plasticity, existence becomes many in different containers, so to speak. Existence is one in itself but becomes many as it is multiplied by the recipients. As Ibn Rushd himself puts it, "from the First Principle [proceeds] a unity that by itself is one single act, but which becomes many through the plurality of *the recipients* (*al-qawābil*), just as there are many deputies under the power of a king, and many arts under one art."[36]

Therefore, all differentiations are attributed to instantiations of one thing (*al-wāḥid*) proceeding from the First.

> The bestower of this conjunction is, therefore, *the bestower of existence*. And since everything conjoined is only conjoined through a unity in it, and this unity through which it is conjoined must depend on a unity, subsistent by itself, and be related to it, there must exist a single unity, subsistent by itself, and this unity must of necessity provide unity through its own essence. This unity is *distributed*

[33] Ibn Rushd finds inconsistencies in the Philosophers' explanation, observing that they also imply that if the first intellect has plurality, then their statement that from the one only one can proceed is mistaken. For example, "since they say that from the One no manifold proceeds, they would have to concede that the manifold cannot proceed from the One, but their statement that from the one only one proceeds contradicts their statement that what proceeds from the First possesses plurality, for from the One one must proceed," ibid., 146.

[34] Ibid., 149. Emphasis mine. [35] Ibid. [36] Ibid., 155. Emphasis mine.

in the different classes of existing things, according to their natures, and from this unity, allotted to the individual things, their existence arises ... By means of this theory Aristotle connects sensible existence with intelligibles [essences], saying that the world is one and proceeds from one. "This one" (*al-wāḥid*) is partly the cause of unity, partly the cause of plurality.[37]

"This one" (*al-wāḥid*) is existence that is bestowed and distributed in accordance with their natures. This is why entities "exist through an absolute unity which is [also] the cause of plurality."[38] As it will be examined in the following chapters, Ibn ʿArabī and Mullā Ṣadrā also understand this "one" proceeding from the First as existence itself. They offer similar explanations of how multiplicity proceeds from the absolutely unitary one. There is God who is the "Absolute Existence." There are also contingent beings who have "relative existence." There is also a third type of existence which is "the absolute expanding existence." This type of existence belongs neither to the Absolute Existence nor to relative existence. It is what connects the two. The Absolute Existence bestows its existence and expands upon contingent beings. It is this act of bestowal or expansion of existence (*sarayān al-wujūd* or *inbisāṭ al-wujūd*) that existentiates contingent beings.[39]

The expanding existence from the Absolute Existence to relative existences is absolutely one, since from the one only one can proceed. However, this one existence becomes delimited, differentiated, and multiplied when it existentiates contingent beings. So, even if what proceeds from the One is only one, the number of recipients of that existence is more than one. In this sense, multiplicity can proceed from the One.[40]

It is evident, therefore, that *there is a unique entity from which a single power emanates through which all beings exist*. And since they are many, it is necessarily from the one (*al-wāḥid*), in so far as it is one, that plurality arises or proceeds or whatever term is to be used.[41]

This conclusion is true, especially when they imagine that the first act proceeding from the First Principle is the unity through which the first effect becomes a

[37] Ibid., 108. Translation modified. [38] Ibid., 154.

[39] Ibn ʿArabī, Qūnawī, and Ṣadrā use similar terms. For example, "God with his existence permeates (*siraya*) the entities without division or hulul or ittihad" in Qūnawī, *Miftāḥ Ghayb al-Jamʿi wa-l-Wujūd fi-l-Kashf al-Shuhūd*, Süleymaniye Yazma Eser Kütüphanesi (Manuscript), Ayasofya, No. 1930, 17b. For Ṣadrā, *al-Asfār*, I: 289–292.

[40] See also in Jurjānī, "Even if we accept the truth of it (the idea that from the One only one can proceed) we assert that this is only possible if the recipient (*qābil*) is not more than one. If the number of recipients is more than one, then from the One many multiplicities could proceed. There is agreement on this." *Sharḥ al-Mawāqif*, VII, 196–197.

[41] Ibid., 109. Translation modified. Emphasis mine.

unique existent, notwithstanding the plurality in it. And indeed, *if they allow an undetermined plurality in the first effect, it must be less or more than the number of existents, or equal to it.*[42]

This explains the procession of multiplicity from the absolute simplicity and oneness of the First. From an ontological perspective, the First is pure act and what emanates from the First is one from one perspective and multiple from another. Plurality is a result of the multiplicity of the recipients of existence.

This is all to say that the First as pure existence-act remains immediately and without mediation present in the world. The First's existence-act is "attached" and "everlastingly mixed with its objects." And, "it is in this way that one must understand the relation of the First to all existents."[43]

At this juncture, we find a participatory theory of causality. Entities participate in the divine existence-act to the extent allowed by their essence-potentialities. By getting their share from the divine existence-act, entities become individual causal agents. Thus, Ibn Rushd writes: "The Philosophers differ in one way, although in another they agree. They all agree in this, the First Agent is immaterial and that its act is the condition of the existence and acts of existents."[44]Again, the root of this pure and eternal act can be found in the very existence of the First. Existence and act are one and the same thing. Pure existence is pure act. "*The starting-point of His acts is at the starting-point of His existence*; for neither of them has a beginning."[45] It is in this sense that entities participate in the divine existence. This is why Ibn Rushd claims, in a fashion resembling Sufi metaphysics:

And this is the meaning of the ancient philosophers, when they say that *God is the totality of the existents which He bestows on us in His bounty and of which He is the agent*. And therefore, the chiefs of the Sufis say: there is no reality besides Him. But all this is the knowledge of those who are steadfast in their knowledge, and this must not be written down and it must not be made an obligation of faith, and therefore it is not taught by the Divine Law. And one who mentions this truth where it should not be mentioned sins, and one who withholds it from those to whom it should be told sins too. And that *one single thing can have different degrees of existence* can be learned from the different degrees of existence of the soul.[46]

The First existentiates by "bestowing" Its existence-act upon multiple essences. It is the difference of the essences of the recipients that multiplies

[42] Ibid. Emphasis mine. [43] Ibid., 199. [44] Ibid., 320.
[45] Ibid., 12. Emphasis mine. [46] Ibid., 282. Emphasis mine.

the *one existence* emanating from the First, which in turn leads to plurality in the world. The First's existence-act permeates the world, is immediately present in the world-process, and grounds all causal activity. This permeation implies a participatory understanding of the relationship between entities and the First and provides metaphysical justification for the causal efficacy of created beings.

4.3 THE QUESTION OF FREEDOM

It will be argued that Ibn Rushd's account of essence-potentiality forms the basis of his conception of freedom. We concluded above that Ibn Rushd ties causal efficacy of entities to their participation in the pure act of the First. The First's pure act is "the condition of the existence and acts of existing beings."[47] Potentialities actualize by participating in the First's pure act. This account provides a metaphysical justification for the causal efficacy of entities while preserving the First as the basis of all subsequent acts. This is why he states:

> And, as we said, we need not doubt that some of these existents cause each other and act through each other, and that in themselves they do not suffice for their act, but that *they are in need of an external agent whose act is a condition of their act, and not only of their act but even of their existence.*[48]

Questions arise here. Whence come the essence-potentialities according to which the world-process is organized? Does God determine essence-potentialities? As far as I am aware, Ibn Rushd nowhere suggests that God determines the potentialities that He actualizes. There are, however, multiple reasons to believe that Ibn Rushd perceives a non-deterministic relation between God and essence-potentialities. This non-determinism appears to allow freedom in the created order.

First, as already alluded to above, where Ibn Rushd rejects the Ashʿarite notion of "habit," he does not accept the idea of arbitrariness in God and in the created order. Recall that the Ashʿarite theory of preponderance asserts that opposites can be differentiated merely through the will of the Agent without any differentiating reason (*tarjīh bi-lā murajjih*). For Ibn Rushd, this implies that "there is no fixed standard for His will either constantly or for most cases, according to which things must happen."[49] And if one replaces the idea of cause with the idea of

[47] Ibid., 320. [48] Ibid., 320. Emphasis mine. [49] Ibid.

habit – and the arbitrariness it suggests – then "there would be no wisdom in the world from which it might be inferred that its agent was wise."[50] In this case, we would have an agent who could act without reason or wisdom. It follows that "in general, if we repudiate the existence of causes and effects, we would have no means of responding to the advocates of chance; I mean, those who assert that there is no Creator and that whatever happens in this world is the product of material causes."[51] Ibn Rushd thus rejects the reduction of the world process to "chance and material causes." Creation is not an arbitrary process and occurs for certain reasons. God creates the world in accordance with these preexisting essence-potentialities. When Ibn Rushd affirms that everything happens for a reason, he has these preexisting essence-potentialities in mind.

Second, as discussed above, Ibn Rushd rejects occasionalism because it leads to rejection of the identity of entities. In Ibn Rushd's terms, these essence-potentialities, sometimes referred to as natures or forms, are, in fact, the roots of the identity of entities. Entities are actualized in accordance with what kind of identity they have.[52] This is to say, the notions of essence, potentiality, nature, and form are used to establish the identity of entities, not to create a deterministic worldview.

Third, Ibn Rushd's theory of knowledge further suggests a nondeterministic relationship between God and essence-potentialities. These essence-potentialities are known by the First, as the First is not only pure act but also pure intellect. Ibn Rushd writes that "all these concepts refer to His essence and to His perception and to His knowledge of His essence, and the knowledge of His essence is His very essence, *for He is pure intellect*."[53] At this juncture, Ibn Rushd offers a quite novel extrapolation from Aristotle's God as "thought thinking itself." Aristotle's God knows itself but does not seem to be interested in anything other than itself. This obviously creates certain difficulties for those who understand God as concerned with even the minutest details of existence. To resolve this tension, Ibn Rushd argues that the First knows all existents through "thinking itself," for the First's essence contains all existents.

50 Ibid., 320.

51 Ibn Rushd, *al-Kashf ʿan Manāhij al-Adilla*, ed. M. Qasim (Cairo, 1961), 200. Cited in Majid Fakhry, *Averroes: His Life, Works and Influence* (Oxford: One World, 2001), 9–10.

52 Ibn Rushd, *Tahāfut al-Tahāfut*, 330.

53 Ibid., 185.

The First amongst all these principles thinks only its own essence and, by thinking its essence, thinks at the same time *all existents* in the noblest mode of existence and in the noblest order and arrangement.[54]

It is true, according to the Philosophers, *that the First thinks only His own essence* – not something relative, namely, that He is a principle – but His essence, according to the Philosophers, *contains all intellects, nay, all existents*, in a nobler and more perfect way than they all possess in reality.[55]

He also holds that the First's knowledge is neither universal nor particular. It is "a unity in act." God knows everything in one single act. This is also to say that in God there is absolute simplicity that exists together with infinite plurality of the known essences-possibilities: "the knowledge of God is *a unity in act*, but the nature of this unity and the representation of its reality are impossible for the human understanding."[56]

Ibn Rushd further suggests that essences-potentialities already exist in the divine knowledge. The world "conforms to God's knowledge." Together with his rejection of the divine arbitrariness, their existence in the divine knowledge indicates that God does not actualize essences-potentialities haphazardly but rather on the basis of their reality as known by the divine knowledge. In Ibn Rushd, as Kogan nicely puts it, "kinesis imitates noesis."[57] As Ibn Rushd states:

God's knowledge of existents is their cause, and these existents are the consequence of God's knowledge, and therefore reality conforms to God's knowledge. If, for instance, knowledge of Zaid's coming reaches the prophet through a communication of God, the reason why the actual happening is congruous with the knowledge is nothing but the fact that *the nature of the actually existent is a consequence of the eternal knowledge*, for knowledge *qua* knowledge can only refer to something which has an actualized nature. *The knowledge of the Creator is the reason why this nature becomes actual in the existent which is attached to it.*[58]

This passage suggests that God existentiates essences according to what they are in the divine knowledge. It does not imply, however, that the divine knowledge also causes essences to become what they are. In other words, God brings the world into existence according to its prefiguration in the divine knowledge, but this prefiguration itself appears to remain uncaused in Ibn Rushd. Essences are known and existentiated but not determined by God. The divine knowledge follows the known. Recall also that Ibn Rushd perceives an entity as a "unity of essence and existence."

[54] Ibid., 130. [55] Ibid., 121. Emphasis mine. [56] Ibid., 207. Emphasis mine.

[57] Kogan, *Averroes and the Metaphysics of Causation*, 201.

[58] Ibn Rushd, *Tahāfut al-Tahāfut*, 325–326.

And therefore, Ghazālī's objection that Ibn Sīnā assimilates existence to a necessary attribute of the essence is not true, because the essence of a thing is the cause of its necessary attribute and it is not possible that a thing should be the cause of its own existence, because *the existence of a thing is prior to its essence.* To identify the essence and the existence of a thing is not to do away with its essence, as Ghazālī asserts, but is only the affirmation of *the unity of essence and existence.*[59]

If the unity of essence and existence constitutes an entity, and if God is described as the "giver of existence," then an entity's creation occurs when these essence-potentialities are existentiated and actualized. The First existentiates essences by giving Its existence or, in other words, by giving Its actuality to potentialities. As Ibn Rushd puts it, the Philosophers believe that "the *existence in the compound is an additional attribute to its essence* and it only acquires this attribute through the Agent." They also believe that in the First, "which is simple and causeless, this attribute is not additional to the essence and that *it has no essence differentiated from its existence.*"[60] Ibn Rushd holds that in the created order, essence precedes existence, for existence is given to essences, which exist in the divine knowledge. In the First, however, existence precedes essence, for It has no essence differentiated from Its existence. The First thus gives existence to essences/potentialities and actualizes them in accordance with what they are in the divine knowledge.

Essence-potentialities, then, are the basis of the world-process. God creates the world according to His preexisting divine knowledge, which includes knowledge of the essence-potentialities. However, essence-potentialities, which make things what they are and give them their identities appear to remain uncaused. It is true that God knows and actualizes essence-potentialities, but God does not cause what kind of essence-potentiality an entity has. The notion of essence-potentiality, therefore, is the basis of freedom of entities in Ibn Rushd's system.

4.4 CONCLUSION

On one hand, Ibn Rushd defends the Aristotelian ideas that everything must have a cause and that causality is the basis of knowledge. On the

[59] Ibid., 236. See also "but the whole of this discussion is built on the mistake that the existence of a thing is one of its attributes. For the existence which *in our knowledge is prior to the essence* of a thing is that which signifies the true," ibid., 236. Emphasis mine.

[60] Ibid., 241. Emphasis mine.

other hand, he contends that participation in the First's existence-act is the basis of the actualization of entities' essence-potentialities. This participation is the basis for the causal agency of entities. The First's causality is always present within entities' causality.

Ibn Rushd's account thus enables a distinction between metaphysical causality and physical causality, as Ibn Sīnā previously outlined. The First, as the metaphysical cause, is the giver of existence-act, for It is itself pure existence and pure act. There is also physical causality, which pertains to matter-motion, and hence intelligibility of the natural order. The notion of metaphysical causality suggests an adoption of Neoplatonistic participatory causality, while the notion of physical causality is based on Aristotelian ideas. As such, Ibn Rushd's account of causality suggests an integration of Aristotelian and Neoplatonistic ideas on causality.

Ibn Rushd also rejects the idea that plurality cannot proceed from the One without intermediation of celestial intellects, an idea that he attributes to Ibn Sīnā. It is not the process of gradual emanation toward celestial intellects that explains the observed multiplicity of the world, but rather the fact that each entity gets its share from one existence emanating from the First in accordance with its particular potentiality. It is here that we see the influence of Ghazālī's criticism of Ibn Sīnā on Ibn Rushd. On this issue, Ibn Rushd also agrees with the Sufi metaphysicians, as he himself acknowledges.

In Ibn Rushd's thought, the actualization of potentialities by God does not happen arbitrarily, as seems to be suggested by Ashʿarite occasionalism. The First shares Its existence and actuality with an entity in accordance with that entity's essence-potentiality. This fact indicates that the eternal will of God does not give "preponderance without a reason." Essence-potentialities of entities, as the uncaused objects of the divine knowledge, provide "reasons" that fashion the share of existence-act the entity is to receive. Hence, the world is existentiated by God in accordance with these essences. From the perspective of the existence-act, an entity is entirely dependent on the divine causality; from the perspective of essence-potentialities, it remains free.

5

Light, Existence, and Causality

The Illuminationist School and the Case of Suhrawardī

This chapter offers an interpretive approach to Shihāb al-Dīn Suhrawardī's account of causality. It also examines how he establishes freedom in the created order in accordance with his understanding of causality. It is argued that Suhrawardī's writings suggest a participatory account of causality. The chapter first examines some salient aspects of Suhrawardī's ontology that are relevant to our discussion. The second section rethinks the question of causality with respect to Suhrawardī's ontology. The third section discusses the question of freedom and the responsibility of moral agents in relation to Suhrawardī's theory of causality.

5.1 CAUSALITY AND ONTOLOGY

It will be argued in the following pages that Suhrawardī's continuous and gradational ontological framework suggests a participatory account of causality. Thus, before we start examining Suhrawardī's view on causality on its own terms, a brief examination of his ontology may prove helpful.

Suhrawardī's ontology starts with a distinction between existence (*wujūd*) and essence (*māhiyya*). From the earliest phase of its development and especially after Ibn Sīnā, this distinction has been one of the most important problems confronting Islamic philosophy. For Suhrawardī, existence is a universal category shared by the Necessary Existent (*wājib al-wujūd*) and contingent existents (*mumkin al-wujūd*): "[e]xistence applies with a single meaning to the Necessary Existent and to everything else."[1] The difference is that the Necessary Existent exists due to itself. In the Necessary Existent, there is no distinction between essence and existence. It can even be said that "[e]xistence is the Necessary Existent itself."[2] Other existents exist because their essences receive the predicate of existence. While in the Necessary Existent existence is a necessary quality, "in others existence is superadded as an accident of essence."[3] Existence of contingent beings is "borrowed" from the Necessary Existent. To use more theological language, contingent beings receive their existence from "above." Existence happens to essences.

An existent being cannot exist without an essence. This means that essence comes before existence in a certain sense, in the order of actualization. Existence becomes realized and intelligible in an existent being. An existent being is contingent upon its essence.[4] This dynamic is also known as the principality of essence (*aṣālat al-māhiyya*). As posited in the following pages, Suhrawardī argues for the principality of essences only in a relative sense, not in the absolute sense. In the created order, essences receive existence or existence happens to them. In reality, however, existence is prior, for God is defined as pure light-existence.[5]

Echoing Ibn Sīnā's distinction between necessary and contingent existence, Suhrawardī argues there are basically two types of light: "light in itself and light due to other than itself."[6] An entity is light due to something other than itself. "[L]ights cannot form an infinite series," and therefore "the accidental lights, the barriers, and the states of each must end in a light beyond which there is no light. This is the Light of Lights."[7] Ibn Sīnā's

1 Suhrawardī, *The Philosophy of Illumination: A New Critical Edition of the Text of Hikmat al-Ishraq*, with English trans., notes, commentary, and intro. J. Walbridge and H. Ziai (Provo, UT: Brigham Young University Press, 1999), 65.

2 Suhrawardī, *Ḥikmat al-Ishrāq*, 65. 3 Ibid.

4 Suhrawardī also discusses this topic in his *al-Talwihāt* among other issues such as universals and particulars. For more on this, see Mahdi Aminrazavi, *Suhrawardī and the School of Illumination* (London: Curzon Press, 1997), 9–11.

5 Ghazālī, before Suhrawardī, also asserted that his purpose is to "clarify that the real light is God and that the name 'light' for everything else is sheer metaphor, without reality." in *Mishkāt al-Anwār* (The Niche of Lights), a dual language edition trans. David Buchman (Provo, UT: Brigham Young University Press, 1998), 3; Ghazālī also comments on the verse in *al-Munqidh min al-Ḍalāl* (Deliverance from Error) and Other Relevant Works of al-Ghazālī, trans. R. J. McCarthy (Boston, MA: Twayne Publishers, 1980).

6 Suhrawardī, *Ḥikmat al-Ishrāq*, 83. Translation mine.

7 *Ḥikmat al-Ishrāq*, 78. Translation mine.

'Necessary Existent' (*wājib al-wujūd*)" becomes the Light of Lights (*al-Nūr al-Anwār*) in Suhrawardī's system.[8]

After equating existence and light, Suhrawardī goes on to construct an ontology based on light. God is the Light of Lights that is evident in Itself and also makes other things manifest. The very nature of light is to manifest itself and also to bring others into manifestation (*ẓāhir bi-nafsihi wa-muẓhir li-ghayrihi*).[9] To make other things manifest is to illuminate their essences. The Light of Lights makes dark essences evident by bestowing its light upon them.

Multiplicity emerges from the undivided unity of the Light of Lights due to the "gloomy essences (*māhiyyā al-muẓlima*) and dark states (*hay'āt al-ẓulmāniyya*)."[10] Harkening back to the Neoplatonistic principle, Suhrawardī holds that "from the One only one can proceed." Being perfectly simple, the Light of Lights can have only one effect, a single light called the "Proximate Light." The Light of Lights is by nature the source of all light and unfolds the first and subsequent lights. The relationships between these lights and the Light of Lights are multiplied. The increase in the number of horizontal relationships between the accidental lights and in the number of vertical relationships between God and the accidental lights brings about entities with their distinct qualities.

Suhrawardī's ontology is *continuous* in that it does not posit any separation between the Light of Lights and accidental lights.

> The existence of a light from the Light of Lights does not happen by the separation of something from it, for you know that separation and connection are specific properties of bodies. Far exalted is the Light of Lights above that! … So, you must also understand that this is so for every accidental shining light or incorporeal light.[11]

There is no real separation between the Light of Lights and the world. Light radiating from the Light of Lights illuminates the gloomy essences of entities and in so doing gets feebler and feebler. However, this erosion of light does not suggest a separation between the Light of Lights and the

8 Ibid. Suhrawardī finds allusions to his conclusion in the Qur'an, such as: "God is the light of the heavens and of the earth" (*Allahu nūru-l-samāwāti wa-l-arḍ*) in Qur'an 24:35. See ibid., 111.

9 Suhrawardī, *Ḥikmat al-Ishrāq*, ed. Henry Corbin, in *Opera metaphysica et Mystica*, vol. II (Paris and Tehran: Adrien-Maisonnevue, 1952), 10–11. Cited in T. Izutsu, *The Concept and Reality of Existence* (Tokyo: The Keio Institute of Cultural and Linguistic Studies, 1971), 62.

10 I have changed the translation from "quiddities" to "essences" for consistency.

11 Suhrawardī, *Ḥikmat al-Ishrāq*, 92.

accidental lights. Feeble light is still light, even though it is not the absolute light. "That which is one in all respects is not divisible in any respect."[12] In accordance with this conviction, Suhrawardī also assumes continuity in the physical world. In contrast to the Ashʿarites and the discrete world suggested by their atomism, Suhrawardī denies the idea of the individual atom (*al-jawhar al-fard*)[13] – asserting that "the space between bodies (atoms) cannot be vacant (*khāliyan*)."[14]

Suhrawardī's ontology is also *gradational* in that entities are differentiated from each other in accordance with their share in the Light of Lights. "Intensity (*ta'akkada*) and perfection (*tamāmiyya*) distinguish necessary existence from contingent existence."[15] Entities partake in the light of God. The intensity and diminution of entities' light is determined by the distance from the Light of Lights, which in turn is determined by the capacities of their essences. As Nasr explains, "The ontological status of all beings, therefore, depends on the degree in which they approach the supreme light and are themselves illuminated."[16]

Accordingly, Suhrawardī reduces the five categories of substance, quality, quantity, relation, and motion into degrees of intensity. They are not distinct "ontic entities," to use Hossein Ziai's expression, but rather differing accentuations of a continuous reality of light.[17] This view reduces these categories into mental concepts without a corresponding extramental reality. Moreover, a number of traditional physical notions are also regarded as mental concepts by Suhrawardī. Substance, for example, is replaced by a continuous and gradational magnitude of light. Hence, epistemologically speaking, what matters most is to go beyond the physical appearances, categories, and mental concepts and discover the light-nature of objects. The discovery of light-nature requires direct

[12] Ibid., 75. [13] Ibid., 63. [14] Ibid., 64.

[15] Ibid., 67. See also "all that is higher in degree of cause is closer to that which is lowest because of the intensity of its being evident. Exalted be the Farthest (*al-ab'ad*) and the Nearest" (*al-aqrab*), the Loftiest (*al-arfa'*) and the Lowest (*al-adnā*)," *Ḥikmat al-Ishrāq*, 106. And "That which results from the Light of Lights must be a single incorporeal light. This, then cannot be distinguished from the Light of Lights by any dark state acquired from the Light of Lights … therefore the Light of Lights and the first light that results from It are only to be distinguished by perfection and deficiency. Just as among the objects of sensation the *acquired light is not the same as radiating light*," ibid., 91.

[16] S. H. Nasr, *Three Muslim Sages: Avicenna-Suhrawardi-Ibn 'Arabi* (Cambridge, MA: Harvard University Press, 1964), 69.

[17] H. Ziai, "The Illuminationist Tradition," in *History of Islamic Philosophy*, ed. S. H. Nasr and O. Leaman (London: Routledge, 2003 [1996]), 465–496. Cf. Marcotte, Roxanne, "Suhrawardī," in *The Stanford Encyclopedia of Philosophy* (Fall 2016 Edition), ed. Edward N. Zalta: https://plato.stanford.edu/archives/fall2016/entries/suhrawardī/.

intuitive experience which can be communicated to a certain degree by rational investigation.[18]

Suhrawardī suggests a *continuous-cum-gradational* ontology.[19] There is no real separation or identification of the Light of Lights and the world. In addition, entities are differentiated from each other in accordance with their share in God's light. As such, the main difference between Suhrawardī's ontology and that of the Ashʿarites, as pertains to our discussion of causality, can be summed up as follows. The Ashʿarites emphasize the "otherness" of the efficient cause with respect to its effect. Their theory of creation ex nihilo and rejection of the eternity of the world can be traced back to this emphasis on the complete otherness of God vis-à-vis the world. If the world is eternal, this would imply that it shares in God's eternity. This would contradict the distinction between God and the world, ending in either reducing God to the world, or elevating the world to the status of God. In both cases one would compromise the distinction between God and the world. The moment one sacrifices temporal priority, one also sacrifices the ontological priority of God. This is the gist of Ghazālī's argument against Ibn Sīnā and Fārābī in the *Tahāfut*. Similarly, the Ashʿarite theory of acquisition (*kasb*) starts from the assumption that there is an absolute distinction between God's will and human will. Subsequently, the theory aims to reconcile both without completely losing human agency in their world, which is dominated by the divine will and power. In almost all salient features of Ashʿarite theory, there is an emphasis on the distinction between God, the cause, and the world, its effect.

[18] H. Ziai, *Knowledge and Illumination: A Study of Suhrawardī's Hikmat al-Ishraq* (Atlanta, GA: Scholars Press, 1990), 81.

[19] Suhrawardī's mystic tendencies fit such an ontology. For similarities between certain Sufi theories and Suhrawardī's teachings, see H. Landolt, "Les idées platoniciennes et le monde de l'image dans la pensée du *Šaykh al-išrāq* Yahyā al-Suhrawardī (ca.1155–1191)," in *Miroir et Savoir. La transmission d'un thème platonicien, des Alexandrins à la philosophie arabo-musulmane*, ed. D. De Smet and M. Sebti (Leuven: Peeters, 2007). Also H. Landolt, "Suhrawardī's *Tales of Initiation*," *Journal of the American Oriental Society*, 107.3 (1987): 475–86; S. Schmidtke, *Theologie, Philosophie und Mystik im zwölferschiitischen Islam des 9./15.Jahrhunderts: die Gedankenwelten des Ibn Abi Gumhur al-Ahsai (um 838/1434–35-nach 905/1501)* (Leiden: Brill, 2000). For the influences of Zoroastrian motifs and Mazdean theology on Suhrawardī, see Suhrawardī, *L'archange empourpré: quinze traités et récits mystiques*, trans., intro., and notes H. Corbin (Paris: Fayard, 1976). For a good analysis of the relationship between Suhrawardī and Greek philosophy, see D. Gutas, "Essay-Review: Suhrawardī and Greek Philosophy," *Arabic Sciences and Philosophy*, 13 (2003): 303–309.

In contrast to Ashʿarite theory, Suhrawardī's ontology of light suggests a continuous-cum-gradational relationship between God and the world. God is essentially light, and other entities are light only by participating in God's light. There is neither real separation nor complete identification between the absolute and non-delimited light and the contingent and delimited light. Entities are differentiated according to their share in light. Accidental lights are not really separated from the Light of Lights. The absolute and non-delimited light becomes delimited in the gloomy essences of entities. This delimitation, however, does not indicate a separation from God. In fact, it implies a unification of God's light and dark essences. The divine light unites with dark essences, illuminating and existentiating them. This difference between Suhrawardī's ontology and that of the Ashʿarites is evident in both accounts' view of causal relations, as will be discussed in the following section.

5.2 SUHRAWARDĪ'S PARTICIPATORY ACCOUNT OF CAUSALITY

Suhrawardī's continuous-cum-gradational ontology suggests a *participatory* theory of causality. According to this ontology, God and the world do not exist separately as two things but rather constitute single thing differentiated according to intensity of light. This relationship of non-separation establishes the causal efficacy and freedom of entities, which participate in (as they are not separate from) divine causality and freedom.

For Suhrawardī, all entities "participate (*madkhulun*) in the luminous reality."[20] There is no separation, although there are degrees of light. Despite the multiplicity caused by the gloomy essences, entities exist in a continuous ontology. In this sense, entities have no positive causal action and are only receivers. What "gives all dusky substances their lights must be something other than their gloomy essences and dark states."[21] This is also to say that the real cause for their light, existence, and subsistence is the Light of Lights.

> Everything other than it is in need of it and has its existence from it ... all sovereignty all power all perfection derives from it.[22]
>
> Entities do not create other objects (*inna-l-jisma lā yūjadu jisman*).[23]
>
> The Light of Lights is the ruling Agent despite all intermediaries, the Cause of their activity, the Origin of every emanation, the Absolute creator, *with or without*

[20] Suhrawardī, *Ḥikmat al-Ishrāq*, 85. [21] Ibid., 78. [22] Ibid., 87. [23] Ibid., 85.

intermediary. There is no effect that does not contain Its effect, although It may not allow the relation of activity to be shared with another.[24]

These passages ascribe causal power to God. The Light of Lights is the cause of everything "with or without intermediary." Despite these passages' attribution of all causal power to God, entities are also causally efficacious due to their participation in God's light. As already mentioned, what bestows existence to the gloomy essences is the existentiating light that emanates from the Light of Lights. Due to the interaction between the non-delimited light and the gloomy essences of entities, light becomes delimited. The absolute light becomes qualified in essences. This process leads to the individuation of light in entities. These individuated lights also radiate (albeit feebler) light. As Walbridge observes, entities that are composed of differing degrees of light remain "unitary concrete entities."[25]

Suhrawardī's account of this process, the radiation of the absolute light from the Light of Lights and the individuation of light in the gloomy essences of the entities, provides the basis for a participatory account of causal efficacy. Entities receive from God an existentiating light that illuminates their dark essences, and they emit the same light down upon lower lights. Entities do not create their own light but merely receive and radiate it. Their light flows from God's light. In this regard, their existence and the continuation of this existence are caused by God. In this state, there is only top-down causality. Yet God's light becomes qualified in the individuated beings. Those beings' participation in the luminous reality of the light of God, albeit in a delimited fashion, allows them to have their own light and, hence, radiate it.

The whole process can be likened to the passage of colorless light through a colored glass. The light will be colored and thus delimited during this process. Colored light, however, is not really separated from colorless light. But it is not identical to colorless light either. A colored light is still light, but it is not the absolute light. In this analogy, the glass itself can be likened to the gloomy essences, for it qualifies the colorless light. Thus, the light the entities emit is God's from one perspective and their own from another. Entities acquire the same absolute light from the Light of Lights, yet they radiate a light in accordance with their essences.

24 Ibid., 114. Emphasis mine.

25 John Walbridge, *The Leaven of the Ancients: Suhrawardī and the Heritage of the Greeks* (Albany: State University of New York Press, 2000), 22–23.

Their qualified light, ultimately, is the light of God. Herein, the same act can simultaneously be attributed to God and the entity: as "the Light of Lights is the cause of the existence and the cause of continuation of all existents, so also are the dominating lights."[26]

An entity, then, is caused by the Light of Lights. The same entity is also a cause, by virtue of the light it participates in and radiates. The Light of Lights is the real illuminating or existentiating cause and the causal efficacy of other beings results from their participation in the divine light. In accordance with Suhrawardī's continuous and gradational ontology, as discussed above, there is a gradation in this participation in accordance with the "intensity and perfection" of their light. Some entities share in the light more fully than others. Which is to say, some entities are causally more efficacious than others.

These individuated lights also interact with each other. Each entity radiates light in accordance with its essence and affects other entities. In this regard, each entity receives light from the Light of Lights with an intermediary. Each entity also receives light from the Light of Lights without an intermediary. An entity is affected by the absolute light on one hand, and by the individuated lights on the other.

> [E]ach higher light shines upon those which are below it in rank, and the lower light receives rays from the Light of Lights by the mediacy of those which are above it, rank on rank. Thus, the second dominating light receives the heaven-sent light from the Light of Lights once from it without intermediary and another time with respect to the Proximate Light … it continues like that *with* (*bi-wāsiṭatun*) and *without intermediary* (*ghayr wāsiṭatun*).[27]

In all cases causal efficacy of intermediaries is due to their participation in the divine light. The non-delimited light emanating from the Light of Lights illuminates the gloomy essences of entities, and entities subsequently radiate light in a delimited form – a process that can be called the individuation of light. If there are intermediaries, they exist as delimitations and individuations of the absolute and non-delimited light. Entities are caused directly by the Light of Lights, but they are also considered causes, for they emit the non-delimited light in an individuated form. The Light of Light causes simultaneously "with and without intermediary."

The same participatory understanding of the concept of causality can be observed in Suhrawardī's discussion of the dependence and

[26] Suhrawardī, *Ḥikmat al-Ishrāq*, 123.

[27] Ibid., 100. Emphasis mine. I have changed the word "propitious" in the original translation to "heaven-sent."

independence of entities. Suhrawardī believes that entities can be regarded as dependent from one perspective and independent from another. For example, "the Proximate Light (the first emanation) is dependent in itself but independent by virtue of the First."[28] In itself any entity is dependent on the existentiating illumination from God. Once an entity receives this illumination from the First, it can also be considered independent. As will be discussed in the following pages, by virtue of their participation in the absolute light to the extent allowed by their essences, entities also participate in the divine independence. Moreover,

> Although the Proximate Light cannot bring into being a dusky substance with respect to its own luminosity, yet still a barrier and an incorporeal light must result from it, since it contains dependence in itself and independence by virtue of the First ... *By the manifestation to itself of its dependence* and the darkening of its own essence in its contemplation of the glory of the Light of Lights in relation to itself, *a shadow results from the incorporeal light*. This is the loftiest barrier, greatest of the barriers, the all-encompassing barrier ... But *with respect to its independence* and its *necessity* by the Light of Lights and its contemplation of its glory and might, *it brings into being another incorporeal light*. The barrier is its shadow, and the self-subsistent light is illumination from it. Its shadow is only due to the darkness of its dependence.[29]

In this passage, Suhrawardī links such notions as necessity and contingency, luminosity and darkness, and independence and dependence. A light is dependent inasmuch as it is contingent in itself. It is independent inasmuch as it is necessary because of something other than itself. To the extent that it is contingent, a shadow results from it. To the extent that it is necessary, light emits from it. To the extent that entities are dependent, they cannot cause something. They themselves are just gloomy essences waiting to be illuminated or to be caused. To the extent that entities are independent, they can cause something. The non-delimited light becomes delimited while illuminating the gloomy essences. Entities, in turn, emit light and bring about effects.

5.3 LIGHT AND MOTION

In certain passages Suhrawardī suggests a connection between physical activity and his metaphysical construction of causality. Suhrawardī writes, for example, that "activity is a property of Light."[30] The activity we observe is due to the nature of light. Thus, light is the cause of

[28] Ibid., 92. [29] Ibid., 95. Emphasis mine. [30] Ibid., 113.

movement. "The light, however, gives being to both movement and heat and by its nature causes them to occur."[31] Furthermore, these motions are intimately related to their capacity for illumination. On the one hand, light causes motion. On the other hand, motion manifests light. Motion also increases the capacity for illumination. The motion of an entity is a condition for illumination.

These motions prepare the capacity for illuminations, while at another time the illuminations necessitate the motions . . . *The motion continues to be the condition of the illumination*, and the illumination at other times necessitates the motion that is after it, and so on perpetually. All the individual motions and illuminations are determined by a continuing love and perpetual desire.[32]

Movement is an attribute of light. When entities move, they are closer to light. Or, they are more like light. In this sense, the more they move, the more they are illuminated. This may also suggest a connection between movement and spiritual advancement. Movement is closer to metaphysical discernment and spiritual realization than to rest.

Motion is also related to "love and desire." This appears to echo Ibn Sīnā's conviction that when entities move, they do so to be more like their source, the Light of Lights.[33] Since motion, which increases their capacity for illumination, makes them more like the Light of Lights, it is their love for the Light of Lights that motivates their motion.[34] This is why there is constant activity in terrestrial and celestial domains. If "the motions of the spheres are infinite, they must be due to something infinitely renewed."[35]

The lights become the cause of movements and heats, and light is evident in both movement and heat – not because they are its cause but because they prepare the receptivity for a light to occur there in from the dominating light that emanates by its substance upon those recipients that are properly prepared to receive it.[36]

These lights are interrelated through the principles of love and dominance. The lower lights have love for the higher lights, and the higher lights

[31] Ibid., 129. See also "desires necessitate motions. Part of the nobility of fire is that it has the highest motion and the most perfect heat and is nearest to the nature of life," ibid., 130.

[32] Ibid., 122. Emphasis mine.

[33] Ibn Sīnā writes, for instance, that objects "desire to imitate the First in inasmuch as He is in act renders the movement of the celestial sphere." *al-Shifāʾ al-Ilahiyyāt*, 315; and "Motion is the very perfection," 322.

[34] Suhrawardī, *Ḥikmat al-Ishrāq*, 121.

[35] Ibid., 122. This passage also suggests that the Light of Lights manifests itself in a renewed fashion.

[36] Ibid., 129.

have dominance over the lower lights. "Every light has dominance in relation to lower light and the lower has love for the higher light."[37] This is also to say that every light has two types of relationships, or exists under the influence of both love and dominion. Every light simultaneously experiences dominance and love. "At the root of the deficient light is passion for the higher light. At the root of the higher light is dominance over the deficient light . . . thus all existence is ordered on the basis of love and dominance (*al-muḥabba wa-l-qahr*)"[38] A light then dominates a lower light and is dominated by a higher light. Similarly, the same light has love for a higher light that causes it and is loved by a lower light that it causes. "You know that light emanates by its nature and it has in its substance a love for its origin and dominance over [that] which is below it."[39]

5.4 NONEXISTENCE AND POSITIVE-NEGATIVE CAUSALITY

Suhrawardī holds that "the removal of impediments" can also constitute a cause. The removal of clouds, for instance, is a cause for the illumination of the earth. What is crucial to understand here is that the removal of clouds is not the real cause of the illumination of the earth. The removal does not have any positive causal agency. The real cause is the sun. Yet, the removal of clouds can also be considered a cause, for the illumination of the earth cannot happen without it. In conclusion, removal of clouds is a cause from one perspective and not a cause from another. "Conditions and the removal of impediments also enter into the cause; for if the impediment is not removed the existence of the thing is still contingent in relation to what is assumed to be its cause."[40]

Similarly, Suhrawardī equates "rest" with a lack of a cause of movement. Rest as a negative quality does not require a cause. Privation itself is a sort of cause. For instance, "movement is closer to the nature of life and luminosity, for movement demands a luminous existential cause whereas a privation – the lack of a cause of movement – is sufficient cause for rest."[41]

[37] Ibid., 97. [38] Ibid., 97–98.
[39] Ibid., 133. Suhrawardī also suggests that in all these vertical and horizontal relations between entities, one observes both necessity and freedom. In participatory accounts of causality, there is both necessity and freedom. "[I]n relation to its effect every luminous cause possesses love and dominance," ibid., 103.
[40] Ibid., 43. [41] Ibid., 129.

As such, the removal of impediments is a cause without having any positive causal activity. This type of causality can be regarded as negative causality. From this perspective, nonexistence is a cause, even if it has no *positive* causal efficacy. "*Nonexistence enters into causality* in the sense that when the mind considers the necessity of the effect, it cannot do this without considering the nonexistence of the impediment."[42] Nonexistence cannot cause anything, for it is simply nonexistent. It has no positive quality to be qualified as a cause.[43] However, from another perspective, nonexistence is a cause, for it causes the observed differentiation of the absolute light. Entities are mixtures of existence and nonexistence or, in other words, light and darkness. To the extent that entities have their share from the light, they have positive causal activity. To the extent that they have their share from darkness, they have negative causal activity. In their positive activity, they participate in the divine light and subsequently emit the light they receive from the Light of Lights, as discussed above. In their negative activity, they delimit the light. Their nonexistence is in this sense a cause too.

> There is multiplicity in the barriers (*barzakh*) ... if there would be no barriers everything would be light.[44]
>
> The agent may be the same, but the perfection and deficiency of the ray may differ by reason of the recipient, as is the case with the rays of the Sun that fall upon crystal, jet, or earth.[45]

Accordingly, entities are not the cause of light but simply receive and participate in light. God gives all "gloomy essences (*māhiyya al-muẓlima*) and dark states" their light.[46] God, the giver of light, is the real existentiating and sustaining cause. The same light is qualified in the essences of the entities. Entities participate in and radiate light in accordance with their essences. Therefore, darkness or nonexistence can genuinely be attributed to entities, whereas light or existence can ultimately only be attributed to God. This attribution does not imply any positive causal activity on the part of entities, since darkness or nonexistence has no positive quality. Yet, nonexistence is the cause of differentiation and, thus, imperfection.

Entities, then, have two types of causal role: positive and negative. Positive, to the extent that they participate in the divine light and

[42] Ibid., 44. Emphasis mine.
[43] Consider: "This is not to say that nonexistence does something," ibid. [44] Ibid., 95.
[45] Ibid., 91. [46] Ibid., 78.

radiate an individuated version of it; negative, to the extent that they delimit the divine light due to their essences. Both in their participation in the divine light and in their delimitation of the divine light, entities are causes.

5.5 FREEDOM: RECIPIENTS AND PARTICIPATION

How does Suhrawardī establish freedom in accordance with this description of causality? There are two possible answers.

First, it has already been mentioned that God illuminates and existentiates the dark essences of entities in accordance with "the suitability of the recipients (*qawābil*)."[47] The essences of the entities lead to delimitation and, thus, differentiation of one light. One light, as we participate in it, becomes multiple. "Many different things may indeed result from the one thing by virtue of differing and multiple states of receptivity."[48] One becomes many in accordance with the recipient's essence.

For the Necessary Existent, existence is a necessary quality, but in the created order "existence is superadded" to essences.[49] This means that essence comes before existence in a certain sense. The idea of the principality of essence (*aṣālat al-māhiyya*) provides the basis for freedom of created entities.[50] Suhrawardī appears to provide no cause for an entity for having the essence it has. It is true that, as the preceding analysis suggests, God causes a possible being to exist as more than a possibility; however, God does not cause a possible being to be what it is. God existentiates entities as they are but does not make them what they are. In other words, God causes their *wujūd* without defining their *māhiyya*. God only illuminates their *māhiyya* by bestowing *wujūd*. Essences that precede existence are, then, *uncaused causes*.

> Generosity is giving that which is appropriate without any recompense ... There is nothing more generous than that which is light in its own reality. *By its essence, it reveals itself to and emanates upon every receptive one.* The true King is *He who possesses the essence of everything* but whose essence is possessed by none. He is the Light of Lights.[51]

[47] Ibid., 96. [48] Ibid. [49] Ibid.

[50] Suhrawardī also discusses this topic in his *al-Talwiḥāt*, among other issues such as universals and particulars. See Mahdi Aminrazavi, *Suhrawardī and the School of Illumination* (London: Curzon Press, 1997), 9–11.

[51] Ibid. Emphasis mine.

Suhrawardī mentions in this passage that God "possesses the essence of everything." This suggests that God knows these essences.

> The Light of Lights is evident to Itself ... and all else is evident to It. "Not the weight of an atom in the heavens or in the earth escapes Him" (Qur'an 34:3), since nothing veils it from anything. Thus, its knowledge and vision are one as are its luminosity and power, since light emanates by its essence.[52]

God's knowing and illuminating-existentiating essences do not mean that God determines essences. God illuminates, creates, and makes manifest these essences according to His knowledge of them. God's creation follows God's knowledge, and God's knowledge follows the known object without determining them. God knows and possesses all possibilities and realizes them in accordance with their essences. If this is true, then although God has the sole existentiating causal power, entities are free in having the essences they have the divine knowledge. If freedom means being an uncaused cause, then entities have a genuine freedom by virtue of having the specific essence they have.

Suhrawardī also suggests that participating in light implies freedom, for to participate in light is to participate in the divine attributes that light implies or necessitates, including existence, life, consciousness, power, and freedom. To the degree that we participate in light, we will have our share in these qualities, including freedom. In participating in the divine freedom, entities will have freedom.

How does light imply other divine attributes? First, for Suhrawardī the Light of Lights is the source of consciousness and self-awareness in the created order. Entities partake in consciousness and self-awareness to the extent that they participate in light. Moreover, "whatever apprehends its own self (*dhāt*) is a light in itself (*nūr li-nafsihī*)."[53] Self-awareness and light are one and the same thing. Hence, the discovery of the light nature of things is possible through discovering the light nature of the self. This is why Suhrawardī's philosophical mysticism starts from the discovery of the light (the self) in the depth of human existence, and then proceeds to the discovery of the light (the Self) in the outer world.[54] What is more important for our discussion is that the divine light is the basis of self-awareness and consciousness of the entities. To participate in the Light of Lights is also to participate in these qualities. Thus, Suhrawardī writes:

[52] Ibid., 105. [53] Ibid., 83.

[54] For a good analysis of Suhrawardī's epistemology and its relevance for modern philosophy, see M. Ha'iri Yazdi, *The Principles of Epistemology in Islamic Philosophy: Knowledge by Presence* (Albany: State University of New York Press, 1992).

> Anything that apprehends its own essence is a pure light, and every pure light is evident to itself and apprehends its own essence.[55]
>
> Ego is nothing but being evident and being light.[56]
>
> It has been shown that your ego is an incorporeal light, that it is self-conscious, and that the incorporeal lights do not differ in their realities. Thus, all the incorporeal lights must apprehend their essences, since that which is necessarily true of a thing must also be true of that which has the same reality.[57]

Similarly, to say light is to say life:

> life and self-consciousness of the Light of Lights are essential not additional to its essence.[58]

Light also implies power and knowledge.

> Thus, the intensity of the Light if Lights and the perfections of Its luminosity are infinite, and nothing else can rule over It by encompassing It. We ourselves are only veiled from It by the perfection of Its light and deficiency of our faculties – not because It is hidden ... By Its light and Its power, It dominates all things. Its knowledge is Its luminosity, and Its power and dominance over all things are Its luminosity as well.[59]

Finally, Suhrawardī equates life with independence. In itself an essence is totally dependent on the existentiating illumination of the Light of Lights, without which it remains a mere essence. Once it receives illumination from the Light of Lights, an entity becomes independent by virtue of participating in the divine light, which entails divine independence. An entity is dependent in itself but independent by virtue of the Light of Lights.[60] In other words, an entity receives its independence from the divine light.

> Although the Proximate Light cannot bring into being a dusky substance with respect to its own luminosity, yet still a barrier and an incorporeal light must result from it, since it contains *dependence in itself and independence by virtue of the First*.[61]
>
> But *with respect to its independence* and its necessity by the Light of Lights and its contemplation of its glory and might, *it brings into being another incorporeal light*.[62]

All divine attributes are perceived as different manifestations of one and the same thing, light. If light entails all these properties and if there is no separation between our light and the Light of Lights despite the gradual descent, then it is possible to argue that entities by sharing in the divine

[55] Suhrawardī, *Ḥikmat al-Ishrāq*, 82. [56] Ibid., 81. [57] Ibid., 86. [58] Ibid., 89.
[59] Ibid., 113. [60] Ibid., 92. [61] Ibid., 95. Emphasis mine. [62] Ibid. Emphasis mine.

light participate in the divine qualities. With God's consciousness, they are conscious. With God's life, they are alive. What is more important for our discussion on freedom is that by participating in the divine freedom, entities also experience freedom. As such, both Suhrawardī's treatment of essences as being uncaused objects of the divine knowledge and the idea of participation in the divine light ground freedom.

5.6 CONCLUSION

Suhrawardī's approach to the question of causality and freedom is rooted in his gradational-cum-continuous ontology. God is light, and other beings are light due to their participation in God's light. The basis for all causal activity is radiation of the divine light upon the gloomy essences. As it illuminates and existentiates essences, the divine light also provides a basis for their causal efficacy. Entities are not the cause of light; they are only recipients of light. Yet, this is not to say that they are causally insignificant. Entities not only receive but also radiate light in accordance with their capacities. The absolute light becomes delimited in the gloomy essences, and these gloomy essences subsequently emanate light in a delimited form. In this sense, the Light of Light reaches entities in two ways, "with and without intermediary." Each entity is caused by the Light of Lights, but it also simultaneously causes other beings.

In this sense, there appears to be an agreement between Ibn Sīnā and Suhrawardī. As discussed in Chapter 2, Ibn Sīnā's distinction between physical and metaphysical causality also leads to a view of the relationship between God and the world as being both with and without intermediation. As opposed to occasionalist rejection of causal intermediation, both Ibn Sīnā and Suhrawardī agree that causal intermediation does not necessarily compromise God's status as the basis for all causal activity. As we will discuss in the following chapters, Qūnawī and Qayṣarī also support this idea that the causal relationship between God and the world is to be understood both "with and without intermediary."

6

The World as a Theophany and Causality

Sufi Metaphysics and the Case of Ibn ʿArabī

This chapter offers a way of approaching the question of causality in Ibn ʿArabī's metaphysical system. Ibn ʿArabī's metaphysics is relational in the sense that entities are comprehended as the totality of their relationships to God. The divine names are theological categories denoting these relations. It is processual in that it perceives the world as the multiplicity of the incessant and ever-changing manifestations of the divine qualities. The world is re-created anew at each moment and entities are societies of divine acts or theophanies. In this framework, causal power is attributed to God, and causality refers to the regularity and predictability of the related theophanic individualities. The relational and processual qualities of Ibn ʿArabī's metaphysics allow him to integrate participatory and occasionalist perspectives on causality. The chapter also examines how Ibn ʿArabī uses the idea of participation and the fixed archetypes (*al-aʿyān thābita*) to establish freedom.[1]

[1] Some parts of this chapter also appeared in Ozgur Koca, "The World as a Theophany and Causality: Ibn ʿArabī, Causes, and Freedom," *Sophia*, 2017, 10.1007/s11841–017-0621-x. Reprinted by permission from Springer. This chapter includes both my own translations and excellent extant translations from T. Izutsu, *A Comparative Study of the Key Philosophical Concepts in Sufism and Taoism* (Tokyo: Keio University; second ed., *Sufism and Taoism* (Los Angeles: University of California Press, 1983 [1966])); and W. Chittick, *The Sufi Path of Knowledge: Ibn al-ʿArabī's Metaphysics of Imagination* (Albany: State University of New York Press, 1989), hereafter *Sufi Path*; and *The Self Disclosure of God: The Principles of Ibn al-ʿArabī's Cosmology* (Albany: State University of New York Press, 1998), hereafter *Self Disclosure*; and Michel Chodkiewicz, ed., *The Meccan Revelations: Ibn al-ʿArabī*, vols 1 and 2, trans. William Chittick and James W. Morris (New York: Pir Press, 2005 [2002]). Chittick's translations are from *al-Futūḥāt al-Makkīyya*, ed. O. Yahia, 14 vols (Cairo: al-Hayʿat al-Misriyyat, 1972–1991),

6.1 IBN ʿARABĪ AND CAUSALITY

What does Ibn ʿArabī say about causality?[2] It is true that oftentimes Ibn ʿArabī's discourse is elusive; he shifts between perspectives, and one will not find in his writings a systematic treatment of the problem of causality. We can, however, discern some elements of his thought that relate to the question of causality. There are also many passages in which the term *asbāb* (causes, means, reasons) appears. These aspects of Ibn ʿArabī's thought, to which I now turn, allow an interpretive approach to the question of how so-called causal relations operate in his metaphysical universe.

6.1.1 Relationality

For Ibn ʿArabī, God-relatedness is the most essential aspect of reality – to the extent that every entity is comprehended as the totality of its relations (*nisab*) to God. What are these relations for Ibn ʿArabī? To demonstrate the exact status of "relations" in his thought and to understand the full significance of this point, we need to look at the function of the divine names in his metaphysics.

There are divine qualities mentioned in the Qurʾan and in the prophetic traditions are the Just, the Compassionate, the All-Powerful, the Subtle, the Transcendent, and so forth. The Qurʾanic name for these qualities is *asmā al-ḥusnā*, the most beautiful names.[3] Ibn ʿArabī offers several ways of understanding the divine names. What is distinctive about his treatment is that he holds that the divine names denote relations or realities of relations (*ḥaqā'iq al-nisab*).[4]

hereafter, *Futūḥāt* (1972–1991). For my own translations, I used *al-Futūḥāt al-Makkīyya* (Cairo, 1911; reprinted, Beirut: Dar Sadir, n.d.). Hereafter, *Futūḥāt* (1911).

[2] For a detailed examination of Ibn ʿArabī's life based on both Ibn ʿArabī's own writings and secondary literature, see Claude Addas, *Quest for the Red Sulphur: The Life of Ibn ʿArabi* (Cambridge, UK: The Islamic Texts Society, 1993). For an examination of the development, refinement, and crystallization of the school of Ibn ʿArabī and its influence on the broader intellectual culture, see Caner K. Dağlı, *Ibn al-ʿArabī and Islamic Intellectual Culture: From Mysticism to Philosophy* (New York: Routledge, 2016). For an accessible look at Meccan Illuminations without requiring specialized knowledge, see James W. Morris, *The Reflective Heart: Discovering Spiritual Intelligence in Ibn ʿArabi's ʿMeccan Illuminations'* (Louisville, KY: Fons Vitae, 2005). Also, Ekrem Demirli, *Ibnu'l Arabi Metafiziği* (Istanbul: Sufi Kitap, 2013).

[3] Qurʾan, 7:180, 59:24.

[4] T. Izutsu, *A Comparative Study of the Key Philosophical Concepts in Sufism and Taoism* (Tokyo: Keio University; 2nd ed., *Sufism and Taoism* (Los Angeles: University of California Press, 1983 [1966])), 99. Hereafter *Sufism and Taoism.*

The nature of this relationality can be understood in epistemological, ontological, and theosophical ways. From an epistemological perspective, the divine names are theological categories denoting the different aspects of the God–cosmos relationship. The divine names are like various perspectives from which we can approach the mysterious relationality between God and the world. As Izutsu writes, "each name is a special aspect of the divine self-disclosure ... They are realities of the relations, i.e., the relation which the One reality bears to the world."[5] The world is a multiplicity of loci on which the divine names are continuously manifested. A being, like a mirror, reflects a specific combination of the divine names. Hence, to understand the divine names is to witness the Real in its manifestations. "Each Name is the Real (*al-Ḥaqq*) as it appears as a particular image (*al-ḥaqq al-mutakhayyal*)."[6] Since each name provides a distinct perspective, the multiplicity of the names provided in the Qurʾan and the prophetic traditions enrich the possibility of understanding and experiencing the ineffable and inexhaustible divine reality in the manifested order.

From a more theosophical perspective, the divine names denote the infinite possibilities hidden in the divine Self (*Dhāt*). As a possibility (*imkān*), a divine quality demands to be manifested. God's manifestation actualizes these possibilities. To use an anthropomorphic analogy, the very act of manifestation eases the "sadness" (*qurba*) of the divine names. "The reality (*ḥaqq*) of names demands that every name become manifest, *ad infinitum*."[7] This is also to say that manifestation is demanded by the divine nature. The divine names require ontological domains on which they can be manifested. The divine quality of the Forgiver requires the existence of things to forgive. Similarly, evil is allowed to exist for the manifestation of the divine wrath and the divine mercy. "[The] Avenger demands the occurrence of vengeance in its objects, while [the] Compassionate demands the removal of vengeance."[8]

From an ontological perspective, the manifestation the divine names brings the fixed archetypes (*al-aʿyān thābita*) into existence. A helpful way of thinking about the fixed archetypes is to see them as "ontological possibilities contained in the Absolute."[9] They are fixed, for in God's

[5] Izutsu, *Sufism and Taoism*, 99.

[6] Ibn ʿArabī, *Fuṣūṣ al-Ḥikam*, ed. A. ʿAfīfī (Beirut: Dār al-Kutub al-ʿArabī, 1946), 38–39; hereafter *Fuṣūṣ*.

[7] Ibn ʿArabī, *Fuṣūṣ*, 65.

[8] Ibn ʿArabī, *Futūḥāt* (1972–1991), II 93.19.

[9] Izutsu, *Sufism and Taoism*, 157.

knowledge everything exists in an eternally unchanging form.[10] In the divine Self these fixed archetypes exist *in potentia*. Therefore, they can neither be said to exist nor not to exist. When the divine names relate to the fixed archetypes, they become *in actu* and "enter" *wujūd*.

Some of these names have a broader scope and connect (*taʿalluq*) to a broader range of entities than others do.[11] For example, the name of All-Knowing is more inclusive then All-Powerful; the former relates to both existence and nonexistence, while the latter relates only to existence. This implies that there is a hierarchy (*tafaḍḍul*) among the divine qualities. Mercy has precedence over wrath.

The number of possible relations between God and the manifested order is infinite. This to say, the number of the divine names is infinite. If "the possible things are infinite, so the names are infinite."[12] Not all of the names are known to us. However, all names in theory can be traced back to those names mentioned in the Qurʾan and the prophetic traditions. These recorded names are the "mothers of names."[13] The possibility of the infinite number of relationships between God and the world does not affect the Divine Unity. "We name him such and such through the effect of what we find within ourselves. So, the effects are multiple within us; hence the names are multiple … but He does not become multiple in Himself through them."[14]

The divine names denote relations between God and the manifested order. The cosmos displays "theophanies" of the divine names. From this viewpoint, the world appears, as Izutsu aptly summarizes, as "nothing but whole sum of the divine names as concretely actualized."[15]

From the perspective of this relational metaphysics, an entity is not an inert and self-contained thing entering into a relationship with God. On the contrary, what makes an entity is its relations. Relations exist before the entities that relate to each other. Reality is defined primarily by relations and only secondarily by the related things or *relata*. The divine

[10] Ibid., 90. This is because things even in their state of pure potentiality hidden in the unmanifested essence have a positive status (*thubūt*) from eternity. This why Ibn ʿArabī thinks the world originates in at once being and nonbeing, *coincidentia opposiorum* (*jam bayn al-naqiḍayn*). It is *huwa la huwa*, He/Not He. Cf. Henry Corbin, *Alone with the Alone* (Princeton, NJ: Princeton University Press, 1998),186.

[11] Chittick, *Sufi Path*, 48.

[12] Ibn ʿArabī, *Futūḥāt* (1972–1991), IV 288.1. Translated in Chittick, *Sufi Path*, 41.

[13] Ibn ʿArabī, *Fuṣūṣ*, 65, trans. in Chittick, *Sufi Path*, 42.

[14] Ibn ʿArabī, *Futūḥāt* (1972–1991), III 387.8, translated in Chittick, *Sufi Path*, 43.

[15] Izutsu, *Sufism and Taoism*, 100.

attributes and names are theological categories describing these relations between the world and God. They designate a specific, manifested divine quality in what we perceive as creation. All that exists is God and God's acts. God's acts manifest the divine qualities. In this regard, the world is nothing but an endless and ever-changing display of the divine names, and an entity is nothing but a nexus of the divine acts or theophanies. An entity is, then, the sum of its relations to God.

6.1.2 Constant Re-Creation and Process

Change is the fundamental principle of reality for Ibn ʿArabī. The concept of the new creation (*al-khalq al-jadīd*) entails that the world is re-created anew at each moment. The world oscillates between existence and non-existence. It comes into being in one moment and perishes in the next.[16] The re-created world is always different from the preceding moment. God not only re-creates the world but also re-creates it differently. The manifestation of the divine qualities never repeats itself (*lā takrār fī-l-tajallī*).[17]

The notion of "process" can be used to describe this aspect of Ibn ʿArabī's metaphysics. Namely, Ibn ʿArabī's metaphysics is processual in that it identifies the natural order with constant change rather than with self-subsisting, permanent substances. In defining the cosmos as constantly renewed creation, Ibn ʿArabī is drawing on a long theological tradition in which the Ashʿarites also participated. The theory of the constant re-creation of the world anew at each moment (*tajdīd al-khalq fī-l-ānāt*) suggested by the Ashʿarite theory of atomism is adapted by Ibn ʿArabī.

Why? Ibn ʿArabī's theosophy provides multiple reasons. First, God is infinite (*al-tawassuʿ al-ilāhī*). To say that God is infinite is to say God has infinite possibilities. For the realization of infinite possibilities, the act of creation must be continuous and not repeat itself. If the source is infinitely rich, then loci must be infinitely variegated in order to manifest the infinite possibilities. God's infinity renders the world a process.

16 For Ibn ʿArabī, such Qurʾanic assertions as "each day He is upon some task (*shaʾn*)" (Qurʾan 55:29) allude to this point. A "day" here, according to ibn ʿArabī, could be the indivisible moment (*an*). "Some days are long and some are short. The smallest of them is the indivisible moment, in respect of which came the verse, 'Each day he is upon some task.'" Ibn ʿArabī, *Futūḥāt* (1972–1991), I. 292.15. Translated in Chittick, *Sufi Path*, 98.

17 This is one of the fundamental principles of Sufi metaphysics. See for example, "After all, you also see God at this very moment in His Effects and Acts. Every instant you see something different, for none of His Acts resembles any other." *Fuṣūṣ*, 113–114.

Second, the idea of creation anew establishes the absolute dependence of the world on God. Nothing in the world can be self-subsistent, for this would imply independence from the infinite God. If the world were to remain in a single state for "two units of time, it would possess the attribute of independence from God."[18]

Third, this cosmological assertion establishes the basis for the attainment of the spiritual and ethical goals of Sufism. The realization of one's absolute dependence on God is a prerequisite for the Sufi ideal of annihilation (*fanāʾ*) in God. To annihilate oneself in God, one should realize the absolute need for God and one's own nothingness. In a world where everything is re-created anew at each moment, God is the sole reason for the continuation of existence. "God is ever creating perpetually, while the engendered existence is in need perpetually."[19]

Fourth, for Ibn ʿArabī, if the world is not re-created at each moment, then this would imply a passivity in God. God "never ceases being the agent." If this is the case, the world must be continuously and necessarily "renewed (*tajaddud*) at each instant," for God to "be the Agent (*fāʿil*) of existence in the possible things."[20] To preserve God's continuous agency, Ibn ʿArabī subscribes to the doctrine of the continuous re-creation of the world.

Ibn ʿArabī employs various anthropomorphic analogies to clarify the concept. For instance, the term the "Breath of the Merciful" (*Nafas al-Raḥmān*) refers to the constant re-creation of the world. God breathes out the word "be" (*kun*) to bring the world into existence. Possibilities that are in God are thus manifested. God breathes out existence, for God is always effusing due to His bounteousness (*fayyāḍ al-jūd*). "The world is made manifest in the Breath of the Merciful to ease the sadness of the divine names."[21] The attribute of mercy here acquires an ontological meaning in that mercy is the most essential aspect of the divine reality and the basis of all existence. What is relevant for this discussion in this analogy is that, like breath, the act of existentiation of the world is a continuous and recurring event.

Moreover, in a world where everything is re-created anew at each moment, the concept of self-subsisting substance/s collapses. Ibn ʿArabī's conviction is particularly evident in his rejection of Ashʿarite atomism.

[18] Ibn ʿArabī, *Futūḥāt* (1972–1991), III. 199; cf. Chittick, *Sufi Path*, 98.
[19] Ibid., II. 280.31; cf. Chittick, *Sufi Path*, 97.
[20] Ibid., IV. 320.3; cf. Chittick, *Sufi Path*, 97.
[21] Ibn ʿArabī, *Fuṣūṣ*, 145, trans. in Izutsu, *Sufism and Taoism*, 213.

For Ibn ʿArabī, Ashʿarite atomism entails the existence of self-subsisting substances. He says that "the Ashʿarites fail to see that the world, in its entirety, is *a sum of accidents* and that, consequently, the whole world is changing from moment to moment, since no 'accident' subsists for two units of time."[22] All things are bundles of accidents. There are no self-subsisting substances in which accidents inhere. Only God is self-subsistent. As Ibn ʿArabī summarizes, "even substance must ultimately be an accident, and as such is not self-subsistent."[23]

To conclude, Ibn ʿArabī considers an object to be an aggregation of accidents that are multiple manifestations of God. This reality escapes human perception, for the act of re-creation is so quick that there is no apparent discontinuity. Considering the centrality of the concept of change in his metaphysics, together with the rejection of the idea of substance, what we observe here is a processual metaphysics in which acts are prior to substance/s. Denial of the idea of self-subsisting substance/s as well as the accentuation of accidents allows Ibn ʿArabī to define an object as a conglomeration of the divine acts. The divine acts, or theophanies, constitute the totality of things.

6.1.3 Causality

How, then, are causal relations, the predictable and continuous interactions of the differentiated entities, conceived in Ibn ʿArabī's relational and processual metaphysical framework?

From the perspective of relationality, an entity is defined by its relation to God, to the extent that these relations make the totality of the entity. Ibn ʿArabī's rejection of self-subsisting substance/s leads to a conception of an entity as a bundle of different qualities and acts. His relational metaphysics traces all of an entity's qualities back to God's qualities. An entity is thus conceived as a manifestation of those qualities.[24] In other words, an entity is the sum of its relations to God.

If the divine names are theological categories describing these relations, it can be said that an object is nothing but a nexus of the divine names. Each object, such as a tree or a rock, displays different configurations of

[22] Ibid., 124–125. Emphasis mine. Trans. in Izutsu, *Sufism and Taoism*, 213.

[23] Ibid., 125–126. Trans. in Izutsu, *Sufism and Taoism*, 214.

[24] The divine qualities exist in God in a state of perfection, and they exist in entities imperfectly, as shadows, as a mixture of light of pure existence and darkness of nothingness.

these names. "In reality, *there is nothing but the names of God in existence*."[25] If this is the case, then an entity's relationships to God, namely the divine names, are the causes of its existence and subsistence.

From the perspective of Ibn ʿArabī's processual metaphysics, the world is re-created anew at each moment. As in Ashʿarite occasionalism, the idea of the continuous re-creation of the world causally disconnects any two moments of cosmic history. There is, then, no causal "glue" connecting now and then, moment one and moment two. The world is perceived as continuous because of the constant effusion of God's existence to the world at each moment. Self-subsistence cannot be attributed to the world, due to the reasons elaborated above. All that exists is God and God's theophanies, instantiations, delimitations, and manifestations that are constantly being renewed. It is important to recall that Ibn ʿArabī understands time as the totality of discrete moments as implied in his theory of the new creation (*al-khalq al-jadīd*). An entity comes into being and perishes immediately afterwards. The illusion of continuity arises from the constant re-creation of the world at distinct moments. Time is to be understood in the form of discrete moments and not as an uninterrupted flux. In this world that pulsates between existence and nonexistence, it is God who attaches any two moments together, not any sort of cosmic causal necessity. This conceptualization is another indication that Ibn ʿArabī attributes all causal power to God.

If God has all causal efficacy, why does Ibn ʿArabī employ the term "secondary causality" (*asbāb*)? What need is there for secondary causality in his cosmology? Ibn ʿArabī states that "God did not establish the secondary causes aimlessly."[26] Despite his rejection of efficacy in secondary causality, Ibn ʿArabī attributes important functions to secondary causality. From a pietistic and spiritual perspective, he explains that the veil of secondary causality preserves the proper *adab* (courtesy, refinement, morals) of the God–servant relationship. The courtesy requires that one not "strip the veils" for those who do not deserve or are not ready for the intimacy.[27] Even if there is no causal power besides God, natural phenomena are created in a consistent fashion beneath the "veil" of secondary causality. God is the engenderer of the (secondary) causes (*mukawwin al-asbāb*).[28] "God established causes and made them like

[25] Ibn ʿArabī, *Futūḥāt* (1911), III. 352. Emphasis mine. Translation mine.
[26] Ibn ʿArabī, *Futūḥāt* (1972–1991), II. 208.16, trans. in Chittick, *Sufi Path*, 44.
[27] Ibn ʿArabi, *Fuṣūṣ*, 185; cf. Izutsu, *Sufism and Taoism*, 256–257.
[28] Ibn ʿArabī, *Futūḥāt* (1972–1991), II. 414.1; cf. Chittick, *Sufi Path*, 45.

veils (*hujūb*). Hence, the causes lead everyone who knows that they are veils back to Him. But they prevent everyone who takes them as lords from reaching the real Lord, i.e. God."[29] The analogy of the veil is important here. Ibn ʿArabī uses the term to refer to something that simultaneously reveals and conceals. Secondary causality conceals, in that God creates behind this veil. It also reveals, in that for those who are willing to explore beyond the veil, secondary causality becomes transparent: "It is He who discloses Himself in the forms of the secondary causes which are a veil, over Him."[30]

From an epistemological perspective, the idea of secondary causality helps one grasp the regularity of the world-process. It can even be argued that causality exists for Ibn ʿArabī as a "regulative idea" that explains the regularity and predictability of natural phenomena. According to Ibn ʿArabī's processual and relational metaphysics, an entity is the sum of its relationships to God, a bundle of the divine acts, a society of divine theophanies. If so, what differentiates an entity from others must be the intensity and modalities of these acts, relations, or theophanies. The concept of causality in this context describes the regularity and predictability of the related societies of the divine acts emanating from God. In other words, it is the rational interpretation of the incessant and ever-changing flow of the manifestations of the divine qualities. Causality is the way we organize this process of unceasing re-creation of the world. God's self-disclosure occurs in a predictable and consistent fashion that is reflected in the human mind in the form of causal relationships. The "cause" is not the necessary precedent but merely the practical *explanans* and the effect is the *explanandum*.

Entities are part of the world-process. Each entity, as an individualized collectivity of the divine theophanies, is "causally" consequential for all other collectivities of theophanies that precede it in time. It will also influence, causally so to speak, the occasions that follow it in time. Although there is no necessary relationship between cause and effect in this schema, a nexus of the divine acts can still be considered to be an

[29] *Futūḥāt* (1972–1991), III. 416.19; cf. Chittick, *Sufi Path*, 45. This idea can be located in the later Sufi tradition. See for example: "these secondary causes are veils upon the eyes, for not ever eye is worthy of seeing His craftsmanship. One must have eyes which cuts thorough secondary causes and tear aside the veils … Oh father secondary causes and means are naught / But a phantom materialized upon the highway." Rūmī, Jalāl al-Dīn, *The Mathnawī of Rūmī*, ed. and trans. R. A. Nicholson, 8 vols (London: Luzac, 1925–1940), IV, 1051–1055.

[30] *Futūḥāt* (1972–1991), II. 469.2; cf. Chittick, *Sufi Path*, 46.

occasion for the following moment in history. In the case of secondary causality, "the created causes are temporally prior to their effects. It is only in this sense they are considered as causes. In reality, they are not causes,"[31] for "the Real does not create things by means of causes, but only together with causes."[32] Here, Ibn ʿArabī comes quite close to Ashʿarite occasionalism, as will be discussed in the last section of this chapter.

It must also be mentioned that the idea that there is no repetition in manifestation (*lā takrār fi-l-tajallī*) adds a further dimension. There is always a difference between any two moments of the world-process. Despite the illusion of repetition, novel elements are always incorporated. What leads to the difference, according to Ibn ʿArabī's relational ontology, is the manifestation of novel theophanies and the disclosure of previously unactualized aspects of the "hidden treasure." Thus, effect becomes a more intense or diminished "ontic event" than a cause that is temporally antecedent.[33] It displays the divine acts, the divine names, and the divine attributes in a more or less comprehensive manner. Since the difference between the two moments cannot be explained other than as the addition of novel divine acts and theophanies, it would be proper to argue that, according to Ibn ʿArabī, effects can never be reduced to causes.[34] That is to say, there is an ever-present disproportionality of cause and effect although they are, from a spatio-temporal point of view, attached to each other. There is always a vertical discontinuity – a difference between cause and effect – alongside the horizontal continuity of the world-process.

To conclude, there are several important aspects of Ibn 'Arabī's conception of causality. He attributes all causal power to God. He thinks

31 Ibn ʿArabī, *Futūḥāt* (1911), IV. 66. Translation mine.

32 Ibid., VI. 71. Translation mine.

33 The concept of isthmus (*barzakh*) is relevant here. This concept is frequently used to refer to the intermediacy of entities between God and nothingness. For Ibn ʿArabī, "a *barzakh* is something that separates (*fāṣil*) two other things while never going to one side, as for example the line that separates shadow from sunlight." *Futūḥāt*, V.I 304.16. For a detailed study of this concept, see Salman H. Bashier, *Ibn Al-ʿArabi's Barzakh: The Concept of the Limit and the Relationship between God and the World* (Albany: State University of New York Press, 2004). Bashier explores the use of the concept of *barzakh* in the construction of God and cosmos relationship.

34 As will be discussed in Chapter 10, Said Nursi similarly writes "*causes are only an apparent veil.* So, by mentioning the aims and results, such verses show that although *causes are superficially joined and adjacent to their effects, in reality there is a great distance between them.*" *Sözler (The Words)*, trans. Sukran Vahide (Istanbul: Sözler Nesriyat, 1992), 435.

causality is a "veil" preserving the proper courtesy between God and man. He treats causality as a "regulative idea" that helps one understand and act in accordance with the apparent (but illusory) predictability and consistency of the divine self-disclosures. He also suggests that effects can never be reduced to causes.

In Ibn 'Arabī's cosmology, all causal efficacy belongs to God, but causal relations remain intact. When a glass falls and breaks, the whole happening is understood as a process of continuous divine theophanies, but one would still act to catch the glass.

6.2 FREEDOM

Several questions arise here. How is it possible to establish freedom and, thus, moral responsibility if all that exist are God and God's acts? If both cause and effect are societies of theophanies, does this not reduce human agency to mere illusion and position God as a completely arbitrary ruler?[35] Although this robust relational and processual metaphysics appears to take all agency from the created order, Ibn ʿArabī's thought in fact offers interesting possibilities to reestablish it in the following ways.

6.2.1 *Freedom, Participation, and "Theophanic Individuality"*

First, Ibn ʿArabī's relational and processual metaphysics leads to what I call a *participatory* account of causal efficacy and freedom: namely, that it is possible to envisage the coalescence of individuals out of the metaphysical flux of the continuous and ever-changing manifestations of the divine qualities. Entities, in this regard, are *individuations* of the collectivities of the divine acts or theophanies. The multiplicity and modalities of these acts or theophanies give entities their distinct identities. The societies of divine theophanies are differentiated as concrete individuals. One can even say that entities are "theophanic individualities."

A *theophanic individuality* is, on the one hand, the totality of its relations to God and, on the other hand, an agent participating in the divine qualities, such as life, power, will, and knowledge. By reducing an

[35] On the implications of causality for morality, see Donald Davidson, "Causal Relations," in *Essays on Actions and Events* (Oxford: Clarendon Press, 1980), 150; Richard Sorabji, *Necessity, Cause and Blame: Perspectives on Aristotle's Theory* (London: Duckworth, 1980), 37.

entity to the totality of its relations to God, Ibn ʿArabī appears to negate causal efficacy in the created order. However, paradoxically, the idea of relationality reaffirms causal efficacy in beings. Relationality necessitates participation. If entities are the totalities of their relations to God, then there is no real separation between God and the cosmos. Since God is essentially existence (*wujūd*), everything other than God exists by participating in God's existence.

If entities are manifestations of the divine names, then they are participants in the divine qualities. Entities' participation in the divine power gives them power; participation in the divine knowledge gives them knowledge; participation in the divine freedom gives them freedom. "We hear through Him, we see through Him, we stand through Him, we sit through Him, we desire through him, and we judge through Him."[36] Therefore, Ibn ʿArabī's metaphysics affirms existence of other individualities participating in God's "individuality."

To use one of Ibn ʿArabī's favorite analogies, this process can be likened to a luminous object's reflection (*mithāl*) in a mirror. He writes that "the creation of the world resembles the formation of an image in the mirror."[37] This image "is neither you nor other than you. The relationship between the object and its image is the same as the relationship between God and the world."[38] Now, there is a difference between a luminous object's mirror image, such as the sun, and a non-luminous object's mirror image, such as a rock. When a rock is placed before a mirror, its shape and colors are reflected in the mirror. But, in the case of the sun, the mirror does not only reflect its shape and colors, but also its light and heat. The mirror reflecting the sun participates in the properties of the sun to the extent allowed by its limited capacity.

Such a participatory view of causality is possible only in a non-dualistic ontological framework, such as that of Ibn ʿArabī. There is no real separation between God and cosmos. God is real existence, and entities' existence is derived from it. Moreover, God is essentially existence, as is implied by the doctrine of the unity of existence (*waḥdat al-wujūd*), usually viewed as characteristic of Ibn ʿArabī's ontology. If God is existence itself, then entities can only exist by participating in God's existence. It is difficult to imagine a similar account in a dualistic framework. If there is a real separation between God's will and human will, as in Ashʿarite occasionalism or Muʿtazilite accounts of causality, then one cannot

[36] Ibn ʿArabī, *Futūḥāt* (1911), VII. 307. Translation mine.
[37] Ibid., VIII. 38. Translation mine. [38] Ibid., VII. 39. Translation mine.

establish a participatory account of causality. In a passage critiquing Ash'arite and Mu'tazilite accounts of will (*irāda*), Ibn 'Arabī asserts:

All existence is a veil of the Real. He is active behind this veil without people noticing it. Ash'arites, who attribute the creation of acts to God, are aware of this. But, due to the veil of *kasb* (acquisition), they cannot see. Similarly, God blinded those who attribute the creation of acts to man (i.e. the Mu'tazilites). They all have a veil before their eyes.[39]

In accordance with his ontology, Ibn 'Arabī suggests a third option.

There is a partnership between God and the servant in acts. There is no rational proof against this. There is also no textual proof attributing acts exclusively to God or the servant. We have three sources of knowledge: unveiling (*kashf*), law, and reason (*'aql*). And none of these sources attribute an act to only God or to only the servant.[40]

If the idea of the individuation of divine theophanies as an entity is intelligible, then one can say an entity is both the sum of its relations to God and a causally efficacious agent participating in God's qualities. This leads Ibn 'Arabī to construct causal relations both vertically and horizontally. They are vertical because the divine names and relations are the causes of beings; they are horizontal because entities, due to their participation in the divine qualities denoted by the divine names, become theophanic individualities and have relations with other entities. Vertical relations, however, are essential and make horizontal relations possible. As a theophanic individuality, what defines an entity is essentially its relations to God and to other theophanic individualities in the world.

Furthermore, according to Ibn 'Arabī's gradational schema, we *participate* in the divinity to different degrees. Entities, as societies of theophanies, are at once manifestations of and participants in the attributes of the infinite God. These attributes include the divine freedom. Thus, entities are free to the extent that they participate in the divine freedom. Differences remain between the divine freedom and entities' freedom. God has absolute freedom due to Himself. The contingent beings have relative freedom due to God. It is in this context that Ibn 'Arabī frequently cites the Qur'anic verse, "you did not throw when you threw (*wa mā ramayta idh ramayta*)" (8:17). For him, this verse simultaneously affirms and negates causal efficacy – although "senses and eye saw that Muhammad threw."[41] The Qur'an simultaneously "attributes

[39] Ibid., IV. 62. Translation mine. [40] Ibid., V. 244. Translation mine.
[41] Ibid., VI. 296. Translation mine.

acts to us and to God."[42] Perhaps one of the best expressions of this view of freedom can be found in Rūmī:

God's free will has given existence to our free will: His free will is like a rider beneath the dust. his free will creates our free will, His commands are founded upon a free will within us.[43]

Thus, with these specifications, it is possible to identify freedom in entities in accordance with Ibn ʿArabī's metaphysics. At the root of this freedom is the intimate relationality between entities and God and, as a consequence, participation of entities in God.

6.2.2 *Freedom and Archetypes*

Ibn ʿArabī's concept of the fixed archetypes offers another perspective from which to approach the question of freedom. The fixed archetypes are usually understood to be the unchanging objects of the divine knowledge. Entities exist in God's knowledge before their existentiation in the cosmos. God gives these nonexisting but possible objects His existence. These possibilities, for their existentiation and for their subsistence at every moment, are totally dependent on the effusion of God's existence onto them. Therefore, as described above, God remains the only causal power.

However, the idea of the fixed archetypes has two important implications for our discussion on causality and freedom. First, Ibn ʿArabī gives us no "cause" for the emergence of these possibilities, as they are, in the divine knowledge. God does not cause them but only knows them. It is therefore possible to argue that these possibilities are *uncaused* objects of God's knowledge. They are not only fixed and unchanging but also uncaused.

[42] Ibid., VI. 213. Translation mine.

[43] Rūmī, *Mathnawī*, V. 3087–3088. Emphasis mine. Rumi and Ibn ʿArabī have similar views on causality. Rūmī expresses his conception of causality by using rich imagery of wind and dust, sea and foam, etc. "Since you have seen the dust of the shape, see the Wind! Since you have seen the foam, see the ocean of the Creative Power!" *Mathnawī*, IV. 1459–1460. "We and our existences are nonexistences. Thou art Absolute existence showing Thyself as perishable things / We are all lions, but lions on a banner: We keep on leaping because of the wind," *Mathnawī*, I. 602–603. And, "He has hidden the Sea and made the foam visible. he has concealed the wind and shown you the dust." *Mathnawī*, V. 1027. Also see "the world is dust, and within the dust the sweeper and broom hidden," Rūmī, *Dīwān Shams-i Tabrīzī*, ed. B. Furuzanfar, 10 vols (Tehran: University of Tehran Press, 1957–1967), n. 13164. Or, "He has stirred up a world like dust; hidden in the dust, He is like a wind," *Dīwān*, n. 28600.

There is no cause for an entity being what kind of entity it is in God's knowledge, although God is the cause of a possible being coming into existence as more than a mere possibility. Ibn ʿArabī writes:

Any possible thing that happens in existence happens according to the divine knowledge. In this sense, if the divine knowledge decrees that something will happen, it happens necessarily. God knows things as they are in themselves. Because the knowledge follows the known (*al-ʿilmu yatbaʿu al-maʿlūm*), the creation of a possible being follows knowledge of that being. *The known precedes the knowledge.* The divine knowledge knows possible beings as they are in their nonexistent condition, in a state of fixity. Therefore, *what gives knowledge to God is the known itself*. In this case God can speak to one in the following way: "this is from you, not from me. I would not know you as you are, if you were not what you are."[44]

In other words, God's power follows God's will, God's will follows God's knowledge, and God's knowledge follows the "uncaused" objects of knowledge. This is why Ibn ʿArabī frequently says that "the known precedes the knowledge." The criterion for knowledge is that there is something to be known. The priority of the known to knowledge allows Ibn ʿArabī to assert God's omniscience without implying strict determinism. If being an "uncaused cause" is the definition of freedom, then one can identify a genuine freedom while at the same time preserving God's status as the sole causal power.

Second, the idea of fixed archetypes also implies that every causal relation occurs in accordance with these possibilities in the divine knowledge and not haphazardly. God is not an arbitrary king in this case. The divine knowledge and creation follow the fixed archetypes as they are God's knowledge. And, again, there is no cause for a fixed archetype to be what it is in God's knowledge.

A question might arise here. If all that exists is an ever-changing process, then how could "fixed archetypes" exist? How can there be fixity? It can be argued that the idea of "fixed archetypes" does not impose a fixity on the manifested order. The archetypes are fixed, for in God's infinite knowledge everything should exist in an eternally unchanging form. But this fixity in God's knowledge does not imply a fixity in the world. What is fixed from the perspective of God's knowledge is experienced as an ever-changing and incessant process in the world. The infinity of God's knowledge implies, on the one hand, that God's knowledge encompasses everything eternally and that things are, in a way, fixed in

[44] Ibn ʿArabī, *Futūḥāt* (1911), VII. 41. Emphasis mine. Translation mine.

the divine knowledge; but on the other hand, it implies that there is an infinity of fixed archetypes or possibilities. If there is an infinite number of possibilities then, as explained in the previous pages, there has to be a constant and never repeating existentiation of these possibilities. Hence, "there is no repetition in manifestation." In other words, the concept of infinity implies simultaneously both fixity in God's knowledge and an ever-changing process in creation.

6.3 CONCLUSION

Ibn ʿArabī's perception of causal relations diverges from the most basic assumptions of the Aristotelian theory of causality, which holds that bodies' actions directly flow from bodies' natures, their formal and material constitution. From the perspective of Ibn ʿArabī's metaphysical cosmology, the idea of nature is at best a misinterpretation of the predictability of the world-process. If entities are bundles of accidents, and if there is no substance in which the accidents can inhere, then the principles of regularity must be sought not in the natures of bodies but in God. This is evident in Ibn ʿArabī's treatment of fixed archetypes and preparedness (*istiʿdād*), which provides a top-down explanation for the regularity of so-called causal relations. The fixed archetypes exist in God's all-encompassing knowledge in unchanging form. The manifestation of the divine qualities occurs *not* haphazardly but according to how these archetypes exist in the divine knowledge. The world-process is organized according to these primordial principles. The concept of *istiʿdād* also implies that God existentiates things in accordance with their preparedness. Both concepts – fixed archetypes and preparedness – replace the Aristotelian notion of natures. Therefore, while in Aristotelian accounts of causality natures are the guarantors of the predictability of natural processes, in Ibn ʿArabī's metaphysics the same function is attributed to the fixed archetypes and *istiʿdād*s.

There are also several important distinctions between Ibn ʿArabī's and Ibn Sīnā's accounts of causality. First, as Chittick observes, Ibn ʿArabī abstains from describing God as the first cause if it implies the inclusion of God in the causal chain. This undermines the divine infinity and God is beyond all delimitations.[45] Second, there is also the problem of the

[45] See for example, Ibn ʿArabī, *Futūḥāt* (1972–1991), I. 90.12, II. 57.26, II. 64.8, IV. 54.8; cf. Chittick, *Self Disclosure*, 17–20.

procession of the many from the One. Ibn Sīnā and Fārābī famously assert that "from the One only one proceeds" (*lā yaṣduru min al-wāḥidi illa shay'un wāḥid*). God is absolutely one and, therefore, the procession of multiplicity from the One has to be explained after a series of emanations. In the emanationist schema, God necessarily remains the distant first cause. However, for Ibn ʿArabī, as he repeatedly states, God is both one/many and many/one. He writes:

The Philosophers say, "from the One only one can proceed" (*lā yūjadu an al-wāḥidi illā wāḥid*). The world is a domain of multiplicity; hence it can proceed only from the multiple. The multiplicity is the divine names. Therefore, *God's unity is the unity of multiplicity*. This unity is demanded by the world. The Philosophers, in saying "from the One only one can proceed," saw that this multiplicity proceeds from the unity in multiplicity. But previously they argued one proceeds from the One. This contradiction forced them to consider the different aspects of the One. Because of the (multiplicity) of these aspects and faces (*wujūh*), multiplicity can proceed from the One. The relationship between the One and different aspects of the One is the same as the relationship of God and the divine names. Hence, multiplicity proceeds from God. For multiplicity, there can be a unity of multiplicity. Similarly, for unity, there can be multiplicity of unity. *God is one/many and many/one*. This is the clearest expression one can offer on this topic.[46]

In this and similar passages, Ibn ʿArabī argues against the gradational emanationist explanation of the procession of multiplicity from the One. God's infinity includes infinite possibilities, as explained above. To say God is to say infinity, and hence also multiplicity. So, the multiplicity does not have to be explained as a procession from the One in a gradual emanationist schema. The multiplicity can proceed from the One/Many or the Many/One without positing a distance between God and the world. Hence, there is no need to denote God as the distant first cause.[47] God gives existence directly, not through a causal chain. This or that thing exists due to God's unmediated causal effect.

As it pertains to the Ashʿarite theory of causation, one can identify certain similarities between the treatments of the question of causality by the Ashʿarites and by Ibn ʿArabī. First, Ibn ʿArabī agrees that the world is re-created anew at each moment. Second, both sides attribute all causal efficacy to God for the same pietistic reason, namely, to establish the

[46] Ibn ʿArabī, *Futūḥāt* (1911), VII. 62. Translation mine.

[47] Recall that this is Ghazālī's and Ibn Rushd's criticism of Ibn Sīnā. Ibn Rushd writes, for example, "one may suppose *a plurality within the First Cause*, and there is no need to assume a second cause and a first effect." *Tahāfut al-Tahāfut*, 147–148.

absolute dependency of everything on God. Third, they also assert that in causal relationships what is regarded as cause is only an occasion for the existence of an effect.[48] Like Ashʿarites, Ibn ʿArabī holds that causes are "occasions for the creation of effects."[49] Causes are "temporally prior" to effects, and only in this sense can they be considered causes.[50]

In my view, despite these similarities, Ibn ʿArabī's account cannot be categorized as a form of occasionalism for the following reasons.

First, Ashʿarite (and Muʿtazilite) treatments of the topic start from the assumption that there is a real separation between human will and the divine will, as suggested by the Ashʿarite theory of acquisition. According to this and similar theories, human will is regarded as a separate entity from God's will. According to Ibn ʿArabī's account, both Ashʿarites and Muʿtazilites misconstrue the relationship of human will and the divine will. Ashʿarites, "due to the veil of *kasb* (the theory of acquisition), cannot see" the real nature of this relationship. God also "blinded those who attribute the creation of acts to man (the Muʿtazilites)."[51] Both Ashʿarites and Muʿtazilites start from the assumption that there is a real separation between the divine will and human will. For Ibn 'Arabī, however, there is but a single knowledge, will, and power in existence. These qualities belong to God. Instances of knowledge, will, and power in our domain are manifestations of these qualities. Human knowledge, will, and power are not, as the Ashʿarites and the Muʿtazilites supposed, distinct from God's knowledge, will, and power. This allows Ibn ʿArabī to address the question of freedom from another perspective. If God alone is essentially existence, other beings can only exist by participating in God's existence. Entities manifest the divine qualities because of their participation in God's existence. By participating in God's existence, they experience freedom. Human freedom is a manifestation of God's freedom. Hence, the same act can be simultaneously attributed to God and to the human agent.

Second, Ibn ʿArabī's treatment of fixed archetypes and preparedness leads to the conclusion that the permeation of *wujūd* does not occur

48 For a comparative study of Ibn ʿArabī and the Ashʿarites on causality, see Ozgur Koca, "Ibn ʿArabī, Ashʿarites and Causality," in *Occasionalism Revisited: New Essays from the Islamic and Western Philosophical Traditions* (Abu Dhabi: Kalam Research and Media, 2017), 41–60; and Ozgur Koca, "Causality as a 'Veil': the Ashʿarites, ibn ʿArabī (1165–1240), and Said Nursi (1877–1960)," *Islam and Christian–Muslim Relations*, 27.4 (June 2016): 455–470.

49 Ibn ʿArabī, *Futūḥāt* (1911), VI. 71. Translation mine.

50 Ibid., IX. 62. Translation mine.

51 Ibid., IV. 162. Translation mine.

arbitrarily. Recall that the idea of "preponderance without reason," for Ashʿarites, resolves the problem of how God creates the world without Himself changing. They also use this idea to explain the differentiation of homogenous atoms, and thus entities, from each other. This process of creation and differentiation of entities happens solely due to the divine preponderance without reason. For Ibn ʿArabī, however, the concepts of the fixed archetypes, essences, preparedness, and capacities suggest that God existentiates entities as they are in the divine knowledge. These fixed archetypes/essences existing as concomitants of the divine infinity are the principles according to which the God's *wujūd* becomes manifest in infinitely variegated particularizations. God does not create from nothing, but rather from these preexisting and uncaused essences. This is a fundamental point of divergence between Ashʿarites and Ibn ʿArabī. His followers, such as Qūnawī and Qayṣarī, agree with him – as will be discussed in Chapter 7.

7

Continuities and Developments in Sufi Metaphysics

The Cases of Qūnawī and Qayṣarī

This chapter focuses on later developments in Sufi metaphysics concerning the question of causality and freedom. It examines the writings of two influential followers of Ibn ʿArabī: Qūnawī and Qayṣarī. Qūnawī was Ibn ʿArabī's adopted son and is widely regarded as his most influential follower.[1] Qayṣarī provides one of the clearest expressions of the principles of the metaphysical framework offered by this school, and his commentaries on Ibn ʿArabī's works were widely used by later Muslim scholars. Both Qūnawī and Qayṣarī contributed to the process of rearticulating Ibn ʿArabī's metaphysics by using logical analysis and metaphysical concepts more freely and explicitly than Ibn ʿArabī himself. This philosophical and accessible articulation made these thinkers highly influential among later generations of Muslim mystics, philosophers, and theologians.

It will be argued that both Qūnawī and Qayṣarī agree with Ibn ʿArabī in their construction of causal efficacy and freedom of entities. The permeation of *wujūd* into essences is the ground of all causal activity. This permeation allows entities to participate in *wujūd* in accordance with their capacities, and participation in *wujūd* establishes entities' causal agency and freedom. Essences are uncreated. God knows these essences without determining what they are. The uncreatedness of essences establishes their realities as uncaused causes of themselves. From the

[1] W. Chittick, "al-Kunawi," in *Encyclopedia of Islam*, ed. P. Bearman, T. Bianquis, C. Bosworth, E. van Donzel, and W. Heinrichs (Leiden: Brill, 2007). Although Qūnawī is relatively unfamiliar in Western scholarship, he influenced many scholars and mystics in modern-day Turkey, North Africa, Iran, India, China, and the Balkans.

perspective of essences, entities remain free. From the perspective of *wujūd*, entities depend absolutely on the permeation of *wujūd* to exist in the world.

What distinguishes both Qūnawī and Qayṣarī is their attempt to understand certain ideas attributed to the Philosophers and Ashʿarites in light of Ibn ʿArabī's articulation of the concepts of *wujūd* and *māhiyya*. Their writings include references both to the ideas of the Philosophers, such as secondary causality and emanationism, and to the ideas of Ashʿarites, such continuous creation, accidents, and "preponderance without reason" (*tarjīh bi-lā murajjih*). This, it will be argued, is not simply a contradiction. In fact, they selectively appropriate these ideas defended by different schools by using the philosophical possibilities suggested by the concepts of *wujūd* and *māhiyya*. The result is a critical reinterpretation of emanationist and occasionalist elements within the larger framework of their metaphysics.

7.1 THE CASE OF QŪNAWĪ

As does Ibn ʿArabī, Qūnawī holds that entities are prefigured in the divine knowledge before their existentiation in the world. Qūnawī calls entities fixed archetypes (*al-aʿyān thābita*), essences (*māhiyya*), knowns (*al-maʿl-ūmāt*), and fixed things (*al-shay al-thābit*).[2] The Real knows essences through self-knowledge "in its own reality (*nafs*)."[3] The Real "knows itself and therefore knows all the entities."[4] Furthermore, God knows essences in their totality both "as universals (*kull*) and particulars (*juzʾ*)."[5]

How and why does God existentiate these "knowns" or "fixed archetypes" or "essences"? God existentiates them by bestowing the gift of existence. This is due to God's compassion and goodness. For God is pure existence, and pure existence is pure goodness and compassion (*al-raḥma nafs al-wujūd*)[6]

Wujūd is given to all essences and, thus, it is the most general category. It is common between the highest and the lowest beings.[7] Due to their

[2] Qūnawī, *Miftāḥ Ghayb al-Jamʿi wa-l-Wujūd fi-l-Kashf al-Shuhūd*, Süleymaniye Yazma Eser Kütüphanesi (Manuscript), Ayasofya, No. 1930, 13b. Also see "the realities of the contingent beings are like hidden letters in the ink or in the speaking mind." *Miftāḥ*, 88b.

[3] Ibid., 89b.

[4] Ibid., 15a. Recall that this is also how Ibn Sīnā and Ibn Rushd solve the problem of the divine knowledge for the Aristotelian tradition, where God is depicted as thought thinking Himself.

[5] Ibid., 16b. [6] Ibid., 31a. [7] Ibid., 13b.

absolute dependence on the divine existentiating act, "nothing can exist due to itself, or due something other than God."[8] Existence is received by entities that "accept to be loci of the light of existence (*nūr al-wujūd*)."[9] Therefore, what existentiates the fixed archetypes or essences known by the divine knowledge is the procession of the divine existence upon essences as an act of pure goodness.

This is to say that existence occurs to essences. God is pure and absolute existence beyond definition. Everything else is essence waiting to be existentiated by receiving a share from the pure divine existence. Hence, entities have both essence and existence. Qūnawī writes of how "the Real's (*al-Ḥaqq*) existence (*wujūd*) is one with (*ʿayn*) Itself (*dhāt*). However, for any other entity, existence is an additional quality (*zāid*)."[10]

The gift of existence is given to essences in accordance with their capacities. Qūnawī sometimes calls this process "pervasion of existence" (*sarayān al-wujūd*) and "expansion of existence" (*inbisāṭ al-wujūd*).[11] The comprehensive existence (*wujūd al-ʿām*) "expands upon the contingent entities realities (essences)."[12] The divine existence pervades into beings without identification (*ḥulūl* or *ittiḥād*).[13] Hence, he asserts that "He, with the light of his pure essence (*bi-nūri al-dhāt al-muqaddas*) permeates (*siraya*) the entities without division (*inqisām*) or penetration (*ḥulūl*)."[14]

Qūnawī also shares Ibn ʿArabī's conviction about the relationship of *wujūd* and the divine attributes. The divine attributes cannot be considered separate from the divine Self. All the names and attributes are concealed in the undifferentiated unity of *wujūd*. The permeation of *wujūd* to essences, however, entails that *wujūd* would have specific relations with each individual essence. These relations are also called the divine names and attributes. In fact, the divine names are theological categories describing the multiplicity of relations between *wujūd* and essences. Thus, the permeation of *wujūd* not only existentiates essences but also manifests the divine qualities concealed in *wujūd*. The names and attributes are not distinct accidents added to *wujūd*. To say *wujūd* is to say all the attributes. Hence Qūnawī states that "these attributes are necessitated by the One without taking away its oneness."[15] This is also

[8] Ibid., 16a. [9] Ibid., 16b. [10] Ibid., 13a.
[11] See for example, ibid., 32b; ibid., 26b. [12] Ibid., 26b. [13] Ibid., 32b
[14] Ibid., 17b. This delimitation, for Qūnawī, does not undermine the divine purity (*quds*) and sovereignty (*ʿizza*), ibid., 18a.
[15] Qūnawī, *Iʿjāz al-Bayān fi Taʾwīl Umm-Qurʾan*, Turkish trans. Ekrem Demirli (Istanbul: İz Yayıncılık-İslam Klasikleri Dizisi, 2009), 157.

why participation in *wujūd* is considered participation in the divine qualities such as power, knowledge, and will. "All the attributes and powers of the servant originate in the names of the Real."[16]

Together with the permeation of *wujūd* into *māhiyyas*, the concealment of the divine attributes in *wujūd* brings us to the general conviction of participatory accounts. The basis of causal efficacy of entities is their participation in existence. At every moment, existence expands and pervades essences. Entities are free due to their participation in *wujūd*, for participation in *wujūd* is to participate in the divine attributes concealed in *wujūd*, including knowledge, will, and power. This participation occurs in accordance with the capacities of essences. To participate in *wujūd* is to participate in the divine freedom.

7.1.1 *The Uncreatedness of Essences and Freedom*

The question of freedom can also be approached from the perspective of essences. As discussed above, Qūnawī describes essences as objects of the divine knowledge. The divine self-knowledge implies that God knows Himself and, through this knowledge, also knows everything else with one undifferentiated knowledge. God existentiates entities in accordance with their fixed archetypes in the divine knowledge. Thus, "the reality of existing beings is their entification (*ta'ayyun*) in the divine knowledge."[17] In a letter he wrote to Naṣīr al-Dīn Ṭūsī, Qūnawī writes, "the forms of beings exist in the Creator, for God knows them. And it is this knowledge that is the reason for their existentiation."[18]

The idea that essences have always existed in the divine knowledge implies for Qūnawī that they are not created (*ḥawādith*) things.[19] Rather, they are uncreated (*ghayr maj'ūl*). Qūnawī also discusses this question in one of his letters to Ṭūsī. The existence of essences in the divine knowledge does not have a beginning, since if they had a beginning in the divine knowledge, it would imply that the divine knowledge has limitations. This contradicts the infinity and eternity of the divine knowledge. Hence,

> Real witnessing and tasting affirms that essences are uncreated. They have a sort of existence. This existence refers to the existence of essences in the knowledge of

[16] Qūnawī, *I'jāz al-Bayān*, 73. [17] Qūnawī, *Miftāḥ*, 13a–b.
[18] Qūnawī, *al-Murasalāt*, Turkish tran. Ekrem Demirli (Istanbul: Kapı Yayınları, 2014), 190.
[19] Qūnawī, *Miftāḥ*, 13b.

> the Real without beginning and end, with their entifications and in an undifferentiated way.[20]
>
> The Real support for these people is due to His knowledge of their uncreated (*ghayr maj'ūl*) capacities. It is with this capacity that they accept *wujūd* from the Real.[21]

The entities' prefiguration in the divine knowledge implies that they have a sort of reality before their existentiation in the world. At this point Qūnawī concludes that, if essences are uncreated, if they have an eternal reality in the divine knowledge, then they must be causes of themselves. Again, "to smell the fragrance of *wujūd*," they depend absolutely on the divine bestowal of *wujūd*. However, the capacity with which they "accept *wujūd*" remains uncreated and uncaused. Therefore, in terms of its essence, an entity is its own cause although, in terms of its existence, it is caused by God. Thus, "the cause of the properties of essences cannot be other than themselves. For these essences, as we discussed, are not created."[22]

Essences are, then, uncaused causes of themselves. If this is true then they are not caused by God to be what they are in the divine knowledge. The divine knowledge only knows them as they are and the permeation of existence existentiates them as they are. Thus, in terms of their existentiation in the world, entities absolutely depend on *wujūd*, and without it they cannot smell the fragrance of *wujūd*. But, in terms of their essences in the divine knowledge, entities are uncreated and uncaused, and hence free.

7.1.2 *Qūnawī, the Philosophers, and the Ash'arites*

Qūnawī presents a participatory account of causality and freedom. In this framework, he critically appropriates certain ideas traditionally attributed to the Philosophers and Ash'arites. I now discuss how he critically integrates these elements into his own system by using the philosophical possibilities presented by the concepts of *wujūd* and *māhiyya*.

Secondary Causality and Emanationism

I have already discussed how Qūnawī constructs causal agency of entities and creaturely freedom on the basis of *wujūd* and *māhiyya*. Qūnawī further argues that the construction of causal agency of entities through their participation in *wujūd* entails that every entity relates to God in

[20] Qūnawī, *Murasalāt*, 68. [21] Ibid., 24. Also see 22. [22] Ibid., 69.

two respects. There is a direct relationship between God and the world, for every entity receives *wujūd* from God without intermediation. There is also an indirect relationship, for the permeation of existence unto essences renders entities real and free causal agents. In other words, *wujūd* reaches entities *with intermediation* through other entities and *without intermediation* from God. In every case, however, all causal activity depends upon the permeation of *wujūd*.

True witnessing confirms that every entity has two types of relationship with the Real: First, through the chain of intermediaries and, second, by removing the intermediaries. For, there is no proof that the divine grace is limited to reach to entities through intermediaries. It is more convenient for the perfection and purity of the Real that it has two types of relationship with beings ... Since plurality is an intrinsic attribute of contingent beings, their relationship with the Real has to occur from two perspectives.[23]

God is not bound by direct or indirect forms of relations. God relates to every entity through veils and without veils. This view appears to affirm secondary causality. In this sense, Qūnawī holds that sometimes the act is attributed to the servant (*ʿabd*) and sometimes to God. What matters is to understand the perspective from which this attribution is made. One then knows "when and how the act relates to whom and whether this attribution is authentic (*ṣaḥīḥ*) or not."[24] This is how one can see both the Real (*al-Ḥaqq*) and the created (*al-khalq*).[25]

The recognition of the reception of *wujūd* with and without intermediation allows Qūnawī to appropriate certain aspects of the Philosophers' emanationism. If *wujūd* can also reach entities through intermediation, then there is no reason to deny the role of intermediating intellects and, thus, secondary causality. Intellects in this context would be defined as unique essences that are existentiated. As with other essences, they exist due to the permeation of *wujūd*. This permeation and participation would bestow upon them causal efficacy that in turn can affect other entities.

Every being's connection with the Real occurs in two respects. One of them is through gradation and intermediation. The first one of these intermediaries is the First Intellect. The other way of connection (without intermediation) is established from the perspective the necessity of the Real.[26]

Qūnawī agrees with Fārābī and Ibn Sīnā on the fundamental idea of emanationism, that "from the One only one can proceed." Yet, there

[23] Ibid., 81. [24] Qūnawī, *Miftāḥ*, 115b. [25] Ibid., 117a.
[26] Qūnawī, *Murasalāt*, 197.

are two important differences to acknowledge here. First, Qūnawī does not think that emanation is the only way that *wujūd* reaches to lower levels. He also affirms that *wujūd* existentiates without intermediation. Second, it is not the intermediation of the intellects that is responsible for the emergence of multiplicity from the One. The intellects are simply essences waiting to be actualized, like all other essences. So, although it is true that "from the One only one can proceed," this one thing should be perceived as the comprehensive existence (*wujūd al-ʿām*) permeating into an infinite number of essences, including celestial intellects, with its infinite plasticity. Multiplicity emerges due to this relationship between *wujūd* and essences. Despite the fact that what proceeds from the Real is an undifferentiated unity, the unity is multiplied when this procession existentiates different entities with different essences. Thus, the one existence, due to the differentiation of the capacities, is multiplied as it manifests in the essences (*al-wujūd al-wāḥid ẓuhūri bi-sababi ihtilafi fi ḥaqāiqi al-qawābil mukhtalifan*).[27] As he puts it:

> According to us, this one thing proceeding from the One, is the general manifestation (*tajallī*) of existence (*wujūd*) that radiates upon the realities of those entities which do not (yet) exist but about the divine knowledge has a verdict of existentiation.[28]
>
> This one thing proceeding from the one Real is the comprehensive existence. In this case the First Intellect and other intellects participate in it (comprehensive intellect), and they relate to God without the intermediation of the sequence.[29]

Wujūd's infinity implies that it connects to each entity with and without intermediation. The comprehensive permeation of *wujūd* becomes the principle of the immediate and un-intermediated relation between God and the world. Secondary causality becomes the principle of the intermediated relation. It is through these modifications that Qūnawī is able to integrate certain emanationist elements into his metaphysics.

Qūnawī and Occasionalism

Qūnawī's construction of causal relations with and without intermediation allows him to appropriate certain ideas of the Philosophers' concerning secondary causality and emanationism. A similar interaction can be observed between Qūnawī and certain occasionalist ideas, such as continuous creation and preponderance (*tarjīh*). He critically reinterprets them in light of the concepts of *wujūd* and *māhiyya*.

[27] Qūnawī, *Miftāḥ*, 39b. [28] Ibid., 13b. [29] Qūnawī, *Murasalāt*, 80.

There are two important points of divergence between Qūnawī and the Ashʿarites. Recall that one of the basic propositions of Ashʿarite occasionalism is the idea that God preponderates the existence of the world over its nonexistence *without any reason*. It is also this preponderance that differentiates entities from each other. For Qūnawī, however, essences are the principle of differentiation. This also to say that God creates not from nothing but rather from uncaused and uncreated essences existing in the divine knowledge. This is because Qūnawī holds that "the absolute nothingness does not turn into existence, for this implies impossibility."[30] Essences, as the principles of the divine existentiation, suggest that the divine creation does not happen solely on basis of the preponderance of the divine will.[31]

The other important point of divergence can be formulated as follows. Ashʿarite occasionalism, by removing causal efficacy from secondary causality, envisages only a vertical relation between God and the world. As discussed above, however, Qūnawī establishes two types of relations between God and the world. *Wujūd* permeates into entities, keeping them in existence, without intermediation. It also reaches them with intermediation. Although it is true that all causal activity and freedom of entities ultimately traced back to their participation in *wujūd*, it is this very participation that also makes them real and free agents. Thus, this acceptance of secondary causality and intermediating intellects adds a stronger horizontal dimension to Qūnawī's system, a dimension that does not exist in Ashʿarite occasionalism.

There are also points of agreement between Qūnawī and the Ashʿarites. Again, Qūnawī accepts that there is a type of relationship between God and cosmos *without* intermediation. The general existence (*wujūd al-ʿām*) is given to all entities continuously, without the intermediation of secondary causality. As such, the Ashʿarite emphasis on vertical causality and divine creation of cause and effect has a place in Qūnawī's system. This allows Qūnawī to integrate certain Ashʿarite ideas, such as the continuous re-creation of the world anew at each moment. For example,

> *Wujūd* is not essential for things other than the Real. *Wujūd* is acquired due to the manifestation of the Real. This is why the world needs the bestowal of *wujūd* for its *continuation*. This help *continues without cessation and discontinuity. If it stops, the world would be annihilated.* For nonexistence is substantial and

[30] Ibid., 221

[31] Again, "what fashions manifestation is the entity manifested." Qūnawī, *Iʿjāz al-Bayān*, 64.

intrinsic in contingent beings. Existence, however, is accidental [in contingent beings] and comes to them only from their Creator.[32]

It is important to note here that Qūnawī does not establish continuous creation of the world on the distinction between substances and accidents, as is the case for Ashʿarite atomism. As examined in Chapter 6, concerning Ibn ʿArabī, and as will be seen more clearly in Qayṣarī's writings, the school of *wujūdiyya* sees both substances and accidents as different manifestations of *wujūd*. The reason for the continuous creation of the world is that both substances and accidents need the continuous permeation of *wujūd* at each moment. The expansion of existence onto an infinite number of essences also creates ever-changing variations. This is why "there is no repetition in manifestation."[33] As such, the school of *wujūdiyya* detaches the idea of continuous re-creation of the world from Ashʿarite atomism.

7.2 THE CASE OF QAYṢARĪ

Qayṣarī's writings offer one of the clearest and most succinct explanations of the basic tenets of the school of *wujūdiyya*. He introduces a participatory theory of causality. Therein, causal efficacy and freedom of entities are established by elaborating of the concepts of existence and essence. Quite distinctively, Qayṣarī reevaluates the ideas of substance (*jawhar*), accidents (*aʿrāḍ*), preponderance (*tarjīh*), and continuous creation in light of the concepts of existence and essence. He also appropriates some of the distinctive features of the Philosophers' cosmology, such as emanation, hyle (*hayūlā*), and nature (*tabiʿa*). Claims of both the Ashʿarites and the Philosophers are assimilated into the larger context of the metaphysics of *wujūd-māhiyya*. Qayṣarī's metaphysics can be seen as a continuation and expansion of those of Ibn ʿArabī and Qūnawī.

7.2.1 *Wujūd* and Causality

For Qayṣarī, *wujūd* is the most evident and comprehensive reality. Yet it is precisely this evident and comprehensive character that also makes *wujūd* the most concealed reality. It cannot be understood in terms of other concepts that, when applied to *wujūd*, necessarily limit the all-encompassing reality of *wujūd*.

[32] Qūnawī, *Iʿjāz al-Bayān*, 68. Emphasis mine. [33] Qūnawī, *Miftāḥ*, 5b–6a.

Hence, Qayṣarī writes that "*wujūd* is the most evident (*aẓhar*) of all things in terms of its being in existence and its realization . . . It, however, is the most concealed (*akhfā*) of all things in terms of its whatness and reality."[34] Thus, the best description that can be given to describe *wujūd* is to say that "*wujūd* is what it is."[35] *Wujūd* defies every attempt at its conceptualization and thus delimitation. For, "it is absolute and delimited, universal and particular, one and many."[36] It is absolute, universal, and one but even its absoluteness, universality, and oneness do not limit *wujūd*, thus it could be delimited, particular, and many.

There is no real distinction between God and God's *wujūd*. If God and *wujūd* were two things, then God would be composite, including *wujūd* as an accident. Moreover, God in this case would need *wujūd* to exist. Hence, it would not be God, who exists due to Himself. And *wujūd* would be an accident inhering in something that already exists, that already has *wujūd*. These are all logical impossibilities. Thus, Qayṣarī writes that "*wujūd* is the same as the divine Self (*wujūd ʿayni dhātihi*)."[37] In possible beings, a distinction between existence and essence can be made, but this is impossible.

God, *wujūd*, and the Necessary Existence are one and the same thing. "God is the Necessary Existence, for its existence is necessary."[38] All entities owe their existence to *wujūd*. They exist due to *wujūd*. *Wujūd*, however, explains its own existence. It exists due to itself. It does not receive its existence from another source. This is also the definition of the Necessary Existence. To be the Necessary Existence, "it should not have borrowed existence" from another being.[39]

Qayṣarī, together with the Philosophers and Ibn ʿArabī, believes that *wujūd* entails all attributes. When the concept of *wujūd* is truly understood, the meaning of all other attributes is also established. Thus, the relationship of the divine attributes and *wujūd* should not be imagined in dualistic terms. There *wujūd* and its attributes are not multiple things. "The (divine) attributes are the same as the Essence."[40] They are all hidden in *wujūd*.

> Every contradicting attribute, such as the Inward and the Outward, is concealed and vanishes in *wujūd*.[41]

[34] Qayṣarī, *Sharḥ Fuṣūṣ al-Ḥikam* (Tehran, 1963 [1383]), 14. 11–12. [35] Ibid., 13. 3–4.
[36] Ibid., 13. 5. [37] Ibid., 24. 21. [38] Ibid., 16. 22.
[39] Qayṣarī, *Risāla fī ʿIlm al-Taṣawwuf*, Turkish trans. Muhammed Bedirhan (Istanbul: Nefes Yayinlari, 2013), 78.
[40] Qayṣarī, *Sharḥ Fuṣūṣ al-Ḥikam*, 24. 15. [41] Ibid., 16. 24.

The reality of *wujūd*, at the level of absolute oneness (*al-martaba al-aḥadiyya*), is that there is nothing together with it, and every (divine) name and attribute disappears in it.[42]

In a fashion similar to Ibn Sīnā, Qayṣarī also analyzes how the divine names and attributes trace back to the undifferentiated unity and necessity of *wujūd*. This analysis is very important for understanding how entities' participation in *wujūd* is also participation in the divine attributes, and how this participation therefore establishes the causal efficacy and freedom of entities.

In Qayṣarī's system, *wujūd* is absolutely simple, for something composite (i.e. not absolutely simple) cannot explain its own existence. Such a composite would need its own parts and another source that gives these parts. Hence, the necessary existent has to be absolutely simple and pure: "*Wujūd* due to its purity and simplicity cannot be divided in itself or in mind."[43] Moreover, *wujūd* is simple because nothing can be added to it. To do so would reduce *wujūd* to the level of possible beings, for addition would imply either that *wujūd* needs something else to exist or that *wujūd* can be more or less perfect than it is. This is also why *wujūd* does not need the attributes of perfection coexisting with it. For, again, all of the divine attributes are concealed in *wujūd*'s unity. Hence, "there is no reality additional or attached to *wujūd*. For, in this case, *wujūd* would need that [additional thing] to exist and this would make it like other beings. This implies infinite regress (*tasalsul*)."[44]

Wujūd is pure good, because every good observed in the phenomenal level must be traceable back to the good. And the very existence of good things at the phenomenal level implies that *wujūd* is bestowed to them by the absolute *wujūd* as an act of generosity and goodness. Thus, "*Wujūd* is pure good (*khayr maḥḍ*), for every good is from it and with it."[45]

Wujūd is self-subsisting, because *wujūd* exists due to itself. It also keeps other beings in existence. Thus, *wujūd* is absolutely independent, and everything else is absolutely dependent on it. "*Wujūd* to be *wujūd* needs nothing but itself. It exists due to itself, hence it is self-subsisting (*al-qayyūm*) and sustains the existence of all beings."[46]

Wujūd is pure light, because it is manifest in itself and causes other beings to be manifest. It is its own light and illuminates other beings. *Wujūd* illuminates the world both ontologically and epistemologically, in that everything exists and is known through the light of *wujūd*.

[42] Ibid., 22. 22–23. [43] Ibid., 15. 10–11. [44] Ibid., 18. 13–14.
[45] Ibid., 15. 15–16. [46] Ibid., 15. 16. Also see Qayṣarī, *Risāla fī 'Ilm al-Taṣawwuf*, 81.

Thus, "*wujūd* is pure light (*nūrun mahḍ*), for, it is evident due to itself, and other beings becomes evident due to *wujūd*. Moreover, everything is known with it. It enlightens the skies of the unseen, the worlds of spirits and bodies. For they become existent and real through *wujūd*."[47]

Wujūd is pure knowledge because it existentiates everything, and something that existentiates everything in accordance with their essences and capacities must know them. Thus, Qayṣarī states that "it encompasses everything with itself (*dhātihi*) and, therefore, it knows everything."[48] Furthermore, every act of knowing and every manifestation of consciousness in the universe originates in *wujūd*. If *wujūd* did not have knowledge, we would not have observed knowledge and consciousness in the universe: "the existence of knowledge in every knowing agent is through *wujūd*. God is the best of all knowers."[49]

Wujūd is the First, because there is no beginning for *wujūd*. If there were a beginning, it would imply that *wujūd* would be a contingent being and would need an external cause. Hence, "there is no beginning to *wujūd*; if there were a beginning this would make it in need of another cause (*ʿillla*) and, hence, a possible being."[50] *Wujūd* is also the Last. There is no end to *wujūd*. If there were an end, then *wujūd* would be qualified with nonexistence, which is impossible. "If *wujūd* would have an end (*intihāʾ*), it would be qualified with its opposite. Thus, *wujūd* is without beginning (*azalī*) and end (*abadī*). So, God is the First, the Last, the Inward, and the Outward (57:3)."[51] *Wujūd* is the Outward and the Inward. It is the Outward, for it existentiates and sustains every entity *in concreto* and in mind. It is the Inward, for it cannot be comprehended by external perceptions.[52]

Since *wujūd* is the First, the Last, the Outward, and the Inward, more specific names can be traced back to *wujūd*. This is because all the divine names are different expressions of these four attributes. For example, the names related to the acts of origination (*ibdāʾ*), creation, or sustenance can be traced back to the First; and the names related to the return (*iʿāda*), accountability, reward, or punishment (*jazāʾ*) can be traced back to the Last.[53] As Qayṣarī puts it, "nothing can fall outside of these four situations; outwardness (*ẓuhūr*), inwardness (*buṭūn*), firstness (*awwaliyya*), and lastness (*akhiriyya*)."[54]

It follows that other attributes such as life, will, and power are also one and the same thing with *wujūd*. He also adds hearing and seeing to this

[47] Ibid., 16. 10–12. [48] Ibid., 15. 20. [49] Ibid., 15. 22. [50] Ibid., 15. 17–18.
[51] Ibid., 15. 18–19. [52] Qayṣarī, *Risāla fī ʿIlm al-Taṣawwuf*, 81.
[53] Qayṣarī, *Sharḥ Fuṣūṣ al-Ḥikam*, 45. 12–15. [54] Ibid., 45. 14.

list, of which he states: "All perfections belongs to it (*wujūd*). Life, knowledge, power, hearing, seeing, and other qualities appear with it. This is why things reach becomes complete with it."[55]

A question arises here. If all the divine names and attributes are concealed in the undifferentiated unity of *wujūd*, then how does multiplicity emerge from it? Again, it is here the concepts of fixed archetypes and essences enter. These concepts refer to two things. One is the reality of every entity in the divine knowledge. Since to say *wujūd* is to say knowledge, God knows the essences of every possible entity in His undifferentiated knowledge. It is important to understand that knowledge of an infinite number of possible beings does not compromise the unity of the divine knowledge. God knows all possibilities in one act of knowing. This is why these possibilities are called "fixed." They are known as they are, and this knowledge does not change.

> Know that the fixed archetypes are nothing but particularized existence. This is due to the reality of the existing beings. These realities have forms in the (divine) knowledge and called the fixed archetypes.[56]

Qayṣarī also uses these concepts to refer to the divine names and attributes. The two meanings here actually entail each other. The existentiation of essences necessitates that the absolute *wujūd* would have unique relation to the individual essences. As discussed in Chapter 6, these relations that God has to essences are called the divine names and the divine attributes. From this perspective, *wujūd*'s particularization in essences not only existentiates essences but also manifests the divine qualities. Thus instantiation, individualization, or particularization are the manifestation of certain divine qualities in this particularized relation. Although *wujūd* is one and undifferentiated, when it relates to the multiple essences, both the divine names and entities are manifested. These two acts are one and the same thing. This is why Qayṣarī uses the concept of essences to refer to both the forms of individual entities in the divine knowledge and the divine qualities manifested in the relationship between existence and essence. Thus, he writes that "there are two aspects of essences ... one is the forms of the names and the other realities of existing beings."[57]

[55] Ibid., 15. 24–25.

[56] Qayṣarī, "Sharḥ Taʾwīlāt Basmala," in *Rasāʾil*, ed. Mehmet Bayraktar (Ankara, 1989), 197–198.

[57] Qayṣarī, *Sharḥ Fuṣūṣ al-Ḥikam*, 65. 13–14.

In some passages, Qayṣarī uses the concepts of "the Most Holy Effusion" (*al-fayḍ al-aqdas*) and "the Holy Effusion" (*al-fayḍ al-muqaddas*) to express the same idea. The Most Holy Effusion refers to the self-disclosure of *wujūd* to itself or, in other words, to self-knowledge of God. This self-knowledge entails the knowledge of the fixed archetypes and essences concomitant with *wujūd*'s infinity. The Holy Effusion refers to the existentiation of these entities *in concreto*. For example,

> Praise be to God who, with the Holy and the Most Holy Effusion, knew essences with His knowledge hidden in the secrecy of His essence ... and showered them with the light of His manifestation ... and brought them out of the domain of the unseen.[58]

The term "effusion" also affirms that entities are existentiated with the expansion, flow, bestowal of *wujūd*. To express the bestowal of *wujūd*, Qayṣarī uses "general expanding existence" (*al-wujūd al-ʿām al-munbasiṭ*).[59] The Real expands upon (*sarayān*) existence with this general existence.[60] The general and undifferentiated existence then becomes particularized and individualized in the essences of entities.[61] *Wujūd* permeates essences, existentiating them in accordance with their form in the divine knowledge. It is this permeation of existence into essences that brings about multiplicity. It is only in this sense that one can talk about the particularization of existence, which appears to us as multiplicity. This multiplicity does not affect the divine unity. In itself *wujūd* is absolutely one, pure, simple.

> In reality *wujūd* is one reality, and there is no multiplicity in this reality. The particularization of this one reality is due to its relation (*iḍāfa*) to essences. This relation [between *wujūd* and essence] is a perspectival (*iʿtibāri*) issue.[62]

Thus far, I have explained the meaning of *wujūd*, the relationship of *wujūd* to the divine qualities, and the relationship between *wujūd* and essences in Qayṣarī's system. It is on the basis of these concepts that causal agency and freedom of entities are to be understood. As discussed, *wujūd* expands upon essences and is the basis of all attributes, such as power, will, knowledge, and life. Thus, when *wujūd* expands upon the created order, entities are also qualified with the attributes concealed in *wujūd*.

[58] Ibid., 3. 1–6. [59] Ibid., 16. 19–20. [60] Ibid., 118. 21.

[61] He also uses Ibn ʿArabī's famous analogy, the "Breath of the Merciful" (*Nafas al-Raḥmān*), to express the expansion of *wujūd* from the Real to the entities. Qayṣarī, *Risāla fī ʿIlm al-Taṣawwuf*, 17.

[62] Qayṣarī, *Sharḥ Fuṣūṣ al-Ḥikam*, 20. 13–14.

It is due to these qualities that an entity becomes causally efficacious and free.

> Every perfection meets with the created order by means of existence (*bi-wāsiṭati al-wujūd*). *Wujūd* is self-subsistent, knowing, willing, alive, and powerful. These attributes are not additional to it. Otherwise, it would need another cause that has life, knowledge, power, and will. These qualities can only emanate from someone who has them.[63]

If "the Generous Giver (*al-wāhib al-jawād*) would not have given these qualities by giving *wujūd*, they would not have them."[64] Hence, the created order has these qualities by receiving and participating in *wujūd*. While participating in existence, entities also participate in such qualities as the divine power and freedom.

> Since the limited (*al-muqayyad*) things are manifestation of the Absolute Existence, the divine qualities are attributed to them by means of participation (*bi-l-ishtirāki*) and by way of gradation (*ʿalā sabīli-l-tashkīk*).[65]

This suggests that entities participate in the divine qualities in a gradational way. In another passage, Qayṣarī uses the term concurrence (*tawāṭuʾ*) to express the same thing. "Predication of attributes on the entities (*taʿayyunāt*) existing in the (divine) knowledge is by way of concurrence (*tawāṭuʾ*)."[66] In light of his treatment of the concept of existence, it can be concluded that entities are conscious and powerful by participating in *wujūd*. They are also free by participating in *wujūd*. The same can be said for other qualities of perfection. In this participation, entities own these qualities – not in the absolute sense but in a limited fashion due to their limited essences. Hence, entities owe their agency and causal efficacy to their participation in *wujūd*.[67]

[63] Ibid., 24. 11–13. See also "things have qualities such as life, knowledge, and will with God who encompasses everything": *Sharḥ*, 183. See also "things have qualities such as life, knowledge, and will with God who encompasses everything," Qayṣarī, "*Sharḥ Taʾwīlāt Basmala*," 183.

[64] Qayṣarī, *Sharḥ Fuṣūṣ al-Ḥikam*, 63. 4–5. [65] Ibid., 25. 14–15.

[66] Ibid., 25. 16–17.

[67] Qayṣarī also explains that the idea of participation in *wujūd* establishes causal efficacy of entities not only in concrete reality but also in mind. For according to Qayṣarī, entities not only in the extramental domain but also in the mental domain owe their existentiation to *wujūd*. *Wujūd* as an all-encompassing concept permeates into mental causality. Thus, he writes that "everything that happens *in concreto* (*khārij*) and in mind (*ʿaql*) happens with *wujūd* ... If there would be no *wujūd*, there would be nothing *in concreto* and in mind," ibid., 14. 13–14.

7.2.2 *Essences and Freedom*

The idea of essences provides another perspective for approaching the question of freedom. Qayṣarī, like Qūnawī, holds that essences are known by God but not caused by God. God knows these essences through Himself. As Qayṣarī writes, "He knows realities of things as he knows himself, not in any other way ... These realities are different from God in terms of their entification (*taʿayyun*), but they are in fact identical with the divine Self."[68] This self-knowledge entails the knowledge of every essence that exists in the infinity and undifferentiated unity of *wujūd*. Since God is present to Himself, every essence is also present to God. God then creates entities not from nothing but from their essences, which are eternally known. Creation is the manifestation of possibilities that already exist in the divine knowledge or, in other words, in the infinity of *wujūd*. In this picture, essences remain absolutely dependent on *wujūd* for their existentiation. For they cannot smell the "fragrance of existence" without the bestowal of *wujūd*.

> Every possible reality, although eternally present in the divine knowledge, did not smell the fragrance (*rāʾiḥa*) of *wujūd* ... Everything existing in the divine knowledge requests, with the tongue of their capacities, existence. There is no exception to this.[69]

It is important to realize that this knowledge does not imply that God determines essences to be what they are. For "the knowledge comes after the known."[70] God knows essences without determining what essences are. God existentiates essences in accordance with their capacities, without imposing these capacities on them.

This metaphysics suggests that essences are coeternal with God. Thus, Qayṣarī writes that essences are "eternal (*qadīm*) and necessary (*wājib*)."[71] In other words, God's knowledge eternally relates to these essences. There is no beginning of the divine knowledge, and hence there is no beginning of the existence of entities in the divine knowledge. Otherwise, it would imply that God did not know essences at one point in time and then started to know them at another point. This is impossible, if the divine knowledge is infinite and unchanging. Hence essences do not have a beginning. Ergo, "in God's knowledge, everything has a form ... These entified forms are infinite ... the

[68] Ibid., 17. 11–12. Also, "the Real knows things as He knows Himself," 49. 3.
[69] Ibid., 63. 1–2. [70] Ibid., 50. 19. [71] Ibid., 25. 17.

divine knowledge relating to these forms is without beginning or an end."[72]

Recall that Qayṣarī also refers to these essences and fixed archetypes as the divine names and attributes. This provides another perspective to understand their coeternity. As a result of the Most Holy Effusion, *wujūd* eternally relates to these essences. It is due to the eternity of these relations between *wujūd* and essences – as concomitants of *wujūd*'s infinity – that the names and the attributes eternally coexist as concealed in *wujūd*. That is to say, there is no temporal gap between *wujūd* and essences. Essences are coeternal with God. Qayṣarī states:

> They (the fixed archetypes or essences) do *not* emerge (in the divine intellect) in a similar fashion as ideas emerging in our intellects when we want to do something ... The Real's knowledge of itself with itself entails that essences exist alongside with the Real, without *temporal posteriority*.[73]

Qayṣarī writes that essences are also, in a sense, absolute. They are absolute, for they are coeternal and uncaused; yet they are contingent, for their existence cannot be without *wujūd*. Only *wujūd* can be absolutely absolute. It is in this sense, "the One in its absolute unity (*dhāt al-aḥadiyya*) is absolute (*muṭlaq*) *wujūd*. Contingent (*muqayyad*) entities are [also] absolute but with particularization and entification (*ta'ayyun*)."[74] Although they are not absolutely absolute, essences can be seen as "relatively (*i'tibāri*) absolute."[75]

Qayṣarī also holds that "there is no middle ground between *wujūd* and nothingness."[76] This provides another reason for Qayṣarī for the coeternity of essences with *wujūd*. A thing either exists or does not exist. If essences are something, then they must exist. Entities we observe in the phenomenal realm are created not from nothing, but from essences that already exist. Creation is a process from one type of *wujūd* to another, not from nothingness to *wujūd*. Essences therefore exist before their existentiation *in concreto*.

These considerations lead to the conclusion that essences are not caused by God to be what they are in the infinity of *wujūd*. It is in this sense that "the [fixed] entities in terms of their being forms (*ṣura*) in the divine knowledge cannot be considered created [or caused] (*maj'ūl*)."[77]

[72] Qayṣarī, "*Sharḥ Ta'wīlāt Basmala*," 181.
[73] Qayṣarī, *Sharḥ Fuṣūṣ al-Ḥikam*, 65. 8–10. [74] Ibid., 25. 14–15. [75] Ibid., 14. 19.
[76] Ibid., 14. 18. [77] Ibid., 64. 24–25.

The essences are created [or caused] only in terms of their existentiation *in concreto*, not in terms of their existence as they are in the divine knowledge. Again, "creation (*ja'l*) of the known forms means their existentiation *in concreto* (*khārij*)."[78] The forms themselves, however, are not caused by God, they are only known by God and then given existence. In the act existentiation of entities, "*wujūd* follows (*tābi'an*) essences. These essences are hidden at the level of absolute oneness (*aḥadiyya*), and they become manifest on the level of relative oneness (*waḥidiyya*)."[79]

To conclude, *wujūd* does not determine essences to be what they are but existentiates them in accordance with what they are. It is this lack of determination of essences – implied by essences' coeternity, relative absoluteness, and uncausedness – that provides a solid grounding for creaturely freedom. From the perspective of existence, God creates us, while from the perspective of essence, we create ourselves.

7.2.3 *Qayṣarī, the Ash'arites, and the Philosophers*

Qayṣarī's writings present a participatory account of causality in which the concepts of existence and essence ground causal agency and the freedom of entities. This view of causality allows him to appropriate certain ideas and concepts traditionally attributed to both the Philosophers and the Ash'arites.

Substance/s and Accidents

Qayṣarī discusses at length how the concepts of substance and accident are to be understood in light of the concept of *wujūd*. *Wujūd* is neither substance nor accident, nor a combination of substance and accident. *Wujūd*, as an all-encompassing reality, is the ground of both substance and accident.

First, Qayṣarī writes that *wujūd* cannot be an accident.[80] An accident inheres in something other than itself. *Wujūd*, however, exists by itself. It does not inhere in something other than itself. If this were the case, that something would have to exist before *wujūd*. Nothing can exist without *wujūd*, nor can *wujūd* cannot precede itself. Hence, *wujūd* exists due to itself and does not inhere in something, as an accident, that existed before it. This would be impossible.

[78] Ibid., 65. 3–4. [79] Ibid., 16. 1–2. [80] Ibid., 13.

If existence were an accident, then it would have to inhere in something that existed before it. This like saying that that a thing precedes itself or comes before itself.[81]

Wujūd is also not substance.[82] Substance is not as all-encompassing as *wujūd*. The very distinction made between substance and accident implies that substance is not the overarching category. The interaction of substance and accident explains the phenomenal world, not the substance itself. If substance is different from accident, and if there are accidents, then the category of substance has limitations. Hence, substance is not the same as *wujūd*. *Wujūd* as the ground of both encompasses and transcends substance and accident.

Wujūd is a more general category than substance and accident. This is why *wujūd* is different from them and is the basis of the definition of both (substance and accident).[83]

What is inhered is substance and what is inhering is accident. Existence encompasses both. For it manifests itself in their forms.[84]

Moreover, *wujūd* is not a composition of substance and accident. If *wujūd* were composed of substance and accident, it would imply that *wujūd* is merely a possible thing. For every possible entity is composed of substance and accident. This is impossible, since *wujūd* cannot be a possible thing. Thus, "*wujūd* is neither substance nor accident. For if it were, then it would be a contingent being which is composed of substance or accident."[85]

As we saw in previous chapters, both the Ashʿarites' and the Philosophers' accounts of causality center on discussions of substance/s and accidents. The Ashʿarites' atomistic definition of substance and the Philosophers' hylomorphic definition of it both provide a basis for causality within their respective systems. In Qayṣarī's account, however, the discussion of substance/s and accidents is not central. At the end of the day, both substance/s and accidents are manifestations of *wujūd*. If the Ashʿarites are correct, then *wujūd* is the basis of atoms and accidents inhering in atoms; if the Philosophers are correct, then *wujūd* is the basis of hyle and the forms. It is this construction of the relationship of *wujūd* and substance-accidents that allows Qayṣarī to appropriate certain elements of Ashʿarite occasionalism and Ibn Sīnā's hylomorphism without giving up the central claims of their *wujūd* metaphysics.

81 Ibid., 13–15. 82 Ibid., 13. 8–9. 83 Ibid., 14. 1–2. 84 Ibid., 74. 4–6.
85 Ibid., 18. 11–12.

For instance, the occasionalist idea that the world is re-created anew each moment is also present in Qayṣarī's system. As discussed in Chapter 6, this idea has already been appropriated by Ibn ʿArabī. Qayṣarī reinterprets the idea of constant re-creation in light of the concept of *wujūd*. Since both substance and accident are instantiations and particularizations of *wujūd*, they do not exist by themselves. They are sustained at all times: "He is the one who keeps things in existence."[86] Ultimately, substances are like accidents. In fact, the world is composed of accidents, which cannot subsist by themselves from one moment to another. Hence, the world receives *wujūd* from God, at each instant. What is important here is that this occasionalist element is assimilated thanks to the comprehensive quality and philosophical-theological implications of the concept of *wujūd*. If the world is a totality of accidents, then Qayṣarī can accept the continuous creation of the world without accepting every other tenet of Ashʿarite atomism.

Preponderance

Remember that the concept of preponderance refers to God's creation of the world and differentiation of entities without a differentiating reason. Ashʿarites generally hold that God creates the world from nothing. To explain the differences in the world without implying a change in God, they defend the notion that God gives preponderance to equal options without any reason. Qayṣarī, together with Ibn ʿArabī and Qūnawī, holds that the act of existentiation does not occur arbitrarily but rather according to the essences, which are known by God. This implies that there is no creation from nothing but rather creation from essences. This represents a fundamental divergence between the two accounts.

Despite this divergence, Qayṣarī continues to use the term preponderance in his writings. However, he does so only in a limited sense. For example, when he is discussing existentiation of the fixed archetypes, he writes that "despite every essence's demand for *wujūd*, the preponderance of some essences over others is a preponderance without a reason (*tarjīh bi-lā murajjih*)."[87] Although everything happens in accordance with what essences are in the divine knowledge, God could preponderate between existentiation and nonexistentiation of essences without a differentiating reason. The difference here is that in Ashʿarite theology there are no preexisting uncreated essences, and God creates the essences of entities in the world without reason. For Qayṣarī, however, there are eternal, preexisting essences and God creates entities from

[86] Ibid., 14. 14. [87] Ibid., 63. 5–6.

these essences. In Qayṣarī's system, the role of preponderance is reduced to preponderance between already existing essences. Some of the possibilities may not be actualized and some of the essences may not be existentiated by God. God does not choose what type of essence an object would have, but He does choose which essences are existentiated.

Miracles

One also observes a similar tendency on the question of miracles. Qayṣarī draws on the standard occasionalist account to explain prophetic miracles. A miracle is a break in God's habit that occurs to affirm a prophet.

> Although *the breaks in the divine habits are decreed in eternity*, they are attributed not to the normal course of event but to the divine power. The miracle does not happen in accordance with the unchanging ways (*sunna*) of God, but as a manifestation of the (divine) power.[88]

Yet Qayṣarī also moves beyond the standard Ashʿarite explanation in arguing that miracles are prefigured in the divine knowledge as essences. The concept of essences or fixed archetypes becomes part of the explanation given for miracles. Qayṣarī accepts the Ashʿarite explanation to a certain degree but also contextualizes it within the larger framework of *wujūd-māhiyya* metaphysics. Together with the Ashʿarites, Qayṣarī asserts that miracles occur as a result of a departure from the regular course of the divine habits, but, unlike the Ashʿarites, he also asserts that even these departures are prefigured in the divine knowledge as essences. Hence, miracles do not occur arbitrarily but as a result of their preexistence in the divine knowledge.

Why do miracles exist as essences in the divine knowledge? Qayṣarī's analysis of the infinity of *wujūd* suggests an answer. This prefiguration of miracles in the divine knowledge is implied by the infinity of *wujūd* for, again, all of essences are concomitants of *wujūd*'s infinity. *Wujūd*'s infinity cannot be delimited by phenomenal regularities and habitual creations. There should also be breaks in habitual patterns. Thus, miracles should also exist as possibilities alongside with regularities and consistencies in natural processes.

Secondary Causality and Emanation

Qayṣarī also appropriates some of the ideas usually attributed to the Philosophers. As discussed above, Qūnawī envisages two types of

[88] Ibid., 148. 17–20.

relationship between God and the world: with and without intermediation. A similar tendency to see two types of relationships between God and the world can also be observed in Qayṣarī's adaption of the idea of *emanation* in light of the concept of *wujūd*. Entities' participation in *wujūd* is the basis of their causal agency and freedom. Each entity receives existence from God's *wujūd*. This further implies that these existing beings not only receive existence but also radiate existence to the extent allowed by their capacities. On the one hand, everything receives existence without intermediation from God; on the other hand, they transmit existence to other entities. Implicit in the causal efficacy of an entity is the transmission of *wujūd*, in a particularized form, to other entities. Although the bestowal of *wujūd* by God implies vertical causality, the transmission of existence by created entities constitutes a horizontal relationship. It is here that emanationism is integrated into Qayṣarī's larger context of *wujūd*. There is an intermediated reception of effusion through intellects and secondary causes, alongside unmediated reception of effusion from God. This explains the use of emanationist concepts such as celestial intellects and souls by the major representatives of the school of *wujūdiyya*. For example,

> Although effusion reaches everything without intermediation, it also reaches them through every entity. Every entity is a medium through which effusion reaches lower entities, just like (celestial) intellects (*al-ʿuqūl*) and abstract souls (*al-nufūs al-mujarrad*) are intermediaries for the lower entities.[89]

Similarly, Qayṣarī appropriates the idea of nature in light of the concept of essence. As discussed extensively above, the idea of fixed archetypes implies that existentiation occurs in accordance with entities' essences in the divine knowledge. In this picture, the concept of essence plays a similar role to the concept of nature. Thus, "anything that is manifested must exist as a potential (*bi-l-quwwa*) before its manifestation."[90] The difference here is that although Aristotle locates these principles in the material constitution of entities, Qayṣarī sees them as metaphysical principles existing in the divine knowledge. Their function, however, is very similar in both systems. They ensure the non-arbitrariness of the divine acts.

The concept of hyle can also be found in Qayṣarī's writings. His general strategy to interpret these concepts in light of the concepts of *wujūd* and essence can also be observed here. He equates hyle with the

[89] Ibid., 65. 23–25. [90] Ibid., 76. 25.

Breath of the Merciful. Recall that the Breath is also the general *wujūd* permeating into essences: "The first thing he made manifest is the general hyle (*al-hayūlā al-kulliya*) which, in the language of the people of God, is called the Breath of the Merciful."[91] Yet, this however, should not be imagined as a self-subsisting substance. As discussed above, neither substance nor accident are self-standing in Qayṣarī's system. They are different particularizations of *wujūd*. Together with the idea of the continuous re-creation of the world, this suggests that hyle, as with everything else, requires the continuous permeation of *wujūd*. As such, the metaphysics of existence-essence allows Qayṣarī to critically appropriate the idea of hyle.

7.3 CONCLUSION

To conclude, the members of the school of *wujūdiyya* examined in this book defend participatory theories of causality. *Wujūd* is the ground of all causal activities. Entities' participation in *wujūd* establishes their causal efficacy and freedom. Essences are uncreated and uncaused principles of differentiation of *wujūd*. God does not determine essences to be what they are but only knows them as they are. As such, the essences are the basis of creaturely freedom.

Qūnawī and Qayṣarī not only defend the fundamental convictions of Ibn ʿArabī but also reinterpret these ideas by using logical analysis and philosophical concepts. They put these ideas in conversation with strong convictions of Ashʿarite occasionalism and emanationism. To this end, they use rich implications of the concepts of *wujūd* and *māhiyya*. The result is a critical appropriation, contextualization, and reinterpretation of such central concepts as substance, accident, preponderance, emanation, intermediation, habits, miracles, natures, and hyle.

This is a world in which both substance/s and accident are regarded as different manifestations of all-encompassing *wujūd*. In this world, God creates not from nothing but from essences. *Wujūd*'s infinity necessitates that God relates to the world *both with and without intermediation*. The same infinity also necessitates that there is both habitual regular creation and breaks in the habits, that is, miracles. This world is re-created anew at each moment, for it cannot subsist for any two moments without the permeation of *wujūd*. There is both vertical causality, for *wujūd* is given without intermediation, and horizontal causality, for *wujūd* also reaches

[91] Ibid., 76. 3–4.

each entity through other entities. To participate in *wujūd* is to participate in the divine attributes, for all attributes are concealed in *wujūd*. Therefore, to participate in *wujūd* is to participate in the divine freedom. This is a world in which entities are at once free due to their uncreated and uncaused essences and absolutely dependent on God to exist and to remain in existence.

8

Toward an Occasionalist Philosophy of Science

The Case of Jurjānī

This chapter focuses on Jurjānī to investigate later developments in the occasionalist tradition.[1] Jurjānī's account is important for two reasons. First, in post-Ghazālīan *kalām*, occasionalism becomes a full-fledged worldview. The notion of "possibility," implied by such concepts as habit, conjunction (*iqtirān*), and proximity (*mujāwara*), becomes central in theological and philosophical inquiries in the *kalām* tradition. Jurjānī's writings provide good examples of how occasionalism can be the central axis of all theological thinking. Second, and more importantly, Jurjānī offers a critical-cum-pragmatic philosophy of science able to appropriate Aristotelian-Ptolemaic-Avicennian natural philosophy and sciences. He defends Ashʿarite occasionalist metaphysics as providing an adequate framework to make sense of conclusions from the medieval natural philosophy.[2] One of the core principles of occasionalism, the idea of "preponderance without reason" (*tarjīh bi-lā murajjih*), is central to Jurjānī's project of critical-cum-pragmatic appropriation of natural sciences.

[1] al-Sayyīd al-Sharīf ʿAli ibn Muḥammad al-Jurjānī (740/1340–816/1413) was an Ashʿarite theologian who authored many books in the fields of theology, jurisprudence, linguistics, and logic, including *Sharḥ al-Mawāqif*, *Ta'rifāt*, *Hāshiya 'ala Lawāmial Asrār*, *Hāshiya 'alā Hidāyat al-Ḥikma*. His most influential work, *Sharḥ al-Mawāqif*, has been studied and commented on around the Muslim world and for almost five hundred years was one of the most popular books in Ottoman schools to introduce Ashʿarite theology. Like other scholars who appeared after the thirteenth century, he was virtually forgotten in the twentieth century, despite the significant contributions he made to Ashʿarite theology.

[2] I use the term "natural philosophy" in the classical sense to refer to philosophical study of nature before the emergence of modern science.

8.1 JURJĀNĪ AND ASHʿARITE OCCASIONALISM

Following the Ashʿarite occasionalist tradition, Jurjānī holds that the relationship between cause and effect is one of possibility (*imkān*) not of necessity (*ijāb*): "Cause renders its effect (*maʿlūl*) possible."[3] Observation shows no real connection between cause and effect but only proximity (*iqtirān*) and conjunction. God is the Agent (*al-Fāʿil*) in that there are no real causal agents other than God. God is also not compelled by any type of necessity in His actions.

> God is sovereign and does what He wishes. Nothing proceeds from Him out of a necessity, and nothing is necessary for Him. Muʿtazilites hold that there are certain things which are necessary upon Him.[4]

If everything is created by God, then why does He hold individual humans accountable for their actions? How can a morally perfect God punish or reward His "servants" for actions He creates? To solve this problem, Jurjānī draws on the Ashʿarite theory of acquisition (*kasb*). Although everything is created by God, human beings have the power to acquire (or not acquire) these created acts. This acquisitive power is again created by God. "If the created (*ḥādith*) power (*qudra*) has a relationship with the act, it is according to us through this acquisition."[5] The way human individuals use this acquisitive power renders them responsible actors. "The act of the servant is created by God from nothing (*ibdāʿan wa iḥdāthan*) and acquired by the servant."[6]

The acquisition occurs together with the divine creative act. "The object of the servant's power (*maqdūr*) is acquisition, and the object of God's power is (causal) efficacy (*taʾthīr*)."[7] There is no causal efficacy in the created power (*al-qudra al-ḥādith*).[8] Acquisition is not a causally efficacious creative act but simply an occasion for God's creation. "What we mean by *kasb* is that the servant's power and choice have no role in the creation of the act, but they occur together with the created act. The servant is a locus (*maḥal*) of the created act."[9]

In accordance with the logic of occasionalism, Jurjānī argues that the created power of the servant and the divine creative act occur in proximity (*iqtirān*) to one another. This is to say that despite the denial of the necessary relationship between cause and effect, what is perceived

[3] Jurjānī, *Sharḥ al-Mawāqif*, ed. Mahmud Omar al-Dimyati, 8 vols (Beirut: Dar al-Qutūb al-Ilmiyya 2012 AD/1433 H.), IV. 207. All translations in this chapter are mine.
[4] Ibid., VIII. 217. [5] Ibid., VI. 86. [6] Ibid., VIII. 163. [7] Ibid., VI. 90–91.
[8] Ibid. [9] Ibid., VIII. 163.

as cause and what is perceived as effect follow each other closely and consistently. The concept of proximity renders the world predictable without implying causal necessity (*ʿilliyya*).[10] "God creates a power and will in the servant to continue his habitual creation."[11] Since the servant's acquisition and God's creation occur in proximity to one another, one can anticipate the consequences of one's decisions.

Jurjānī also offers some arguments in support of the theory of acquisition. First, as other Ashʿarites have argued, observation does not provide any relationship between the act and the power of the servant.[12] Second, if all possibilities are actualized and existentiated by the divine power, the acts of the servant – as possible entities – must also be created by God. Third, to be the real creator of an act, one should know and will everything about that act. However, this is almost never the case. To own the act of "moving a finger," for example, one should know and will the acts of every particle, muscle, and bone participating in this act. Unless one controls these acts knowingly and willingly, one cannot be called an agent in the real sense. This is true for all acts of which the servant claims to be the cause, such as speaking, walking, and eating. All-knowing God is the real and only cause.[13] Furthermore, if one is to possess his or her acts, then one should also be able to change them as he or she wishes. This, again, is generally not the case. Hence, the created power and will of the servant do not suffice to attribute causal efficacy to human beings.[14]

Jurjānī also argues that positing causal efficacy in the created power leads to contradictions, for "it is impossible that two efficacious agents (*qādir*) simultaneously affect one object (*maqdūr*)."[15] In this view, it is impossible that the divine will would be inefficacious. If there is causal efficacy in the servant's acquisition, it would imply that in certain cases there will be a contradiction between the preferences of the divine will and human will. In these cases, the divine will has to be the determinant.[16] Therefore, there is no need to posit causal efficacy in human acquisition. It can only acquire what the divine will chooses and creates. This view, Jurjānī believes, does not annihilate the efficacy of human power and will, but it does seriously limit it.

[10] Ibid., VIII. 68–71. [11] Ibid., VIII. 163.

[12] See for example his discussion of the concept of *tawḥīd*, ibid., VIII, 162–163.

[13] Ibid., VIII, 164. [14] Ibid., VIII. 164–165. [15] Ibid., VIII. 164.

[16] Ibid., VI. 63–66. As discussed above, Ibn ʿArabī offers a third option. There is no real separation between the divine will and the servant's will.

> Even if the efficacy of the servant is accepted, it must be rejected that the two powers are equal. God is more powerful than the servant. Therefore, the efficacy of the divine power negates the efficacy of the servant's created power. This, however, does not annihilate the servant's power. Yes, this implies poverty on the part of the servant, but this fits his/her reality. Such poverty contradicts divinity, not servanthood.[17]

Furthermore, Jurjānī interprets some Qur'anic verses as supporting his occasionalist convictions. These verses include: "you cannot wish unless He wishes" (76:30), "God creates you and what you do" (37:96), "God is the creator of everything" (13:16), "God does what He wishes" (14:27), "God guides whomever he wishes and misguides whomever He wishes" (6:125), and "God sealed their hearts" (2:7). These and similar verses for Jurjānī indicate God's overwhelming power over human acts.[18]

To provide a cosmological context for these views, Jurjānī harkens back to Ash'arite cosmology, especially to the account of accidents and substances. Jurjānī defines an accident as "an existent inhering in (or subsisting with) something that occupies space (*mawjūdun qāimun bi-mutaḥayyiz*).[19] An accident cannot subsist by itself (*lā yaqūmu bi-nafsihi*).[20] Things like colors, tastes, humidity, coldness, warmth, and heat do not exist by themselves but only occur to or in something else.[21] Thus, accidents necessarily need a locus (*maḥal*) in which to inhere.[22]

These accidents subsist in atoms, which "are in space."[23] Atoms cannot be divided, for "what can be divided is a body (*jism*). What is indivisible is called an atom (*al-jawhar al-fard*). A body is composed of at least two atoms."[24] Atoms are also dimensionless and shapeless. Jurjānī writes that "atoms do not have a shape; on this theologians (*mutakallimūn*) are in agreement." This is because "shape implies boundaries," and "we [theologians] do not accept that atoms have an end." Something that has a shape or dimension can be divided. If atoms have a shape, then one "imagines a container and contained. In this case an atom (*al-jawhar al-fard*) becomes divisible. This we reject." Furthermore, Jurjānī rejects the idea of divisibility in both theory and practice. If an atom has a shape, then "even though it is not divisible in practice, it would be divisible in imagination (*wahm*)."[25] At the same time it must also mentioned that, drawing on Baqillānī's account, Jurānī grants the

[17] Ibid., VIII. 83–84. [18] Ibid., VIII. 166–167. [19] Ibid., V. 8. [20] Ibid., V. 28.
[21] Ibid. [22] Ibid., V. 32–33. [23] Ibid., VI. 288. [24] Ibid., VI. 288.
[25] Ibid., VI. 290.

possibility that "even if an atom had a shape, it would have to be unlike anything we know."[26]

Theologically speaking, what is more important for Jurjānī – and earlier Ashʿarite occasionalism – is that accidents cannot stay in existence for two consecutive moments by themselves. For, if they could, it would imply self-subsistence and independence. If the world were self-subsistent, it could exist by itself without a creator, a proposition that cannot be accepted. "If God were nonexistent – exalted is He – one could still imagine that the world would continue in its existence."[27] Yet, things are completely dependent on the continuous creative and sustaining divine act, for "everything which needs a cause (*mua'ththir*) is created (*ḥādith*)."

Ashʿarī and his followers agree that accidents do not exist by themselves for two moments. Accidents are not self-subsistent and are discrete and renewed. When one accident goes (to nonexistence), a similar accident replaces it. It is *al-Qādir al-Mukhtār* that designates every accident for the specific time it occurs with His pure will.[28]

How about substances? Are not they self-subsistent? The Ashʿarite answer to this is negative. As with accidents, substances are also created anew at each moment: "When God does not renew the accidents with which substance continues to exist, substance is also annihilated."[29] This is to say that substances depend on accidents for their existence.

Since accidents are continuously renewed, and since the existence of substances depends on the accidents, then substances need a cause (*muaʾththir*) for their subsistence. Hence, accidents and substances are in need of God for their continuation at each moment.[30]

Jurjānī also argues that the fact that we experience the world as an uninterrupted flux does not disprove the constant renewal of the world. The world is not a continuous block but rather is composed of discrete atoms and moments. Time is also atomized and renewed.[31]

Experience does not lead to the conclusion that what is experienced is one and continuous. For it is possible that what is experienced might be a continuation of discrete but similar entities. Water coming out of a pipe is seemingly one and

[26] Ibid., VI. 291–292. [27] Ibid. [28] Ibid., V. 38–39. [29] Ibid., V. 41–42.
[30] Jurjānī also notes that some Muʿtazilite theologians such as Naẓẓām agree with the Ashʿarites on this particular issue.
[31] Ibid., V. 103–115.

continuous, but in reality it is discrete but similar moments following each other in a regular fashion.[32]

Jurjānī's occasionalist theory of causation is also grounded in the Ashʿarite theory of the divine attributes. Two ideas are especially important for understanding this connection: (1) coeternity and (2) the all-pervasiveness of the divine attributes. First, according to the Ashʿarites, the divine attributes are coeternal with God. They are not created in time. Despite their coeternity with God, they are not identical to God. They exist as neither-separate-nor-identical qualities of the divine Self.

The Ashʿarites believe that God has existent (*mawjūd*), eternal (*qadīm*) attributes belonging to His essence. God, according to this view, is knowing (*ʿālim*) with a knowledge, powerful (*qādir*) with a power, and willing (*mūrīd*) with a will. Other attributes are also like this ... the Philosophers and Shiʿites, on the other hand, deny that God has attributes that are distinct from His essence and hold that God is knowing and powerful with His essence.[33]

For Jurjānī, Shiʿites, Philosophers, and Muʿtazilites deny these attributes in their belief that the divine attributes are not separate entities but simply different expressions of the undifferentiated unity of God. These groups do not accept the Ashʿarite view that there are separate attributes alongside the divine Self. For Muʿtazilites, the moment one imagines a separate entity qualifying God, one implies a multiplicity of eternals (*taʿaddud al-qudamaʾ*), which in turn implies association (*shirk*). Therefore, for Muʿtazilites, as Jurjānī asserts, "accepting the multiplicity of eternals (*qadīm*) is disbelief (*kufr*), and it is for this reason Christians are called disbelievers."[34]

Jurjānī disagrees and responds that "disbelief is to posit multiple eternal essences (*dhawāt*), not to posit eternal attributes (*ṣifāt qudamaʾ*) of one eternal essence."[35] Hence, Jurjānī accepts that a being can have the same quality as God, in this case eternity, without being divinized. The eternity of the divine attributes does lead to the conclusion that there is more than one eternal entity. The problem here arises if one accepts multiple Gods and essences, not one essence with multiple attributes.[36]

Second, as an Ashʿarite himself, Jurjānī holds that the divine attributes are eternal and infinite in the sense that they have no boundaries in space and time. He writes, for example, that "the divine power is infinite,"[37] for "the number of possibilities is infinite, and God can create all

[32] Ibid., V. 50. [33] Ibid., VIII. 52. [34] Ibid., VIII. 52–53. [35] Ibid., VIII. 55–56.
[36] Ibid., VIII. 55. [37] Ibid., VIII. 67.

possibilities."[38] There is also agreement that the divine power is a meaningful notion only in the realm of possibilities. Thus, although the divine power is infinite from the perspective of possibilities, it cannot existentiate impossibilities. "Nonexistence is not within the domain of the (divine) power."[39] This formulation means that all logical impossibilities are nonexistent and, therefore, beyond the existentiating influence of the divine power. Aside from these cases, the divine power is the real, existentiating cause of all possibilities. Jurjānī goes on to state that

> finitude is negated from (the divine) power ... The meaning of its [the divine power's] infinity is that there can be no boundary for the divine power beyond which it cannot pass. If the number of its objects (*ta'alluqāt*) is finite, this does not change the fact that its objects could be finite in actuality (*bi-l-fi'il*), yet it is infinite in potentiality (*bi-l-quwwa*).[40]

The divine will similarly is all pervasive. Things are possible in themselves and God gives preponderance (*tarjīh*) to their existence. Without this preponderance, they would not exist.

> Will (*irāda*) is different from knowledge and power. This gives preponderance to one of the two objects of power (*maqdūr*) ... from the perspective of power there is no difference between the realization of two possibilities. It could happen at this or that time. It does not make any difference for power. Thus, there has to be a willer (*mukhaṣṣiṣ*)... The willer is not the divine power. It is also not the divine knowledge. For the knowledge follows the known. In other words, knowing that something will happen at a certain time depends on the things happening at that time. Knowledge is like a shadow or narration of the known. Thus, this willer is different from power, knowledge as well as life (*ḥayy*), hearing (*sam'*), seeing (*baṣar*), and speech (*kalām*).[41]

The divine knowledge is also all encompassing. It encompasses more than other attributes, for, unlike other attributes, it relates to all possibilities and impossibilities.

> The divine knowledge comprehends all possible, necessary, and impossible notions (*mafhūm*). This is why it is more comprehensive than the divine power. For the divine power does not relate to the necessary and the impossible. It only relates to the possible ... What necessitates knowledge is the divine Self (*dhāt*).[42]

The fact that God knows infinite possibilities as well as impossibilities does not imply a multiplicity in the divine Self. For "the multiplicity is in

[38] Ibid., VIII. 69. Also: "God is all powerful due to Himself (*dhāt*). The notion of power is necessitated by the divine Self itself," ibid., VIII. 69.

[39] Ibid., VIII. 65. [40] Ibid., VIII. 67. [41] Ibid., VIII. 94–95. [42] Ibid., VIII. 80–81.

the *relata* (*ta'alluqāt*) which are relative. It is possible that the *relata* can be infinite in number. But the divine knowledge itself one."[43] Therefore, the divine knowledge is one (*wāḥid*) but relates to an infinite (*ghayr mutanāhi*) number of things.[44]

God knows particulars and the specific times at which they occur. But this knowledge does not relate to them as they appear in the created or in anteriority or posteriority. Their knowledge (in relation to time) changes. But God knows them with a pure (*munazzah*) knowledge that is independent of time and continues from the preeternal to the eternal.[45]

The divine knowledge is one. Jurjānī posits that "we reject the multiplicity of knowledge. Multiplicity occurs in the known (*ma'lūmāt*). One knowledge relates to multiple things. There is no problem in the increase in the multiplicity of the known."[46] God knows Himself and thus knows everything.[47] This knowledge does not imply change in God as argued by the Mu'tazilites, since God "knows things in their absence and presence. When the known moves from absence to presence, this does not change God's knowledge." For example, "someone who knows that Zayd will enter the city tomorrow does not experience a change in his knowledge when Zayd (actually) enters the city."[48] Thus, God knows everything without changing. There is no anteriority or posteriority for God. Knowing particulars (*juz'iyyāt*) thus does not imply change. The past, present, and future are like one point in God's knowledge.[49]

What is important for our discussion here is the following. First, Ash'arite theology treats these attributes as distinct eternal entities qualifying the divine Self. This is different from Mu'tazilite doctrine, which dissolves the attributes in the divine Self. Then, Ash'arite theology locates the divine will at the center of its theological project. This accentuation of the divine will (and freedom) in turn leads to a rejection of any type of necessity in the divine or created order. It is here that the roots of occasionalist doctrine lie. Second, these attributes are all pervasive in that they are the real causes of qualities like power, will, knowledge, and life in the world. Seeing these attributes as the real causes of all earthly qualities leads to the conclusion that finite beings are not causally efficacious entities producing their own qualities. In this theological framework, finite beings do not own or produce their acts but merely acquire them.

[43] Ibid., VIII. 90. [44] Ibid., VIII. 67. [45] Ibid., VIII. 80–81. [46] par. 1314.
[47] Ibid., VIII. 77. [48] Ibid., VIII. 86. [49] Ibid., V. 80–1.

In accordance with his occasionalist denial of any type of necessity in the divine order, Jurjānī rejects the construction of a rational framework for evaluating the divine actions. The accentuation of the divine will manifests itself in ethics in the discussion over good (*ḥusn*) and evil (*qubḥ*). "It is not necessary (*wājib*) for God to do what is best for His creation. Nothing is necessary for God. Exalted is He from this (necessity)."[50] Here Jurjānī responds to the Muʿtazilites, who believe that God's moral perfection necessitates that God must do the most beneficial thing (*aṣlaḥ*) for His servants. For Ashʿarites, this requirement contradicts the divine freedom.[51] In sharp contrast to Muʿtazilite theologians, who argue that "God cannot do an evil act[, for] to do evil consciously is wickedness, unconsciously is ignorance [and n]either quality can be attributed to God,"[52] Jurjānī writes that "God does not have to do the best for the creation."[53] For, "there is no evil in relation (*nisba*) to God. For He has dominion over all things. As a sovereign, He does what He wishes."[54] As in nature, in the realm of ethics, the divine will dominates and the idea of necessity is rejected.

Yet, Jurjānī does not believe in an arbitrary God. The notion of *ḥikma* allows him to say that while God does what He wishes, what He wishes is wise and good. This fact follows from his pure generosity and grace and is not due to any type of necessity. Jurjānī states that "the Community (*Umma*) agreed (*ijmaʿ*) that God does not do what is ugly."[55]

> Ashʿarites defend that the divine acts do not occur due to a need (*gharāḍ*) or purpose. Philosophers and metaphysicians agree with Ashʿarites on this. Muʿtazilites, however, argue that the divine acts are necessitated by teleological causes. The jurists (*fuqahā'*) hold that the relationship between benefits and acts is not necessary, [but] is purely the divine grace (*faḍl*) and generosity (*iḥsān*).[56]
>
> It is due to God's generosity that we find benefits in the divine commands (*aḥkām*). For you (Muʿtazilites) it is obligatory (*wājib*) for God to observe the servants' benefits.[57]

Whatever comes from God is good, even though human rationality cannot necessarily recognize it. It follows that reason cannot give objective criteria to judge the divine acts. One learns what is good and bad

[50] Ibid., VIII. 114. [51] Ibid. [52] Ibid., VIII. 71–72. [53] Ibid., VIII. 218.

[54] Ibid., VIII. 72.

[55] Can God lie? For Muʿtazilites the answer is no. For Ashʿarites, He could, for the capacity to lie is not always a bad quality. But they do not attribute petty lies to God. God remains morally perfect. For Jurjānī's discussion of this question, see ibid., VIII. 201–216.

[56] Ibid., VIII. 224. [57] Ibid., VIII. 214–215.

from revelation, not from reason. Thus, Jurjānī writes that "the goodness or evilness of things does not occur in reason, nor is it confirmed by the law (*sharī'a*). Before the law, things cannot be categorized as good or evil."[58]

Jurjānī also applies occasionalist logic to the question of eschatology. "If the servant is not the performer of his acts, then how can he be rewarded or punished?" Jurjānī answers thus: "praise or condemnation comes in accordance with being the loci of the act (*maḥāl*), not as it pertains to being the real agent ... According to us, we cannot ask why God creates burning after contact with fire but not with water. Similarly, we should not ask why God gives reward or punishment after certain acts but not others."[59] There is therefore no necessary relationship between acts and salvation. Salvation is determined on the basis of the divine freedom.

Another important topic that cannot be examined in depth here is Jurjānī's application of occasionalist logic concerning pietistic courtesy. He writes that "God is the creator of both evil and good. Yet, God is not called evil, just as even though God creates monkeys and pigs," He is not called the creator of monkeys and pigs. This is for two reasons. The word evil implies that the majority of His acts are evil (which is wrong). Calling someone evil means that evil is his nature and dominates his behavior. Second, the law does not suggest this. "We receive God's names from the law."[60] So, although God is the creator of everything, one should not attribute the creation of evil to God.

Jurjānī's occasionalist doctrine of causality shapes his views on a number of other topics, such as miracles, epistemology, and prophetology. His account of miracles, for example, draws on Ash'arite occasionalism. Jurjānī sees miracles as breaks in God's habitual creation. God creates cause and effect on a habitual path and in certain cases breaks from these habits to prove the truthfulness of a prophet. This is precisely the Ash'arite explanation of miracles.

> According to us, a miracle is the act of *al-Fā'il al-Mukhtār*. God creates a miracle to show the truthfulness of his messengers. For they call for something that brings happiness in both worlds. God's will relates to their claim for prophethood to confirm (*taṣdīq*) their message.[61]

[58] Ibid., VIII. 201–202. On the contrary, for Mu'tazilites things have intrinsic qualities that can be discovered by pure reason. Revelation confirms the findings of reason. See ibid., VIII. 202–203.

[59] Ibid., VIII. 172. [60] Ibid., VIII. 72. [61] Ibid., VIII. 246.

His example is the following:

> If a man claims to be a messenger sent by the King, and if he subsequently asks the King to change his habits by sitting on the *diwan* instead of the throne, and if the King actually fulfills his wish, this confirms the truth of his claim.[62]

The same occasionalist logic can be seen in his prophetology, where "there is no necessary relation between capacity (*isti'dād*) and being a prophet."[63] To be a prophet is entirely based on the divine will. God chooses whomever He wants to be a prophet.

Similarly, Jurjānī applies occasionalist logic to epistemology. He defines reasoning (*naẓār*) as a systematic process of moving from the known to the unknown (*majhūlāt*).[64] However, this mental process for producing knowledge is not a necessary one. If there is a relationship between reasoning and knowledge, this is due to the habitual creation of God. God creates knowledge together with reasoning. There is no necessary but only a possible relationship in epistemological as well as natural processes.

8.2 JURJĀNĪ'S OCCASIONALIST APPROPRIATION AND CRITIQUE OF THE NATURAL PHILOSOPHY

Jurjānī approaches the natural philosophy and sciences of his time from the occasionalist point of view described above. He follows a careful strategy to critically appropriate certain conclusions of the Aristotelian-Ptolemaic-Avicennian scientific tradition without forsaking his occasionalist convictions. Furthermore, he suggests that an occasionalist cosmology could help transcend certain predicaments of the *philosophia naturalis*. One does not need to adhere to the Philosophers' metaphysics in order to reach the results of such sciences as physics and astronomy. Moreover, occasionalist metaphysics is superior to Ibn Sīnā's metaphysics in terms of offering an "adequate" explanation of sensual phenomena.[65]

[62] Ibid., VIII. 253. [63] Ibid., VII. 201. [64] See for example, ibid., I. 196–210.

[65] I borrow the term "adequate" from Alfred N. Whitehead. He argues that the strength of a metaphysical theory could be judged based on (1) its *internal consistency*, (2) its *adequacy* to explain sensual phenomena in their own terms, and (3) its *tenability* in the light of what we know about the physical world. A. N. Whitehead, *Process and Reality*, ed. David Ray Griffin and Donald W. Sherburne (New York: Free Press, 1978), 3–7.

8.2.1 *Wisdom (Ḥikma)* versus Cause (*ʿIlla*)

Jurjānī makes a distinction between the concepts of cause and wisdom. The scientific study of the world deals with phenomena and does not reveal the real cause of the natural process. However, scientific study could still show how things work and relate to each other. In other words, natural philosophy is the study of wisdom in the natural order. This wisdom comes from God's generosity, not from any type of necessity imposed on God. Despite his rejection of necessary causal relations, Jurjānī holds that God creates not arbitrarily but rather "wisely."

What is interesting here is that this shift from cause to wisdom enables Jurjānī to appreciate and borrow the method and content of scientific research and at the same time deny its philosophical premises. Here Jurjānī diverges from the preceding Ashʿarite tradition, which has a neutral, if not negative, position when it comes to natural philosophy.[66] Famously, Ghazālī criticizes the Philosophers' metaphysics but remains indifferent toward their physics. For Ghazālī, mathematics and physics are not really connected with religious matters. One should "neither deny nor affirm them."[67]

Jurjānī offers something quite new within the Ashʿarite tradition by proclaiming that science can actually be a tool to discover the wisdom (*ḥikma*) of natural processes. The more one studies science, the more one understands the beauty and complexity of the created order. God remains the sole causal power, but at the same time, everything Aristotle, Ibn Sīnā, and others say about the natural world can illustrate the *ḥikma* in the organization of the world.

> Futility (*ʿabath*) is devoid of benefit and meaning. But the divine acts are full of wisdom and perfect. They have innumerable benefits and wisdoms. But these wisdoms (*ḥikma*) are not necessitating causes.[68]

Jurjānī thus does not agree with Ījī, who writes of Ptolemaic modeling of planetary motion that "these are imagined things without an extra-mental reality ... These things can neither be proved nor disproved ... These are weaker than spider webs. See this and do not be afraid of their rumbling

[66] Jurjānī might have borrowed this from Maturidite theology. For the use of the wisdom/cause distinction in Māturīdī, see Ulrich Rudolph, *Al-Māturīdī and the Development of Sunnī Theology in Samarqand*, trans. Rodrigo Adem (Boston, MA: Brill, 2014), 297–299.

[67] See Ghazālī, *Tahāfut*, 5–6.

[68] Jurjānī, *Sharḥ al-Mawāqif*, VIII. 227.

noise."[69] Jurjānī disagrees with this description. After explaining the rational basis of the sphericity of the celestial objects and such notions as poles, epicycle, deferent, and equants, he comments thus:

> These and similar things, although they do not exist in an extramental world, as healthy disposition (*al-fiṭra al-salīma*) testifies, are in accord with what is happening in reality. If they are mere concepts, they are imagined in consistency with what is really happening. These are not like other misguided (*fāsid*) imaginations such as teeth of giants, ruby mountains, or two-headed men. With these concepts, we can figure out the speed, slowness, and the direction of the celestial objects in a way that can be understood with the senses and can be measured with tools. The properties of celestial spheres (*aflāk*) and the earth (*al-arḍ*), the richness and the profundity of *wisdom*, and the bewildering quality of the created order can be understood. Then the learned can say, "O Lord, you did not create this in vain."[70] And it is this benefit that lies beyond their [the Philosophers'] words. So, we should value their words and not take into consideration those who belittle their value.[71]

Jurjānī determines that "we should not hold it [Ptolemaic astronomy] in low esteem." For explanation of the wisdom and order in the universe depends largely on the natural philosophy of the Greeks and its adoption by Muslim Philosophers. Jurjānī defends the principles of such sciences as astronomy and physics, but at the same time, as an occasionalist, he states that causality is to be employed within the confines of these sciences and not to be extrapolated beyond them. It is in this intellectual milieu that the astronomer and theologian ʿAlī Qushjī (d. 1474) writes that "what is stated in the science of astronomy does not depend upon physical and metaphysical premises."[72] As Ormsby states, this "astonishing remark is only conceivable in a world-view which admitted causality as an indispensable construct while simultaneously abolishing it from reality."[73]

8.2.2 *Possibility and Impossibility*

How is rational knowledge possible within an occasionalist framework? It would seem that the occasionalist denial of any necessary connection between cause and effect leads to a totally unpredictable view of natural

[69] al-Ījī, *al-Mawāqif*, 389–390. [70] A reference to Qurʾan 3:191.

[71] Jurjānī, *Sharḥ al-Mawāqif*, VII. 109–110. Emphasis mine.

[72] Gerhard Endress, "Mathematics and Philosophy in Medieval Islam," in *The Enterprise of Science in Islam: New Perspectives*, ed. Jan P. Hogendijk and Abdelhamid I. Sabra (Cambridge, MA: MIT Press, 2003), 159–160.

[73] Eric Ormsby, *The Makers of the Muslim World: Ghazālī* (Oxford: One World, 2007), 81.

processes and hence renders science and knowledge impossible. Is it not true that if one denies the necessary connection between cause and effect, then one should allow the possibility that at this moment there are in front of us "lofty mountains" that we do not see? Jurjānī's responds to this hypothetical as follows:

> It is possible that habits of God might change and even contradict each other. But we still deny such contradiction, and there is no sophistry (*safsata*) here. This is true in the case of "lofty mountains" that we do not see. We deem it possible that they might exist, yet we deny without doubt their (actual) existence. For possibility (*imkān*) does not necessitate actuality (*wuqūʿ*) … Thus, believing in these possibilities is not absurdity.[74]

This is to say that not all possibilities will be actualized. Creation of these absurd possibilities is within the domain of the divine power. So long as they are not logical impossibilities, the divine power can create them. Thus, as an occasionalist, Jurjānī accepts that such absurdities are possible. Yet we also know that God does not realize all possibilities but only some of them – those that are consistent with his habitual creation. How do we know that? The cosmic history of the world shows that God did not actualize these absurd possibilities, and this history assures us that God will not do so in the future. Jurjānī's position here echoes that of Ghazālī, who also argues that the consistency of the natural processes "fixes unshakably in our minds the belief in their occurrence according to the past habit."[75] If regularity dominates the past, it will also dominate the present and the future.

As such, the occasionalist theory implies the possibility of certain breaks in nature without requiring them. Certain things are possible but will not be actualized in reality. Thus, for Jurjānī, the occasionalist theory does not negate the predictability of natural processes and the possibility of a rational understanding of the world.

8.2.3 *Method versus Metaphysics*

Jurjānī does not have an alternative science based on Ashʿarite occasionalist cosmology, but he does hold that Ashʿarite cosmology can be a basis for a critique of Aristotelian, Ptolemaic, and Avicennian

[74] Cited in Ömer Türker, "Introduction" in *Sharḥ al-Mawāqif* (Turkish trans. Ömer Türker) (Istanbul: Türkiye Yazma EserlerKurumu Başkanlığı, 2015), 78.

[75] Ghazālī, *Tahāfut*, 170.

natural philosophy. To this end he pursues a twofold strategy. First, Jurjānī argues that the natural philosophy and metaphysics offered by the Philosophers fail to explain the position and differentiation of celestial objects, geological formations, animals, characters, and forms, and so on. In other words, if one explains natural phenomena by starting from such notions as emanation, necessity, intellects (*ʿaql/ʿuqūl*), hierarchy of intellects, souls (*nafs/nufūs*), natures, and substance/accidents, then one cannot explain the "uncaused differences" among objects.

Most of the Philosophers' errors are based on their two teachings: (1) the rejection of the All-Powerful Willer (*al-Qādir al-Mukhtār*) who created this world with his pure will (not out of necessity) and (2) the affirmation that the First does not know particulars (*juzʾiyyāt*).[76]

The Philosophers' system severely limits the selective capacity of the divine will. Ashʿarites, however, as Ibn Rushd describes elsewhere, understand differentiation to be "the distinguishing of one thing either from a similar one or from an opposite one without this being determined by any wisdom in the thing itself that makes it necessary to differentiate one of the two opposite things."[77]

There is a degree of arbitrariness in the world which can only be accounted for by God's giving preponderance to one possibility over others without any cause. The element of the divine freedom that Jurjānī draws from Ashʿarite occasionalism can actually explain the arbitrary nature of the world. The more deterministic account of the Philosophers cannot explain this arbitrary nature, according to Jurjānī. So, in Ashʿarite cosmology the probabilistic and diversified nature of the world is explained through the accentuation of the divine will and preponderance without reason.

Second, Jurjānī approaches certain scientific theories as working hypotheses that can be accepted as a basis for further research in order to arrive at a better explanation. A proposed scientific theory is not the ultimate truth but only an expedient truth. This way of seeing the dominant scientific theories of his time as tenable and useful tools allows him to hold onto his occasionalist metaphysics while using Aristotelian, Ptolemaic, and Avicennian theories to understand the order and wisdom in the world's organization. Let me provide some examples.

[76] Jurjānī, *Sharḥ al-Mawāqif*, VII. 216. [77] Ibn Rushd, *Tahāfut al-Tahāfut*, 412.

Astronomy

Jurjānī rejects the causal influence of the motion of stars on terrestrial bodies. The motion and arrangement of constellations of extraterrestrial objects are believed to affect happiness and misery in the terrestrial domain. Proceeding from his occasionalist convictions, Jurjānī argues that although we can talk about certain conjunctions between celestial movements and terrestrial happenings, this proximity (*iqtirān*) does not prove a causal relationship. The proximity between the two could imply merely a conjunction and not a necessary connection.

Moreover, even if there is a conjunction, the Philosophers' attempt to establish a relationship between the celestial and terrestrial domains based on the motion of the stars fails to account for certain problems. Jurjānī uses the example of a "twin brother." The happiness and misery of two individuals who are born on the same day from the same mother cannot be explained in terms of celestial movements. They are equal in all regards, but still one may observe a great difference between the fate, appearance, and character of twin brothers. The differentiation of the twin brothers cannot be explained merely in terms of celestial causality. In an occasionalist metaphysical framework, however, God does as he wishes. He can bestow different characters, appearances, and fates to twin brothers without any causal history. Hence, one must reject the necessary connection between celestial causality and terrestrial effect. One must also see that the causal network provided by the Philosophers fails to explain certain features of the world. Jurjānī then affirms that "there is no other causal influence than God," who "does as He wishes"[78]

The Location of Celestial Objects

Jurjānī summarizes the Philosophers' cosmology as follows:

> The first intellect has three dimensions. It is an existent, it exists necessarily due to the Necessary Existent, and it is possible in itself. From these (three) dimensions something emanates. As much as it is an intellect emanates from it; as much as it is necessary a soul emanates from it; as much as it is possible a body emanates from it. This body is the celestial sphere (*falak*) . . . Similarly, from the second intellect emanates a third intellect, soul, and body . . . The tenth intellect is called the active intellect (*al-ʿaql al-faʿāl*). This intellect affects (*taʾthīr*) the hyle (*hayūlā*) of the lower realm and emanates (*fayḍ*) forms (*ṣūra*), souls (*nafs*), and accidents (*aʿrāḍ*) to simple elements (*al-ʿanāṣir*) and their components (*murakkabāt*). The reason for this emanation (from the tenth intellect) is the capacity (*istiʿdād*) of these

[78] Jurjānī, *Sharḥ al-Mawāqif*, VIII. 70.

compounds. And these compounds in turn are caused by the motion of celestial spheres, the motion of stars, and their locations.[79]

Is this metaphysical framework adequate to explain why celestial objects are located where they are? For Jurjānī, the answer is no. One of the problems of astronomy in his time is to explain how outer planets sometimes seem to stop and move backwards in retrograde motion. Ptolemy in his *Almagest* develops the concepts of "epicycles," "deferent," "equant," and "eccentric" to solve the problems of older models. Ptolemy's model allows astronomers to discern a close approximation of the location of heavenly bodies. In the Islamic world, however, during the Middle Ages, there are attempts to criticize Ptolemy's system. Ibn al-Haytham, for instance, writes that "Ptolemy assumed an arrangement that cannot exist, and the fact that this arrangement produces in his imagination the motions that belong to the planets does not free him from the error he committed in his assumed arrangement, for the existing motions of the planets cannot be the result of an arrangement that is impossible to exist."[80]

What is important for our discussion is that for medieval Muslim intellectuals it was clear that neither Ptolemy's nor Aristotle's nor Plato's models were able to fully explain the complicated movements of the sun, planets, stars, and moon. Astronomical records and observations showed that heavenly bodies move across the sky not uniformly but at varying rates and modes, to an extent that they even stop and move backwards. However, Muslim philosophers' Neoplatonistic and emanationist cosmology does not give us any metaphysical reason for why this is the case.

It is in this context that Jurjānī determines that Ashʿarite metaphysics provides a more convincing metaphysical explanation of the planetary motion. He argues that the position of celestial spheres is "either necessary or possible. It cannot be necessary, for their essences (*māhiyya*) are the same." So, it must be possible. In sharp contrast to the Philosophers'

[79] Ibid., VII. 262–263.

[80] Quoted in E. Rosen, *Copernicus and the Scientific Revolution* (Malabar, FL: Krieger Publishing Co., 1984), 174. See also N. Swerdlow and O. Neugebauer, *Mathematical Astronomy in Copernicus's* De Revolutionibus, 2 vols (New York: Springer-Verlag, 1984), 46–48. See also A. Ede and L. B. Cormack, *A History of Science in Society: From the Ancient Greeks to the Scientific Revolution* (North York, ON: University of Toronto Press, 2012); G. E. R. Lloyd, *Principles and Practices in Ancient Greek and Ancient Chinese Science* (Aldershot: Ashgate, 2006); C. J. Tuplin and T. E. Rihill, *Science and Mathematics in Ancient Greek Culture* (Oxford: Oxford University Press, 2002).

account, Jurjānī holds that celestial objects are where they are due to God's uncaused preponderance.[81] The same occasionalist logic is intact here.

In this case their position cannot be based on a necessitating agent. Because an agent cannot prefer one option over another if there is no reason for preponderance. In this case such preponderance (*tarjīḥ*) can only be due to a chooser (*murajjiḥ*) who chooses without any reason. If they (the Philosophers) accept this in the beginning, they would be able to transcend many predicaments, especially in the case of the location of celestial spheres. For all these difficulties stem from the assumption that the Necessary (*al-Wājib*) necessitates the world due to itself (*mūjiban bi-l-dhāt*).[82]

It is useful to recall here that this paragraph goes back to Ghazālī's rejection of the world's necessary emanation from the One. In the first discussion of the *Tahāfut*, Ghazālī argues that God gives existence to the world without any reason. As he puts it, the function of the will is "to differentiate a thing from its similar."[83] The divine will, therefore, must have given preponderance to the existence of the world without any necessitating reason. This undermines the Philosophers' conviction that the world emanated from the One necessarily. Ashʿarites reject the idea of necessity and affirm that the creation of the world is possible. God can differentiate two equal options without there being any differentiating quality between them.

Even before Ghazālī, Juwaynī applied this logic to explain the positions of the celestial bodies. For Juwaynī, it is possible that the celestial objects could have been in different sizes and places. If this is possible, then there has to be a willer and assigner (*mukhaṣṣiṣ*) who assigns their actual location, sizes, and all the other properties they have.[84] Jurjānī agrees with Juwaynī and Ghazālī on this point:

God wills everything, and for this reason He is the creator of everything ... The one who creates everything without discontent is the one who wills them. It has already been established that God is the creator of all possibilities (*mumkināt*). This also implies that it is God who gives preponderance (*tarjīḥ*) to their existence or their nonexistence in a specific time. The root of this preponderance is the divine will.[85]

As with the creation of the world, the alternative location of the celestial spheres is also possible. The Philosophers' metaphysics, which starts from

[81] Jurjānī, *Sharḥ al-Mawāqif*, VII. 96–97. [82] Ibid., VII. 97.
[83] Ghazālī, *Tahāfut*, 23. [84] His account is given in Shahrastānī, *Nihāyat al-Iqdām*, 13.
[85] Jurjānī, *Sharḥ al-Mawāqif*, VIII. 193.

the idea of necessity, does not account for the unintelligible differentiation of the position of the celestial objects. For an Ashʿarite, however, God can choose without any reason and thus can differentiate the position of celestial spheres as He wishes. For Jurjānī, the necessitarian worldview of the Philosophers does not allow such differentiation. The occasionalist cosmology provides a more compelling explanation.

There are many stars in the eight celestial spheres, and it is very problematic to explain this multiplicity by tracing it back to one aspect of the second intellect (*al-ʿaql al-thānī*). Moreover, in our world the forms and accidents are infinitely diverse. This again cannot be traced back to the active intellect (*al-ʿaql al-faʿāl*). In short, their claims are weak, and this is clear to the insightful.[86]

Jurjānī does not question the credibility of human observation here. He and the Philosophers agree on the location of the celestial spheres. However, he does question the Philosophers' metaphysical framework and suggests that it is inadequate to explain physical phenomena. He concludes that Ashʿarite metaphysics, which is based on the divine will and freedom, can account for the uncaused differentiations of the celestial objects.

Mountains

As discussed above, the motion of celestial objects is believed to affect the variations of terrestrial bodies.[87] In a similar fashion, when explaining the formation of mountains, Jurjānī relies on the same occasionalist logic. The differentiation of geological forms is due to God's preponderance. The Philosophers' metaphysics gives us no explanation for the specification of the "hard and soft" parts on the earth.

Despite the fact that different parts of the earth have the same relation (*nisba*) to the celestial spheres as the Philosophers argue, and that they are givers of specific properties to these parts, the formation of soft and hard parts of the earth needs a specifying (*takhṣīṣ*) cause. It is here that reason stops (can provide no explanation). This cause is the Agent Willer (*al-Fāʿil al-Mukhtār*). O, why do we not accept this in the beginning![88]

86 Ibid., VII. 263.

87 A good example of this line of thinking comes from Ibn Rushd, who writes that "the differences arising in the sublunar world in the elements, as for instance the difference between fire and earth, and in short the opposites, are based on the differentiation of matter and on their varying distances from their movers, which are the heavenly bodies": *Tahāfut al-Tahāfut*, 261.

88 Jurjānī, *Sharḥ al-Mawāqif*, VII. 160–161.

Thus, for Jurjānī, natural philosophy's model of natural processes cannot explain the formation of mountains. Neither can the motion of the celestial spheres, since different parts of the world have the same relation to celestial objects. Again, it must be God who differentiates things, even if there is no reason for differentiation. God's uncaused preponderance alone can explain these natural phenomena.

Animals

One observes in the design of animals the best possible choices, which can only be attributed to God, the Agent Willer (*al-Fāʿil al-Mukhtār*), who gives preponderance to certain possibilities over others. Again, the same occasionalist logic attributes the seemingly uncaused differentiations of animals to God's preponderance, rather than to necessary causal relations.

> When one contemplates the wonders among the animals and plants these cannot be attributed to blind forces, whether they be simple or composite. This is especially so with respect to what happens in the wombs of animals, which includes planning, measurements, and best choices ... In the books written on this topic one reads about thousands of benefits. What we do not know is more than what we know. Again, someone who sees this knows without doubt and necessarily that these acts can only be attributed to someone who knows comprehensively, knows all of the hidden secrets, and acts with wisdom and power. And the book of God says, "It is He who forms those in the wombs" ... When the Agent Willer (*al-Fāʿil al-Mukhtār*) is accepted and everything is traced back directly to Him, one finds great benefit.[89]

Galaxies

On another occasion, Jurjānī touches on the difference of opinion among astronomers concerning certain issues such as the formation of galaxies (*majarra*) and the dark spots on the moon. Jurjānī observes that these phenomena are contested issues. Some argue that a galaxy is "a burnt spot on the celestial spheres due to the heat of the sun"; others argue that it is a "smoky vapor (*bikhārun dukhāni*)" or a "conglomeration of little stars (*kavākibun ṣighār*)."[90] By drawing the reader's attention to this debate, Jurjānī aims to show "the tentativeness and groundlessness of what the natural philosophers say."[91] This opens up a space for him to discredit natural philosophy while using its theories as tentative hypotheses.

[89] Ibid., VII. 196–197. [90] Ibid., VII. 140. [91] Ibid.

Elements and Atoms

Jurjānī notes that there are four fundamental elements according to natural philosophy: earth, water, fire, and air. As an Ashʿarite, however, he rejects that the compound entities are made not of these four (or fewer) elements but rather of atoms that are indivisible and infinite. Jurjānī argues that differences between the compounds can better be explained by starting from the idea of atoms and accidents inhering in these atoms. God assigns certain accidents to an atom while re-creating them anew at each moment. For Jurjānī, this worldview provides a more dynamic and fluid ground for the explanation of the extreme differences in the world. In this case the differences between entities would be due not to their substantial natures (*al-ṭabāiʿu al-jawhariyya*) but rather to the attributes of atoms given by God.[92]

There is a fundamental difference between the two cosmologies. The Philosophers explain physical processes by starting from celestial intellects and spheres and their interaction with hyle (*hayūlā*). Ashʿarites see objects as a conglomeration of atoms. These atoms carry different accidents, which are created anew at each moment by God. Bodies are the same in their essences, for they all are composed of homogenous atoms.

> They (the Philosophers) repeatedly deny the All-Powerful Willer (*al-Qādir al-Mukhtār*). For this reason, they attribute the differences of bodies to their capacities and natures (*istiʿdād*). Bodies have different causal power due to their different forms and natures. In the last analysis, the difference in natures is explained in terms of the motion of stars and their locations. Theologians (*mutakallimūn*), however, say the following: Bodies are homogenous in their essence. That is to say that they have a common reality (*ḥaqīqa*). For all these bodies are composed of atoms (*jawhar al-fard*), and these atoms are similar, and there is no difference between them. The difference, in this case, among the bodies is not due to their natures (which are caused by celestial movements). It is due to the acts of the All-Powerful Willer, which cause the different accidents in bodies. For this reason, bodies are similar in their substance but different in their accidents.[93]

Elsewhere he writes that

> If an object is devoid of all accidents, it remains undifferentiated. It becomes unindividuated and unspecified ... This object cannot be said to be an existent. What exists outside is only what is differentiated and specified.[94]

The Ashʿarite theory of atomism goes against the basic assumptions of Aristotelian physics and its theory of form (*ṣūra*) and hyle (*hayūlā*).

[92] Ibid., VI. 143. [93] Ibid., VII. 226. [94] Ibid., VII. 241.

Jurjānī argues that an atomistic view of the universe cannot coexist with hylomorphism.[95] "Once the atom (*jawhar al-fard*) is accepted, there is no need for forms or *hayūlā* or the combination of the two."[96] Furthermore, "if it is accepted that an entity is composed of atoms, then there are only atoms in it. It is not that some of these atoms would be form and others matter."[97]

Human Soul

Jurjānī agrees with the Philosophers on the immateriality of the soul. He writes that "the soul is abstract and immaterial."[98] It must be mentioned that the Muʿtazilite and pre-Ghazālīan Ashʿarite traditions reject the idea of the immateriality of the soul. Those thinkers thought that immateriality belongs only to God, and entities cannot be like God, neither in their essence nor their attributes. After Ibn Sīnā's celebrated doctrine of the modalities of being led to a change in this view. According to Ibn Sīnā's doctrine, it is possible to think about eternal entities without undermining God's role as the first cause. Ghazālī explains that the Philosophers argue that "the Creator's priority to the world" is like "the sun's priority to light." There is only a priority "in essence and rank (*rutba*), not in time (*zamān*)."[99] From here, Ibn Sīnā draws the conclusion that the world is eternal. Ibn Sīnā's theory of the modalities of being specifies that other beings can share in God's eternity without being God. The same logic is applicable to other attributes, such as God's immateriality. Like God, the soul can be immaterial without contravening God's uniqueness.

To this extent, Jurjānī agrees with and borrows the Philosophers' views. However, his occasionalist convictions also lead to significant divergences. Jurjānī rejects a causal relationship between the soul (*al-nafs*) and body (*al-badan*). The Philosophers attempt to find a link between the immaterial soul and the material body through a complex mechanism that involves the heart, or more precisely the "an empty chamber on the left side of the heart."[100]

Jurjānī rejects that there is any necessary relation between mental and bodily states. Thus, there is no need to imagine a contact point between the two. He suggests that this relationship "is the direct creation of the All-Powerful Willer (*al-Qādir al-Mukhtār*), and [that] there is no need to

[95] Ibid., VI. 285–286. [96] Ibid., VI. 286. [97] Ibid., VI. 287. [98] Ibid., VII. 254.
[99] Ghazālī, *Tahāfut*, 12.
[100] Ibid., VII. 260. The Philosophers' theory here anticipates Descartes' "pineal gland."

accept these powers given by the soul (to limbs of the body)."[101] This rejection again stems from Ashʿarite occasionalism. In the relationship of the body and the soul, one does not observe any causal influence as suggested by the Philosophers. God creates mental and bodily states and attaches them to each other in a self-imposed habitual pattern.[102] There is no causal connection, neither between the soul and the body, nor between bodily states, nor between mental states.

8.3 CONCLUSION

As an Ashʿarite theologian, Jurjānī defends an occasionalist view of the world. The accentuation of the divine will and power in Ashʿarite occasionalism leads the conclusion that the relationship between cause and effect is not necessary, but possible. Observation shows only constant conjunction, not any necessary connection. Finite beings are devoid of causal efficacy. God creates both cause and effect and attaches them to each other in a self-imposed habitual pattern. These conclusions also shape Jurjānī's view on a number of other theological issues ranging from ethics and eschatology to prophetology and epistemology.

Jurjānī is aware that the natural philosophy/sciences of his time, especially physics and astronomy, were elaborated starting from premises quite distinct from those of Ashʿarite cosmology. For example, the Aristotelian doctrine of "natures" implies a necessitarian worldview that clearly contradicts the Ashʿarite rejection of necessary relation between cause and effect. Moreover, the central doctrine of Aristotle's philosophy of nature – that the natural body consists of primary matter (*hylē*) and form (*morphē*) – as well as the continuous cosmology this hylomorphism implies are inconsistent with the discrete and discontinuous world of Ashʿarite atomism. Despite these and similar fundamental disagreements, Jurjānī draws on Aristotelian natural philosophy and Ptolemaic astronomy. In his attempt to both criticize and draw on Aristotelian-Ptolemaic-Avicennian natural philosophy, Jurjānī develops what one might call a critical philosophy of science. On the basis of the wisdom-cause (*ḥikma-ʿilla*) distinction, he aims to incorporate the findings of natural philosophy without accepting its necessitarian premises. He also sees natural

[101] Ibid.

[102] Interestingly, Jurjānī's defense here anticipates Malebranche's occasionalist answer to Descartian soul–body dualism. See for example, Malebranche, Oeuvres complètes de Malebranche, ed. André Robinet (Paris: Vrin, 1958–1984), 20 vols, 2: 316.

philosophy as a tool to discover the "wisdom" in the world and, thus, departs from the indifference or condescension vis-à-vis natural sciences that characterized some of earlier Ash'arite accounts. Furthermore, Jurjānī displays a quite pragmatic attitude toward scientific theories offered by natural philosophy and suggests that they are only practical working hypotheses and not ultimate truths. He also criticizes some of the convictions of medieval natural philosophy and argues that Ash'arite occasionalist metaphysics can provide a more adequate explanatory framework and transcend certain predicaments of the natural philosophy of his time. To construct this explanatory framework, he employs the idea of "preponderance without reason." The results of natural philosophy in such sciences as astronomy, geology, and physics are in no case dependent upon adherence to the Philosophers' metaphysics. Jurjānī's attempt could shed some light on the complex relationship of Ash'arite occasionalism with medieval natural philosophy and sciences.

9

Causality and Freedom in Later Islamic Philosophy

The Case of Mullā Ṣadrā

This chapter examines Mullā Ṣadrā's account of causality and freedom from the perspective of the central concepts of his metaphysics.[1] Existence (*wujūd*), for Ṣadrā, is "the ground of all metaphysical questions."[2] So, an analysis of Ṣadrā's account of causality and freedom must begin with his conception of existence. The metaphysical treatment of the concept of existence allows Ṣadrā to develop of an account of causality in which the causal efficacy and freedom of entities are established through the expansion of and participation in existence. The chapter then considers the significance of the concept of essence in Ṣadrā's metaphysics and how he uses this concept to establish freedom in the created order.

9.1 EXPANSION OF EXISTENCE AND CAUSALITY

In Ṣadrā's system, *wujūd* is "the immutable principle within every existent."[3] Due to its manifestness and clarity, "it is the least in need of

[1] For some basic guides to Ṣadrā's life, works, and thought, see the following European language sources: Hossein Ziai, "Mullā Ṣadrā," in *History of Islamic Philosophy*, ed. S. H. Nasr and O. Leaman (London: Routledge, 1996), I: 635–642; Ibrahim Kalin, "An Annotated Bibliography of the Works of Mullā Ṣadrā with a Brief Account of his Life," *Islamic Studies*, 42 (2003): 21–62; Sajjad H. Rizvi, *Mullā Ṣadrā Shirazi: His Life, Works and the Sources for Safavid Philosophy* (JSS Supplements 18, Oxford: Oxford University Press, 2007); John Cooper, "Mullā Ṣadrā Shirazi," in *The Routledge Encyclopaedia of Philosophy*, ed. E. Craig (London: Routledge, 1998), 6: 595–599.

[2] Mullā Ṣadrā, *Kitāb al-Mashā'ir*, trans. Seyyed Hossein Nasr, ed., intro., and annot. Ibrahim Kalın (Provo, UT: Brigham Young University Press, 2014), 3.

[3] Ṣadrā, *Mashā'ir*, 4. And "that which is other than it is like a reflection (*'aks*), a shadow (*ẓill*), and an apparition (*shabḥ*)," ibid., 4.

definition."[4] *Wujūd* does not have a "mental existence,"[5] for it cannot be conceived through anything that is "more manifest or better known than it."[6] *Wujūd* is not only "the most general among all concepts" but also "the most particular of all particular things." This is because "through *wujūd* is made concrete all that is concrete" and "is determined all that is determined and particularized."[7] *Wujūd* is a "simple reality" (*amrun basīṭun*);[8] it is "not a genus, nor a species, nor an accident."[9] *Wujūd* "does not at all need, in its realization or actualization, anything added to it."[10] It is completely realized, and there is no potentiality waiting to be actualized in it; it is pure actuality. *Wujūd* is the "reality by which all things are created."[11] The reality of existence is identical to God. "God is simple being because He is described by existence, and existence is a unique, simple reality. It is simplicity devoid of essence."[12] Echoing the conviction of Muslim philosophers and Sufi metaphysicians examined in this book, Ṣadrā describes God as pure existence without essence. Purity entails ultimate perfection. God is not limited in an essence and therefore it is not possible to describe the pure reality of God. It is the introduction of essences that causes imperfection, impurity, and "contamination." God is beyond these qualities.

That simplicity is uncontaminated by multiplicity, privation, imperfection or any such negative property. *God's existence is pure and unencumbered by complexity* such as an essence that might raise questions of genera, division, composition and definition. The reality of existence (*ḥaqīqat al-wujūd*) is identical to God. Existence without essence is the utmost perfection because of its purity.[13]

Since pure *wujūd* has no essence, it exists by itself. It explains its own existence and does not need a cause to exist. Simplicity, purity, and actuality locate *wujūd* in the beginning of all ontological and causal activity. Since all things other than God have an essence, they need a cause to exist. This also explains the divine perfection and creaturely imperfection. God is pure existence without essence and therefore perfect.

[4] Ibid., 6. Sabzawārī, Ṣadrā's influential commentator, says that "its [*wujūd*'s] notion is one of the best-known things, but its deepest reality is in the extremity of hiddenness." *The Metaphysics of Sabzawari*, trans. M. Mohaghegh and T. Izutsu (New York: Caravan Books, 1977), 31–32. Quoted in Ibrahim Kalın, "Mullā Ṣadra's Realist Ontology of the Intelligibles and Theory of Knowledge," *Muslim World*, 94.1 (2004): 81–106. 26p.

[5] Ibid., 7. [6] Ibid. [7] Ibid. [8] Ibid., 8. [9] Ibid., 9. [10] Ibid., 8.

[11] Ibid., 9.

[12] Mullā Ṣadrā, *al-Ḥikmat al-Muta'āliya fi-l-Asfār al-'Aqliyyat al-'Arba'a*, ed. Muhammad Rida Al-Muzaffar, 9 vols (Beirut: Dār Iḥyā' al-Turāth al-'Arabī, 1981), VI. 45.

[13] Ṣadrā, *Asfār*, VI. 17–18. Emphasis mine.

Everything other than God lacks the purity and simplicity of *wujūd* and is therefore imperfect.

Ṣadrā also holds that these entities are existentiated by receiving "existence" from the "pure existence" through the expansion of *wujūd*. An entity gets its share of existence (*ḥiṣaṣ al-wujūd*) from God's pure and undelimited existence in accordance with its essence or capacity. According to Ṣadrā, there are three types of existence and their relationship explains how entities are existentiated. The first is the "absolute existence" (*al-wujūd al-muṭlaq*). The absolute existence is beyond definition and pertains only to God. The second type of existence is the "relative existence." All created entities have relative existence, for they cannot claim self-sufficiency. As it pertains to themselves, they are nothing but shadowy essences. They need a self-sufficient giver of existence to exist. They cannot properly be said to exist until they get their share from the absolute existence. As Ṣadrā puts it:

> The meaning of contingency in particular beings, which radiate from the True One, goes back to their deficiency and essential poverty and their being essentially related to [the Creator] whereby their origination is impossible without their self-sufficient maker. They have no essence in themselves except that they are related to the First Truth and dependent on It as God the Exalted said "God is rich and you are poor." (Qur'an 47:38)[14]

This brings us to the third type of existence, which connects the first two types of existence. This is called "the absolute expanding existence." Ṣadrā suggests that this type of existence refers to the act of bestowal of existence upon contingent beings. The absolute existence "expands" upon contingent beings and therefore becomes particularized (*takhaṣṣus*) in the essences of entities. The absolute expanding existence hence belongs to the domain of neither absolute existence nor relative existence. What proceeds from the One is existence itself, which becomes differentiated when it relates to entities. Ṣadrā calls this process the "pervasion of existence" (*sarayān al-wujūd*) or "expansion of existence" (*inbisāṭ al-wujūd*).[15] For Ṣadrā, such Qur'anic verses as "the compassion embraces all things" (7:156) express how *wujūd* permeates and embraces everything.

[14] Ṣadrā, *Ḥudūth al-'ālam*, ed. S. H. Musawiyan (Tehran: Bunyād-i Ḥikmat-i Islāmi-yi Ṣadrā (Sadra Islamic Philosophy Research Institute, AH. 1378/1959), 28–29.

[15] Ṣadrā, *Asfār*, I: 67, 146, 289–292, 381. Ṣadrā borrows these terms from earlier Sufi metaphysicians. See for example, Qūnawī, *Miftāḥ*, 17b, 26b, and 32b. and Qayṣarī, *Sharḥ Fuṣūṣ al-Ḥikam*, 118. 21.

> *Wujūd* has three degrees: (1) *wujūd* that is not related to anything other than itself and that is not limited any particular limit and deserves to be the principle of all things; (2) *wujūd* that is related to something such as intelligences the souls of the heavens, the basic natures (heat, dryness, and humidity), celestial bodies, and material substances; and (3) extended *wujūd*, whose comprehension and extension englobes the temples of individual concrete things and essences ... in a manner that is understood by the gnostics and that they call *the "Compassionate Breath,"* a name derived from His saying, transcendent is He: "And My Mercy embraces all things" 7:156 ... This wujūd is *the principle of the existence of the universe*, its life and its light, and *penetrates* into all that there is in the heavens and the earths. It *exists in all things according to that thing* in such a way that in the intellect, it is intellect; in the soul it is soul; in nature it is nature; in the body it is body. Its relation to the Divine Being – exalted be He – is analogous to the relation of sensible light, and the rays shining upon bodies in the heavens and the earth, to the sun.[16]

Wujūd "penetrates" all levels of being. What existentiates beings is the "expansion of the light of *wujūd* upon the temples (*hayākil*) of contingent beings and the receptivity (*qawābil*) of the essences."[17] As such, "all of the universal essences exist through it."[18] Furthermore, "everything else becomes possessor of reality through it."[19] Due to this expansion, entities participate in the divine existence. And it is this participation that is the basis of their causal agency and freedom.[20] Their participation in existence is the basis of their motion and physical activity.

9.2 SUBSTANTIAL MOTION AND PHYSICAL MOTION

One of the cardinal principles of Ṣadrā's metaphysics is that existence is pure act. He writes that "pure act of the Necessary Being is the sheer reality of *wujūd*."[21] For "there is no possibility in it."[22] If there is no possibility in it, then is nothing waiting to be actualized – it is pure actuality. A being with possibility cannot be the Necessary Being.[23]

16 Ṣadrā, *Mashāʿir*, 97. 17 Ibid., 9. 18 Ibid. 19 Ibid., 11.

20 Thus, I agree with Rizvi, who has already noted that Mullā Ṣadrā's account of causality bears resemblance to Neoplatonic "eidetic causality" in that the One is "the processual sustainer" and "participates in things and thus causes them in a sense." Sajjad H. Rizvi, "Mullā Ṣadrā and Causation: Rethinking a Problem in Later Islamic Philosophy," *Philosophy of East and West*, 55.4 (2005): 575. However, Rizvi's article does not provide sufficient textual support for this reading. It also fails to deal with the question of how Ṣadrā establishes creaturely freedom if the One "participates in things and causes them in a sense." For the concept of "eidetic causality," see D'Ancona Costa, "Plotinus and Later Platonic Philosophers on the Causality of the First Principle," 361.

21 Ṣadrā, *Mashāʿir*, 51. 22 Ibid. 23 Ibid.

The Necessary Being by itself constitutes *a superabundance of actuality and perfect actuality containing all modes of existence*, all modes of becoming, all cases of perfection. It has no analogue, no similitude, nothing comparable, nothing opposite, and nothing like unto it in *wujūd*. Rather, its essence, by the perfection of its excellence, necessitates that it be the support of all perfections and the source of all good.[24]

It is evident that for all things the principle and source of *the act of existing* is the pure reality of *wujūd*, which is not mixed with anything other than *wujūd*.[25]

It is also this continuous act that constantly renews the world. In other words, the world is constantly created anew at each moment due to the participation of all entities in the divine actuality. As Ṣadrā explains:

There is absolutely no ipseity or individual – be it celestial or elemental, simple or composite, substance or accident – but *that its nonexistence precedes its being in time, and its being likewise precedes its nonexistence in time.*[26]

... the Eternal is connected to that which originates in time ... For the ipseity of this Nature is such that It is ceaselessly being renewed and passing away, originating and ending.[27]

... there is nothing among the corporeal things ... except that its identity is renewed and its existence and individuality are not permanent.[28]

God causes the continuity of the world through constant re-creation and incessant renewal. In this way, God, who possesses the "quality of permanence and stability" due to His pure actuality, originates and subsists the world, whose "essence and ipseity are in incessant renewal."[29] The cosmic manifestation of this continuous re-creation of the world is universal substantial motion (*ḥaraka jawharīya*). All individuals that are in existence undergo motion and flux due to substantial motion, which is the result of the never-ending act of the divine existence. The continuous motion is a proof that "the Nature of corporeality is a substance whose being is [perpetually] flowing, continually renewed."[30] At this juncture, Ṣadrā relates the idea of the incessant renewal and substantial motion to

[24] Ibid., 52. Emphasis mine. [25] Ibid., 50. Emphasis mine.

[26] Mullā Ṣadrā, *The Wisdom of the Throne* (*al-Ḥikmat al-ʿArshiyya*), trans. James Winston Morris (Princeton, NJ: Princeton University Press, 1981), 119. Emphasis mine.

[27] Ṣadrā, *The Wisdom of the Throne*, 121–122. [28] Ṣadrā, *Mashāʿir*, 68.

[29] Ibid. 69. Agreeing with Ibn ʿArabī and his students, Ṣadrā holds that the following verses support this view: "Are they in doubt about the new creation?" 50:15; "From changing your forms and crating you again in forms that you know not" 56:61; also 27:88; If He so will, He can remove you and put (in your place) a new creation" 14:19; also 35;16; 39:67; 19:40.

[30] Ṣadrā, *The Wisdom of the Throne*, 123. He Here also claims that there is an agreement of "the most ancient philosophers concerning the transience and passing away of the world and the continual renewal of everything," ibid., 123.

physical motion. It is this "continual renewal of the state [of being] of a thing is the meaning of *motion*."[31]

Motion is an intellectual and relational entity, consisting of passing of a thing from potentiality to actuality. It is from *wujūd* in becoming and an origination that is realized gradually. Time is the quantity of this passage and renewal. *As for motion, it is the gradual passage from potentiality to actuality, and the time is the measure of it.*[32]

All existing beings undergo a process of reaching their telos and actualizing their potential. It is this journey from potentialities to actualities that is the basis of physical motion. And it is the permeation and expansion of *wujūd* as pure actuality that is the basis of actualization of potentialities. *Wujūd* is then the source of all acts and all effects in the cosmos and the proximate cause of all motion and all actualization.

To conclude, Ṣadrā places motion and time in this larger context of *wujūd* and offers a connection between the divine actuality and physical activity. The source of the entities' acts is the divine actuality. Participation in existence grounds their causal efficacy in terms of motion and physical activity. In this sense, Ṣadrā, in a quite similar fashion to Ibn Rushd, finds the basis of causal efficacy of beings in *wujūd* as pure existence and pure act.[33] To participate in existence is to participate in its actuality. The reality of existence-*qua*-existence is nothing "but full realization, actuality and manifestation."[34] This is why Ṣadrā writes that

[31] Ṣadrā, *Mashāʿir*, 69. [32] Ibid. Emphasis mine.

[33] In a quite similar fashion to Ibn Rushd and Ibn ʿArabī, Ṣadrā envisages a type of plurality in the simplicity of God: "The Pure One is the cause of all things and not of all things. Rather it is the beginning of everything and not all things. All things are in it and not in it. All things flow from it and subsist and are sustained by it and return to it. So, if someone says: how is it possible that things are from a simple one that has no duality or multiplicity in it in any sense? I say: because a pure simple one has nothing in it, but because it is a pure one, all things flow from it. Thus, when there was no existence, being flowed from it." In *Asfār*, VII: 351. Cited in Sajjad Rizvi, "Mullā Ṣadrā," *The Stanford Encyclopedia of Philosophy* (Summer 2009 Edition), ed. Edward N. Zalta: https://plato.stanford.edu/archives/sum2009/entries/Mullā-Ṣadrā/. Existence needs to be understood by bringing the opposites together. This "single and continuous existence is also conjoined and changing existence." Existence has "oneness that comprises all of its parts." Therefore, "if we say 'it is one', we would be right. If we say 'it is many', we would be right. If we say 'it is the same from the beginning of change to the end', we would be right. If we say 'it is changing at every moment', we would be right. If we say 'it is existent with all of its components', we would be right. And if we say 'it is nonexistent', we would be right": Ṣadrā, *Ḥudūth*, 70–71. Cited in, Ibrahim Kalın, *Mullā Ṣadrā* (New Delhi: Oxford University Press, 2014), 82.

[34] *Ṣadrā, Asfār*, I. 259.

"existence, insofar as it is existence ... is the agent of all agents, the form of all forms, and the goal of all goals."[35] However, a question arises here: If *wujūd* is "the agent of all agents," then how can entities be free? How can their agency be established? In my view, the question of freedom in Ṣadrā can be approached from two perspectives, from the perspective of existence and from the perspective of essence. I discuss these points in the next section.

9.3 EXISTENCE AND FREEDOM

In the previous section, we considered how Ṣadrā establishes the idea of participation through the concept of expansion and permeation of existence. The other important aspect of Ṣadrā's philosophy as pertains to this discussion is his understanding of the relationship of the divine attributes and *wujūd*. Recall that Ashʿarites make a distinction between God's attributes and God's essence in order to avoid the implication of eternal associates with God. They conclude that the divine attributes are coeternal with God. They are neither identical with nor separate from God. Ṣadrā, however, together with the Philosophers and Sufi Metaphysicians, argues that the divine attributes are identical to the divine existence. All attributes are concealed in and implied by *wujūd*. God is existence, loving, willing, knowing and so forth, all at the same time. To say *wujūd* is to say knowledge, will, power, life.

His attributes – transcendent is He – are the same as His essence (*dhāt*) ... That is to say, His *wujūd* – transcendent is He – which is His very reality, is itself the attributes of perfection ... The attributes, despite their plurality and multiplicity, exist by a single *wujūd*.[36]

Furthermore, "all of His qualities and attributes exist through a single *wujūd*, and it is the *wujūd* of the divine Self."[37] On the divine attribute of knowledge, for example, Ṣadrā writes the following:

Knowledge possesses a reality in the same way that *wujūd* possesses a reality. Just as the reality of *wujūd* is a single reality and, with its oneness, attaches itself to all things, it is necessary that *wujūd* repels nonexistence from all things, being the *wujūd* of all things. In the same way, the reality of knowledge is a single reality

[35] Ibid., I, 54. Notice that in this passage he reformulates Aristotelian efficient, formal, and final causes in terms of his own ontology.

[36] Ṣadrā, *Mashāʿir*, 59.

[37] Ṣadrā, *Asfār*, III. 142. For more on this, see Fazlur Rahman, *The Philosophy of Mullā Ṣadrā* (Albany: State University of New York Press, 1975), 141–146.

and, with its oneness, the knowledge of everything: "It leaves nothing, neither small nor big, but has enumerated them." (Qur'an 18:49)[38]

What is true for knowledge also applies to the divine attribute of power. For instance, "His power with its oneness is of necessity the power over all things, because His power is the reality of power. If it were not connected to all things, then His power would cause one thing to exist rather than another."[39] What is true for knowledge and power is also true for other divine attributes. Hence, "the same reasoning holds true for His will, His love, His life, and so on."[40]

This conception of the divine attributes provides the basis for the idea that when *wujūd* permeates into existence, all other attributes also permeate it. When *wujūd* expands, will, consciousness, and life also expand. These qualities, however, do not permeate the levels of the created order to the same degree. Entities participate in these qualities in accordance with their share from *wujūd*. In a similar fashion to Suhrawardī, Ṣadrā elaborates a gradational ontology. Entities are multiple because of the "gradation" (*tashkīk*) of existence. Existence expands upon essences and causes the modulation and gradation of existence (*tashkīk al-wujūd*) in the essences of entities. They are situated in the framework of this gradational ontology according to their intensity (*al-aqdamiyya wa-l-ashaddiyya*) of existence.[41] Entities participate in existence to differing degrees. This explains the emergence of perfection and imperfection in the world. Every existent is a differentiated manifestation (*takhaṣṣūs*) of existence, which entails infinitely variegated forms. Essences are principles of differentiation that cause entities to be in different degrees of intensity and diminution or perfection and imperfection:

essence is united with existence *in concreto* in a kind of essential unity. When the mind analyzes them into two things, it asserts the precedence of one over the other *in concreto*. Now, this [reality that precedes the other] is existence because it is the principle in being the reality emanating from the [First] Principle (*al-mabda'*). As for the essence, it is united with and predicated of existence not like an attached accident but in its own reality [as essentially united with existence]. Insofar as the mind is concerned, the essence precedes the latter [i.e., existence] because essence is the principle in mental judgments.[42]

Expansion of *wujūd* is expansion of knowledge, will, and power to all beings, including inanimate ones. However, these qualities exist in a

[38] Ṣadrā, *Mashā'ir*, 60. [39] Ibid., 61. [40] Ibid. [41] *Ṣadrā, Asfār*, I. 42–43.
[42] Ibid., I. 56. Cited in, Kalın, *Mullā Ṣadrā*, 94.

hierarchy. Human beings are the culmination of this process, and they experience will, power, and knowledge at the highest possible level. Other entities, animate and inanimate, get their shares from the divine qualities to the extent that they participate in existence. This also implies that consciousness exists throughout the cosmos in a gradational way, which is consistent with the model of the universe as a living being.[43]

The abode of existence is one, and *the whole universe is a big living being*. Its dimensions are conjoined with one another, but not in the sense of the conjunction of measurement and the unification of surfaces and environs. Rather, what is meant is that each degree of existential perfection must be adjacent *to a degree that befits* it in (a similar) existential perfection.[44]

To conclude, in Ṣadrā's system, creaturely freedom and agency are established through the concepts of expansion of and participation in existence. Expansion of *wujūd* implies that the divine attributes concealed in *wujūd* are given to the created order in accordance with entities' capacities. Participation in *wujūd* implies participation in the divine qualities such as knowledge, will, and power. By participating in *wujūd*, we also participate in the divine freedom. Therefore, we are free.

9.4 ESSENCE AND FREEDOM

The question of freedom in Ṣadrā's system can also be approached from the perspective of essences. It has already been mentioned that the notion of modulation or gradation of existence (*tashkīk al-wujūd*) in Ṣadrā's ontology explains the differentiation of beings. Existence is a "simple reality," yet it is differentiated through "intensification and diminution" and made "*more perfect and stronger*" in some beings than others.[45] What exactly causes this differentiation? Does existence particularize itself? Or does existence become particularized by permeating into essences? Do essences really exist? What role do they play in Sadrean metaphysics?

Some modern commentators on Ṣadrā's philosophy argue that Ṣadrā replaces Suhrawardī's essentialist metaphysics with an existentialist

[43] This idea of universe as a "living being" has a long history among Muslims and ancient Greeks. For a short history of this idea see Richard Sorabji, *Animal Minds and Human Morals: The Origins of the Western Debate* (Ithaca, NY: Cornell University Press, 1993), 12–16.

[44] Ṣadrā, *Asfār*, II. 342. [45] Ibid., I, 36.

metaphysics. It is suggested in these writings that Ṣadrā defends the primacy of existence to transcend the predicaments created by Suhrawardī's primacy of essence. Surprisingly, they claim that Suhrawardī and the entire early Islamic philosophical and mystical tradition devalue existence as an accident and reduce it to a mental concept, a predicate, or an attribute that adds nothing to and extracts nothing from the actual reality of things. Suhrawardī constructs existence as a secondary intelligible (*maʿqūl thānī*), and Ṣadrā establishes existence as the principal reality.[46] These claims, however, lack textual support in Suhrawardī's writings and also appear to overlook earlier treatments of the concept of existence (*wujūd*) by other philosophers and mystics, some of which were explored in the previous chapters, before Ṣadrā.

It is true that Ṣadrā's ontology revolves around the concept of existence and rejects that essences are the fundamental reality of things. Existence cannot be reduced to a common attribute, predicate, a secondary intelligible, or a universal to be found only in the mind. It must be remembered, though, that neither Suhrawardī nor Ibn ʿArabī and his followers such as Qūnawī and Qayṣarī describe existence as a predicate that adds nothing to and extracts nothing from the reality of things. They all agree with Ṣadrā that existence must be prior to essence, for the simple reason that God is pure existence and devoid of essence. Essences are perceived as concomitants of *wujūd*'s infinity and as objects of the divine knowledge. Essences derive their existence from God. God bestows *wujūd* to essences which, by themselves, cannot smell the "perfume of *wujūd*." All of these ontologies examined in previous chapters affirm the primacy of existence and establish the reality of essences as absolutely dependent on existence.

Thus, Ṣadrā's position on essences is more complex than a simple rejection. Establishing existence as the principal reality does not lead to total rejection of essences. Here it will be helpful to consider Ṣadrā's

[46] For the defense of this position, see Fazlur Rahman, *The Philosophy of Mullā Ṣadrā*, 27, 33, 141–146; Seyyed Hossein Nasr, *Sadr al-Din al-Shirazi and his Transcendent Theosophy* (Tehran: Imperial Iranian Academy of Philosophy, 1977); M. Aminrazawi, ed., *The Islamic Intellectual Tradition in Persia* (Richmond: Curzon Press, 1996), 135; Ibrahim Kalin, "Editor's Introduction" to Mullā Ṣadrā, *Kitāb al-Mashāʿir*, trans. Seyyed Hossein Nasr (Provo, UT: Brigham Young University Press, 2014), xx. Sajjad Rizvi argues that reading Suhrawardī through a Sadrean lens is rather anachronistic, for the question of the primacy of existence or essence was not formulated before Ṣadrā. "Islamic Subversion of the Existence–Essence Distinction? Suhrawardī's Visionary Hierarchy of Lights," in *Asian Philosophy*, 9.3 (1999): 224. In fact, our reading of Suhrawardī indicates that what Suhrawardī means by light is not different from what Ṣadrā means by existence.

perspectivalism, which holds that the reality of essences is such that it lends itself to be approached from multiple points of view or, what Ṣadrā calls "perspective" (*iʿtibār*). As he notes, without the principle of multiplicity of perspectives "wisdom would have been lost."[47] Accordingly, I would argue that Ṣadrā accepts the reality of essences from one perspective and rejects it from another. Since essences are, in fact, particularizations of existence, there are no essences *in concreto*. However, they exist in the divine knowledge as the principles of instantiations. So, essences do exist in a certain sense, and this suffices to render them principles of differentiation in Ṣadrā's metaphysics. It is this nature of essences that makes them the basis of creaturely freedom and agency.

In a way, Ṣadrā denies the existence of essences. When we say, "a rock exists," *in concreto* the existence and the essence of rock are not two distinct things. *Wujūd* exists "as the rock," or the rock appears as a particular modality of existence. In this sense, there is only *wujūd* and its individuations. Thus, essences can only be mental concepts that emerge when entities are analyzed by the mind. In fact, existence and essence form a single unity *in concreto*.

Essences, however, exist in the divine knowledge. Hence, when *wujūd* appears as a rock, *wujūd* particularizes itself in accordance with the essences of entities as they are the divine knowledge. Thus, this is not arbitrary self-determination of *wujūd*. Existence penetrates essences as they are known by God. The modulation of existence occurs in accordance with entities' essences or archetypes, or capacities in the divine knowledge. According to Ṣadrā's account of the divine knowledge, The Necessary Being, which is pure *wujūd*, knows itself and through this knowledge knows all beings. It is "present to itself" and "intellects the totality of things."

> The necessary being intellects its own essence, because its essence is simple and disengaged from mixture with deficiency, contingency, and nonexistence. It is present to itself without any veil. Knowledge is nothing other than the presence of *wujūd* without any veil. Every perception is produced by a mode of disengaging from matter and its veils, because matter is the source of nonexistence and absence ... Its essence is the subject that *intellects itself and the object of its own intellection*, by the most exalted intellect ... through its own essence, *it intellects the totality of things in an intellection that contains absolutely no multiplicity*.[48]

[47] Ṣadrā, *Īqāẓ al-Nāʾimīn*, ed. Muhammad Khwansari (Bunyād-i Ḥikmat-i Islāmi-yi Ṣadrā (Sadra Islamic Philosophy Research Institute, AH.1384), 54.

[48] Ṣadrā, *Mashāʿir*, 55. Emphasis mine.

Wujūd implies knowledge. As discussed above, all of His qualities and attributes exist through *wujūd*. God, the pure *wujūd*, knows Himself and the totality of beings without undermining the divine simplicity and purity. God knows all essences, for without this knowledge, particularization of *wujūd* in entities would not be possible. These essences, known by God, are existentiated with the bestowal of existence.

His knowledge, which is His presence to Himself, cannot be mixed with the absence of anything. How could this be, since He is the Reality that *bestows reality* upon all realities.[49]

All existences have a single origin, which is the Reality that *bestows reality upon all realities* . . . It is the Origin; what is other than it is its manifestations (*ẓuhurāt*) and theophanies (*tajalliyāt*).[50]

Because of his conviction that mental existence without existentiation *in concreto* is possible, Ṣadrā states that an "essence might be actualized in mind without having to be actualized *in concreto*."[51] In this sense, existence and essence are a single unity *in concreto* and cannot be separated, yet they can exist separately in the mind. As objects of the divine knowledge, essences do not have real existence. They are known but not existentiated. These "fixed essences" exist only in the divine knowledge until they receive their share from the *wujūd*.

Who made the clouds of doubt in my heart through the rising of the Sun of the Truth, and Who established *me* on the "firm doctrine" in this life and in the Hereafter. Existences are the principal realities, *whereas the "fixed essences" have never smelled the perfume of real existence.*[52]

Therefore, existence and essence do not relate to each other as two independently existing entities. *Wujūd* exists by itself, and essences exist due to *wujūd*. *Wujūd* is not an accident. The relationship between existence and essence is not comparable to the relationship of substance and accident. *Wujūd* does not inhere in an entity as an accident that already exists. *Wujūd* appears *as* the entity with all of its qualities. As such, essences are absolutely dependent on *wujūd* for their existentiation. Only *wujūd* exists by itself, and "all essence other than *wujūd* is existent through *wujūd*."[53]

Now, we say that it [*wujūd*] emanates upon all that is other than itself, without this emanation producing an association with it; for what is other than it is, in

[49] Ibid., 60. [50] Ibid., 58. Emphasis mine.
[51] Ibid., 13. Kalin's translation uses "quiddity" instead of "essence." I have modified the translation for consistency.
[52] Ibid., 37. Emphasis mine. [53] Ibid., 50.

reality, contingent essences and deficient essences – existences that depend upon something other than themselves … *Now all that whose wujūd depends upon another is in need of that other and finds its full completion with it, and this other is its origin and its end.*[54]

Despite their absolute dependence on *wujūd*, essences remain vitally important. Essences do not exist by themselves as independent entities and cannot "taste the smell of existence" without the existentiating act of *wujūd*. They do, however, have an existence in relation to *wujūd*. This is why Ṣadrā presents essences as principles of differentiation.

The reality of *wujūd*, while being individualized by itself, is differentiated according to the differentiation of contingent essences (*bi-ḥasabi ikhtilāfi māhiyyāti*), each of which is united with one of its stages.[55]

In other contexts, Ṣadrā describes the process of existentiation of essences using concepts and analogies drawn from earlier Muslim philosophers and mystics.

When the Sun of the Truth rises and its penetrating Light spreads in all regions of contingent beings, *expanding upon* the "temples" (*hayākil*) of *essences*, it becomes evident and manifest that all to which the name *wujūd* is given is nothing but a state among the states of the One, the self-Subsistent, and a flash among the flashes of the Light of lights.[56]

The relation between it (the Necessary Being) and that which other than it is analogous to the relation between the rays of the sun – supposing that it subsisted by itself – with the bodies that are illuminated by it and are dark in themselves.[57]

On the one hand, there is only *wujūd*, for *wujūd* appears in the form of essences. On the other hand, there are also essences, for "light spreads in all regions of contingent beings and expanding upon the temples of essences." Entities are thus modalities of *wujūd*. However, there are also essences, and although they do not exist without *wujūd*, they nevertheless have a sort of existence. Existence is bestowed upon the temples of essences. Hence, "when the agent has bestowed existence on essence, it has bestowed its *wujūd*. And when it has bestowed *wujūd*, it has bestowed this *wujūd* by itself."[58] Since the light of *wujūd* "shines upon all

[54] Ibid., 53.

[55] Ibid., 10. One of the terms frequently used by Ṣadrā in these contexts is *ja'l*. See for example, *Asfār*, I. 65–66. This term signifies, as Kalin writes, "putting something into a specific state or condition in conformity with its essential properties." See *Mashā'ir*, 81, n. 26. If this is true, the creation occurs in accordance with its essential qualities, not arbitrarily.

[56] Ibid., 58. [57] Ibid., 53. [58] Ibid., 25.

contingent beings," there is only *wujūd* modifying itself in essences. But this does not render essences nonexistent, for "the sun of the Truth *manifests itself in all essences that are contingent*."[59] Lāhijī explains this point as follows:

The relation of effusion to the source of effusion is like the relation of a ray to the source of the ray itself. Existences are illuminative effusions from the *wujūd*, which is the true reality and is purely self-subsisting to the essences of contingent beings and fixed essences (*al-māhiyyāt al-thābitāt*). Relations between existences are themselves the realization of things; the essences have no realization in principle and by themselves. *They have not smelled the perfume of existence primarily and by themselves*; rather, the judgement of existence applies to them only in relation to what is attached to them [in the extramental world]. There are two ways of looking at contingent beings and particular things that exist in the world: [The first is] a summary consideration, by which they are judged to exist and [by which] they do exist. [The second is] detailed consideration, because every contingent being is a composite pair and has two aspects: the aspect that looks toward its Lord, and the aspect that looks toward itself. The aspect of the Lord is *wujūd* [and is] included in the [which states that] "everything is perishing except its [His] Face." The aspect of itself is the essence included in the things that perish by themselves and have not smelled the perfume of existence ... That is why it has been said that essences are nonexistent by themselves and existent [only] in judgement.[60]

Essences exist only in a certain sense and are nonexistent "by themselves." Everything has two aspects. With respect to themselves, things are mere essences that "have not smelled the smell of (real) existence." With respect to their Lord, they have real existence as a result of the bestowal of existence. This dual nature implies that entities have a type of existence before their existentiation and the bestowal of *wujūd* turns them into real beings.[61] This why Ṣadrā also frequently asserts that a thing exists as composition of essence and existence.

Every existent *in concreto* is other than *wujūd*; and there is in it a blemish of *composition* ... in contrast to pure *wujūd*. And because of this, the Philosophers have said: All contingent beings – that is, all things that possess essence – are a compound pair, and there is nothing among the essences that is a simple.[62]

The *wujūd* of all existents is their very essence *in concreto* and is united with it in some kind of *unification*."[63]

[59] Ibid., 20.
[60] Muhammad Jaʿfar Lāhijī, *Sharḥ Risālat al-Mashāʿir*, ed. Sayyid Jalal al-Din Ashtiyani (Tehran: Muassasa-yi Intisharat-i Amir Kabir, 1376/1997), 147. Translated by Kalin in *Mashāʿir*, 87–88, n. 56.
[61] Also see, Lāhijī, *Sharḥ Risālat al-Mashāʿir*, 161.
[62] Ṣadrā, *Mashāʿir*, 12.
[63] Ibid., 30.

> Therefore, it is necessary that *wujūd* be exactly that something by which the essence is made to exist and with which the essence is united *in concreto*.[64]

It should also be mentioned that Ṣadrā's terminology concerning permeation of existence upon entities, which includes "pervasion of existence" (*sarayān al-wujūd*), "expansion of existence" (*inbisāṭ al-wujūd*), and "Breath of the Compassionate," suggests that *wujūd* is given, expands upon, flows into, and encompasses something that already has a kind of existence, albeit only in the divine knowledge. For, "*if wujūd* were not to exist in, and also [if] *māhiyya were* not to exist in itself, then how could ever be existent?"[65] As such, there appears to be an agreement between Ṣadrā and other thinkers examined in this book. This is why he writes thus:

> According to the verifiers (*muḥaqqiqīn*) among the sages (*ʿurafāʾ*) and the theosophers (*mutaʾallihīn*) among the Philosophers (*ḥukamāʾ*), it is clear and firmly established that the existence of everything is nothing but *the reality of its identity*, which is related to the existence of the Real and Self-Subsisting One and which is the basis of judgment for the being-ness of things. The most appropriate way to describe this is to say that [their existence] is a mode of their actual identity, which is related to the Divine Existence.[66]

Moreover, Ṣadrā's positions on a number of theological issues are also based on the assumption that essences exist in a certain sense. For example, when discussing the emergence of evil in the world, he writes (as cited above) that "*God's existence is pure and unencumbered by complexity* such as an essence ... The reality of existence (*ḥaqīqat al-wujūd*) is identical to God. Existence without essence is the utmost perfection because of its purity (*amran basīṭan*)."[67] Ṣadrā identifies the perfection of God with pure existence. Imperfection is related to essences. Existence without essence is the utmost perfection. Imperfection occurs at lower levels because of the impurity of essences.[68]

It is also important for our discussion that Ṣadrā does not see the relationship between existence and essences as one of temporality. That is, existence does not precede essence in terms of temporal priority; it does so through existential priority. This why Ṣadrā writes that "neither

[64] Ibid., 18. [65] Ibid., 15. [66] Ṣadrā, *Asfār*, I. 116. [67] Ibid., VI. 17–18.

[68] See also: "Contingent beings are differentiated from each other by perfection and deficiency, self-sufficiency and poverty. Now, deficiency and poverty are not things that are postulated by the reality of *wujūd* itself ... Deficiency, shortcomings, contingency, and the like come only from what is secondary and caused (entities), and the emanated is not equal to the source of emanation." Ṣadrā, *Mashāʿir*, 54.

māhiyya nor *wujūd* possesses antecedence or precedence in relation to the other."[69] In addition,

The anteriority of *wujūd* to *māhiyya* is not the same as the anteriority of cause to effect . . . Rather, it is like the anteriority of the essential to the accidental, of the real to the metaphorical.[70]

Here, Ṣadrā's perception of essences comes close to those of Ibn ʿArabī, Qūnawī, and Qayṣarī, who argue that essences are coeternal objects of the divine knowledge. The infinity and eternity of the divine knowledge imply that essences have always existed in the divine knowledge. "The origination of an essence follows from the origination of its concrete individual instances, and *its eternity likewise follows from their eternity*."[71] Essences are, then, originated in one sense and eternal in another. In terms of their existence *in concreto*, they are originated in time. In terms of the divine knowledge, however, essences are eternal and uncreated. They are "forms in the divine Decree" according to which God continuously create the world.[72]

What is with God (in His knowledge) are the actual primordial realities (*al-ḥaqāʾiq al-muḥaṣṣala al-mutaʾaṣṣila*) (of contingent things), from which those things are descended at the level of shadows.[73]

The idea that essences are uncreated and eternal leads to the conclusion that God eternally knows essences but does not cause the type of essence an entity has. Thus, although entities are completely dependent on God for their existentiation, they can be regarded as causes of themselves with respect to their essences. This is why Ṣadrā states that "what is essential in something is *not caused by anything but its own essence*."[74] It is important to note here that God does not cause but only knows essences as they are in the divine knowledge. God is the cause of the existentiation of essences *in concreto*. Without God, essences cannot "smell" the perfume of real existence. If essences are not caused, they can be understood as uncaused causes of themselves. In other words, an entity is not caused by God in terms of its essence but in terms of its existence. It is here that one can speak of the self-determination of entities. As Ṣadrā puts it,

69 Ibid., 25. 70 Ibid. 71 Mullā Ṣadrā, *The Wisdom of the Throne*, 124.
72 Ibid., 125.
73 Ibid., 105. For a more extensive discussion of Ṣadrā's views on the divine knowledge, see Fazlur Rahman, *The Philosophy of Mullā Ṣadrā*, 146–163.
74 Ibid., 122.

actually existing beings are many in the external world, but the source of their existence and the owner of their realization is one and single. And it is the reality of expanding being itself, not something else. *The source of their plurality is self-determination.*[75]

God knows the essences of entities and existentiates them without determining their essences. If entities are uncaused causes of themselves, in a certain way, this can be the basis of creaturely freedom. Essences can be seen as the principles of agency and freedom of the created order. Thus "the Pure One is the *cause of all things and not of all things*."[76] It is "the cause of all things" to the extent that they have existence. It is "not the cause of all things" to the extent that essences are uncreated and uncaused. From the perspective of existence, God is the only causal power. From the perspective of essences, entities are their own causes and, thus, free.

9.5 CONCLUSION

In Ṣadrā's ontology, entities are particularizations of an all-inclusive reality of existence. Existence expands upon specific individual beings. It is this expansion that is the basis of entities' causality, agency, and freedom. When existence expands and permeates all levels of existence, it also actualizes potentialities of entities/essences. The actuality of existence is the basis for the actualization and, thus, of the acts and motion of entities. Provided existence is the basis for all attributes, the expansion of existence implies expansion of will, consciousness, and power. Hence, to participate in existence is to participate in will, consciousness, and power to the extent allowed by the capacities of entities. Existence in Ṣadrā's framework plays a very similar role to that played by "light" in Suhrawardī's system. Both thinkers agree that to exist is a mode of participation. Things exist by participating in the all-inclusive reality of existence or of light. This participation in turn grounds both thinkers' views on causality. A similar continuity can also be observed in their treatment of the question of freedom. Ṣadrā, like Ibn ʿArabī, Qūnawī, and Qayṣarī, uses essences to establish agency and freedom in the created order.

[75] Ṣadrā, *Asfār*, I, 321. Cited in, Kalın, *Mullā Ṣadrā*, 86.

[76] An interesting metaphor to think about the relationship of existence an essence is that of ink and different letters written with it. Ink manifests itself in many forms of letters. Letters here are multiple modifications of the ink. One needs to see both the ink and the letters. Although the letters cannot exist without the ink, a meaning can be assigned to them as modifiers of existence. See for example, Ḥaydar Āmulī, *Jāmiʿ al-Asrār wa-Manbāʿ al-Anwār*, Henry Corbin and Uthman Yahya (Tehran-Paris: Bibliothèque iranien, 1969), 106–107.

10

Occasionalism in the Modern Context

The Case of Said Nursi

Said Nursi is a Muslim scholar who wrote the *Risale-i Nur* (Epistles of Light), a voluminous work of Qurʾanic exegesis.[1] Nursi adheres to basic principles of Ashʿarite occasionalism and argues that God creates both cause and effect concomitantly on a self-imposed habitual path. He holds that secondary causality is inefficacious. The concept of habituality secures regularity and horizontal continuity of natural processes. In this view, the concept of natural law is a mental construction without an extramental reality and a misinterpretation of the regularity and consistency of the divine creative act. Entities are composed of atoms, which are loci of the divine attributes. Miracles are breaks in the habitual creation of God.

There are three factors that make Nursi's work worthy of attention in this study. First, as modern works, Nursi's writings indicate that occasionalism is still a viable option for some Muslim thinkers. This modern iteration also suggests that occasionalism can be seen as a living and vibrant tradition with a high degree of adaptability. In previous chapters,

[1] Nursi was a prolific author, but he did not write in a systematic fashion. To understand Nursi's metaphysical cosmology and theory of causation, we have to collect bits and pieces from this large corpus (5,913 pages) and bring them together in a coherent fashion. To the extent that he is clear, I will follow him. When he is not clear, I will have to offer my interpretation – not in an arbitrary fashion but by taking into consideration the sources that shaped his worldview and his corpus in its totality. I will also point to some parallels between Nursi and Western thinkers. For more information on Nursi, see Zeki Saritoprak, "Bediüzzaman Said Nursi," in *The Islamic World*, ed. Andrew Rippin (London and New York: Routledge, 2008), 396–402; Zeki Saritoprak, "Said Nursi," in *Islamic Studies*, ed. Andrew Rippin (New York: Oxford University Press, 2011).

I have examined how occasionalist theologians in the middle period, such as Rāzī and Jurjānī, interacted with the medieval philosophy of nature, how they reformulated Ashʿarite atomism in light of Euclidian geometry after Ibn Sīnā's criticism, and how their skepticism toward Aristotelian and Ptolemaic models produced highly original philosophy of science. These thinkers' works reflected the tendencies of the occasionalist tradition in the context of premodern science. Similarly, Nursi's work presents an interesting case to understand certain aspects of occasionalism's engagement with modern science. In fact, Nursi's case introduces one of the earliest and most comprehensive attempts to reconcile modern science and occasionalist worldview. Nursi was active when materialist and positivist interpretations of modern science circulated among Ottoman intellectuals at the end of the nineteenth and the beginning of the twentieth century. August Comte's, Claude Bernard's, and F. Ludwig Büchner's writings were quite influential in these circles. In particular, Büchner's *Force and Matter* (*Kraft und Stoff*) was widely circulated and played an important role in the propagation of scientific materialism among the younger generations of the Ottoman intellectual elite, some of whom, including the likes of M. Kemal Atatürk, were to become the founding fathers of the new Turkish Republic.[2] It was quite common to associate the new sciences (Tr. *fünūn-u cedīde*) imported from Europe with materialism and positivism. It is in this context, Nursi attempts to offer occasionalism as a framework in which the findings of the new sciences can be interpreted.[3]

Second, Nursi's case presents an intriguing interaction between occasionalism and Ibn ʿArabī's metaphysics in the contemporary context. He attempts to enhance and reiterate classical Ashʿarite positions on

[2] For more information about the late nineteenth- and early twentieth-century reception of scientific materialism and positivism by Ottoman intellectuals, see Şükrü Hanioğlu, *Atatürk: An Intellectual Biography* (Princeton, NJ: Princeton University Press, 2011); Süleyman Hayri Bolay, *Türkiye'de Ruhçu ve Maddeci Düşüncenin Mücadelesi* (Ankara: Nobel Kitap, 2008).

[3] Although Nursi is the most influential representative of late Ottoman occasionalism, there are also other, lesser-known occasionalists such as Ali Sedad and Hamdi Yazir; see Nazif Muhtaroğlu and Ozgur Koca, "Late Ottoman Occasionalists and Modern Science," in *Occasionalism Revisited: New Essays From the Islamic and Western Philosophical Traditions*, Ed. Nazif Muhtaroglu (Abu Dhabi: Kalam Research and Media, 2017), 83–101; Nazif Muhtaroglu, "Ali Sedad Bey's (d.1900) Kavāid al-Taḥavvulāt fī Ḥarakāt-al-Zarrāt (Principles of Transformation in the Motion of Particles)" in *Oxford Handbook of Islamic Philosophy*, eds. Khaled El-Rouayheb and Sabine Schmidke (New York: Oxford University Press, 2017), 586–606.

secondary causality, atoms, and physical laws by using Ibn ʿArabī's theory of the divine names – the basic premise of which is that the world is a multiplicity of loci for the unceasing and ever-changing manifestations of the divine qualities. For example, for Nursi, although secondary causality is inefficacious, as occasionalists believe, it still functions as a *veil* between God and the world, as Ibn ʿArabī and his followers hold. Moreover, it is the very existence of this veil that makes the world a more expository "loci" for the continuous manifestations of the divine names and attributes. Similarly, he agrees with the Ashʿarites that entities are composed of indivisible atoms. He then draws on Ibn ʿArabī's work to depict atoms as loci for the manifestations of the divine names. Atoms are marked by poverty and need, which make them perfect loci to reflect the divine qualities. As such, his theory of causality represents an interesting meeting point of *kalām* and Sufi metaphysics.

Third, Nursi also introduces a highly innovative idea that I call causal disproportionality. As far as I am aware, this concept does not exist in any of the previous occasionalists' writings. The concept of causal disproportionality suggests that effect/s are never reducible to their cause/s. There is always a vertical distance between cause and effect. Furthermore, within this distance, the divine qualities and names are continuously manifested. As such, all causal relations are mirrors reflecting the divine qualities. To justify the belief in the ever-present disproportionality of cause and effect, Nursi advances several arguments, which will also be examined in the following pages.

10.1 NURSI'S OCCASIONALISM AND SUFI METAPHYSICS

Nursi upholds the basic tenets of the Ashʿarite occasionalist doctrine of causality. For Nursi, it is God who creates both cause and effect and attaches them to each other.

> The All-Glorious Maker, Who is powerful over all things, has created causes, and so too does He create the effects. Through His wisdom, He ties the effect to the cause
> (*Sâni-i Zülcelâl esbabı halk etmiş, müsebbebâtı da halk ediyor. Hikmetiyle, müsebbebâtı esbaba bağlıyor*).[4]

[4] Said Nursi, *The Flashes: From the Risale-i Nur Collection*, trans. Şükran Vahide (Istanbul: Sözler Neşriyat, 1995), 244. I generally rely on Şükran Vahide's translations but modify them occasionally. Note that her translations are also available at www.nur.gen.tr/en .html.

As with earlier Muslim occasionalists, Nursi distinguishes between causal proximity and causal connection. He writes that "constant conjunction is one thing, necessary connection is another (*iktiran ayrıdır, illet ayrıdır*)."[5] Causal relations in the world are orderly and consistent. The regularity of cause and effect relationships might be deceiving in that when "the two things *come together* or *are together*" we suppose that "the two things cause one another."[6] Since in causal relationships one constantly observes that the nonexistence of one thing is the cause of the nonexistence of the effect, one then wrongly supposes that the existence of one thing is also the cause of the existence of the other. This is a mistake, for "God creates cause and effect together *directly*. In order to demonstrate His wisdom and the manifestation of His Names, by establishing an apparent causal relationship and connection through order and conjunction, He makes causes and nature a veil to the hand of His power."[7]

For Nursi, the true meaning of the statement "there is no god but God" entails that everything is absolutely dependent on God in its creation and subsistence. The robust oneness of God negates the idea of intermediation, and thus secondary causality, between God and cosmos. No aspect of divinity is shared. If it were, it would imply 'independence' from God. Things are in a state of absolute need and poverty under God. Thus, Nursi concludes, "the divine unity and majesty demand that causes withdraw their hands and have no true effect (*esbab ellerini çeksinler tesir-i hakikîden*)."[8] This is because "just as it is impossible for the Necessarily Existent One to have any partner or counterpart, so too is the interference of others in His sovereignty and in His creation of beings impossible and precluded."[9]

As discussed above, Ashʿarites understand the divine attributes as neither separate from nor identical to God. The attributes are all pervasive and thus are the real causes of events. This robust understanding of the divine attributes and names leads to the negation of causal power on the part of created beings. Nursi echoes this Ashʿarite claim when he argues that "no aspect of it (the earth) – whether particular or universal – can be outside the divine will, choice, and purpose. However, as is required by His wisdom, the Possessor of absolute power makes apparent causes a

5 Ibid., 182. 6 Ibid. Emphasis mine.
7 Ibid., 244. Emphasis mine; translation modified.
8 Nursi, *The Words: From the Risale-i Nur Collection*, trans. Şükran Vahide (revised edition) (Istanbul: Sözler Neşriyat, 2004), 301.
9 Nursi, *The Flashes*, 241.

veil to His disposals."[10] Nursi's discussion of the name of the Creator sheds further light on our topic. Nursi holds that for one to penetrate the real meaning of this name, one has to travel through certain stages. The true understanding of this name necessitates that God is the creator of all beings. As Nursi puts it:

> If you want to draw close to Him through His Name of Creator, you have to have a relationship through the particularities of your own Creator, then in regard to the Creator of all mankind, then through the title of Creator of all living creatures, then through the Name of Creator of all beings. Otherwise you will remain in shadow and only find a minor manifestation.[11]

Nursi's denial of the ontological independence of secondary causality can also be understood in relation to his ethical/spiritual concerns. According to Nursi, the emphasis on the divine unity in Islam sets the gaze on the real cause of phenomena, God, and thus paves the way toward an "authentic worship" (*ubûdiyet-i halise*), the most important characteristics of which are sincerity in faith/acts, submission to the will of God, and breaking the ego. Nursi writes:

> Islam is the religion of the true affirmation of divine unity and, thus, dismisses intermediaries and causes (*İslâmiyet, tevhid-i hakikî dinidir ki; vasıtaları, esbabları ıskat ediyor*). It breaks egotism and establishes sincere worship. It cuts at the root of every sort of false dominicality, starting from that of the soul, and rebuffs it (*Nefsin rubûbiyetinden tut, ta her nevi rubûbiyet-i batılayı kat'ediyor, reddediyor*).[12]

The foundation of worship for Nursi is supplication and beseeching Almighty God with a sincere heart and deep realization of one's own impotence and poverty, breaking the ego and showing deep humility before God in His presence, and offering thanks for everything.[13] This goal can be attained by someone who comprehends the absolute dependence of everything on God. However, secondary causality, if not

[10] Nursi, *The Words*, 187.

[11] Nursi, *The Words*, 215. He also argues that it is an error to emphasize just one of these attributes and downplay others. They all are equally substantial. He believes that excessive emphasis on *wujūd* might lead to pantheism, where the distinction between God and cosmos no longer exists, and therefore such attributes and names as Generous, Forgiver, etc., lose their literal meaning.

[12] Nursi, *The Letters: From the Risale-i Nur Collection*, trans. Şükran Vahide (Istanbul: Sözler Neşriyat, 1994), 500.

[13] For Nursi's understanding of the basis and essence of worship, see Nursi, *The Letters*, 521–532.

understood correctly, may be illusionary and distracting. It can prevent one from fixing one's gaze on God. The central tenets of Islamic spiritual life, such as the purity of intention and certainty, can only truly be realized if one locates secondary causality in its proper place. For example, if one understands that all natural phenomena are created directly by God, this leads to a state of "living in the presence of God" (*huzûr-u daimî*), which is the definition of perfection in religion.[14]

> By attaining a sense of the divine presence through the strength of certain, affirmative belief and through the lights proceeding from reflective thought on creatures that leads to knowledge of the Maker; by thinking that the Compassionate Creator is all-present and seeing; and by not seeking the attention of any other than He, and realizing that looking to others in His presence or seeking help from them is contrary to right conduct in *His presence*, one may be saved from such hypocrisy and gain sincerity.[15]

In accordance with the Ash'arite tradition, Nursi holds that God creates on a self-imposed habitual path. The world is consistent and natural phenomena are predictable. What we perceive as natural laws are actually habits (Tr. *âdet*) of God.[16] This is why Nursi also calls the body of laws governing the physical world "şeriat-i fitriyye" or "şeriat-i kübrâ."

> Through His will, He has determined a manifestation of the Greater Shari'a, the Laws of Creation, which consists of the Divine laws concerning the ordering of all motion in the universe, and determined the nature of beings, which is only to be a mirror to that manifestation in things, and to be a reflection of it. And through His power, He has created the face of that nature which has received external existence.[17]

By referring to the body of laws governing the physical world as a type of "şeriat," Nursi suggests that the physical laws govern the behavior of not only inanimate but also animate, and not only nonconscious but also conscious beings.[18] Physical interactions are law-like and physical laws are helpful devices to understand and interpret the world. However, the physical laws do not govern the world; they are simply mathematical structures that allow us to grasp the law-like manner in which God

[14] Nursi, *The Words*, 441. [15] Nursi, *The Flashes*, 218. Emphasis mine.

[16] See for example, Nursi, *The Flashes*, 64. Thus, studying the nature is the same as studying some character traits of God.

[17] Nursi, *The Flashes*, 247.

[18] However, as we discuss in the following pages, this robust understanding of physical laws does not lead Nursi to a denial of human freedom. He locates human will in a non-nomological domain beyond causality, where physical laws do not apply.

creates in the world.[19] The law-like relations that we typically think of as holding between cause and effect are actually grounded in the self-imposed habits of God. The attribution of a creative power to the physical laws, which exist as abstract mathematical structures, is an error. Nursi provides a comparison to explain this point. A man enters into "a palace in an empty desert adorned with all the fruits of civilization." Then attempts to provide an explanation for the existence of palace without reference to "no one from outside."

Later, he saw a notebook in which had been written the plan and programs of the palace's construction, an index of its contents and the rules of its administration. For sure, the notebook too, which was without hand, eye, or implement, like the rest of the objects in the palace, was completely lacking in the ability to construct and decorate the palace. But since he saw that in comparison with all the other things, the notebook was related to the whole palace by reason of its including all its theoretical laws, he was obliged to say: "There, it is this notebook that has organized, ordered and adorned the palace, and has fashioned all these objects and set them in their places."[20]

Physical laws have mental existence (*vücud-u ilmî*) with no corresponding extramental existence (*vücud-u haricî*) out there in the world.[21] Drawing

[19] A similar thought was also expressed by Thomas Reid: "Supposing that all the phenomena that fall within the reach of our senses, were accounted for from the general laws of nature, justly deduced from experience; that is, supposing natural philosophy brought to its utmost perfection, it does not discover the efficient cause of any one phenomenon in nature. The laws of nature are the rules according to which the effects are produced; but there must be a cause which operates according to these rules. *The rules of navigation never navigated a ship*. The rules of architecture never built a house." (EAP 1.6, 38) https://plato.stanford.edu/entries/reid/.

[20] Nursi, *The Flashes*, 242.

[21] Nursi is not alone among contemporary Muslim thinkers in seeing the natural laws as principles regulating our interaction with the world without any ontological reality. Muhammad Baqr al-Sadr (1935–1980) states the following: "According to our view of causality, which asserts that causality is a rational principle above experimentation the situation is completely different with regard to various aspects. First, causality is not limited to the natural phenomena that appear in the experiment. Rather, it is a general law of existence at large, which includes the natural phenomena, matter itself, and the various kinds of existence that lie beyond matter. Second, the cause whose existence is confirmed by the principle of causality need not be subject to experimentation, or be a material thing. Third, the fact that experimentation does not disclose a specific cause of a certain development or of a certain phenomenon does not mean a failure on the part of the principle of causality, for this principle does not rest on experimentation, which can be shaken in the case of the absence of experimentation. In spite of the failure of experimentation to discover the cause, philosophical confidence in the existence of such a cause remains strong, in accordance with the principle of causality. The failure of experimentation to discover the cause is due to two things: either to the fact that

on the Ashʿarite tradition, Nursi argues that our belief in the material existence of the natural laws is a result of accumulated habits developed in response to accumulated sensory experiences. When one encounters the world of experience, one also witnesses the consistency in the world. This consistency leads to the construction of the idea of law. There is nothing wrong with having such regulatory ideas. What is problematic for Nursi is to understand these ideas as the causes of the consistency in the world. This is philosophically unjustifiable, for this consistency itself led to the construction of these ideas in the first place.[22]

> The immaterial laws of the ordering of the universe proceed from the Pre-Eternal Monarch's wisdom … the theoretical laws of the sovereignty, and the rules and ordinances of the Shariʿa of Creation are immaterial and exist only as knowledge.[23]

There is nothing material about the physical laws. They are simply highly successful definitions of the material reality that is sensually experienced. Immaterial laws by themselves cannot govern material existence. Therefore, scientific explanations given in terms of physical laws are not exhaustive, although they are practically useful. Philosophical and theological questions remain. To act as though we have exhausted the issue at hand is an error. There is difference between naming and understanding. It is a problem "to attach a scientific name to a most profound, unknowable, and important truth which has purposes in a thousand respects, and act as though through the *name* it has been understood."[24]

Nursi rejects the Aristotelian idea of natures for similar reasons. Recall that for Aristotle a causal explanation should bring together the inner principles (natures) and external principles (*dunameis*). A being's nature results from the matter it is made of and its formal constitution. Natures

experimentation is limited and does not extend to the material reality and occurrence of specific attachments, or to the fact that the unknown cause lies outside empirical thought, and is beyond the world of nature and matter." *Our Philosophy*, trans. Shams C. Inati (Create Space Independent Publishing Form, 2014), 311.

22 It may be helpful to draw the reader's attention to the parallels between Nursi's point of view and British Empiricism. The basic idea is that the mind operates on the material provided by the senses to reach more complex and abstract ideas. But sometimes we mistakenly believe that the ideas that exist in the mind also exist in the extramental world. We, however, cannot philosophically justify this jump from the mental to the extramental existence. Thus, in Berkeley one ends up losing the ideas of substance and time, and in Hume the ideas of self and causality.

23 Nursi, *The Flashes*, 243. 24 Nursi, *The Words*, 188.

can be taken as the basis for an exhaustive causal explanation.[25] As discussed in Chapter 1, Ash'arites reject this logic, for the idea of natures implies, as Frank aptly summarizes, that "the natural action of the material constituents of bodies; i.e., their specific behavior, active and passive, as it is determined by and directly flows from the nature of their materiality."[26] For Ash'arites, this would imply limits to God's free action and creative power. They therefore offer the concept of habit as an alternative to the concept of natures.

Nursi draws on the Ash'arite tradition in his rejection of natures. He holds that the idea of nature is a misinterpretation of the regularity in the world. The real cause of regularity is the divine attributes of power, will, and knowledge. Neither physical laws as external principles nor natures as internal principles have extramental material existence. One constructs the idea of natures in mind, and then, unjustifiably, posits them as the explanation of regularity.

> But to set up in place of divine power those laws, which proceed from the divine attributes of knowledge and speech and only exist as knowledge (*yalnız vücud-u ilmîsi bulunan*), and to attribute creation and material existence (*mevcud-u haricî*) to them; then to attach the name *nature* to them (*sonra da onlara "Tabiat" namını takmak*), and to deem force, which is merely a manifestation of dominical power, to be an independent almighty possessor of power, is a thousand times more low-fallen ignorance than the ignorance in the comparison.[27]

Therefore, Nursi concludes:

> The imaginary and insubstantial (*mevhum ve hakikatsız*) thing that Naturalists call nature, if it has an external reality, can at the very most be a work of art; it cannot be the Artist (*bir san'at olabilir, Sâni' olamaz*). It is embroidery, and cannot be the Embroiderer (*Bir nakıştır, Nakkaş olamaz*). It is a set of decrees; it cannot be the Issuer of the decrees (*Ahkâmdır, hâkim olamaz*). It is a body of the laws of creation and cannot be the Lawgiver (*Bir şeriat-ı fıtriyedir, Şâri' olamaz*). It is but a created veil to the dignity of God and cannot be the Creator (*Mahluk bir perde-i izzettir, Hâlık olamaz*). It is passive and created and cannot be a Creative Maker (*Münfail bir fıtrattır, Fâtır bir fâil olamaz*). It is a law, not a power, and cannot possess power (*Kanundur, kudret değildir; Kâdir olamaz*). It is the recipient and cannot be the source (*Mistardır, Masdar olamaz*).[28]

[25] Aristotle, *Metaphysics*, 8.4, 1044a32–b1, 9.8, 1049b5–10, and 9.1, 1046a11–13. Aristotle, *Physics*, 2.1, 192b20–23, 2.7, 198a24–27.

[26] Richard M. Frank, "Notes and remarks on the *ṭabā'i* in the teaching of al-Māturīdī," in *Melanges d'islamologie a la memoire d'Armand Abel*, ed. P. Salmon (Leiden: E. J. Brill, 1974), 138.

[27] Nursi, *The Flashes*, 243. Translation modified. Emphasis mine.

[28] Ibid., 244. Translation modified.

To defend his conception of laws, Nursi poses the following question: How does one explain the existence of laws in the first place? Why do regularity (mathematicity) and the resulting aesthetics exist in the world? The laws, as he has contended so far, are immaterial principles or descriptive formulae with no causal influence in the world. If this is the case, then one is left with two options. The source of regularity can either be traced back to matter itself, or to God. Matter consists of particles. If these particles are acting in a way that produces mathematicity and aesthetics in the world, then they should have almost God-like qualities. For example, each particle should be omniscient to be able to act with an eye on the whole cosmos to be consistent with all other particles. They should also be morally perfect to collaborate with each other to sustain the world-process. If there is no one omniscient and omnibenevolent God who sees and governs the acts of these particles, then each particle must be a god to produce the same effect.

At this juncture, Nursi develops analogies that he borrows from Sufi metaphysics. Nursi asks his reader to imagine sunlight reflected by the surface of the sea.

> The sun's manifestations and reflections appear in all small fragments of glass and droplets on the face of the earth. If those miniature, reflected imaginary suns are not ascribed to the sun in the sky, it is necessary to accept the external existence of an actual sun in every tiny fragment of glass smaller than a match-head, which possesses the sun's qualities and which, though small in size, bears profound meaning; and therefore, to accept actual suns [as being the same in] number [as the] pieces of glass. In exactly the same way, if beings and animate creatures are not attributed directly to the manifestation of the Pre-Eternal Sun's names, it becomes necessary to accept that in each being, and especially animate beings, there lies a nature, a force, or quite simply a god that will sustain an infinite power and will, and knowledge and wisdom. Such an idea is the most absurd and superstitious of all the impossibilities in the universe. It demonstrates that a man who attributes the art of the Creator of the universe to imaginary, insignificant, unconscious nature is without a doubt less conscious of the truth than an animal.[29]

The existence of light on a surface can be easily explained by attributing it to the sun. This would be the easiest and most logical explanation. If one chooses to explain the existence of light without taking the sun into account, then one would have to explain it by attributing it to the particles of the sea. This would be absurd, for in this case one would have to accept

[29] Ibid., 239.

countless suns. Each individual being reflecting or refracting light would have to produce its own light. There is a third possibility here: One can deny the existence of light. But this would be contrary to countless experiences. There is light (whether in mathematicity, aesthetics, beauty, or morality) in this world. It is undeniable. This line of thought ends in the following conclusion: If there is not one God, then every particle has to be "a god" acting with an eye on the whole cosmos and collaborating with other particles with utmost moral perfection for the continuation of beauty, aesthetics, and order in the world.

> Like the stones of a dome, the particles stand together in perfect balance and order demonstrating the eye and the tongue, for example, each to be a wondrous building, extraordinary work of art, and miracle of power. If these particles were not officials dependent on the command of the master architect of the universe, then each would have to be both absolutely dominant (*hâkim-i mutlak*) over all the other particles in the body and absolutely subordinate (*mahkûm-u mutlak*) to each of them; and both equal to each and, with regard to its dominant position, opposed; and both the origin and source of most of the attributes that pertain only to the Necessarily Existent One (*hem yalnız Vâcibü'l-Vücuda mahsus olan ekser sıfât*), and extremely restricted; and both in absolute form, and in the form of a perfectly ordered individual artifact that could only, through the mystery of unity, be the work of the Single One of Unity.[30]

Notice that Nursi combines occasionalism and Ibn ʿArabī's metaphysics to provide this explanation. On the one hand, as an occasionalist, he defends the idea that physical laws are practical tools to understand the consistency of natural processes, even though they lack causal efficacy. On the other hand, he argues, to explain the manifestation of light, that either the light of the divine sun is manifested in the mirror of the world or that each part constituting the mirror (the world) is a separate sun. Ergo, any attempt to explain the existence of light without reference to the sun is absurd.

What does Nursi think about Ashʿarite atomism? As discussed in Chapter 1, Ashʿarite atomism provides a basis for the idea of the constant re-creation of the world and, thus, occasionalism.[31] Nursi shares with Ashʿarite atomism the view that the world consists of discrete and fragmented particles. These act according to the laws of nature, which are nothing but representations of God's habitual creation

[30] Ibid., 237. Emphasis mine.

[31] Nazif Muhtaroglu aptly observes that occasionalism does not presuppose a specific physical ontology, but it certainly postulates certain limitations on any model of physical ontology. Nazif Muhtaroglu, *Islamic and Cartesian Roots of Occasionalism*, 26.

in the world.[32] The change one observes in the world is an outcome of continuous motion and resulting association and dissociation of these atoms. The realm of atoms is a "field" where God harvests new universes.

Then too the making of the world of minute particles into a boundless, broad arable field and every instant sowing and harvesting it and obtaining the fresh crops of different universes from it, and those inanimate, impotent, ignorant particles being made to perform innumerable orderly duties most consciously, wisely, and capably – this also shows the necessary existence of the All-Powerful One of Glory and Maker of Perfection, and His perfect power and the grandeur of His sovereignty and His unity and the perfection of His dominicality.[33]

As alluded to above, like Ibn ʿArabī, Nursi presents atoms as neutral and homogeneous loci of the manifestation of God's names. To this end, Nursi rearticulates Ashʿarite atomism in the language of Sufi metaphysics. God creates, equips, moves, and governs atoms.[34] In themselves, atoms do not own anything. Their need and poverty testify that they are not the source of creation; they are not the cause of orderliness and beauty. God uses these submissive loci to create new worlds continuously. As homogenous and neutral beings marked by poverty and need, they cannot be the ultimate causal explanation. As darkness underlies light, the poverty of atoms underlies and thus manifests God's power, knowledge, and will.[35] The disproportionality between their natures and the "loads" they carry makes them more expository loci of manifestation.[36]

He creates the spring as easily as He creates a single flower. For He has no need to gather things together. Since He is the owner of the command of "'Be!' and it is;" and since every spring He creates from nothing the innumerable attributes, states, and forms of the innumerable beings of spring together with the elements of their physical beings; and since He determines the plan, model, index, and program of everything in His knowledge; and since all minute particles are in Motion within the sphere of His knowledge and power; He therefore creates everything with infinite ease as though striking a match. And nothing at all confuses its motion

[32] Said Nursi, *Mesnevi, Risale-i Nur Külliyatı*, 2 vols (Istanbul: Nesil Yayinlari, 2002), 2:1342. Translation mine. This is a compilation of Nursi's works in two volumes. I use this text for hitherto untranslated passages from the *Risale-i Nur*. This text is also available online in Turkish: www.risaleinurenstitusu.org.

[33] Nursi, *The Words*, 689. See also *The Letters*, 250.

[34] For Nursi's account of atoms, see Nursi, *The Words*, 570–582.

[35] Nursi, *Mesnevi*, 2:1290.

[36] The concept of "disproportionality" will be examined more extensively in the following pages.

so much as an iota. Minute particles are like a regular, disciplined army in the same way that the planets are an obedient army.[37]

Nursi applies the same line of thought to subatomic particles, or *aether* in his parlance. Aether fills the world and consists of particles that are subtler than atoms. As such it refers to the subatomic realm, which is also discrete and fragmented. For Nursi, the verse "His throne was over the water" (Qur'an 11:17) refers to aether. "After its creation, aether became the primordial locus of the first creative manifestations of the Glorious Maker."[38] It is absolutely submissive in front of the divine names, which mold, determine, limit, and transform it into reality. Here the term "water" refers to the neutral and dynamic nature of the ultimate underlying substance. For Nursi, aether is the first locus of the divine action or, to use his metaphor, the primordial mirror where the first manifestation of the divine names occurs. It surrenders to the will of God. It grounds the whole reality, and everything else emerges from it.

And yet they attribute preeternity and everlastingness, which are the Necessarily Existent One's most particular qualities and are necessary and essential to Him, to things like aether and particles, which are matter that is material, unbounded and numerous, is the least stable level of existence and the least tangible, the most changing and the most varying and the most dispersed through space ... This extraordinary ignorance requires endless impossibilities because aether is matter that is unconscious, lifeless and without will and is finer than the matter of which particles consist, which drowns the materialists, and is denser than the index of primordial matter into which the ancient philosophers thrust themselves. To attribute to this matter, which may be fragmented and divided without limit and is equipped with the qualities and duties of being passive and the ability to transmit – to attribute to its minute particles, which are far minuter than particles of other matter, the actions and works that exist through a will and power that sees, knows, and directs all things in all things is mistaken to the number of particles of aether.[39]

10.2 SECONDARY CAUSALITY AND THE IDEA OF "VEIL"

In Nursi's writings there is another interesting meeting point of occasionalism and Sufi metaphysics. The rejection of the necessary connection

[37] Nursi, *The Flashes*, 307.

[38] Translation mine. Said Nursi, *İşaratü'l-İcaz* (Istanbul: Yeni Asya Neşriyat, 1994), 237–238. For an extensive analysis of Nursi's account of aether, see Durmus Hocaoglu, "Nursi ve Descartes Felsefelerinde Tabiat Uzerine Mukayeseli Calisma" accessed Nov. 12, 2013: www.koprudergisi.com/index.asp?Bolum=EskiSayilarGoster=YaziYaziNo=500; also see Mucahit Bilici "Kayyumiyet ve Esir Maddesi" accessed Nov. 12, 2013: www.koprudergisi.com/index.asp?Bolum=EskiSayilarGoster=YaziYaziNo=278.

[39] Nursi, *The Flashes*, 438.

between cause and effect in Nursi leads to reconstruction of causality as a veil (*perde*). To this end he draws on Ibn ʿArabī's formulation of causality as a "veil" that at once hides and manifests the relations of the self-disclosures of God depending on the observer's propensities and intentions. Moreover, from an ethical perspective, the veil of causality preserves the necessary courtesy and refinement of the God–servant relationship. Similarly, secondary causality for Nursi is also veil with multiple epistemological, theosophical, and ethical functions.

Why does God create behind the structure of causality? This question is of great importance to Nursi and seems relevant to any occasionalist thinker. However, the only Ashʿarite theologian (as far as I am aware) who deals with this question is Ghazālī, and he does so only indirectly. He reminds us that the Qurʾan sometimes attributes an act to the causal agent such as human beings or physical entities. "God, exalted be He, related acts in the Qurʾan one time to the angels, one time to the servants, and another time to Himself."[40] How do we reconcile the denial of causal efficacy in beings with these Qurʾanic statements? For Ghazālī, the difficulty can be addressed by understanding the secondary causes as loci of the divine actions. Here the beings are perceived as causally inefficacious, neutral, and receptive mirrors on which God's attributes are continuously reflected. The real cause is God, and beings are loci of the divine attributes. The beings in a way mediate the divine causal power but, as Marmura observes, "mediation does not necessarily mean the attribution of causal efficacy to the mediator."[41] The language of mediation implies that there is a kind of medium between God's acts and human observation without causal efficacy. This brings us very close to the idea of causality as a veil. However, Ashʿarite theologians do not use the term "veil" to talk about causality.

To my knowledge, the first Muslim thinker to employ the term "veil" when conceptualizing causality is Ibn ʿArabī. As discussed in the preceding pages, for Ibn ʿArabī the illusion of causal necessity exists for very important reasons. He writes that "God did not establish the secondary causes aimlessly."[42] "God established causes and made them like veils. Hence, the causes lead everyone who knows that they are veils, back to Him. But they prevent everyone who takes them as lords from reaching

[40] Ibid., 192.

[41] Michael Marmura, "Ghazālīan Causes and Intermediaries," *Journal of the American Oriental Society*, 115 (1995): 92.

[42] See fn. 538. Ibn ʿArabī, *Futūḥāt*, II. 208.16 translated in Chittick, *Sufi Path*, 44.

the real Lord, i.e. God."[43] The concept of causality refers to something that reveals and hides God at the same time. God acts behind the structure of causality. And it is not always easy to see God as the engenderer of the causes behind the veil of causality.[44] It is, however, a transparent veil for those who are willing to see what is behind it: "It is He who discloses Himself in the forms of the secondary causes which are a veil, over Him."[45] The analogy of the veil also suggests that secondary causality has an ethical function, in that it preserves the necessary courtesy, refinement, and morals of the relationship between God and His servant. The courtesy requires that we not "strip the veils" for those who do not deserve or are not ready for such intimacy with reality.[46] The idea of causality must be preserved in the conventional parlance, for perceiving the true beauty and wisdom of natural phenomena is not always possible for everyone. In a very similar fashion to Ibn ʿArabī, Nursi reconstructs the idea of causality as a veil. In an already-cited passage he writes of how "God creates cause and effect together *directly*. In order to demonstrate His wisdom and the manifestation of His Names, by establishing an apparent causal relationship and connection through order and conjunction, He makes causes and nature a veil to the hand of His power."[47]

First, Nursi argues that "causes have been placed so that the dignity of power may be preserved in the superficial view of the mind." Causes have been created to be the "veils" of the creative acts in states which are "incompatible with the dignity and perfection of the Eternally Besought One." The world is the domain of evil as well as good. We witness many things in the world which, from an aesthetic point of view, are unsightly, improper, and even repugnant. Everything takes place in relation to divine power, will, and knowledge. How do we preserve God's moral perfection while at the same time admitting God is the creator of evil as well as good?

The gist of Nursi's response to this question is that "the acquisition of evil is evil, but the creation of evil is not evil (*kesb-i şer şerdir, halk-ı şer şer değildir*)."[48] From God comes only good, but when human beings appropriate good, they may turn it to evil for themselves. To use his example, sunlight is good, but it also causes corruption and decay for things that are not in proper relation with it. God creates rain, which is good.

[43] Ibid., III. 416.19. [44] Ibid., II. 414.1. [45] Ibid., II. 4469.2.
[46] Ibn ʿArabī, *Fuṣūṣ*, 185; cf. Izutsu, *Sufism and Taoism*, 256–257.
[47] Nursi, *The Flashes*, 244. Emphasis mine. [48] Nursi, *The Words*, 478. Emphasis mine.

One can benefit from rain thoroughly. But one can make himself or herself sick by developing an improper relationship with the rain, such as through overexposure.[49] The examples suggest that evil emerges as a necessary concomitant of good but only in relation to us, not God. "In the inner face, that of reality, which looks to their Creator, everything is transparent and beautiful."[50] So even in the cases of (apparent) evil and impropriety, it is fitting that "the divine power should itself be associated with it," provided that in this process God remains the source of pure good. That is to say, God is the creator of both good and evil, but that status does not affect God's moral perfection.

However, not everyone can see the beauty and purpose behind the apparent evil. Here enters causality. Causes have been put as intermediaries, "so that unjust complaints and baseless objections should be directed at them and not at the Absolutely Just One. For the faults arise from them, from their incapacity and lack of ability."[51] Most human beings see secondary causality and attribute evil to it. Causality acts like a veil for those who cannot see the good behind apparent evil. In their perception, causes, not God, are associated with evil, and divine dignity and perfection are preserved. For some, the veil of causality is removed. They understand that God creates both good and evil, but this does not lead them to undermine the moral perfection of God, since "the creation of evil is not evil; the acquisition of evil is evil." For those who can perceive the good behind evil, there is no need for a veil, and thus, the veil of causality disappears. For those who fail to see this, the veil of causality remains.

> The Angel Azra'il (Peace be upon him) said to Almighty God: "Your servants will complain about me while I am carrying out my duty of taking possession of the spirits of the dying; they will be resentful toward me." So, Almighty God said to him through the tongue of wisdom: "I shall leave the veil of disasters and illnesses between you and my servants so that the complaints will be directed at them, and they will not be indignant at you." So, see illnesses are a veil; what are imagined to be the bad things at the appointed hour are attributed to them, and what are in reality the good things in the spirits of the dying being seized are attributed to the Angel Azra'il and his duty. The Angel Azra'il is also a veil; he is a veil to the divine power when spirits are seized which is apparently unkind and are inappropriate to the perfection of mercy.[52]

Thus, the illusion of causality is necessary to preserve the necessary courtesy, refinement, and morals (Ar. *adab*, Tr. *edeb*) of the God–servant

[49] Ibid., 479. [50] Ibid. [51] Ibid., 301. [52] Ibid.

relationship. God's moral perfection is preserved in "the superficial view of the mind." The servant observes causality to embody the *adab* necessitated by the nature of this relationship. He/she glorifies God in all circumstances; secondary causality becomes the first resort of complaint.

Second, causality also has an epistemological function. To borrow a term from Kant, the idea of secondary cause is postulated as a *regulative* idea for practical purposes.[53] In reality, although we know that secondary causality is devoid of causal efficacy, the illusion allows us to make sense of the world, to grasp the regularity of the world, to preserve the predictability of the world. So, for practical purposes we can act in the world *as if* causality is real.

> By relating causes to effects, God has deposited an order in the universe through His will and obliged man through his nature, illusions, and imagination, to comply with the order and be bound to it. Moreover, He directed all things toward Himself and is far above the effect of the causes in His dominions. He charged man in belief and faith, to comply with this sphere with his conscience and his spirit, and be bound to it. For in this world, the sphere of causes predominates over the sphere of belief, while in the next world the truths of belief will be manifested as supreme over the sphere of causes.[54]

God creates both cause and effect but does not do so in a chaotic manner. God attaches cause and effect to each other on a self-imposed habitual pattern. This world is predictable and consistent, because in this world God's habituality prevails. These habitual patterns help human beings make sense of the world and interact with it in a more efficacious manner. To discover the habitual creation of God, one first must realize the law-like flow of natural phenomena. Here, the idea of causality, though a mental construction without any extramental reality, serves as an epistemological tool to perceive the regularity and consistency in the world.

Many people mistakenly take secondary causality to precede divine causation. The idea of causality provides a more intelligible grounding between the religious elite and the common people. It is linguistically necessary to employ the language of secondary causality to communicate with others. Nursi thus allows metaphorical use of language of secondary causality out of linguistic necessity.

From an epistemological perspective, secondary causality is a regulative idea. It does not have a real existence but still helps one interact with

[53] See for example, Immanuel Kant, *Critique of Pure Reason*, trans. Norman Kemp Smith (New York: St. Martin's Press, 1965), A180/B222.

[54] Nursi, *İşaratü'l-İcaz*, 26. Translation mine.

the world in a more meaningful manner. As a reflection of God's habitual creation in the mind, it enables one to decode the law-like flow of phenomena. It also serves as an epistemological bridge to reach higher theological truths. It is a means to an end, not an end in itself. It is a temporary station to set off a journey for the discovery of higher metaphysical truths – not (or should not be) a permanent epistemological frame. But only a minority goes beyond the veil of causality and discovers the truth: that God creates both cause and effect. The majority of people think secondary causality is real. So, for the sake of communication with others, it is a linguistic necessity to employ the language of secondary causality. Herein one acts as if the secondary causality were real without attributing causal efficacy to it.

Last, causality has theosophical significance. For Nursi, the world is a multiplicity of mirrors reflecting the divine names. The more expository the mirror, the better. This is why the world is so variegated, in constant motion, oscillating between rigor and mercy. The apparent intermediaries between God and the world allow a greater diversification and reflection of the divine names. If God would create effects directly without causal relationships, most of the divine names such as wisdom would be concealed from our sight. Causality, or in other words, the consistency and graduality of natural processes, allow one to perceive God's wisdom, will, and subtlety in the mirror of creation. All the divine names, as discussed above, demand to be manifested in their loci and thus be known by conscious beings. By creating beneath the structure of secondary causes, gradually and consistently, God transforms the world into a more comprehensive mirror and allows a richer manifestation of the divine names.

> The Absolutely Powerful One is in no need of impotent intermediaries to share in His dominicality and creation ... He creates cause and effect together directly. By establishing an apparent causal relationship and connection through order and sequence, he demonstrates His wisdom and manifests His names. He makes causes and nature a veil to the hand of His power so that the apparent faults, severities, and defects in things should be ascribed to them, and in this way His dignity be preserved.[55]

A world where creation takes place instantaneously and chaotically would be a less comprehensive and expository mirror. The consistency and graduality of the flow of phenomena allow rich manifestation of such divine qualities as wisdom, will, subtlety, dignity, and majesty. "He forms

[55] Nursi, *The Flashes*, 244.

certain beings out of elements of the universe in order to demonstrate subtle instances of wisdom, such as displaying the perfections of His wisdom and the manifestations of many of His names."[56]

We have seen that the veil of causality in Nursi's thought has theosophical, epistemological, and ethical functions. From an ethical point of view, the veil of causality is necessary in order to develop an authentic relationship with God in accordance with the courtesy and refinement necessitated by the nature of that relationship. From an epistemological point of view, causality is a regulative idea, a temporary epistemological station enabling one to reach a higher theological and spiritual elevation. God, by creating beneath the structure of secondary causality in an ordered fashion, enables human cognition to understand and to interact with the world in a more meaningful and efficacious manner. From a theosophical point of view, the regularity and graduality of natural processes transform the world into a more comprehensive and expository mirror for the reflection of the divine names, which demand to be manifested unceasingly. As such, although Nursi does not assign causal efficacy to secondary causality, he presents a worldview in which the veil of causality is fundamentally important.

10.3 MIRACLES AND THE DIVINE NAMES

Another interesting interaction between Nursi's occasionalism and Sufi metaphysics can be seen in his approach to the question of miracles. His explanation for miracles accords with Ashʿarite tendencies examined in previous chapters. He holds that a miracle is "the confirmation by the creator of the cosmos of his declaration of prophethood." When a prophet asserts that God has appointed him to this position, the proof of that appointment can be manifested in one of two ways. Either the word "yes" is uttered by God, or God changes "His usual practice and attitude" at his request. This would confirm his claim "even more soundly and more definitely than the word 'yes'."[57]

Nursi adds that these breaks in God's "usual practices and attitudes" can also be understood from the perspective of Sufi metaphysics. As already discussed, the concepts of physical laws are helpful

[56] Ibid., 253.

[57] Nursi, *The Letters*, 115–116. For an extensive discussion on Nursi's understanding of miracles, see Umeyye Isra Yazicioglu, *Understanding the Qurʾanic Miracle Stories in the Modern Age* (University Park, PA: Penn State University Press, 2013).

epistemological tools to understand and interact with the world. There should, however, be exceptions to the comprehensiveness of physical laws (Tr. *şüzûzât-ı kanuniye*). There should be both laws and exceptions to these laws. The laws make the natural phenomena predictable and thus knowledge of such phenomena possible. On the other hand, contingency makes the world ontologically open. The world is predictable because it operates in a law-like manner, but its possibilities are not exhausted by physical laws, since the contingency embedded in the warp and woof of the world keeps "surprising" human cognition. Necessity and contingency are intertwined.

Why? Because, necessity and contingency are both needed for the manifestation of God's names and attributes. The comprehensiveness of law-like behavior of natural phenomena results from such divine attributes as power, majesty, and wisdom. These attributes require a degree of regularity in the world. Power and majesty impose orderliness, and wisdom requires regularity, for knowledge is possible only if the natural phenomena are predictable. On the other hand, the attribute of will entails that God's acts are not to be confined by dictates of these natural laws. Such confinement would contradict divine freedom. God has the power and freedom to break the laws without completely annihilating regularity in the world in order to manifest the divine freedom. Power, wisdom, and majesty impose necessity (order, causality, predictability, law-likeness); will and mercy require contingency (liberation, openness, miracles). One observes both in the world. This dual nature makes the world a more comprehensive mirror for the reflection of all of God's attributes.

> The All-Powerful and All-Knowing One, the All-Wise Maker, shows His power and His wisdom in a way that chance can in no way interfere in His works. The system and order of His rules and practices in the universe are demonstrated in the form of laws. So, too, *through exceptions to the laws*, the wonders of His practices, superficial changes, differences in individual characteristics, and changes in the times of appearance and descent (*şüzûzât-ı kanuniye ile, âdetinin hârikalarıyla, tegayyürât-ı sûriye ile, teşahhusâtın ihtilâfâtıyla, zuhur ve nüzûl zamanının tebeddülüyle*), He shows His volition, will, choice, that He is the Agent with choice, and that He is under no restrictions whatsoever.[58]

From the perspective of the God–servant relationship, the "openness" of the world negates the monotony of the world-process and "proclaims that everything is in need of God."[59] Miracles allow one to see the real cause, God, behind the illusory veil of secondary causes. If, as Nursi holds, God had

[58] Nursi, *The Words*, 217. Emphasis mine. [59] Ibid.

not created the world as ontologically open, then one might easily have been deceived by the illusion, predictability, and monotony of causal relations.

10.4 FREE WILL

How does Nursi reconcile the idea of free will with the determinism suggested by occasionalism? As discussed earlier, Muslim theologians have exerted great effort to explain human freedom within an occasionalist framework. Muʿtazilites generally see genuine causal efficacy in human power, while Ashʿarites generally deny that efficacy. However, we also see that Ashʿarites attempt to ease the determinism of their position by postulating the theory of acquisition.

Nursi deals with the problem of free will by drawing on this Ashʿarite tradition. However, he also borrows certain concepts from Maturidite theologians. If occasionalism holds that both cause and effect are created by the divine power, then human choice must also be created by God. In this case, human freedom is lost. To escape this conclusion, Nursi sees human choice as a perspectival matter (*emr-i itibarî*) or a relative matter (*emr-i nisbî*).

> According to the Māturīdī, inclination, the essence of the power of choice, is a perspectival matter (*emr-i itibarî*) and may be attributed to God's servants. But Ashʿarī considered inclination to have existence and so did not attribute it to the servants. However, according to Ashʿarī, the power of disposal within inclination is a relative matter (*emr-i nisbî*), which makes the inclination and the disposal together a relative matter lacking a definite external existence.[60]

The key term here is "relative matters." To understand what Nursi means by this concept, a quick look at its history is necessary. The first Muslim theologian who applied the theory of relative matters (Ar. *amrun iʿtibāriyyun*) appears to be Ṣadr al-Sharīʿa.[61] Like Māturīdī, this scholar understands choice (*ikhtiyār*) to be the essence of human will. Human choice differentiates (*takhṣīṣ*) between opportunities.[62] What is distinctive about Sharīʿa is that he locates human will somewhere between existence

60 Ibid., 482.

61 For a very good analysis of this scholar's defense of free will in an occasionalist framework, see Nazif Muhtaroğlu, "An Occasionalist Defense of Free Will," in *Classical Issues in Islamic Philosophy and Theology Today* (New York: Springer, 2010), 45–62.

62 Taftazānī and Ṣadr al-Sharīʿa, *Sharḥ al-Talwīh ʿala Tawḍih li Matni al-Tankīh fi Uṣūl al-Fiqh*, vol. 1 (Beirut: Dar al-Kutub al-Ilmiyyah, n.d.), 349.

and nonexistence. Human will is neither an existent nor a nonexistent thing (*lā mawjūdun wa-lā maʿdum*).[63] Thus, it is a "relative matter." "Spatial orientation" is another example of a relative matter.[64] Terms like "rightness and leftness" or "aboveness and underness" are relative matters in that they exist as relational entities. When we build a wall, relative matters such as the rightness or leftness of the wall emerge. Rightness or leftness can be defined in relation to the wall, but they are not in the same ontological category as the wall. The wall is an existent, but rightness and leftness of the wall are neither existent nor nonexistent. They do not have external existence and exist only as relative matters in the eye of the observer. The basket is on the right side from one perspective and on the left from another. These, for Sharīʿa, are relative matters located between existence and nonexistence.

Sharīʿa locates human will in this intermediate ontological category. But how does this escape the deterministic conclusions of occasionalism? The argument continues as follows. Since human will is not a created being in the true sense of the word, divine power does not apply to it. As such, relative matters are located beyond the scope of an act of creation. This is also consistent with occasionalism, as Sharīʿa is still able to say that the divine power creates every existent being. Ibn Humām joins Sharīʿa in placing human choice in this distinctive ontological category that falls outside of the domain of the divine power.[65]

Nursi employs the same terminology. For Nursi too, human will is a relative matter located in this intermediate ontological realm between existence and nonexistence. As such, human will is beyond the scope of the divine power and, thus, is free.

> Relative matters do not require causes for their existence. [If this were the case] necessity would intervene and nullify the will and power of choice. Rather, if the cause of relative matters acquires the weight of preference, a relative matter may become actual and existent.[66]

Here, Nursi implies that a relative matter does not require a cause to exist. In the intermediate ontological location, human will as a relational entity has freedom, because it falls outside of the domain of the divine attribute

[63] Ibid., 332, 337, 338.

[64] For a good introduction to this issue, see Muhtaroglu, *Islamic and Cartesian Occasionalism of Occasionalism*, 332.

[65] Kamāl al-Dīn Ibn Humām, *Kitāb al-Musāyara* (Istanbul: Çağrı Yayınları, 1979), 112–113.

[66] Nursi, *The Words*, 482.

of power. The divine power creates the existent beings. But human will is neither existent nor nonexistent. The human will invites the divine will and power. In this sense, human choice is an "occasion" that coincides with the divine will.

To bolster his position, Nursi adopts the distinction between the world of creation (Tr. *alem-i halk*) and the world of command (Tr. *alem-i emr*) from the Islamic spiritual tradition.[67] The world of creation is the domain of divine power and will. The divine power creates everything in the world of creation, but it does so by observing the causal sequence. Nursi suggests that in the world of command, however, creation takes place instantaneously, without causality.[68] The human soul and natural laws are located in the world of command, which is beyond human cognition.

By postulating a realm beyond causality and thus beyond the scope of the divine power, Nursi saves human will from determinism while at the same time preserving the strict occasionalist relation between cause and effect in the world of creation. To put it simply, in the world of creation or, in other words, in the world of causality, Nursi is a thoroughgoing occasionalist. In the world of command, where causality does not exist, Nursi is able to attribute freedom to the human soul.

Nursi's strategy to attribute freedom to human will without sacrificing the basic tenets of occasionalism is thus twofold. First, he locates human will in an intermediate realm between existence and nonexistence, beyond the scope of divine power. Second, he postulates a realm where causality does not exist. The human soul, which is located in this realm, tastes freedom but without that freedom being caused by the divine power.

Nursi is aware that this account does not really explain the nature of the interaction of human will and the divine will. To understand the mechanism of that interaction, one must know the real nature of soul, which according to Nursi comes from "the world of command" and, thus, remains unknown to us.[69] For Nursi, humans actually do not know

[67] Considering Ahmad Sirhindī's influence on Nursi, it is probable that Nursi borrows this distinction directly from him. See for example, Ahmad Sirhindī, *Maktūbāt*, vols 1–2, trans. Kasim Yayla (Istanbul: Merve Yayinlari, 1999), 34th Letter. This distinction, however, was established much earlier than Sirhindī.

[68] He writes: "Like fixed and constant natural laws, spirit comes from the world of the Divine command and attribute of will," *The Words*, 735. The distinction between the two ontological categories is seconded by such verses as "to God belongs creation and command" (A'raf, 54).

[69] A Qur'anic verse states, "the spirit is of my Lord's commands, and you have been granted any knowledge of it but a little" (17:85). For Nursi's analysis of *rūh*, see Nursi, *The Words*, 533–556.

how to reconcile free will and divine will. But we do know, experientially, that we have free will. The fact that we do not know how to solve this problem does not negate the possibility of the two existing together.[70]

> Of necessity, everyone perceives in himself a will and choice; he knows it through his conscience. To know the whatness of things is one thing; to know they exist is something different (*mevcudatın mahiyetini bilmek ayrıdır, vücudunu bilmek ayrıdır*). There are many things which although their existence is self-evident, we do not know their true nature ... The power of choice may be included among these. Everything is not restricted to what we know; our not knowing them does not prove the things we do not know do not exist.[71]

As such, I believe, Nursi's strategy to deal with the problem of free will comes surprisingly close to that of Kant. Recall that Kant distinguishes between the causal deterministic framework we impose upon the world as we perceive it and the world as it exists in itself, positing human freedom as a part of the latter. This duality allows Kant to affirm at once strict causality in a world of phenomena and freedom apart from the world of noumena. The world of noumena escapes the human cognitive capacity, but it is exactly this aspect of it that allows Kant to locate freedom there. Similarly, Nursi asserts that the world of creation is the domain of causal relations. His occasionalism applies in this domain of reality. Soul and will are located in the world of command, which is beyond causality. The "whatness" of the soul and will is thus inexplicable, and the relation of the human will to the divine will is thus incomprehensible. But the fact that we do not know how to reconcile the human and divine wills does not necessitate the denial of the existence of such a relationship. Nursi's strategy is to show why the problem is insoluble and why it still makes sense to believe in human freedom, and he attempts to do this without sacrificing the basic tenets of occasionalism.[72]

70 Similarly, Whitehead writes that "we must bow down to those presumptions, which, in despite of criticism we still employ for the regulation of our lives," in *Process and Reality*, corrected edn, ed. David R. Griffin and Donald W. Sherburne (New York: Free Press, 1978), 151. As Thomas Reid puts it, the very act of denying these principles would entail "metaphysical lunacy." See *An Inquiry Into the Human Mind on the Principles of Common Sense* [1764]: *A Critical Edition*, ed. Derek Brookes (University Park, PA: Penn State University Press, 1997), 268–269.

71 Nursi, *The Words*, 480. Translation modified.

72 There is, though, at least one major difficulty in the proposed solution. The whole argument rests on the assumption that an intermediate ontological domain between existence and nonexistence is possible. But how is an intermediate realm between existence and nonexistence intelligible? This question goes unaddressed in Nursi's treatment of causality. I discuss this challenge further in Chapter 11.

10.5 THE DISPROPORTIONALITY OF CAUSE AND EFFECT

Aside from the attempt to rearticulate occasionalist theory in the language of Sufi metaphysics, what makes Nursi's approach unique within the Islamic occasionalist tradition is his emphasis on the ever-present disproportionality of cause and effect.[73] In the following statement, Nursi adds a further dimension to his occasionalist theory of causality.

> It sometimes happens that in order to disallow apparent causes the ability to create and to demonstrate how far they are from this, a [Qu'rani]) verse points out the aims and fruits of the effects so that it may be understood that *causes are only an apparent veil*. So, by mentioning the aims and results, such verses show that although *causes are superficially joined and adjacent to their effects, in reality there is a great distance between them*. The distance from the cause to the creation of the effect is so great that the hand of the greatest causes cannot reach the creation of the most insignificant effects. Thus, it is within this long distance between cause and effect that the divine names rise like stars (*İşte sebep ve müsebbeb ortasındaki uzun mesafede esmâ-i İlâhiye birer yıldız gibi tulû eder*). The place of their rising is this distance. To the superficial glance, mountains on the horizon appear to be joined to and contiguous with the sky, although from the mountains to the sky is a vast distance in which the stars rise and other things are situated; so too the distance between causes and effects is such that it may be seen only with the light of the Qur'an through the telescope of belief.[74]

Here, Nursi reiterates what we have already discussed, namely that "causes are only an apparent veil." What is interesting in this passage, however, is that he asserts there is also a "long distance" between cause and effect. In similar passages, he introduces the idea of disproportionality of cause and effect. Effects are "joined or adjacent" to causes but can never be reduced to them. There is always a *vertical discontinuity* or *gap* in causal relationships.[75]

We should take note of the following statement: "it is within this long distance between cause and effect that the divine names rise like stars."

[73] I also discuss the concept of the disproportionality of cause and effect in Ozgur Koca, "The Idea of Causal Disproportionality in Said Nursi (1877–1960) and Its Implications," *Journal of Islamic Philosophy*, 11 (2019): 5–32.

[74] Ibid., 435. Emphasis mine. Translation modified.

[75] See also: "All the instances of physical beauty proceed from the non-physical beauties of their own realities and meanings; and as for their realities, they receive effulgence from the divine names and are shadows of them of a sort ... This means that all the varieties and sorts of beauty in the universe are the signs, marks, and manifestations – by means of names – of a faultless, transcendent Beauty which is manifested from beyond the veil of the Unseen." Nursi, *The Rays: From the Risale-i Nur Collection*, trans. Şükran Vahide (Istanbul: Sözler Neşriyat, 2002), 94.

Here Nursi again borrows an idea from Ibn ʿArabī. He holds that the world is a multiplicity of loci for the unceasing and ever-changing manifestations of the divine names. The divine names ground everything as theological categories describing the relationship between the manifested reality and the source of manifestation. Again, this is why Nursī writes that "the divine names constitute the true reality of things."[76] If God creates cause and effect in a way that they are "joined and adjacent to their effects" and that "in reality there is a great distance between them," and if the divine qualities and names are continuously manifested "within the distance" between cause and effect, then all causal relations are loci manifesting the divine qualities. Nursi thus transforms causality into a mirror reflecting the divine names.

But, how can one justify the belief in the ever-present disproportionality of cause and effect? Nursi provides several arguments to answer this question, though these are spread throughout his voluminous writings and not presented in a systematic way. Some of these arguments predate Nursi and were used by earlier Ashʿarite theologians. But Nursi makes innovative use of them. In the classical Ashʿarite literature, these arguments are used to establish the theory of acquisition and "non-observation of necessary connection." Nursi's primary concern here is to use the same arguments to establish the vertical distance between cause and effect in all causal relations. For example, in the Epistle of Nature (*Tabiat Risalesi*), Nursi posits that there are four possible ways to explain the continuity of creation, order, aesthetics, and wisdom in the world.

> Indeed, since beings exist and this cannot be denied, and since each being comes into existence in a wise and artistic fashion, and since each is not outside time but is being continuously renewed, then ... you are bound to say either that: (1) the causes in the world create beings; (2)that beings form themselves; (3) that its coming into existence is a requirement and necessary effect of its nature; or (4) that it is created through the power of One All-Powerful and All-Glorious. Since reason can find no way apart from these four, if the first three are definitely proved to be impossible, invalid, and absurd, the way of divine unity, which is the fourth way, will necessarily and self-evidently and without doubt or suspicion, be proved true.[77]

This is the case for even the most commonplace natural occurrences. How, for example, can one explain the freefall of a stone that occurs according to certain mathematical formulae? Kinematic equations give distance (d) travelled in a given time (t) on a planet with a local gravitational

[76] Nursī, *The Words*, 655. [77] Nursi, *The Flashes*, 233–234.

acceleration (g) (d: $\frac{1}{2}gt^2$); average velocity after elapsed time (v_a:1/2gt); instantaneous velocity (v_i) of the object that has traveled a distance (d) on a planet with mass (m) and radius (r) (v: $(2GM(1/r-1/r+d))^{1/2}$). There is obviously mathematicity, symmetry and, arguably, beauty in this motion. To use Nursi's logic, in this case the mathematicity and beauty of the freefall of a stone can be attributed to: (1) pure chance; (2) the stone itself or the interactions of elementary particles; (3) natural laws; or (4) an omnipotent and omniscient God.

Pure chance (1) obviously cannot be the cause of the emergence and *continuation* of the mathematicity and beauty in the world.[78] Seeking the source of mathematics and aesthetics in the stone itself or in the elementary particles (2) that constitute the stone leads to dire logical conclusions. For if the mathematics and aesthetics emerge as a result of the collaboration and interaction of countless particles in the universe, then one has to attribute God-like qualities to the elementary particles. They must have limitless intellect, wisdom, and ethical perfection, because the order and beauty in the world is possible only if the particles move with perfect knowledge of the whole universe.[79] Consider Nursi's favorite example mentioned above: There is light in the world. If one attempts to explain the existence of light without taking the sun into account, then one would have to imagine that every shiny thing, "every bright small fragment of glass and droplet on the face of the earth," is the producer of its own light. Denying the sun ends in the postulation of countless suns. If there is not one God, then there have to be countless Gods to explain the existence of every positive quality in the world.[80] Therefore, Nursi concludes that the elementary particles cannot be perceived as the real cause without erroneously exalting them to the level of God or gods. Atoms are not the real cause of things but are loci reflecting the infinite mind and power of God.

Similarly, natural laws (3) do not provide a satisfactory answer to why the world functions in an orderly way and why this order leads to design

[78] Ibid., 234–236.

[79] See for example: "Nothing can exist without everything else. Throughout the universe the mystery of cooperation is both concealed and pervasive; intimated in every part of it are mutual assistance and the reciprocal answering of needs. Only an all-encompassing power could do this, and create the particle, situating it suitably to all its relations. Every line and word of the book of the world is living; need drives each, acquaints one with the other … Every living word has a face and eye that looks to all the sentences." Nursi, *The Words*, 731.

[80] Nursi, *The Flashes*, 239.

and beauty. As discussed earlier, Nursi holds that the natural laws are descriptions of the regularities in natural processes. These regularities can be decoded by scientific inquiry and encapsulated in mathematical formulae. As such they are mental constructions without a corresponding extramental reality. The regularity of the observed order leads to emergence of these ideas in mind. There is no reason, however, to believe that descriptions of regularities (the natural laws) are the causes of these regularities. Rather, they are causally inefficacious abstract entities.[81] Nursi develops these ideas as a critique of the common understanding of physical laws as having prescriptive force and governing natural processes, however blindly. The gist of Nursi's argument converges with David Ray Griffin's inquiry: "If there is nothing except particles and motion, then whence does mathematics come?"[82]

If these three options (chance, particles, natural laws) do not provide an exhaustive answer for the existence and continuation of order, design, and beauty, then one can posit a disproportionality in causal processes. None of the causes (chance, particles, natural laws) explains the effects (order, design, beauty) that are spatio-temporally attached to them.

Nursi's arguments concerning the disproportionality of cause and effect are not limited to those examined above. His corpus includes multiple approaches to the problem. I review a few below.

The first approach is what I call the *argument from consciousness*. How do I move my arm? I simply will to move it, and it moves. Do I deserve to be named as the cause of this event? For Nursi, the answer is no. In actuality, this apparently simple bodily motion happens through the participation of countless particles in complex neurological, physical, and chemical processes. To be the real cause of something (in this case the motion of my arm), I would need to know every single step – namely, all the physical and chemical reactions – that takes place at the subatomic, atomic, molecular, and cellular levels. But we do not know what truly happens at these levels in our bodies to bring about even the simplest bodily movements.

[81] Nursi would agree with Penelope Mady, who asks: "How can entities that do not even inhabit the physical universe take part in any causal interaction whatsoever? Surely to be abstract is to be causally inert." *Realism in Mathematics* (Oxford: Claredon Press, 1990), 37.

[82] David R. Griffin, "Interpreting Science from the Standpoint of Whiteheadian Process Philosophy," in *The Oxford Handbook of Religion and Science*, ed. Philip Clayton and Zachary Simpson (New York: Oxford University Press, 2006), 453.

Recall that earlier Ash'arites made the same point.[83] It is also important to note that a similar argument developed in French occasionalism in the seventeenth century. Arnold Geulincx, for example, writes that "You are not the cause of that which you do not know how to bring about."[84] Malebranche presents his own version of the argument: "But I deny that my will is the true cause of my arm's movement, of my mind's ideas, and of other things accompanying my volitions, for I see no relation whatever between such different things. I even see clearly that there can be no relation between the volition I have to move my arm and the agitation of the animal spirits, i.e., of certain tiny bodies whose motion and figure I do not know and which choose certain nerve canals from a million others I do not know in order to cause in me the motion I desire through an infinity of movements I do not desire."[85]

Very similarly, Nursi concludes that the human mind cannot be considered the real cause of things that it does not exhaustively comprehend, from bodily movements to natural processes. As he puts it, "these acts require consciousness. But *your consciousness does not relate to them.* Their cause is, thus, a Conscious Maker, and neither you nor your causes."[86] What is more important for the present discussion is that the act cannot be attributed to consciousness, even though they (the act and consciousness) are spatio-temporally attached to each other and occur conjointly. There is an *epistemological vertical gap* between the act itself and the consciousness.

I call the second approach the *argument from will.* Nursi states: "Human will is the most noble and strongest among causes. Despite the fact that human will relates to such commonplace and voluntary acts as eating and drinking, we are not the cause of them."[87] His argument in this and similar passages is as follows: There is always a disproportionality

[83] For different versions of this argument, see Bāqillānī, *al-Inṣāf*, 205; Juwaynī, *al-Irshād*, 174, Juwaynī, *al-'Aqīda al-Niẓāmiyya*, 191; Ghazālī, *al-Iqtisād*, 87–88; Nasafī, *al-Tabṣirāt al-Adilla*, II. 613–618; Rāzī, *Muḥaṣṣal*, 195.

[84] Arnold Geulincx, "*Metaphysica vera*," in *Arnoldi Geulincx antverpiensis Opera philosophica*, ed. J. P. N. Land, vol. 2 (The Hague: Martinum Nijhoff, 1893), 2:150–151.

[85] In *Oeuvres complètes de Malebranche*, ed. André Robinet, 20 vols. (Paris: Vrin, 1958–1984), III: 226. As Steven Nadler has also pointed out, the principle applies to all cases of causal efficacy: S. Nadler, "Knowledge, Volitional Agency and Causation in Malebranche and Geulincx," *British Journal for the History of Philosophy*, 7 (1999): 263–274.

[86] Nursi, *Mesnevī*, *Risale-i Nur Külliyatı*, 2: 1347. Emphasis mine. Translation mine.

[87] Ibid.

between will and motion. When I will to move my lips, I do so. But how does this happen? I do not observe a necessary connection between the act of willing and the act of moving my arm. My preponderance does not suffice to cause the event that is adjacent to it. It follows that there is always a *vertical gap* between preponderance or preference (cause) and effects.

I call the third approach the *argument from spatio-temporal continuity*, which is an implicit aspect of Nursi's occasionalism. The existence of a being a little while ago does not lead to the conclusion that it must still exist now. There is no necessary connection between the past and the present, or the present and the future. Recall that according to the Ashʿarite tradition, God constantly recreates atoms and the accidents that inhere in these atoms; the world is re-created anew at each moment. In one example, Nursi compares the world to a running river.[88] The river reflects the sun as it flows. When the connection between the river and the sun is cut as it flows under a bridge, the river stops reflecting the sunlight. In this sense, the river does not own (Tr. *mazhar*) the light but merely reflects (Tr. *memer*) it. The world is a multiplicity of constantly moving finite mirrors. Each mirror comes and goes, but the light persists.[89] The mirrors borrow their light (subsistence) from God. And if they borrow everything from God, then they are not the real cause of anything. This example reflects Nursi's belief that individual beings that join the flow of time do not have subsistence by themselves. In agreement with Santayana, Nursi suggests a type of "solipsism of the present moment."[90] The existence of beings in the past does not lead to the conclusion that they must exist now. Our experience in the world provides no evidence for a causal connection between past and present. There is always a disproportionality between past and present.

To conclude, a recurring theme throughout Nursi's corpus is the ever-present disproportionality in all causal relationships between cause and effect. Even the best explanations in terms of physical laws and secondary causality give us no reason to terminate our philosophical research at that

[88] "With divine permission, all creatures are unceasingly flowing in the river of time; they are being sent from the World of the Unseen; they are being clothed in external existence in the Manifest world; then they are being poured in orderly fashion into the World of the Unseen, and it is there that they alight. At their Sustainer's command, they continuously come from the future, stop by in passing pausing for a breath, and are poured into the past," Nursi, *The Flashes*, 281.

[89] Ibid., 280–281.

[90] See George Santayana, *Skepticism and Animal Faith* (New York: Dover, 1955), 14–15.

point. The vertical gap remains between the cause (chance, atoms, natural laws, will, past) and the effect (mathematicity, beauty, order, motion, consciousness, present).

10.6 CONCLUSION

Nursi's account of causality indicates that occasionalism is a living tradition and continues to interact with dominant scientific and philosophical paradigms. The case of Nursi also suggests that occasionalism continues produce synthesis with other strong currents in Islamic intellectual history. Nursi repeatedly draws on and reformulates certain occasionalist ideas with the help of Ibn ʿArabī's account of the divine names, which asserts that the world is a multiplicity of loci for the manifestations of the divine names. Nursi applies Ibn ʿArabī's ideas to his explanations of secondary causality, atoms, miracles, and physical laws without departing from the central tenets of Ashʿarite occasionalism. The result is an original synthesis of Ashʿarite *kalām* and Sufi metaphysics in the modern context.

Nursi also hints at what I have called the *disproportionality* of cause and effect. As far as I am aware, Nursi's is the first elaboration of this idea in the occasionalist tradition. Disproportionality means that effect/s are never reducible to their cause/s. Such qualities as mathematicity, beauty, order, motion, consciousness, and the present cannot be reduced to chance, atoms, physical laws, will, or the past. Nursi also advances several arguments to establish this point. Some of these arguments are novel, while others are borrowed from earlier Ashʿarite theologians. Nursi holds that there is a perpetual ontological and epistemological distance between cause and effect in all causal relations, and that it is within this distance that the divine qualities and names are unceasingly manifested. As such, all causality is transformed into a locus.

11

Islamic Theories of Causality in the Modern Context

The Religion and Science Debate

So far, I have examined the emergence and development of different accounts of causality in the Islamic tradition. In this chapter, I consider these accounts in the context of the modern discussion of the reconciliation of religious and scientific claims about the nature of the world. One of the most important parts of the debate is the problem of how we can make sense of the divine causality in accordance with the scientific methodology. It is this question that concerns us here. I aim to explore whether the examined theories on causality are viable options for thinking about the divine causality without undermining the rigor of the scientific approach to the world.

11.1 THE DIVINE CAUSALITY AND SCIENCE

How should one understand the divine causality in the age of science? How does God act in the world? Many thinkers draw a helpful distinction between "General Divine Action" (GDA) and "Special Divine Action" (SDA) to approach this question.[1] Nicholas Saunders offers a detailed examination of various ways to consider GDA and SDA, especially the latter. For him, GDAs are "those actions of God that pertain to the whole of creation universally and simultaneously. These include actions such as the initial creation and the maintenance of scientific regularity and the

[1] Paul Draper posits an analogous distinction between "direct" and "indirect" divine action in "God, Science, and Naturalism," in *The Oxford Handbook of Philosophy of Religion*, ed. William J. Wainwright (Oxford: Oxford University Press, 2005), 281.

laws of nature by God." SDA refers to "those actions of God that pertain to a *particular* time and place in creation as distinct from another. This is a broad category and includes the traditional understanding of 'miracles', the notion of particular providence, responses to intercessory prayer, God's personal actions, and some forms of religious experience."[2]

There have been criticisms of both proposed concepts. G. D. Kaufman, for example, argues that "it is no longer possible for us to think of individual or particular events by themselves in our modern experience."[3] The scientific evidence about the interconnectivity of all events make SDAs not only "difficult to believe" but also "inconceivable." SDA proposals also have elicited criticisms of a possible lack of justice, capriciousness, excessive anthropomorphism, and apathy on the part of God.[4] GDA proposals have also been met with critique. If God is acting by maintaining the laws of nature, this leads to the denial of any causal feedback and autonomy on the part of the created order and, hence, makes God directly responsible of all events – raising difficult questions about free will, moral responsibility, and theodicy.[5] Due to these difficulties concerning both GDA and SDA proposals, Saunders suggests that "we need to seek a middle ground between these two views: one in which GDA is the continuous background to specific instances of SDA in which God may act in a personal manner."[6]

Attempts have been made to address this challenge. Many thinkers have examined theological and philosophical implications of certain scientific theories to make sense of divine action in the age of science.[7] Arthur Compton, Eric Mascall, Edmund Whittaker, George Thomson, Robert Russell, and Nancy Murphy trace the philosophical implications of quantum mechanics to argue that divine action is intelligible without violating the law-like behavior of natural phenomena.[8] The probabilistic

[2] Nicholas Saunders, *Divine Action and Modern Science* (Cambridge, UK: Cambridge University Press, 2002), 21 (emphasis mine).

[3] G. D. Kaufman, "On the Meaning of 'Act of God,'" *Harvard Theological Review*, 61 (1968): 188.

[4] M. Wiles, *Reason to Believe* (London: SCM Press, 1999), 16–17.

[5] For a lengthy discussion, see Saunders, *Divine Action and Modern Science*, 17–47.

[6] Ibid., 31.

[7] There are a number of excellent works providing the history of the discussion, such as Ian G. Barbour, *When Science Meets Religion* (New York: Harper Collins, 2000); Ted Peters, *Science and Theology: The New Consonance* (Oxford: Westview Press, 1998); Ian G. Barbour, *When Science Meets Religion* (New York: Harper Collins, 2000), 31.

[8] Cf. Nancey Murphy, *Reconciling Theology and Science: A Radical Reformation Perspective* (Kitchener, Ontario: Pandora Press, 1997); Robert J. Russell, Nancey

laws of quantum mechanics imply that there are indeterminacies at different levels of reality. These indeterminacies are intrinsic in nature. According to the mainstream theory of quantum mechanics the wave-function is in a state of superposition of several possibilities. God acts by affecting "subatomic particles as a quasi-physical force" and manipulates the quantum system.[9] This is to say, quantum systems always have more than one potential, and God may be understood as realizing one of these potentials but not others. In the end, the wave-function collapses into a choice of one of the desired possibilities. This in turn gives rise to certain changes in the higher levels of the classical world.[10] For example, the quantum events taking place within a DNA molecule might cause certain genetic mutations that are amplified by the germ line and influence an organism's evolutionary trajectory. Thus, the probabilistic laws of quantum mechanics would be the definition of the way God acts in the world.[11] As Tracy puts it, "this providential determination of otherwise undetermined events will not transgress natural law, as long as this divine action operates within the statistical regularities."[12]

Some of these authors have used chaos theory to suggest that nonlinear systems provide a way of thinking about divine action. These systems are very highly sensitive to small changes in the initial conditions, rendering the outcome practically unpredictable. Chaos theory is, however, quite different from quantum theory. It functions within a framework defined by classical mechanics and does not suggest new postulates or ontological and intrinsic indeterminacies in natural processes. It is not a "novel theory of physics." The central question here is the computability of chaotic systems. John Polkinghorne has given special attention to the theological implications of chaos theory. Given our inability to know all initial

Murphy, and Arthur Peacocke, eds, *Chaos and Complexity: Scientific Perspectives on Divine Action* (Vatican City State: Vatican Observatory Publications, 1995).

9 R. J. Russell, "Does 'the God Who Acts' Really Act? New Approaches to Divine Action in the Light of Science," *Theology Today*, 54.1 (1997): 64–65.

10 It is important to understand that these potentials are already provided by the system and not introduced from outside.

11 Nancy Murphy, "Divine Action in the Natural Order: Buridan's Ass and Schrodinger's Cat," in *Chaos and Complexity: Scientific Perspectives on Divine Action*, ed. Robert Russell, Nancy Murphy, and Arthur Peacocke (Vatican City State: Vatican Observatory Publications, 1995), 344–348; also see Saunders, *Divine Action and Modern Science*, 155.

12 T. F. Tracy, "Particular Providence and the God of the Gaps," in *Chaos and Complexity: Scientific Perspectives on Divine Action*, ed. R. Russell, N. Murphy, and A. Peacocke (Vatican: Vatican Observatory and Berkeley: The Center for Theology and the Natural Sciences, 1995), 315.

conditions, chaotic systems remain incalculable. In fact, mathematical formulations describing these dynamic systems reach a state of infinite density, in which there is no difference between alternating options. Since the initial conditions are unknown, we might think of God as differentiating two nearby options by introducing some infinitesimal input affecting the overall outcome of the whole system without adding extra energy. This very small input is amplified by the dynamics of the chaotic system and subsequently changes the behavior of all systems.[13]

Some have applied system biology and emergence theory to argue against what they view as scientific reductionism that holds that lower-level structures always determine upper-level occurrences. These theories point to the idea that the world works top down as well as bottom up. For the proponents of this approach, this insight provided by science calls for a paradigm shift and reconceptualization of the divine action.[14] Arthur Peacocke uses the scientific concept of supervenient properties, which "emerge" from lower levels but are not reducible to those levels. These emergent properties exercise a top-down causal influence on lower levels.[15] As such, the idea of emergence allows us to think about the relationship between God and cosmos in a panentheistic way. God both includes and transcends the world. God is neither separate from nor reducible to the world. This relationship can be likened, to use Peacocke's analogy, to the relationship of a composer and their music.[16] As the composer cannot be reduced to his work, God, cannot be reduced to the world. However, there is an

[13] For a defense of this position, see John Polkinghorne, *Science and Providence: God's Interaction with the World* (Boston, MA: Society for Promoting Christian Knowledge, 1989); and *Science and Theology: An Introduction* (Minneapolis, MN: First Fortress Press, 1999); and *Belief in God in the Age of Science* (New Haven, CT: Yale University Press, 2002).

[14] For a defense of this position, see Philip Clayton, *In Quest of Freedom: The Emergence of Spirit in the Natural World* (Gottingen: Vandenhoeck and Ruprech, 2009); and *Mind and Emergence: From Quantum to Consciousness* (Oxford: Oxford University Press, 2004).

[15] Arthur Peacocke, *Theology for a Scientific Age: Being and Becoming–Natural, Divine, and Human*, 2nd ed. (London: SCM Press, 1993), 159–160; See also Philip Clayton, *God and Contemporary Science* (Edinburgh: Edinburgh University Press, 1997), 232–269; and "Panentheism Today: A Constructive Systematic Evaluation," in *In Whom We Live and Move and Have Our Being: Panentheistic Reflections on God's Presence in a Scientific World*, ed. P. Clayton and A. Peacocke (Grand Rapids, MI: Wm B. Eerdmans Publishing Co., 2004), 263–264; and "Natural Law and Divine Action: The Search for an Expanded Theory of Causation," *Zygon*, 39 (2004): 632–633.

[16] Arthur Peacocke, *Theology for a Scientific Age*, 173–177; also, *Creation and the World of Science: The Reshaping of Belief*, 2nd edn (Oxford: Oxford University Press, 2004), 105–106.

immanent relationship between the composer and the piece of music. As Philip Clayton states, "the infinite God is ontologically as close to finite things as can possibly be thought without dissolving the distinction of Creator and created altogether."[17]

The proposed theological interpretations of quantum mechanics, chaotic systems, and emergence theory have also elicited criticism. First, it has been argued that scientific theories are constantly evolving and therefore tentative. There are unsettled issues in all these fields. Hence, a theological interpretation offered on the basis of the current status of a scientific theory renders any reconciliatory attempt tentative and, thus, problematic. To respond to this objection, one can argue that the fact that scientific theories continuously evolve does not lead to the conclusion that any attempt for reconciliation of religion and science is problematic. Theological interpretation of a given theory should just take this tentativeness into account. Moreover, there are fundamental truths that science has discovered about the world that do not appear to be tentative, including that the laws of nature can be expressed as mathematical formulae and that the world is fine-tuned for life.

Second, it has also been said that scientific theories lend themselves to multiple philosophical readings. Quantum theory, for example, allows indeterministic interpretations but does not require them. A deterministic interpretation of the theory is also possible.[18] The theory also seriously limits the influence of indeterministic interactions at the subatomic level on the development of the world. Saunders, for instance, contends that through quantum mechanics it takes millions of years to achieve even the simplest effects.[19] The probabilistic nature of the subatomic world seems to be averaged out by deterministic laws on higher levels.

Third, it has also been suggested that the proposed theological interpretations of modern scientific theories may lead to an excessively anthropomorphic understanding of God, which competes against the created causes, "either pushing them aside in interventionist miracles or delicately bringing divine influence to bear at points where the system of infinite causes is incomplete."[20] This is a theological problem. But if

17 Philip Clayton, "The Pantheistic Turn in Christian Theology," *Dialog*, 38 (1999): 290.

18 As suggested, for example, by David Bohm.

19 N. T. Saunders, "Does God Cheat at Dice? Divine Action and Quantum Possibilities," *Zygon*, 35.3 (2000): 541–542.

20 Thomas F. Tracy, "Theologies of Divine Action," in *The Oxford Handbook of Religion and Science*, ed. Philip Clayton and Zachary Simpson (New York: Oxford University Press, 2006), 608.

one's theological premise allows a degree of anthropomorphism or some event to place God "in a subordinate position to creation,"[21] as is the case in some kenotic accounts, this may not appear to be a problem.

What we can safely say here is that the question of divine causality remains unresolved. The proposals are open to criticism, rendering this an ongoing and vibrant debate.

A closer look at the discussions among modern Muslim scholars also reveals a number of tendencies pertinent to the reconciliation of religious beliefs and scientific findings. In the late nineteenth and early twentieth century, Jamal al-Din Afghani, Muhammad Abduh, and Said Nursi argued that there cannot be a real conflict between the revealed text, the Qur'an, and the created text, the world, for the author of both texts is God. Therefore, religion and science can, in principle, be harmonized. "Apparent" conflicts may be resolved by reinterpreting the text on the basis of scientific findings (while not disregarding the tentativeness of those findings). Furthermore, in their writings, science holds theological and spiritual significance. Said Nursi, as examined above, believes that science unearths the hidden treasures of the divine names manifested in the world. The art, harmony, beauty, mathematicity, and design in the world reflect divine qualities. The real conflict between religion and science arises when science is used for destructive purposes and domination, as in colonialism. Hence, the reconciliation of religion and science is primarily an ethical matter.[22]

Another major tendency emerges among Muslim scholars in the late twentieth century. This is the argument that science is a social construct. Ismail al-Faruqi and Ziauddin Sardar, for example, draw on the insights of contemporary philosophy of science as elaborated by such philosophers as Popper, Polanyi, Kuhn, Feyerabend, and Lakatos as well as postmodern criticism of absolutist truth claims. In this literature, science appears as a time-bound and culture-specific activity. This allows

[21] Saunders, "Does God Cheat at Dice? Divine Action and Quantum Possibilities," 541–542.

[22] Science here is imagined as an ethically value-free domain. For a lengthy discussion, see Ibrahim Kalin, "Three Views of Science in the Islamic World," in *God, Life and the Cosmos: Christian and Islamic Perspectives*, ed. Ted Peters, Muzaffar Iqbal, and Syed Nomanul Haq (Aldershot: Ashgate, 2002), 43–75. For a refutation of this position, see Taner Edis, *An Illusion of Harmony: Science and Religion in Islam* (Amherst, NY: Prometheus Books, 2007).

questioning of the epistemic status of science and rejects the hierarchy created between religious and scientific truth claims.[23] Relativization of scientific epistemology also allows Faruqi to argue that in an Islamic framework not only the interpretations of scientific findings but also the very methodology of science changes. He then launches an ineffectual project for the "Islamization" of science. There has been criticism of this account as well, on the basis that the project of the Islamization of science implies certain localization of scientific activity and hence overlooks the universality of its methodology. Nidhal Guessoum, for instance, posits that science already has a solid foundation and efficient methodology. The whole attempt to localize or reinvent science is both ineffectual and unnecessary.[24]

There are also scholars such as Seyyed Hossein Nasr, Alparslan Açıkgenç, and Osman Bakar who argue that the tension between religion and science cannot be resolved without modifying the metaphysical premises of modern science, which is intrinsically secular and inevitably desacralizes the world. The only way to prevent this outcome is to revitalize the traditional sacred outlook of sciences – whether Chinese, Hindu, or Islamic – that might study the world as efficiently as modern science without absorbing its metaphysical assumptions. Nasr, for example, together with the members of the Traditionalist (Perennialist) School such as Frithjof Schuon, René Guénon, and Titus Burckhardt, argues that the premodern and modern sciences have differences in their conceptions of nature, methods, cosmological presumptions, and epistemological stance as well as the parametric framework through which they process the "facts" found by observation and experimentation.[25] Their arguments are not always clear, but Nasr and others do seem to suggest that the modern worldview is to be deconstructed by changing our most fundamental assumptions about the nature of reality, assumptions that

[23] See Ismail al-Fārūqī, *Islamization of Knowledge: General Principles and Work Plan* (Washington, DC: IIIT, 1982); and Ziauddin Serdar, *Explorations in Islamic Science* (London: Mansell Publishing Ltd, 1989).

[24] Nidhal Guessoum, *Islam's Quantum Question: Reconciling Muslim Tradition and Modern Science* (London and New York: I.B.Tauris, 2011), 110–139.

[25] Nasr's contribution to the field is immense. See his *An Annotated Bibliography of Islamic Science*, 3 vols (Lahore: Suhail Academy, 1985); *Science and Civilization in Islam* (Cambridge, UK: Cambridge University Press, 1987); *An Introduction to Islamic Cosmological Doctrines* (Cambridge, UK: Cambridge University Press, 1964). For the defense of this position by other authors, see Alparslan Acikgenc, *Islam Medeniyetinde Bilgi ve Bilim* (Istanbul: Turkiye Diyanet Vakfi, 2006); Osman Bakar, *Classification of Knowledge in Islam* (Cambridge, UK: The Islamic Text Society, 1998).

are dictated by the dominant dualist-mechanistic-anthropocentric paradigm.[26]

More recent scholarship provides some criticism of these accounts. Guessoum asserts that Nasr's project relies on vague principles. The ideas of the robust unity of God and the role of intuitive knowledge do not add anything innovative to our understanding of scientific processes. We do not need to deconstruct science to resacralize it. The overall purpose is to reconcile "religious tradition with rational and scientific modernity … without being schizophrenic."[27] Similarly, Golshani argues that Nasr's metaphysical discussion is unnecessary because "science and metaphysics are complementary rather than contradictory."[28] Furthermore, Stefano Bigliardi observes that the "new generation" of Muslim authors do not advocate any kind of "Islamization" of science.[29]

What is more important for our discussion is that there are also certain proposals regarding how to think about divine causality in accordance with scientific methodology in the world. For instance, Guessoum defends methodological naturalism as a viable option. Guessoum does not see any contradiction between "adopting both a theistic worldview and a thoroughly naturalistic methodology for science." He argues that methodological naturalism is "a neutral standpoint and approach, and it has proven to be fruitful, appearing to correspond to how the world functions." Moreover, theologies that are consistent with methodological naturalism can also be constructed by tapping into rationalist tendencies within Islam, such as Muʿtazilite theology.[30] Guessoum also believes that God interacts with us "through the spirit … not through the physical mechanisms."[31] In accordance with his methodological naturalism, Guessoum rejects miracles.[32]

[26] For a good study of Nasr's account, see Ibrahim Kalın, "The Sacred versus the Secular: Nasr on Science," in *Library of Living Philosophers: Seyyed Hossein Nasr*, ed. L. E. Hahn, R. E. Auxier, and L. W. Stone (Chicago, IL: Open Court Press, 2001), 445–462.

[27] Guessoum, *Islam's Quantum Question*, xxvi.

[28] Mahdi Golshani, *From Physics to Metaphysics* (Tehran: Institute for Humanities and Cultural Studies 1997), 75.

[29] Stefano Bigliardi, *Islam and the Quest for Modern Science: Conversations with Adnan Oktar, Mehdi Golshani, Mohammed Basil Altaie, Zaghloul El-Naggar, Bruno Guiderdoni and Nidhal Guessoum.* Transactions (Istanbul: Swedish Research Institute in Istanbul, 2014), 180.

[30] http://muslim-science.com/islam-science-methodological-naturalism-divine-action-and-miracles/.

[31] Bigliardi, *Islam and the Quest for Modern Science*, 175, 176.

[32] Ibid., 173.

Similarly, Golshani argues that miracles are actually rare natural phenomena. They take place through "different laws of nature which we do not know." Golshani is clear that these phenomena do occur and that reports of them should not be interpreted metaphorically. It is possible that the miracles described in the sacred texts actually took place due to "unknown physical causes."[33] However, Guessoum finds Golshani's argument logically flawed, for if a miraculous event is taking place through natural laws, albeit unknown, it cannot bear the label "miraculous" anymore.[34] There cannot be natural miracles.

Mohammed B. Altaie goes back to Ashʿarite theology, especially Ghazālī's writings, to argue for divine action in the world. He suggests that the celebrated Ashʿarite doctrine of the re-creation of the world anew at each moment can be used to explain divine action at the quantum level. He writes that "properties of matter and energy are renewed billions of times in a second … and the one who is renewing these properties is God."[35] Accordingly, Altaie accepts that miracles stem from the "probabilistic nature of the physical world."[36] They are extremely rare but do exist. Similarly, Bruno Guiderdoni accepts the possibility of miracles as singular and unrepeatable events. Precisely due to their singularity and rarity, "science cannot say anything about miracles," since science can only explain repeatable events. Yet Guiderdoni does not see "God intervening as an agent" because such an account "lowers our idea of God." Although God can change the laws of nature, "He deliberately chooses not to change them."[37]

This short overview suggests that the primary issues for Muslim scholars in the reconciliation of religion and science are ethical, epistemological, and metaphysical. These scholars argue that conflict arises when foundational texts are read with false assumptions and arbitrarily; when the power of science is used without ethical consideration; when the limitations of scientific epistemology are not understood, or when the underlying metaphysical assumptions of science are not realized.

[33] Ibid., 57–58.

[34] Ibid., 173. Guessoum also implies that although God can violate His own laws, He does not necessarily do so. "God put together the laws so that things function in an orderly manner," ibid., 175.

[35] Ibid., 98. [36] Ibid., 84. [37] Ibid., 146–147.

11.2 SCIENCE AND ISLAMIC OCCASIONALISM

I turn now to discuss the possible bearings of Islamic occasionalism on what we may call the heart of the contemporary debate over religion and science: the reconciliation of the divine causality and scientific methodology. My investigation identifies strengths and weaknesses of Islamic occasionalism in addressing this challenge.

One of the greatest merits of Islamic occasionalism is that its framework entails several presuppositions that overlap with the guiding principles of scientific inquiry. Namely, an occasionalist can argue, without contradicting the internal logic of the theory, that interactions in the world are regular, physical occurrences are lawful, and physical calculations and predictions are possible. The consistency of natural processes is a basic concept in Islamic occasionalism, as the notion of habit suggests. Although occasionalism denies necessary connection, it affirms constant conjunction in a way that can secure the regularity and uniformity of cause-and-effect interactions. The denial of causal necessity in things does not necessarily imply chaotic happenings in the world. The theory explicitly states that God creates on a self-imposed habitual pattern and does not rule over the world in an arbitrary manner. If this is the case, as Griffel observes, to the extent that there is no break in God's habits, the world of Islamic occasionalism remains *indistinguishable* from a universe governed by physical laws.[38]

But what about miracles? How can an occasionalist deal with the possibility of breaks in God's habits without undermining the guiding principles of natural sciences? Ibn Rushd has already insisted that the moment one denies necessary connection in causality, one cannot make any reliable predictions about the world. Islamic occasionalism can offer three possible solutions to this challenge.

1. The first is to marginalize extraordinary events to an extent that the normal operation of the laws of nature remains the central explanatory framework for the physical world, and to appeal to the supernatural, as William Dembski suggested elsewhere, only when there are very strong reasons to believe that "empirical resources are exhausted."[39]

[38] Frank Griffel, "Al-Ghazali," *The Stanford Encyclopedia of Philosophy* (Winter 2016 Edition), ed. Edward N. Zalta: https://plato.stanford.edu/archives/win2016/entries/al-ghazali/.

[39] William Dembski, "On the Very Possibility of Intelligent Design," in *The Creation Hypothesis*, ed. J. P. Moreland (Downers Grove, IL: InterVarsity Press, 1994), 132.

In fact, Ghazālī himself proposes a similar solution. Anticipating Ibn Rushd's criticism, Ghazālī accepts that if a necessary connection between cause and effect is denied, then it is possible that "if someone leaves a book in the house, this book, on his returning home, could change into an intelligent slave boy or into an animal."[40] Provided that this is not a logical impossibility and that God is all-powerful and absolutely free, then, in fact, a book could turn into "a slave boy or an animal." However, this does not happen, nor should we expect it to, for the following reason:

> God created for us the knowledge that He does not enact these possibilities (*mumkināt*) . . . The continuous habit (*istimrār al-ʿāda*) of their occurrences repeatedly, one time after another, *fixes unshakably* in our minds the belief in their occurrence according to the past habit.[41]

In this passage, Ghazālī aims to marginalize the extraordinary events without denying their possibility. The consistency of the natural processes "fixes *unshakably* in our minds the belief in their occurrence according to the past habit." According to this version of occasionalism, the world is not governed by an "arbitrary king." This at least is not the conclusion scholars like Ghazālī mean to suggest. Our "unshakable" belief in the regularity in this world depends on the consistency of the cosmic history of the world. If regular occurrences dominated the past, they will also dominate the present and the future.[42]

What is important for our discussion is that despite his criticism of necessary connection, Ghazālī still bows to the idea of consistency, which we use to regulate our lives.[43] Ghazālī is skeptical only about the metaphysical framework of causality, not the structure of causality. In his system, natural processes remain regular and law-like. Although God can change the laws of nature, He chooses not to change them. Thus, a "common-sense" view of causality is necessary.[44] While we fail

[40] Ghazālī, *Tahāfut*, 170. [41] Ibid.

[42] Ghazālī is not alone in holding this conviction. Many in the later occasionalist *Kalam* tradition agree with him. See for example, Jurjānī, *Sharḥ al-Mawāqif*, trans. Omer Turker, a Parallel Turkish–Arabic text, 3 vols (Istanbul: Turkiye Yazma Eserler Kurumu Baskanligi, 2015), 512.

[43] A. N. Whitehead also writes of how "we must bow to those presumptions, which, in despite of criticism, we still employ for the regulation of our lives," *Process and Reality*, 151. Quoted in David Ray Griffin, "Science and Process Philosophy," in *The Oxford Handbook of Religion and Science*, ed. Philip Clayton and Zachary Simpson (Oxford: Oxford University Press, 2006).

[44] At this juncture, it can also be noted that the Scottish "common sense" school shares a similar sentiment. The most famous member of the school, Thomas Reid, shares much of the skepticism of Hume regarding causality. He agrees that we have no sensory

to demonstrate the necessary connection, we must still run our lives *as if* there were a necessary connection. One could choose, from a metaphysical point of view, to believe the truth of occasionalist claims, but one would still, from a practical point of view, live life with the predictability of the world in mind. As such, Ghazālī endorses the view that, in an occasionalist framework, despite a qualified skepticism about the nature of causal relations, the idea of consistency of natural processes is still, to borrow a Kantian concept, a necessary postulate of practical reason.[45]

A similar tendency to accept but marginalize miracles can also be observed among earlier Muslim occasionalists. Bāqillānī, for example, argues that God breaks the normal course of events and creates miracles only to protect His prophets.[46] This is to say that miracles are meaningful only in the context of prophetic missions. As, according to Islamic prophetology, the prophetic missions ended in the seventh century, one should not expect any subsequent breaks in the apparent natural order.

At this juncture, we may also note the possibility for an occasionalist to make a distinction between metaphysical opinion and scientific method, given that the primary concern of occasionalism is the metaphysical framework of efficient causality, not the structure of efficient causality. This comes from the basic insight of occasionalism that observation reveals only constant conjunction and cannot prove necessary connection. The dichotomy between necessary connection and constant conjunction always remains, even after the best scientific explanation. Accordingly, an occasionalist could believe that the natural sciences provide a greater degree of explanatory possibility vis-à-vis the physical world than any other known method without offering metaphysical truth, for the way phenomenal causes exercise influence is beyond our comprehension. In fact, in later occasionalist tradition there is a move in this direction. For example, Ibn Khaldūn – who is widely viewed as an occasionalist,[47] and

experience of necessary relation between cause and effect. But this does not make our common sense of causality mistaken. See Ryan Nichols and Gideon Yaffe, "Thomas Reid," *The Stanford Encyclopedia of Philosophy* (Winter 2016 Edition), ed. Edward N. Zalta: https://plato.stanford.edu/archives/win2016/entries/reid/.

45 See for example, Kant, *Critique of Practical Reason* (1788), trans. and ed. M. J. Gregor (Cambridge, UK: Cambridge University Press, 1996), 5:135–136.

46 Bāqillānī, *al-Bayān*, 52–55.

47 For some evaluations of Ibn Khaldūn's theory of causality, see Edward Omar Moad, "Ibn Khaldūn and Occasionalism," in *Occasionalism Revisited: New Essays from the Islamic*

the first philosopher to study history and society as an object of systematic science – writes that "even if [those sciences] are not adequate to achieve the intention [metaphysical certainty] of the Philosophers, they constitute the *soundest norm of speculation we know*."[48] Although physical sciences cannot achieve metaphysical certainty, they can present greater or lesser approximations about the physical world. This separation between metaphysical truth and scientific methodology makes it easier for an occasionalist to subscribe to occasionalism as a metaphysical opinion while acknowledging the methodological value of scientific research.

It may even be argued that Ashʿarite occasionalism shares certain qualities with empiricism, given the former's skepticism toward causal connections on the grounds that they cannot be located in observation. This occasionalist attitude might have certain advantages for scientific research because of its emphasis on observation. As indicated in Chapter 5, this skepticism in fact leads to a questioning attitude toward some of the mental constructions of Ptolemaic Astronomy and Aristotelian physics. ʿAlī Qushjī, for example, criticizes the idea of celestial spheres as being purely mental construction without any basis in the senses. This might have played a role in stripping scientific activity of certain unnecessary philosophical concepts.

These and similar incidents in the history of Islamic occasionalism indicate that a coherent occasionalist study of the world should resort to natural causes when explaining physical phenomena. This form of occasionalism only appeals to the supernatural when there are very strong reasons to believe that empirical resources are exhausted. The acceptance of these extremely low-probability events that occur perhaps only once in the universe's lifetime does not really affect how one studies the world here and now. On the other hand, such occasionalism can also bring together both general and specific divine action proposals, since God's

and Western Philosophical Traditions, ed. Nazif Muhtaroglu (Abu Dhabi: Kalam Research Media, 2017), 61–82; Syed Farid Alatas, *Ibn Khaldun* (Oxford: Oxford University Press, 2012), 105–116; H. A. R. Gibb, "The Islamic Background of Ibn Khaldun's Political Theory," *Bulletin of the School of Oriental Studies, University of London*, 7.1 (1933): 23–31; Aziz al-Azmeh, *Ibn Khaldun in Modern Scholarship: A Study in Orientalism* (London: Third World Centre for Research and Publishing, 1981), 79–81; Henry A. Wolfson, "Ibn Khaldun on Attributes and Predestination," *Speculum*, 34.4 (1959): 586.

48 Ibn Khaldūn, *Muqaddima*, ed. N. J. Dawood and trans. Franz Rosenthal (Princeton, NJ and Oxford: Princeton University Press, 2004), 405.

universal action is "the continuous background" of extremely rare but possible specific divine actions.[49]

2. The second possible answer is to argue that, although Islamic occasionalism *accepts the possibility of breaks in God's habits, it certainly does not require them*. Occasionalism sees the divine action behind all causal activity. The way the world operates is the same as the way God creates. Hence, although Muslim occasionalists allow the possibility of an intervention, they do not require it to affirm the divine action. The theory is not designed to seek God in extraordinary events or miracles but in causality itself. Both Jesus's walk on water and a ship's floating on water, in this view, can be called miracles. In fact, the concepts of intervention and miracle are quite marginal according to the internal logic of the theory, the primary goal of which is to explain the normal, law-like flow of natural processes without positing necessary causal connections and without establishing causal intermediation between God and the world. To put it another way, occasionalism aims to view all ordinary events as miracles, in that God's conjunction of cause and effect is miraculously predictable and frequent. The main goal is to find God "in what we know." Given that Islamic occasionalism does not need violations of the laws of nature in order to argue for divine action, the theory actually comes close to scientific methodology as it pertains to the study of the world.

3. The third possible answer, which is closely related to the second, is to argue that occasionalism can adopt an entirely different view of miracles. Many authors have proposed a rational and naturalistic view of miracles. In this literature, miracles do not appear as "violations of the laws of nature" but as "extremely rare events that fall under the laws of nature." They are "consistent with, but transcend, natural processes."[50] In Muslim intellectual history, this view of miracles can be traced back to Ibn Sīnā and Ibn Rushd. For example, Ibn Rushd defends the position that while miracles result from extremely rare causal sequences, we may not be able to identify what those causes are. Despite this conviction, he

[49] Ummeyye Isra Yazicioglu argues that Said Nursi's distinction between "universal and general principles" and "special favours and manifestations" implies that "the very structure of the universe is such that, instead of being resigned to the ruthless precision or "constraints" of natural laws, one can hope for a special dispensation in unique situations, and act with that hope." *Understanding the Qur'anic Miracle Stories in the Modern Age* (University Park, PA: Penn State University Press, 2013).

[50] Terence L. Nichols, "Miracles in Science and Theology," *Zygon*, 37.3 (2002): 703–716.

also argues that miracles should not be questioned, at least publicly, because of their function in the religious and ethical education of the masses (i.e. confirming prophethood). In addition, several modern Muslim thinkers such as Guessoum and Golshani have adopted naturalistic explanations of miracles.[51]

Can an occasionalist accept the view of miracles as consistent with natural laws? I believe the answer is in the affirmative. There is no need for Islamic occasionalism to depict miracles as violations of natural laws, despite the general tendency among Ashʿarites to see them as such. God could create miracles as violations of natural laws or consistent with natural laws. If Muslim occasionalists' main idea is that both cause and effect are created by God without intermediation and attached to each other on a self-imposed habitual path, then these premises are preserved in both cases – even when one sees miracles as extremely rare events that are consistent with the known/unknown laws of nature. So long as God is preserved as the creator of cause and effect, both natural and supernatural views of miracles appear to be in accordance with the logic of occasionalism. If this is true, then Islamic occasionalism could endorse the idea that the world is to be studied *as if* there are no causal gaps or breaks in God's habits or violations of the laws of nature.

At this point, a critic might argue that if science has shown that the world follows laws in all its processes and phenomena, why can we not just say that God acts indirectly by sustaining the world and its laws and letting things work out according to these laws? It is true that from the perspective of deistic and similar alternative accounts, one can make the case that one should study the world *as if* it is governed by secondary causality. The aim of this discussion, however, is not to make Islamic occasionalism compete with other proposals that explain the divine creative action. It simply examines whether this theory of causality – which throughout Islamic intellectual history (and in the present) has offered for many Muslims a theologically and metaphysically compelling account of the world – can contribute to this discussion of divine creative action.

Another criticism might be that Islamic occasionalism is simply mental acrobatics. Occasionalism rests on the notion that the "constant conjunction" (between events) does not constitute "necessary connection"; that natural laws are God's habits; and that the world is re-created anew at each moment. The premises are not necessarily intuitive.

[51] See Bigliardi, *Islam and the Quest for Modern Science*, 57–60, 81, 145–146.

Moreover, when the "conjunction" is always there, it is difficult to argue that there is no connection. Thus, a critic might hold, occasionalism is merely sophistry. Perhaps the only response that Islamic occasionalism could offer here is to say that an argument should not be discarded simply because it sounds far-fetched. As a metaphysical doctrine, its strength can only be evaluated by exploring its internal consistency and adequacy to explain sensual phenomena on its own terms.[52]

A critic might also contend that the idea of indistinguishability of divine causation and secondary causation leaves us with no argument for God's existence. Islamic occasionalism postulates that God affects the universe as a whole in all points of time and space. But if all instances of change and continuity in the world are the work of God, how can we infer the existence of God from natural phenomena? If every event is the result of God's creative act, then nature cannot be really said to provide a framework for investigating divine activity. In other words, if God is everywhere, then there is no way of saying God is "here." As Walker writes, "if God's action is applicable to every class of events (natural, miraculous) and, in some cases, to everything, then the words 'God's action' seem to have lost any substantive content either as that which excites wonder, on the one hand, or as individual enough to be construed as the separate class of acts, called 'God's acts', on the other."[53] Can Islamic occasionalism provide an answer here? A possible response is that the regularity, elegance, and beauty of nature and its laws are enough of an "argument" for God's existence here and everywhere and all the time. Not specific instances but the totality of the world justifies the argument.

The critic may also argue that if Islamic occasionalism's reconciliation rests on the assertion that natural laws are, in reality, reflections of God's habitual creation, then the theory provides nothing more than a way of thinking about God's causality and a scientific understanding of causality as being on two parallel tracks. However, it is not appropriate to see this as a way of reconciliation. Are we not just offering a lexical equivalence to materialistic naturalisms? First, this criticism can be raised against all accounts of the world that locate God in all points of time and space, including Plotinus's One, Tillich's Ground of Being, Neville's Creator, and Ibn 'Arabī's *al-Ḥaqq*. Second, I believe the objection is premised on the wrong assumption of what the reconciliatory strategy of Islamic

[52] Here, I follow Alfred N. Whitehead's proposal in *Process and Reality*, 3–7.

[53] I. Walker, *The Problem of Evil and the Activity of God* (London: New Blackfriars, 1982), 29.

occasionalism actually is. The theory does not offer two parallel tracks (theological and scientific) relating to and explaining the same natural phenomena. Its strategy is rather to locate scientific discourse in a larger metaphysical framework without negating its legitimacy, authority, and distinctive methodology. Maybe the more proper analogy here would be concentric circles instead of parallel tracks.

Despite these advantages, there are certain theological and philosophical challenges to Islamic occasionalism. It cannot be considered a viable worldview unless they are resolved. I briefly discuss these challenges next.

First, Islamic occasionalism can be a viable option only if the reality of free will is established. Is human choice created? If occasionalism envisages that both cause and effect are created by the Divine Power, then human choice, as a cause, must also be created by God. In other words, human choice is not an uncaused cause of itself. In this case we would lose genuine human freedom. Can this problem be solved?

As discussed in Chapter 10, some scholars attempt to solve this problem by placing human choice between existence and nonexistence. Nursi, for example, drawing on Ṣadr al-Sharīʿah, describes human will as neither existent nor nonexistent. As such, human choice is defined as a relative matter (*amrun iḍāfiyyun* or *amrun ʿitibarīyyun*).[54] Relative matters, such as rightness or leftness, can only exist in relation to an object. They cannot be put in the same ontological category with the object existing *in concreto*. Rightness or leftness do not have external existence and exist as relative matters only in the mind. But how does this solution escape the seemingly deterministic conclusions of occasionalism? The argument continues that if human will-choice is not truly an existing thing, it cannot be considered created or caused. If human will is beyond the scope of the act of creation, it should be free. This solution is also consistent with the principles of occasionalism, for God still creates every existing entity.

But this proposition does not appear to solve the problem, for even if relative matters are beyond the scope of divine power, they still emerge as a result of the application of the divine power in the natural world. The rightness and leftness of a wall emerge as a result of the creation of that wall. Relative matters, as relational entities, are then determined by the creation of other beings to which they are related. This implies that free will, as a relative matter, is still a determined quality. Moreover,

[54] Nursi, *The Words*, 482. For Ṣadr al-Sharīʿa, *Sharḥ al-Talwīh*, 332, 337, 338, 349. See also Ibn Humām, *Kitāb al-Musāyara*, 112–113.

how can a relative matter, which does not qualify as fully existing, be robust enough to anchor genuine freedom? More generally, how are we to make sense of the putative intermediate realm between existence and nonexistence? How can there be a third possibility between existence and nonexistence (*principium tertii exclusi*)? These are difficult questions that Islamic occasionalist tradition must address in order to establish the reality of free will in a way consistent with the logic of occasionalism.

Second, the failure sufficiently to ground the existence of free will within the logic of occasionalism leads to dire conclusions. If there is absolutely no reality to secondary causality, then it follows that God's habits have, in fact, no real role in the world. The idea of habitual creation is intelligible in a world where there is some reality to secondary causes. If God did everything without taking the created beings' causal contributions into consideration, then the creation of cause and effect would be entirely arbitrary. There would be only an *appearance of habit*. In fact, metaphysically speaking, God would remake the world out of nothing at every instant. Neither the state of the universe nor any previous acts of God have any bearing on the next instance. Islamic occasionalism thus becomes somewhat inconsistent when it comes to God's habits. The very idea of habit suggests a kind feedback from the created order, which occasionalist logic does not allow. Thus, when we lose creaturely feedback, we also lose habits. God becomes an arbitrary king. There is no reality of human will, or any other will, and therefore no responsibility. In fact, there would be no creation at all; we would lose the world, because if beings are making no causal contribution to the world, their real existence would be unintelligible. The world thus becomes an illusion.

Third, Islamic occasionalism implies God's direct involvement with evil in the world. If God causes every event within creation, then he causes evil too. There is obviously a contradiction between of God's moral perfection, absolute power, and knowledge and the abundance of suffering in the world. To respond to this challenge, an Islamic occasionalist might argue that if the reality of free will and autonomy of beings are preserved within the occasionalist framework, then the doctrine could counter this objection. However, as we just discussed, this is a difficult task to accomplish for Islamic occasionalism. Without providing a convincing answer here, Islamic occasionalism remains susceptible to serious challenges relating to theodicy.

Fourth, it can also be argued that in the world of occasionalism there seems to remain no distinction between God and the world. If God is all causality, then what prevents us from completely eliminating events and things that appear to us as cause and effect? William Hasker writes: "It can be argued on both epistemological and metaphysical grounds that the material substance posited by occasionalists is redundant and should be eliminated, leading to a Berkeleyan immaterialism. Epistemologically, occasionalism holds that material substances make no causal contribution towards our perceptions of objects."[55] Similarly, Murphy argues that "if God were completely in control of each event, there would be no-thing [*sic*] for God to keep in existence."[56] To respond to this point, an occasionalist might contend that the doctrine does not eliminate the world so long as it can sustain the autonomy of beings. However, as I touched on above, this is not an easy task within the framework of occasionalism without establishing an intermediate realm between existence and nonexistence.

11.3 PARTICIPATORY ACCOUNTS AND SCIENCE: A PHENOMENOLOGY OF CAUSALITY?

It can be said that occasionalism suggests a one-dimensional understanding of causality because it insists that causal power is attributed solely to God and not shared with the created order. Some of the accounts examined in this book offered by Muslim philosophers and mystics, however, suggest that causality needs to be discussed in a participatory framework as a two-dimensional reality. If the created order participates in the divine causality, then causal efficacy can simultaneously be attributed to both God and the created order.

As argued above, in the cases of Ibn Sīnā and Ibn Rushd, this two-dimensionality manifests itself in the form of "physical and metaphysical causality." Physical causality deals with motion and rest. Metaphysical causality starts from the concept of existence and constructs a more intimate relation between God, as the giver of existence, and entities that

55 William Hasker, "Occasionalism," excerpted on Sept. 6, 2012 www.muslimphilosophy.com/ip/rep/K057. Cf. George Berkeley, *A Treatise Concerning the Principles of Human Knowledge* and *Three Dialogues between Hylas and Philonous* (La Salle, IL: Open Court, 1986 [1710, 1713]).

56 N. Murphy, "Divine Action in the Natural Order: Buridan's Ass and Schrodinger's Cat," in *Chaos and Complexity: Scientific Perspectives on Divine Action*, ed. R. Russell, N. Murphy, and A. Peacocke (Vatican: Vatican Observatory and Berkeley: The Center for Theology and the Natural Sciences, 1995), 341.

constantly receive and participate in existence. Suhrawardī and Mullā Ṣadrā also agree that causality needs to be understood in the larger context of the relationship between existence (*wujūd*) and essence (*māhiyya*) and conclude that participation in existence is the basis of the causal efficacy of created beings. Similarly, Ibn ʿArabī and his followers suggest the same two-dimensionality by starting from the concept of causality-as-veil. Causality stands between the human mind and the world and, like a translucent veil, both conceals and exposes what is behind it. As such, causality alludes to both the intelligibility and transcendence of the world.

The two-dimensionality suggested in these accounts bears on our discussion of the reconciliation of religion and science. It can be argued that the two-dimensionality of causality suggests that explanations for any given natural phenomena can be derived by commencing from either of two perspectives: *metaphysically*, starting from the notion of existence as an all-encompassing notion; and *physically*, starting from motion and rest. From the perspective of physical causality (motion-rest), natural processes remain predictable and allow us to trace causal chains. From the perspective of metaphysical causality (existence), one can intuit that the extramental reality is more than its representation in physical causality, and that there is always an element of transcendence beyond phenomena. This way of seeing things accommodates both modes of explanation as complementary. It also allows us to evaluate physical causality within the larger context of metaphysical causality without undermining the premises of the scientific activity. The world can be studied as a predictable and consistent system.

What is important to realize here is that scientific investigation of the world does not begin with the question of existence (*wujūd*), which is the starting point of inquiries into metaphysical causality. The question of existence remains at the margins in scientific investigation and thus can easily be overlooked. The scientific inquiry and the study of metaphysical causality require different perspectives.

At this juncture, it may be argued that the two-dimensionality of causality invites a *phenomenology of causality*. Namely, the purpose of phenomenological study is to develop an awareness of what is unnoticed in the world, what is at the margin or periphery of our attention. This goal has been articulated as an awareness of the directedness of consciousness by Husserl, an awareness of Being as the ever-present background of all cognitive experience by Heidegger, and an awareness of the transcendence of the "face" by Levinas. It is not my intention to engage with this tradition of philosophy.[57] However, to clarify my point, it will be useful to examine Heidegger's ideas more closely.

Heidegger asserts that "the propositions of metaphysics have been strangely involved in a persistent confusion of beings (existents) and Being (Existence)."[58] It is this confusion that leads to what Heidegger calls "the oblivion of Being." To transcend this predicament, "our thinking, instead of implementing a higher degree of exertion, is directed toward a different point of origin. The thinking that is posited by beings as such, and therefore representational and illuminating in that way, must be supplanted by a different kind of thinking which is brought to pass by Being itself and, therefore, responsive to Being.[59] This is an invitation for "the transition from representational thinking to a new kind of thinking that recalls (*das andenkende denken*)."[60] As opposed to "representational thinking" about the world, one should recall the "ground" of beings, which is more fundamental and real than the entities around us. This deeper understanding comes from phenomenology in the sense that all entities we experience are phenomena, beneath which lies their "being-in-itself." Thinking that recalls

[57] The focus is on the meanings of things in our consciousness or as objects appear in our "life-world." Husserl's notion of "intentionality," which he borrows from Brentano, introduces the idea of the directedness of consciousness toward its object. There is no consciousness without this intentional directedness or, in other words, "consciousness is always consciousness of something." This intentional directedness allows one to focus on one's concrete "lived experience" and avoid the pitfalls of speculative thought where consciousness lacks a concrete object to be directed. Edmund Husserl, *Logical Investigations*, trans. J. Findlay (Abingdon, UK: Routledge, [1900] 1970), V. 9–11, 14. Heidegger rejects the primacy of the idea of intentional directedness in explaining the structure of consciousness. There are many aspects of lived experience toward which consciousness is not directed but that exist as the background of conscious states. This background is the unconscious or semiconscious existential engagement in the world. Therefore, Heidegger starts from the daily experience, from "facticity," a term he borrows from Wilhelm Dilthey. We are essentially defined by being-in-the-world and cannot study our experience or consciousness by "bracketing" the question of Being. This study can be done by a conscious agent who experiences Being and for whom the meaning of Being is an issue, *Dasein*. We are to study beings in relation to Being, the all-comprehensive context, the ever-present background of all conscious activities.

[58] Heidegger, "What Is Metaphysics?" in *Existentialism from Dostoevsky to Sartre* (New York: New American Library, 1975), 269.

[59] Ibid., 270, In scientific activity we are related to beings, or what-is. "The world relationship runs through in all the sciences constrains them to seek what-is in itself, with a view of rendering it according to its essence (*Wasgehalt*) and its modality (*Seinsart*), an object of investigation and basic definition," ibid., 243.

[60] Ibid., 277.

Being suggests a different and better way of relating (*verhalten*) to the natural phenomena.

Here, Heidegger identifies science as a kind of representational thinking. What phenomenology proposes is to go beyond representational thinking by using *das andenkende Denken*, a thinking that *recalls*. In this mode of thinking, one recalls what one is already aware of: Being.[61] And it is metaphysics that "inquires over and above what-is (beings), with a view of winning it back again as such and in totality for our understanding."[62] Science, however, due to its distinctive and exclusive focus on beings, does not "find Being." As Heidegger puts it, "all it [science] encounters, always, is what-is, because its explanatory purpose makes it insist at the outset on what-is. But Being is not an existing quality of what-is, nor, unlike what-is, can Being be conceived and established objectively."[63]

This phenomenology attempts, momentarily, to erase the world of representation of *beings* given by science by recalling the more primordial experience of Being itself.[64] Being thus becomes the proper theme of metaphysics, whereas scientific research focuses on beings and, thus, marginalizes the question of Being. Being is pushed aside in scientific inquiry, which retreats from thinking about Being itself, despite the fact that scientific inquiry presupposes this much more "primordial" foundation of the awareness of Being.[65]

[61] "As long as man remains *animal rationale* he is also *animal metaphysicum*. As long as man understand himself as the rational animal, metaphysics belongs, as Kant said, to the nature of man," ibid., 267. This helps us approach such statements as "Dasein is ontically distinguished by the fact that, in its very Being, that Being is an issue for it." Heidegger, *Being and Time*, trans. J. Macquarrie and E. Robinson (Oxford: Basil Blackwell, 1962 [first published in 1927]), 4: 32.

[62] Ibid., 254. [63] Ibid., 259–260.

[64] As such, "the path of the question of Being is illumined by the phenomenological attitude," ibid., 239.

[65] According to Levinas's phenomenological descriptions, the element of irreducibility or transcendence is glimpsed in the immediacy of the face-to-face encounter with the Other. The infinity of the human individual is manifested and concealed by the human face in "the nakedness of the face." Emmanuel Levinas, *Totality and Infinity: An Essay on Exteriority*, trans. Alphonso Lingis (Boston, MA: Martinus Nijhoff Publishers, 1979), 74. One perceives "the glean of transcendence like a theophany," ibid., 24. The element of transcendence "appears, but remains absent," ibid., 181. The face is a locus from which the transcendence of the Other is intuited. The face-to-face experience is described as a fissure, a confrontation with something that is both familiar and ambiguous, ibid., 42. This allows one to think about "the presence of a content in a container that exceeds its capacity," ibid., 289.

At this juncture, it can be argued that a way of thinking about the world through "Being" could be complementary to a scientific methodology that approaches the world through "beings." These two modes of thinking – representational thinking and thinking that recalls – could have a complementary relationship. They accentuate two intimately related and complementary aspects of reality.

Most of the authors examined in this book (Ibn Sīnā, Suhrawardī, Ibn Rushd, Ibn ʿArabī, Qūnawī, Qayṣarī, and Ṣadrā) are concerned with "recalling" existence (*wujūd*) in existents. The centrality of the notion of existence in these accounts and the distinction between metaphysical and physical causality might allow application of a similar phenomenology. One can argue that our common sense of physical causality is alienated from the question of existence. Existence, however, can be recalled in the study of metaphysical causality. As such, metaphysical causality does not appear to clash with physical causality. Horizontal regularity and continuity of natural causal processes could exist alongside one another with an element of transcendence. All existents and their relationships are located within the larger context of existence and must be studied by two distinct but complementary modes of causal thinking. Existents' interaction with each other is to be examined through physical causality and rigorous scientific inquiry. The basis of these interactions – existence – is glimpsed through metaphysical causality, inquiry into which can help one develop an awareness of what normally eludes attention and recognize the element of transcendence in natural processes. The trace of transcendence, like a theophany, is intuited in all causal relationships through the very notion of existence. The phenomenology of causality could accentuate this element that escapes an inattentive mind.

As such, participatory accounts of causality may present interesting and viable ways of reconciling religious and scientific modes of thinking about the world. They may allow us to make sense of the human experience of "existence" in causality, study a meaning that is more than what is explicated in science, and also manage to preserve the rigor and efficiency of scientific investigation of the world.

Islamic occasionalism also offers interesting possibilities for thinking about the divine creative action in the world. Despite its skepticism about the necessary connection between cause and effect, occasionalism can accommodate a common-sense view of the world and accept that God's habitual creation secures the regularity of the natural processes and paves the way for serious engagement with the natural sciences. No doubt, it accepts the possibility of special divine actions, but it does not require them for its account of divine causality. The universal sustenance of the world remains the continuous background against which special divine action takes place. Moreover, occasionalism also marginalizes the role of special divine actions – such that the normal operation of the laws of nature remains the principal framework for explaining the physical world and the guiding principles of how we regulate our lives. However, Islamic occasionalism also faces serious theological and philosophical difficulties. It does not seem to secure free will, despite repeated efforts of Muslim theologians to save it from this conclusion. The theory appears to remain susceptible to the difficult issues of theodicy. It is also somewhat inconsistent, to the extent that if the reality of free will is not clearly established, then the term "God's habits" loses its meaning. Its theoretical possibilities may not yet have been exhausted; however, despite its advantages, these theological and philosophical difficulties need to be resolved before Islamic occasionalism can offer a compelling account of divine causality in the world.

Due to these considerations, I believe that participatory accounts of causality centered on the question of existence offer a more promising path than occasionalism for reconciling religious and scientific modes of explaining the world.

Conclusion

In this book, I have examined the works of key figures in the Islamic intellectual tradition in an effort to reveal their insights on causality and freedom. As we have seen, Muslim theologians, philosophers, and mystics hold a complex array of views on these pressing matters. A closer look at these views allows us to identify and explore certain major trends that link them together. The first of these is the occasionalist tradition, which emerges within the context of the Ashʿarites' attempt to articulate a theology of possibility. Theologically, Ashʿarite theory of the divine attributes offers a basis for an understanding of divine action centered on divine will and freedom. The idea that the divine attributes are neither identical to nor separate from God allows the Ashʿarites to construct the relationship between God and the world through the divine attributes. Of all the attributes, the divine will is primary in defining the God–cosmos relationship. Cosmologically, the Ashʿarites are aware that to ground this theology of possibility, they need to reject the idea of causal necessity in the world. They construct an atomistic physical cosmology to eliminate the causal "glue" from the world-process. In their discrete and causally detached world, no necessary relationship can be constructed between any two occurrences. Every relation is intrinsically possible. The world needs the divine will in order to remain attached, consistent, and not collapse. It is in this context that Ashʿarite occasionalism introduces such concepts as conjunction (*iqtirān*), proximity (*mujāwara*), and possibility (*imkān*) to bolster a theology of possibility.

Powerful theological tools such as the idea of "preponderance without reason" (*tarjīh bi-lā murajjih*) also emerge in the context of Ashʿarite occasionalism. Early occasionalists use this idea to explain how homogeneous atoms are differentiated from each other. Different accidents are assigned to atoms based entirely on the preponderance of the divine will without reason. Later occasionalist theologians continue to find novel applications for this idea. Ghazālī uses it to defend the idea of creation ex nihilo without reason and thus without any "change" in God. This application is in fact one of the key points in his refutation of Ibn Sīnā. Jurjānī then applies it to offer a theological criticism of medieval natural philosophy and to argue that the Ashʿarite occasionalist theological framework explains differentiation of celestial and terrestrial objects better than the Philosophers' necessitarian system, which looks for a reason for every cosmic event. In modern times, Nursi uses the idea of preponderance to address the question of free will.

Similarly, certain occasionalist arguments against causal efficacy and necessity in the created order persist. One repeatedly encounters in occasionalist writings the "argument from consciousness." Despite this continuity, we also find the same idea applied in different ways. For example, early occasionalists use this argument to reject any necessary relationship between cause and effect. However, Nursi – a modern occasionalist – uses it to argue that effect/s can never be reduced to cause/s and that there is always an ontological distance, a disproportionality, in causal relations.

One also observes that certain occasionalist doctrines are reformulated in the face of strong criticism and then survive. Rāzī's reformulation of atomism after Ibn Sīnā's hylomorphic criticism is one such instance. Moreover, Nursi's attempt to integrate Ashʿarite occasionalism and Ibn ʿArabī's metaphysical cosmology indicates that occasionalism interacts with and synthesizes other major currents of Islamic thought. This shows occasionalism's ability to adapt to different philosophical paradigms.

Something similar can be observed in occasionalists' interactions with medieval scientific models. In the hands of Rāzī and Jurjānī, occasionalism develops a pragmatic-cum-skeptic attitude toward the Aristotelian-Ptolemaic-Euclidian paradigm of science. Rāzī's appropriation of Euclidian geometry, Jurjānī's appropriation of Ptolemaic celestial models, and Nursi's defense of occasionalism in the context of modern science are all marked by this skeptical yet pragmatic attitude. In this view, scientific theories are approximate, not exhaustive, definitions of the world. They have practical functionality yet should not alter our theological commitments. The ability of occasionalist scholars to defend central tenets of the school within different philosophical and scientific paradigms suggests that occasionalism can be considered a living tradition with a certain degree of adaptability.

Occasionalism appears to be the dominant way of understanding causality and freedom among theologians. By contrast, the Philosophers (*mashshāʾiyyūn* and *ishrāqiyyūn*) and Sufi metaphysicians examined in this book move toward different versions of participatory accounts. I believe this trend results from how the Philosophers and Sufis construct the relationship between God and cosmos on the concept of existence (*wujūd*) rather than the divine will. They hold that existence is undifferentiated, pure unity and the source of all divine attributes, such as knowledge, power, mercy, and will. Since all entities participate in existence, their causality and freedom are understood in relationship to existence. Entities' causal efficacy derives from their participation in existence. If all of the divine qualities are concealed in existence, then every entity participating in existence is also qualified with these qualities. Existence, then, becomes the basis of all causality.

For the defenders of participatory accounts, the intermediary-secondary causes remain efficacious. Their participatory view of causality attributes causal efficacy to intermediary-secondary causes while asserting that existence is, in fact, the basis of all causality. This leads to a two-dimensional view of causality. In Ibn Sīnā's writings we observe this two dimensionality in his distinction between physical and metaphysical causality. Ibn Sīnā understands causality both from the perspective of "motion or rest" and from the perspective of "existence." This is because he holds that God is not only the principle of motion and rest in the world but also the principle and giver of existence. The act of bestowal of existence is the basis of motion-rest in the world. When entities receive existence to the extent allowed by their essences (*māhiyya*), they actualize their potentialities. This continuous actualization manifests itself in the form of universal motion. Physical causality pertains to only motion and rest and does not concern the "question of existence." It is in metaphysical causality that existence becomes relevant as the basis of all causal activity. In a way, Ibn Sīnā goes beyond the four Aristotelian causes and sees existence as the permanent background for the efficient, formal, material, and final causes. This perspective in fact integrates the Aristotelian view of causality into the larger Neoplatonistic participatory account of causality, for everything happens because of – and is therefore related to – existence as an all-encompassing reality. As such, Ibn Sīnā offers a novel and influential synthesis of Aristotelian and Neoplatonistic accounts in a larger metaphysical framework based on the concept of existence and essence.

A similar understanding of causality can be observed among other philosophers and mystics examined in this book. Ibn Rushd, despite his

Aristotelian tendencies and his disagreements with Ibn Sīnā, again tends to fit his physical description of causality within a larger framework of metaphysical causality. His conception of the First as pure existence-act provides the foundation for his perception of causality. On the one hand, together with Aristotle, Ibn Rushd holds that everything must have a cause and that natures/essences/forms necessitate an entity's behavior. On the other hand, his construction of the God–cosmos relationship in terms of the relationship of pure existence-act and essence-potentiality further suggests that the First is present in all causality in that potentialities become actualized by participating in the First's pure act. This indicates that despite his Aristotelianism, Ibn Rushd understands physical causality within the larger context of participatory causality.

Similarly, Suhrawardī holds that the light of God reaches entities "with and without an intermediary." The absolute light becomes particularized in the gloomy essences, and these gloomy essences transmit light in a delimited form. Each entity is illuminated by the Light of Lights and then shares its light with other entities in a particularized fashion. In this schema, once again the intermediaries remain causally efficacious, although the divine light remains the basis of all causal activity. The representatives of the school of *wujūdiyya* examined in this book agree with Suhrawardī on this point. Qūnawī and Qayṣarī believe that *wujūd*'s infinity necessitates that it relates to the world both with and without intermediaries. *Wujūd*'s relationship to the world cannot be limited to intermediation, as suggested by emanationism, or to non-intermediation, as suggested by occasionalism.

Another point of agreement among the proponents of participatory accounts can be found in their understanding of creaturely freedom. They agree that pure existence is the source of all divine qualities. The evidentiality, comprehensiveness, purity, and simplicity of existence entails that God, the pure existence, is also pure good, pure knowledge, self-subsisting – the first, the end, the outward, the inward, and so on. When entities participate in existence as a result of the divine bestowal of existence, they also participate in the divine qualities, including consciousness, will, and freedom. *Wujūd* thus becomes the principle of creaturely freedom.

There is also consensus on the role of essences in establishing creaturely freedom. "Essence" refers to an entity's prefiguration in the divine knowledge. The infinity of *wujūd* entails that essences must exist in it in some form. An entity's essence is known preeternally but is not determined by God. The uncreated and uncaused nature of essences suggests creaturely freedom. This perspective also implies that essences by themselves cannot smell the fragrance of existence and that for their existentiation they require the bestowal of existence. When the uncausedness of essences is brought together with their ontological poverty and need, entities can be understood as absolutely dependent on existence and yet also free to be what they are. God knows and existentiates essences but does not impose what kind of essence an entity possesses. This freedom is based on *wujūd*'s infinity. An entity is free due to its uncaused essence and its participation in existence. Its essence is actualized *in concreto* through its participation in existence.

These agreements suggest that one can identify another strong current within the Islamic intellectual tradition, aside from occasionalism. These accounts can be characterized as participatory due to their emphasis on the bestowal of and participation in existence. They also include certain Aristotelian elements, owing to their acceptance of intermediary-secondary causality. These accounts subsume secondary causality, which pertains to the world-process as it appears to us, under metaphysical causality, which pertains to existence (*wujūd*) as the background of the world-process and all appearances. Existence is understood as the framework and source of all causal activity. This synthesis is formed within an Islamic religious framework. Based on these observations, these accounts of causality and freedom can be called Islamic participatory accounts.

Despite these continuities, one also observes differences of opinion among the defenders of participatory accounts. Disagreeing with Ibn Sīnā, Ibn Rushd contends that one does not need emanationism to explain the emergence of multiplicity from the One. On this point, he is in agreement with Ghazālī and the Sufi metaphysicians. Each entity gets its share from "one existence" proceeding from the One without needing the pluralizing effect of celestial intellects. Aside from Ibn Rushd, thinkers such as Ibn ʿArabī, Qūnawī, Qayṣarī, and Mullā Ṣadrā all explain the emergence of multiplicity in a similar fashion. The expansion of *wujūd* upon essences with or without intermediation explains how "one existence" becomes individualized in entities in accordance with their essences.

The Sufi metaphysicians who take part in these debates are distinguished by their willingness to put participatory accounts in conversation with certain occasionalist ideas. This happens in the writings of Ibn ʿArabī, Qūnawī, and Qayṣarī. To incorporate certain occasionalist ideas, they elaborate on the rich implications of the concepts of existence and essence. The result is a critical evaluation and appropriation of such central occasionalist concepts as the constant re-creation of the world, the possibility of breaks in the habitual creation, and preponderance without reason. Substance/s and accidents are here understood as different manifestations of the all-inclusive reality of *wujūd*. *Wujūd*'s infinity necessitates that the world is re-created at each moment, for it cannot subsist from one moment to another without the continuous bestowal of existence.

Some of the important distinctions between occasionalist and participatory accounts of causation and freedom can be summarized as follows. First, as already mentioned, participatory accounts accept that entities have real causal efficacy due to their participation in existence and their uncreated and uncaused essences. There is both vertical causality, for *wujūd* is given without intermediation, and horizontal causality, for this act of giving renders entities causally efficacious and free. Second, the concept of essences, fixed archetypes (*al-aʿyān thābita*), or preparedness (*istiʿdād*) indicates that the expansion of existence upon essences does not occur solely on the basis of "preponderance without reason." God existentiates entities as they are in the divine knowledge. In other words, God does not create ex nihilo, but creates from uncaused and uncreated essences. This marks a fundamental divergence from occasionalist theology of possibility. Third, occasionalists usually approach the problem of freedom from the perspective of their theory of acquisition (*kasb*), according to which human will and God's will are separate entities. Participatory accounts, however, approach the relationship of human will and God's will from a non-dualistic perspective and hold that human freedom is not separated from the divine freedom. It is actually a manifestation of the divine freedom. Freedom can simultaneously be attributed to God and to human beings.

Concerning the modern relevance of these theories, the following may be observed. Islamic occasionalism continues to interact with the philosophical and scientific paradigms of modernity. The fundamental tenet of the occasionalist worldview is that necessary causality can be expressed in terms of constant conjunction. So long as we are unable to definitively distinguish between necessary causation and constant conjunction, occasionalism will continue to exist. However, one can argue from the perspectives of theology and philosophy that occasionalism presents serious difficulties. It does not seem to be able to secure free will, despite efforts by its exponents to do so. Such ideas as preponderance without reason suggest a high degree of arbitrariness in God's acts and the world. There are also problems related to theodicy, the possibility of knowledge, and the possibility of identity.

By contrast, Islamic participatory accounts are centered on the concept of existence and offer a two-dimensional treatment of the question of causality. Entities' relationships with each other can be examined in terms of physical causality and through scientific methods. From the perspective of metaphysical causality, existence remains the basis of all causality. Participatory accounts focus on existence as the all-encompassing background of the world process and locate physical relationships of entities within the larger framework of existence.

As such, in my view, Islamic participatory accounts present richer possibilities for contemplating the relationship of religious and scientific modes of thinking about the world than do Islamic occasionalist accounts. I would further suggest that such participatory accounts may have interesting implications for how we think about a range of topics, from morality to politics. To examine this properly requires future studies.

Bibliography

Abrahamov, B. "Ghazālī's Theory of Causality," *Studia Islamica*, 67 (1988), 75–89.

"The *Bi-lā kayfa* Doctrine and Its Foundations in Islamic Theology," *Arabica*, 42 (1995), 365–379.

Abū Ḥanīfa, al-Ṇu'mān ibn Thābit. *İmamı Azamın Beş Eseri*, trans. Mustafa Öz. Istanbul: Marmara Universitesi Ilahiyat Fakultesi Vakfi, 1992.

Abū Rīda. *Min Shuyūh al-Mu'tazila Ibrahim ibn Sayyār al-Naẓẓām*. Cairo: Dar al-Nadim, 1989.

Acikgenc, Alparslan. *Islam Medeniyetinde Bilgi ve Bilim*. Istanbul: Turkiye Diyanet Vakfi, 2006.

Adamson, Peter. "From Necessary Existent to God," in *Interpreting Avicenna: Critical Essays*, ed. Peter Adamson, 170–189. Cambridge, UK: Cambridge University Press, 2013.

Addas, Claude. *Quest for the Red Sulphur: The Life of Ibn 'Arabi*. Cambridge, UK: Islamic Texts Society, 1993.

Alami, Ahmed. *L'ontologie modale: Étude de la théorie des modes d'Abū Hāshim al-Jubbā'ī*. Paris: Vrin, 2001.

Alon, Ilai. "Ghazālī on Causality," *Journal of American Oriental Society*, 100.4 (1980), 397–405.

Alousi, Husām Muhīddīn. *The Problem of Creation in Islamic Thought*. Baghdad: National Print Co., 1968.

Aminrazavi, Mahdi. (ed.), *The Islamic Intellectual Tradition in Persia*. Richmond: Curzon Press, 1996.

Suhrawardī and the School of Illumination. London: Curzon Press, 1997.

Āmulī, Ḥaydar. *Jāmī' al-Asrār wa Manbā' al-Anwār*, Henry Corbin and Uthman Yahya. Tehran-Paris: Bibliothèque iranien, 1969.

Anawati, G. C. "Fakhr al-Din al-Razi," *Encyclopedia of Islam* 2, 2010, https://referenceworks.brillonline.com/entries/encyclopaedia-of-islam-2/fakhr-al-din-al-razi.

Annas, Julia. "Aristotle on Inefficient Causes," *Philosophical Quarterly*, 32 (1982), 311–326.
Aquinas, Thomas. *Quaestiones disputatae de potentia*, ed. P. M. Pession. Turin: 1965.
Aristotle. *The Complete Works of Aristotle*, ed. Jonathan Barnes, 2 vols. Princeton, NJ: Princeton University Press, 1984.
Metaphysics, trans. Joe Sachs. Santa Fe, NM: Green Lion Press, 1999 (2nd ed. 2002).
Physics, Books I–II, trans. William Charlton. Oxford: Clarendon Press, 1970 (2nd ed. 1992).
Ashʿarī. *al-Ibāna ʿan Uṣūl al-Diyāna*, ed. Abbas Sabbagh. Beirut: Dar al-Nafaais, 1994/1414.
The Elucidation from Islam's Foundation (Kitāb al-Ibāna ʿan Uṣūl al-Diyāna), trans. Walter C. Klein. American Oriental Series, vol. 19. New York: Kraus Reprint Corporation, 1967.
Kitāb al-Lumaʿ, ed. Hammuda Ghuraba. Cairo: Mattba'at Misr Sharikah Musahimah Misriyah, 1955.
Maqālāt al-Islamiyyīn wa Ikhtilāf al-Muṣallīn, ed. Helmut Ritter. Wiesbaden: Franz Steiner Verlag, 1963/1382.
"A Vindication of the Science of Kalam (*Risāla fī Istiḥsān al-Khawḍ fī 'Ilm al-Kalām*)," in *The Theology of Ashʿarī*, ed. Richard J. McCarthy, 117–134. Beirut: Imprimerie Catholique, 1953.
Baghdādī, ʿAbd al-Qāhir ibn Tāhir al-. *Uṣūl al-Dīn*. Istanbul: Dar al-Funun Ilahiyat Fakültesi, 1928.
al-Farq bayn al-Firaq, ed. M. Zahid al-Kawthari. Cairo: Maktab Nashr al-Thaqafah al-Islamiyya, 1948.
Bakar, Osman. *Classification of Knowledge in Islam*. Cambridge, UK: The Islamic Text Society, 1998.
Barbour, Ian G. *When Science Meets Religion*. New York: Harper Collins, 2000.
Bāqillānī. *al-Inṣāf*, ed. Imaduddin Ahmad Haydar. Beirut: Alam al-Kutub, 1986/1407.
Kitāb al-Bayān, ed. Richard McCarthy. Beirut: al-Maktab al-Sharqiyya, 1958.
Kitāb al-Tamhīd, ed. Imaduddin Ahmad Haydar. Beirut: Muassasa al-Kutub al-Thakafiyya, 1987/1407.
Bashier, Salman H. *Ibn al-ʿArabi's Barzakh: The Concept of the Limit and the Relationship between God and the World*. Albany: State University of New York Press, 2004.
Belo, Catarina. *Chance and Determinism in Avicenna and Averroes*. Boston, MA: Brill, 2007.
Benevich, Fedor. "The Classical Ashʿarite Theory of *Aḥwāl*: Juwaynī and His Opponents," *Journal of Islamic Studies*, 2.2 (2016), 136–175.
Berkeley, George. *A Treatise Concerning the Principles of Human Knowledge* and *Three Dialogues between Hylas and Philonous*. La Salle, IL: Open Court, 1986 [1710, 1713].
Bertolacci, Amos. "The Doctrine of Material and Formal Causality in the 'Ilāhiyyāt' of Avicenna's 'Kitāb al-Shifāʾ'," *Quaestio*, 2 (2002), 125–154.

"The Reception of Avicenna in Latin Medieval Culture," in *Interpreting Avicenna: Critical Essays*, ed. Peter Adamson, 242–269. Cambridge, Cambridge University Press, 2013.

Bigliardi, Stefano. *Islam and the Quest for Modern Science: Conversations with Adnan Oktar, Mehdi Golshani, Mohammed Basil Altaie, Zaghloul El-Naggar, Bruno Guiderdoni and Nidhal Guessoum*. Istanbul: Swedish Research Institute in Istanbul, 2014.

Brunschvig, Robert. "Mu'tazilisme et optimum," *Studia Islamica*, 39 (1974), 5–23.

Chittick, W. "al-Kunawi" in *Encyclopedia of Islam*, ed. P. Bearman, T. Bianquis, C. Bosworth, E. van Donzel, and W. Heinrichs. Leiden: Brill, 2007.

The Self Disclosure of God: The Principles of Ibn al-ʿArabī's Cosmology. Albany: State University of New York Press, 1998.

The Sufi Path of Knowledge: Ibn al-ʿArabī's Metaphysics of Imagination. Albany: State University of New York Press, 1989.

Clayton, Philip. *God and Contemporary Science*. Edinburgh: Edinburgh University Press, 1997.

Mind and Emergence: From Quantum to Consciousness. Oxford: Oxford University Press, 2004.

"Panentheism Today: A Constructive Systematic Evaluation," in *In Whom We Live and Move and Have Our Being: Panentheistic Reflections on God's Presence in a Scientific World*, ed. P. Clayton and A. Peacocke, 249–264. Grand Rapids, MI: Wm B. Eerdmans, 2004.

"The Pantheistic Turn in Christian Theology," *Dialog*, 38 (1999), 289–293.

In Quest of Freedom: The Emergence of Spirit in the Natural World. Gottingen: Vandenhoeck and Ruprecht, 2009.

Coope, Ursula. "Aristotle's Account of Agency in *Physics* III.3," *Proceedings of the Boston Area Colloquium in Ancient Philosophy*, 20 (2004), 201–221.

Cooper, John. "Mullā Ṣadrā Shirazi," in *The Routledge Encyclopaedia of Philosophy*, ed. E. Craig, 595–599. London: Routledge, 1998.

Corbin, Henry. *Alone with the Alone*. Princeton, NJ: Princeton University Press, 1998.

Opera metaphysica et Mystica. Paris-Tehran: Adrien-Maisonnevue, 1952.

Costa, D'Ancona. "Plotinus and Later Platonic Philosophers on the Causality of the First Principle," in *Cambridge Companion to Plotinus*, ed. Lloyd P. Gerson, 356–385. Cambridge, UK: Cambridge University Press, 1996.

Courtenay, William J. "The Critique on Natural Causality in the Mutakallimun and Nominalism," *Harvard Theological Review*, 66 (1973), 77–94.

Dağlı, Caner K. *Ibn al-ʿArabī and Islamic Intellectual Culture: From Mysticism to Philosophy*. New York: Routledge, 2016.

Davidson, Donald. "Causal Relations," in *Essays on Actions and Events*, 149–162. Oxford: Clarendon Press, 1980.

Davidson, H. A. *Proofs for Eternity, Creation, and the Existence of God in Medieval Islamic and Jewish Philosophy*. Oxford University Press, 1987.

Dembski, William. "On the Very Possibility of Intelligent Design," in *The Creation Hypothesis*, ed. J. P. Moreland, 113–138. Downers Grove, IL: InterVarsity Press, 1994.

Demir, Osman. *Kelamda Nedensellik: Ilk Dönem Kelamcılarında Tabiat ve İnsan*. İstanbul: TC Kültür ve Türizm Bakanlığı, 2015.

Demirli, Ekrem. *Ibnu'l Arabi Metafiziği*. Istanbul: Sufi Kitap, 2013.

Dhanani, Alnoor. "The Impact of Ibn Sina's Critique of Atomism on Subsequent Kalam Discusssions of Atomism" *Arabic Sciences and Philosophy*, 25 (2015), 79–104.

The Physical Theory of Kalām: Atoms, Space, and Void in Basrian Mu'tazilī Cosmology. Leiden: Brill, 1994.

"Problems in Kalām Physics," *Bulletin of the Royal Institute of Interfaith Studies*, 4 (2002), 73–96.

Draper, Paul. "God, Science, and Naturalism," in *The Oxford Handbook of Philosophy of Religion*, ed. William J. Wainwright, 272–303. Oxford: Oxford University Press, 2005.

Druart, T. A. "Ibn Sina(Avicenna) and Duns Scotus," in *John Duns Scotus, Philosopher. Proceedings of The Quadruple Congress on John Duns Scotus*, ed. M. B. Ingham and O. Bychkov, 13–27. Munster: Aschendorff, 2010.

Dummett, Michael. "Is Time a Continuum of Instants?" *Philosophy*, 75 (2000): 497–515.

Dutton, Blake D. "Al-Ghazāli on Possibility and the Critique of Causality,"*Medieval Philosophy and Theology*, 10 (2001), 23–46.

Ede, A. and Cormack, L. B. *A History of Science in Society: From the Ancient Greeks to the Scientific Revolution*. North York, ON: University of Toronto Press, 2012.

Edis, Taner. *An Illusion of Harmony: Science and Religion in Islam*. Amherst, NY: Prometheus Books, 2007.

Endress, Gerhard. "Mathematics and Philosophy in Medieval Islam," in *The Enterprise of Science in Islam: New Perspectives*, ed. Jan P. Hogendijk and Abdelhamid I. Sabra, 159–160. Cambridge, MA: MIT Press, 2003.

Fakhry, Majid. *Averroes: His Life, Works and Influence*. Oxford: One World, 2001.

Islamic Occasionalism. London: George Allen and Unwin Ltd, 1958.

Falcon, Andrea. *Aristotle and the Science of Nature: Unity without Uniformity*. Cambridge, UK: Cambridge University Press, 2005.

"Aristotle on Causality," in *The Stanford Encyclopedia of Philosophy* (Spring 2015 Edition), ed. Edward N. Zalta: https://plato.stanford.edu/archives/spr2015/entries/aristotle-causality/.

Fārābī, Abū Naṣr Muḥammad al-. *al-Madīna al-Fāḍila*, ed. Albert Nasri Nadir. Beirut: Dar al-Mashriq, 1985.

Fārūqī, Ismail al-. *Islamization of Knowledge: General Principles and Work Plan*. Washington, DC: International Institute of Islamic Thought, 1982.

Fīrūzābādī, Abu Ṭāhir. *al-Qāmūs al-Muḥīṭ*. Beirut: Muassasat al-Risala, 1986.

Frank, Richard M. "al-Aḥkām in Classical Ash'arite Teaching," in *De Zenon d'Élée à Poincaré. Recueil d'études en hommage à Roshdi Rashed*, ed. R. Morelon and A. Hasnawi, 753–777. Louvain: Éditions Peeters, 2004.

"*Al-Ma'nā*: Some Reflections on the Technical Meanings of the Term in the Kalâm and Its Use in the Physics of Mu'ammar," *Journal of the American Oriental Society*, 87.3 (Jul.–Sep. 1967), 248–259.

"The Ash'arite Ontology I: Primary Entities," *Arabic Sciences and Philosophy*, 9 (1999), 163–231.

Beings and their Attributes: The Teaching of the Basrian School of the Mu'tazila in the Classical Period. Albany: State University of New York Press, 1978.

"Bodies and Atoms: The Ash'arite Analysis," in *Islamic Theology and Philosophy: Studies in Honor of George F. Hourani*, ed. Michael E. Marmura, 39–63. Albany: State University of New York Press, 1984.

Creation and the Cosmic System: Ghazālī Avicenna. Heidelberg: Carl Winter Universitatsverlag, 1992.

"Elements in the Development of the Teaching of Al- Ash'arī," *Le Museon*, 104 (1991), 141–190.

Ghazālī and the Ash'arite School. Durham, NC: Duke University Press Books, 1994.

The Metaphysics of Created Being According to Abū al-Hudhayl al-'Allāf. Istanbul: Netherlands Historische-Archeologisch Instituut, 1966.

"Notes and remarks on the *ṭabā'i'* in the teaching of al-Māturīdī," in *Melanges d'islamologie a la memoire d'Armand Abel*, ed. P. Salmon, 137–149. Leiden: E. J. Brill, 1974.

"Reason and Revealed Law: A Sample of Parallels and Divergences in Kalam and Falsafa," in *Recherches d'Islamologie. Recuil d'articles offert a Georges C. Anawati et Louis Gardet par leurs collegues et amis*, ed. R. Arnaldez and S. Van Riet, 123–138. Louvain: Peeters, 1977.

"The Structure of Created Causality According to al-Ash'arī," *Studia Islamica*, 25 (1966), 53–59.

Freeland, Cynthia A. "Aristotle on Bodies, Matter, and Potentiality," in *Philosophical issues in Aristotle's Biology*, ed. Allan Gotthelf and James Lennox, 392–407. Cambridge, UK: Cambridge University Press, 1987.

Freudenthal, Gad and Mauro Zonta, "The Reception of Avicenna in Jewish Cultures, East–West," in *Interpreting Avicenna: Critical Essays*, ed. Peter Adamson, 214–241. Cambridge, UK: Cambridge University Press, 2013.

Gardet, L. "La pensé religieuse d'Avicenne' (Ibn Sīnā)," in *Études de Philosophie Médiévale*, 41. Paris: Vrin, 1951.

Geulincx, Arnold. "Metaphysica vera," in *Arnoldi Geulincx antverpiensis Opera philosophica*, ed. J. P. N. Land, vol. 2. Hague: Martinum Nijhoff, 1893.

Ghazālī. *al-Iqtiṣād fī-l-I'tiqād*, ed. Ibrahim Cubukcu and Huseyin Atay. Ankara: A. U. Ilahiyat Fakultesi Yayinlari, 1962.

al-Iqtiṣād fī-l-I'tiqād (Moderation in Belief), trans. Michael Marmura in "Ghazālī's Chapter on Divine Power in the *Iqtiṣād*," in *Arabic Sciences and Philosophy*, vol. 4 (1994).

Al-Maqsad al-Asnā fī Sharḥ al-Ma'ānī Asmā' Allāh al-Ḥusnā (The Ninety-Nine Beautiful Names of God) trans. David B. Burrel and Nazer Daher. Cambridge, UK: The Islamic Texts Society, 1992.

al-Munqidh min al-Dalāl and Other Relevant Works of Ghazālī, trans. R. J. McCarthy. Boston, MA: Twayne Publishers, 1980.

Iḥyā' 'Ulūm al-Dīn, 16 parts (Cairo: Lajnat Nashr al-Thaqafa al-Islamiyya. Reprinted Beirut: Dar al-Kitab al-Arabi, n.d. [c.1990]).

The Incoherence of the Philosophers (*Tahāfut al-Falāsifa*), a Parallel English-Arabic Text, ed. and trans. M. E. Marmura. Provo, UT: Brigham Young University Press, 1997.

Kitāb al-Arbaʿīn. Cairo, 1916.

Mishkāt al-Anwār (The Niche of Lights), a dual-language edition trans. David Buchman. Provo, UT: Brigham Young University Press, 1998.

Gill, Mary Louise. "Aristotle's theory of causal action in *Physics* III. 3," *Phronesis*, 25 (1980), 129–147.

Gilson, É. "Avicenne et les Origines de la Notion de Cause Efficiente," *Atti Del XII Congresso Internazionale di Filosofia*, 9 (1958), 121–130.

History of Christian Philosophy in the Middle Ages. London: Random House, 1955.

"Notes pour l'histoire de la cause efficiente," *Archives d'Histoire doctinrale et littéraire du Moyen Age*, 37 (1962), 7–31.

Gimaret, Daniel. *La doctrine d'al-Ashʿarī*. Paris: Cerf, 1990.

Théories de l'acte humain en théologie musulmane. Paris: J. Vrin, 1980.

Goichon, A. M. *La distinction de l'essence et de l'existence d'après Avicenne*. Paris: Desclée de Brouwer, 1937.

Goldziher, Ignaz. *The Zahiris: Their Doctrine and Their History*, trans. Wolfgang Behn. Leiden: E. J. Brill, 1971.

Golshani, Mehdi. *From Physics to Metaphysics*. Tehran: Institute for Humanities and Cultural Studies, 1997.

Goodman, L. E. *Avicenna*. London: Routledge, 1992.

"Did Ghazālī Deny Causality?," *Studia Islamica*, 47 (1978), 83–120.

Griffel, Frank *Al-Ghazā'lī's Philosophical Theology: An Introduction to the Study of his Life and Thought*. New York: Oxford University Press, 2009.

"Al-Ghazali," *The Stanford Encyclopedia of Philosophy* (Winter 2016 Edition), ed. Edward N. Zalta: https://plato.stanford.edu/archives/win2016/entries/al-ghazali/.

Griffin, David R. "Interpreting Science from the Standpoint of Whiteheadian Process Philosophy," in *The Oxford Handbook of Religion and Science*, ed. Philip Clayton and Zachary Simpson, 453–471. New York: Oxford University Press, 2006.

Grünbaum, Adolf. *Modern Science and Zeno's Paradoxes*. Middletown, CT: Wesleyan University Press, 1967.

Guessoum, Nidhal. *Islam's Quantum Question: Reconciling Muslim Tradition and Modern Science*. London and New York: I.B.Tauris, 2011.

Gutas, D. "Essay-Review: Suhrawardī and Greek Philosophy," *Arabic Sciences and Philosophy*, 13 (2003), 303–309.

Günaltay, M. Şemsettin. *Kelam Atomculuğu ve Kaynağı Sorunu*, ed. and noted by Irfan Bayın. Ankara: Fecr, 2008.

Halkin, A. S. "The Hashwiyya," *Journal of the American Oriental Society*, 54 (1934), 1–28.

Hanioğlu, Şükrü. *Atatürk: An Intellectual Biography*. Princeton, NJ: Princeton University Press, 2011.

Hasker, William "Occasionalism," www.muslimphilosophy.com/ip/rep/K057.

Hayri Bolay, Süleyman. *Türkiye'de Ruhçu ve Maddeci Düşüncenin Mücadelesi*. Ankara: Nobel Kitap, 2008.

Heidegger, Martin. *Being and Time*, trans. by J. Macquarrie and E. Robinson. Oxford: Basil Blackwell, 1962 (first published in 1927).

"What is Metaphysics?," in *Existentialism from Dostoevsky to Sartre*. New York: New American Library, 1975.

Hocaoglu, Durmus. "Nursi ve Descartes Felsefelerinde Tabiat Uzerine Mukayeseli Calisma": www.koprudergisi.com/index.asp?Bolum=EskiSayilarGoster=YaziYaziNo=500.

Hourani, George E. "The Dialogue between Ghazālī and the Philosophers on the Origin of the World," *The Muslim World*, 48 (1958), 183–191.

"'Ibn Sīnā's 'Essay on the Secret of Destiny'," *Bulletin of the School of Oriental and African Studies*, 2.1 (1966), 25–48.

Hume, David. *Treatise of Human Nature*, ed. L. A. Selby-Bigge, rev. P. H. Nidditch. Oxford: Oxford University Press, 1978.

Husserl, Edmund. *Logical Investigations*, trans. J. Findlay. Abingdon, UK: Routledge, 1970 [1900].

Ibn ʿArabī. *al-Futūḥāt al-Makkīyya*, 9 vols. Cairo, 1911; reprinted, Beirut: Dar Sadir, n.d.

al-Futūḥāt al-Makkīyya, 14 vols, ed. O. Yahia. Cairo: al-Hayʿat al-Misriyyat al-ʿAmma liʿl-Kitab, 1972–1991.

Fuṣūṣ al-Ḥikam, ed. A. ʿAfīfī. Beirut: Dar al-Kutub al-ʿArabi, 1946.

The Maccan Revelations: Ibn al-ʿArabī. Vols. 1 and 2, ed. Michel Chodkiewicz, trans. William Chittick and James W. Morris. New York: Pir Press: 2005 [2002].

Ibn Fūrak, Abū Bakr Muḥammad. *Mujarrad*, ed. Daniel Gimaret. Beirut: Dar al-Mashriq, 1987.

Kitāb al-Ḥudūd fi-l-Uṣūl, ed. Muhammad Sulaymani. Beirut: Dar al-Gharb al-Islami, 1999.

Ibn Ḥazm, Abū Muḥammad ʿAlī ibn Aḥmad ibn Saʿīd. *al-Taqrīb li-Ḥadd al-Mantiq*, ed. Ihsan Abbas. Beirut: Dar al-Maktaba al-Hayat, 1959.

al-Iḥkām fī Uṣūl al-Aḥkām. Beirut: Dar al-Afak al-Jadid, 1980.

al-Faṣl fi-l-Milal wa-l-Ahwāʾ wa-l-Niḥal, ed. Ibrahim Nasr and Abdurrahman Umayra, Riyad-Jidda, 1982/1402.

ʿIlm al-Kalām, ed. Ahmad Hijazi, Cairo: al-Maktaba al-Thakafiyya, 1989.

Ibn Humām, Kamāl al-Dīn. *Kitāb al-Musāyara*. Istanbul: Çağrı Yayınları, 1979.

Ibn Khaldūn, Abū Zayd 'Abd al-Raḥmān ibn Muḥammad. *Muqaddima*, ed. N. J. Dawood, trans. Franz Rosenthal. Princeton, NJ and Oxford: Princeton University Press, 2004.

Ibn al-Manẓūr, Jamāl al-Dīn Abū al-Fadl. *Lisān al-ʿArab*. Beirut: Dar Sadr, n.d.

Ibn Mattawayh, *al-Tadhkira fī Aḥkām al-Jawāhir wa-l-Aʿrāḍ*, ed. Daniel Gimaret. Cairo: al-Ma'had al-'Ilm al-Faransi, 2009.

Ibn Maymūn (Maimonides). The *Guide for the Perplexed (Dalālat al-Ḥāʾirīn)*, trans. M. Friedlander, 2nd ed. Skokie, IL: Varda Books, 2002.

Ibn al-Murtazā. *al-Munya wa-l-Amal*, ed. Isamuddīn ibn Muhammad Ali. Alexandria: Dar al-Maʿrifa al-Jamiyya, 1985.

Ibn al-Nadīm, Abū al-Faraj Muḥammad. *al-Fihrist*. Beirut: Dar al-Marifa, 1978.

Ibn Rushd, *al-Kashf ʿan Manāhij al-Adilla*, ed. M. Qasim. Cairo, 1961.

Decisive Treatise and Epistle Dedicatory (*Kitāb Faṣl al-Maqāl* and *Risala al-Ihdā'*), trans. Charles Butterworth. Provo, UT: Brigham Young University, 2008.

Tahāfut al-Tahāfut, trans. Simon Van den Bergh. London: Messrs. Luzac and Company, Ltd, 1954.

Ibn Sīnā. *al-Shifā' al-Ilāhiyyāt* (The Metaphysics of The Healing: A Parallel English-Arabic Text), ed. and trans. Michael E. Marmura. Provo, UT: Brigham Young University Press, 2005.

al-Ishārāt wa-l-Tanbīhāt (Pointers and Reminders with Naṣīr al-Dīn Ṭūsī's Commentary) ed. Suleyman Dunya. Cairo: Dar al-Ma'arif, 1957–1960, 3 vols.

Avicenna's De anima, ed. F. Rahman. London: Oxford University Press, 1959.

Dānesh Nāma-i 'Alā'ī, MS Nuruosmaniye Library, No. 2258/2682.

Kitāb al-Shifā'/Ṭabī'iyyāt (1): *al-Samā' al-Ṭabī'ī*, ed S. Zāyid. Cairo, 1983.

Kitāb al-Najāt, ed. Majid Fakhry. Beirut: Dar al-Afaq al-Jadida, 1985.

Kitāb al-Ta'līqāt, ed. S. H. Mousavian. Tehran: Iranian Institute of Philosophy, 2013.

The Physics of the Healing, trans. J. McGinnis. Provo, UT: Brigham Young University Press, 2009.

Iqbal, Muhammad. *The Reconstruction of Religious Thought*. Stanford, CA: Stanford University Press, 2013.

Ivry, A. "Destiny Revisited: Avicenna's Concept of Determinism," in *Islamic Theology and Philosophy*, ed. Michael E. Marmura. Albany: State University of New York Press, 1984.

Izutsu, T. *A Comparative Study of the Key Philosophical Concepts in Sufism and Taoism*. Tokyo: Keio University; second ed., *Sufism and Taoism*, Los Angeles: University of California Press, 1983 [1966].

The Concept and Reality of Existence. Tokyo: Keio Institute of Cultural and Linguistic Studies, 1971.

Jabrī, Mohammad Abed al-. *The Formation of Arab Reason*, trans. Centre for Arab Unity Studies. Hamra: The Centre for Arab Unity Studies, 2011.

Jāḥiẓ, Abū 'Uthman al-. *Kitāb al-Ḥayawān*, ed. Abdussalam Muahmmad Harun. Beirut: Dar Ihya al-Turasi al-Arabi, 1969.

Janssens, J. "The Problem of Human Freedom in Ibn Sīnā," in *Actes del Simposi Internacional de Filosofia de l'Edat Mitjana*, 112–118. Vic-Girona: Patronat d'Estudis Osonencs, 1996.

Jolivet, Jean. "Aux origines de l'ontologie d'Ibn Sīnā," in *Etudes sur Avicenne*. ed. Jolivet and R. Rashed, 19–28. Paris: Les Belles Lettres, 1984.

Jurjānī, al-Sayyīd al-Sharīf 'Ali ibn Muḥammad al-. *al-Ta'rīfāt*. Lipsiae: Sumptibus F. C. G. Vogelii, 1845.

Sharḥ al-Mawāqif, ed. Mahmud Omar al-Dimyati, 8 vols. Beirut: Dar al-Qutub al-Ilmiyya, 2012/1433 H.

Sharḥ al-Mawāqif, trans. Omer Turker, a Parallel Turkish–Arabic text, 3 vols. Istanbul: Turkiye Yazma Eserler Kurumu Baskanligi, 2015.

Juwaynī, 'Abd al-Malik al-. *Luma' al-Adilla*, ed. Fawqiya Husayn Mahmud. Cairo: al-Dar al-Kawmiyya, 1965/1385.

al-ʿAqīda al-Niẓāmiyya, ed. Muhammad Zubaidi. Beirut: Dar Sabil al-Rashad, 2003/1424.

al-Kitāb al-Irshād, ed. Asad Tamīmī. Beirut: Muassasa al-Kutub al-Thakafiyya, 1985/1405.

al-Shāmil fī Uṣūl al-Dīn, ed. A. S. al-Nashshar, Faysal Budayr Awn, and Suhayr Muhammad Mukhtar. Alexandria: Munshaʾat al-Maʿarif, 1969.

Kalın, Ibrahim. "An Annotated Bibliography of the Works of Mullā Ṣadrā with a Brief Account of his Life," *Islamic Studies*, 42 (2003), 21–62.

Mullā Ṣadrā. New Delhi: Oxford University Press, 2014.

"Mullā Ṣadra's Realist Ontology of the Intelligibles and Theory of Knowledge" *Muslim World*, 94.1 (2004), 81–106.

"The Sacred versus the Secular: Nasr on Science," in *Library of Living Philosophers: Seyyed Hossein Nasr*, ed. L. E. Hahn, R. E. Auxier, and L. W. Stone, 445–462. Chicago, IL: Open Court Press, 2001.

"Three Views of Science in the Islamic World," in *God, Life and the Cosmos: Christian and Islamic Perspectives*, ed. Ted Peters, Muzaffar Iqbal, and Syed Nomanul Haq, 43–75. Aldershot, UK: Ashgate, 2002.

Kant, Immanuel. *Critique of Pure Reason*, trans. Norman Kemp Smith. New York: St. Martin's Press, 1965.

Critique of Practical Reason [1788], trans. and ed. M. J. Gregor. Cambridge: Cambridge University Press, 1996.

Kaufman, G. D. "On the Meaning of 'Act of God,'" *Harvard Theological Review*, 61 (1968), 175–201.

Khayyāṭ, ʿAbd al-Raḥīm ibn Muḥammad al-. *Kitāb al-Intiṣār wa-l-Rad ʿalā Ibn al-Rāwandī al-Mulḥid*, ed. H. S. Nyberg and A. Nader. Beirut: al-Matbaa al-Katolikiyya, 1957.

Kindī, Yāʿqūb ibn al-Isḥāq al-. *Rasāʾil al-Kindī al-Falsafiyya*, ed. M. A. H. Abu Riadah. Cairo: Dar al-Fikr al-Arabi, 1950.

Koca, Ozgur. "Causality as a 'Veil': the Ashʿarites, ibn ʿArabī (1165–1240), and Said Nursi (1877–1960)," *Islam and Christian-Muslim Relations*, 27.4 (2016), 455–470.

"Ibn ʿArabī, Ashʿarites and Causality," in *Occasionalism Revisited: New Essays from the Islamic and Western Philosophical Traditions*, ed. Nazif Muhtaroglu, 41–60. Abu Dhabi: Kalam Research and Media, 2017.

"The Idea of Causal Disproportionality in Said Nursi (1877–1960) and Its Implications," *Journal of Islamic Philosophy*, 11 (2019), 5–32.

"Revisiting the Concepts of Necessity and Freedom in Ibn Sīnā (Avicenna) (c. 980–1037)," *Sophia*, 2019, https://doi.org/10.1007/s11841-019-0706-9.

Said Nursi's Synthesis of Ashʿarite Occasionalism and Ibn 'Arabī's Metaphysical Cosmology: "Diagonal Occasionalism," Modern Science, and Free Will. Ph.D. dissertation, Claremont Graduate University, 2013.

"The World as a Theophany and Causality: Ibn ʿArabī, Causes, and Freedom," *Sophia*, 2017, 10.1007/s11841-017-0621-x.

Kogan, Barry S. *Averroes and the Metaphysics of Causation*. Albany: State University of New York Press, 1985.

Koutzarova, T. *Das Transzendentale bei Ibn Sīnā*. Leiden: Brill, 2009.

Kukkonen, Taneli. "Creation and Causation," in *The Cambridge History of Medieval Philosophy*, ed. R. Pasnau and C. Van Dyke, 232–246. Cambridge, UK: Cambridge University Press, 2010.

Kutluer, Ilhan. "er-Redd ale'l-Kindi el-Feylesuf Adli Risalenin Tahlili," *Sakarya Üniversitesi İlahiyat Fakültesi Dergisi*, 3 (2001), 23–40.

Lāhijī, Muhammad Ja'far. *Sharḥ Risālat al-Mashā'ir*, ed. Sayyid Jalal al-Din Ashtiyani. Tehran: Muassasa-yi Intisharat-i Amir Kabir, 1376/1997.

Landolt, H. "Les idées platoniciennes et le monde de l'image dans la pensée du *Šaykh al-išrāq* Yahyā al-Suhrawardī (ca.1155–1191)," in *Miroir et Savoir. La transmission d'un thème platonicien, des Alexandrins à la philosophie arabo-musulmane*, ed. D. De Smet and M. Sebti. Leuven: Peeters, 2007.

"Suhrawardī's Tales of Initiation'," *Journal of the American Oriental Society*, 107.3 (1987), 475–486.

Levinas, Emmanuel. *Totality and Infinity: An Essay on Exteriority*, trans. Alphonso Lingis. Boston, MA: Martinus Nijhoff Publishers, 1979.

Mady, Penelope. *Realism in Mathematics*. Oxford: Claredon Press, 1990.

Makdisi, George. "Ash'ari and the Ash'arites and Islamic Religious History I," *Studia Islamica*, 17 (1962), 37–80.

Ibn 'Aqil: Religion and Culture in Classical Islam. Edinburgh: Edinburgh University Press, 1997.

Malebranche, N. *Oeuvres complètes de Malebranche*, ed. André Robinet, 20 vols. Paris: Vrin, 1958–1984.

Marmura, Michael E. "Some Aspects of Avicenna's Theory of God's Knowledge of Particulars," *Journal of the American Oriental Society*, 83 (1962), 299–312.

"Avicenna and the *Kalam*," *Zeitschriftfür Geschichte der Arabisch-Islamischen Wissenschaften*, 6 (1990), 172–206.

"Divine Omniscience and Future Contingents in Al-Farabi and Avicenna," in *Divine Omniscience and Omnipotence in Medieval Philosophy. Islamic, Jewish and Christian Perspectives*, ed. Tamar Rudavsky, 81–94. Dordrecht: D. Reidel, 1984.

"Ghazālīan Causes and Intermediaries," *Journal of the American Oriental Society*, 115 (1995), 89–100.

"Ghazālī on Bodily Resurrection and Causality in Tahafut and the Iqtisad," *Aligarh Journal of Islamic Thought*, 1 (1989), 46–75.

"Ghazālī's Second Causal Theory in the 17th Discussion of his Tahafut," in *Islamic Philosophy and Mysticism*, ed. Parviz Morewedge, 85–112. New York: Caravan Books, 1981.

"The Metaphysics of Efficient Causality in Avicenna," in *Islamic Theology and Philosophy*, ed. Michael E. Marmura, 171–189. Albany: State University of New York Press, 1984.

Māturīdī, Abū Manṣūr al-, *Sharḥ al-Fiqh al-Akbar*. Hyderabad: Dairat al-Ma'arif al-Uthmaniyya, 1946.

Kitāb al-Tawhīd, ed. Bekir Topaloglu and Muhammad Aruci. İslam Araştırmaları Merkezi, 2003.

Mehmet Dag, *Cuveyni'nin Alem ve Allah Görüşü*, Ph.D. thesis. Ankara Üniversitesi, 1976.

Michot, J. [Yahya]. *La destinée de l'homme selon Avicenne*. Louvain: Peeters, 1986.

Moad, Edward Omar. "Ghazālī on Power, Causation, and Acquisition," *Philosophy East West*, 57.1 (2007), 1–13.

"Ibn Khaldūn and Occasionalism," in *Occasionalism Revisited: New Essays from the Islamic and Western Philosophical Traditions*, ed. Nazif Muhtaroglu, 61–82. Abu Dhabi: Kalam Research Media, 2017.

Morris, James W. *The Reflective Heart: Discovering Spiritual Intelligence in Ibn ʿArabi's "Meccan Illuminations."* Louisville, KY: Fons Vitae, 2005.

Muhtaroglu, Nazif. "Ali Sedad Bey's (d.1900) *Kavāid al-Taḥavvulāt fī Ḥarakāt al-Zarrāt* (Principles of Transformation in the Motion of Particles)," in *Oxford Handbook of Islamic Philosophy*, ed. Khaled El-Rouayheb and Sabine Schmidke, 586–606. New York: Oxford University Press, 2017.

"Islamic and Cartesian Roots of Occasionalism." Ph.D. dissertation. University of Kentucky, 2012.

"An Occasionalist Defense of Free Will," in *Classical Issues in Islamic Philosophy and Theology Today*, ed. Anna Tymieniecka and N. Muhtaroglu, 45–62. New York: Springer, 2010.

and Özgür Koca, "Late Ottoman Occasionalists and Modern Science," in *Occasionalism Revisited: New Essays from the Islamic and Western Philosophical Traditions*, ed. Nazif Muhtaroglu, 83–101. Abu Dhabi: Kalam Research and Media, 2017.

Murphy, Nancey. "Divine Action in the Natural Order: Buridan's Ass and Schrodinger's Cat," in *Chaos and Complexity: Scientific Perspectives on Divine Action*, ed. R. Russell, N. Murphy, and A. Peacocke, 325–358. Vatican: Vatican Observatory and Berkeley, CA: The Center for Theology and the Natural Sciences, 1995.

Reconciling Theology and Science: A Radical Reformation Perspective. Kitchener, ON: Pandora Press, 1997.

Muzaffar. Muḥammad Riḍa al-. *ʿAqāʾid al-Imāmiyya*, translated into Turkish by Abdulbaki Gölpınarlı. Istanbul: Zaman Yayınları, 1978.

Nader al-Bizri, "God: Essence and Attributes," in *The Cambridge Companion to Classical Islamic Theology*, ed. Tim Winter, 121–140. Cambridge, UK: Cambridge University Press, 2008.

Nadler, Steven. "Knowledge, Volitional Agency and Causation in Malebranche and Geulincx," *British Journal for the History of Philosophy*, 7 (1999), 263–274.

Nasafī, Muḥammad al-. *Tabṣirat al-Adilla*, ed. Claude Salame, 2 vols. Damascus: Institut Français de Damas, 1990–1993.

Nasr, S. H. *An Annotated Bibliography of Islamic Science*. 3 vols. Lahore: Suhail Academy, 1985.

An Introduction to Islamic Cosmological Doctrines. Cambridge, UK: Cambridge University Press, 1964.

Sadr al-Din al-Shirazi and his Transcendent Theosophy. Tehran: Imperial Iranian Academy of Philosophy, 1977.

Science and Civilization in Islam. Cambridge, UK: Cambridge University Press, 1987.

Three Muslim Sages: Avicenna-Suhrawardī-Ibn 'Arabi. Cambridge, MA: Harvard University Press, 1964.

Nichols, Ryan and Gideon Yaffe, "Thomas Reid," in *The Stanford Encyclopedia of Philosophy* (Winter 2016 Edition), ed. Edward N. Zalta: https://plato.stanford.edu/archives/win2016/entries/reid/.

Nichols, Terence L. "Miracles in Science and Theology," *Zygon*, 37.3 (2002), 703–716.

Nīsābūrī, *al-Masāʾil fi-l-Khilāf bayn al-Baṣriyyīn wa-l-Baghdādīyyīn*, ed. Ridwan Sayyid, Maʿn Ziyada. Beirut, Maʿhad al-Inma al-Arabi: 1979.

Nursi, Said. *The Flashes: From the Risale- i Nur Collection*, trans. Şükran Vahide. Istanbul: Sözler Neşriyat, 1995.

The Letters: From the Risale- i Nur Collection, trans. Şükran Vahide. Istanbul: Sözler Neşriyat, 1994.

Mathnawi al-Nuriya (Epitomes of Light: *The Essentials of The Risale-i Nur*). Caglayan A. S. Izmir: Kaynak Publications, 1999.

The Rays: From the Risale-i Nur Collection, trans. Şükran Vahide. Istanbul: Sözler Neşriyat, 2002.

Risale- i Nur Külliyatı. 2 vols. Istanbul: Nesil Yayinlari, 2002.

The Words: From the Risale-i Nur Collection, trans. Şükran Vahide (revised edition). Istanbul: Sözler Neşriyat, 2004.

Ormsby, Eric L. *The Makers of the Muslim World: Ghazālī*. Oxford: One World, 2007.

Theodicy in Islamic Thought: The Dispute over Ghazālī's 'Best of All Possible Worlds.' Princeton, NJ: Princeton University Press, 1984.

Pazdawī, Abū al-Yusr Muḥammad al-. *Uṣūl al-Dīn*, ed. Hans Peter Lins. Cairo: Dar Ihya al-Kutub al-Arabiyya, 1963.

Peacocke, Arthur. *Creation and the World of Science: The Reshaping of Belief*, 2nd ed. Oxford: Oxford University Press, 2004.

Theology for Scientific Age: Being and Becoming—Natural, Divine, and Human, 2nd edn. London: SCM Press, 1993.

Perler, D. and U. Rudolph. *Occasionalismus: Theorien der Kausalität im arabisch-islamischen und im europäischen Denken*. Göttingen: Vandenhoeck and Ruprecht, 2000.

Peters, Ted. *Science and Theology: The New Consonance*. Oxford: Westview Press, 1998.

Pines, Sholomo. *Mazhab al-Zarra*, trans. Muhammad Hadi Abu Rida. Cairo: Maktabat al-Nahdat al-Islamiyya, 1946.

Plato, *Complete Works*, ed. John M. Cooper with introduction and notes, ass. ed. D. S. Hutchinson. Cambridge, MA: Hackett, 1997.

Polkinghorne, John. *Belief in God in the Age of Science*. New Haven, CT: Yale University Press, and Nicholas Saunders, 1998 (2002).

Science and Providence: God's Interaction with the World. Boston, MA: Society for Promoting Christian Knowledge, 1989.

Science and Theology: An Introduction. Minneapolis, MN: First Fortress Press, 1999.

Qāḍī ʿAbduljabbār. *al-Mughnī fī Abwābi al-ʿAdl wa-l-Tawhīd*, ed. Ibrahim Madkur, Taha Husayn, and various editors. 16 vols. Cairo: al-Dar al-Misriyya li al-Telif wa al-Tarjuma, 1962–1965.

al-Muḥīṭ bi-l-Taklīf, ed. Umar Sayyid Azmi and Ahmad Fu'ad al-Ahwani. Cairo: al-Sharika al-Misriyya, n.d.

al-Mukhtaṣar fī Uṣūl al-Dīn. Cairo: Dar al-Hilal, 1971.

Sharḥ al-Uṣūl al-Khamsa, ed. Abd al-Karim Uthman. Cairo: Maktabat Wahbah 1965.

Qayṣarī, Dāwūd al-. *Risāla fī ʿIlm al-Taṣawwuf*, trans. into Turkish by Muhammed Bedirhan. Istanbul: Nefes Yayinlari, 2013.

Sharḥ Fuṣūṣ al-Ḥikam. Tahran, 1963 [1383].

"Sharḥ Taʾwīlāt Basmala," in *Rasāʾil*, ed. Mehmet Bayraktar. Ankara, 1989.

Qūnawī, Ṣadraddīn al-. *al-Murasalāt*, Turkish trans. Ekrem Demirli. Istanbul: Kapı Yayınları, 2014.

Iʿjāz al-Bayān fī Taʾwīl Umm-Qurʾan, Turkish trans. Ekrem Demirli. Istanbul: İz Yayıncılık-İslam Klasikleri Dizisi, 2009.

Miftāḥ Ghayb al-Jamʿi wa-l-Wujūd fi-l-Kashf al-Shuhūd, Süleymaniye Yazma Eser Kütüphanesi (Manuscript), Ayasofya, no. 1930.

Rahman, Fazlur. *The Philosophy of Mullā Ṣadrā*. Albany: State University of New York Press, 1975.

Rashed, M. "Théodicée et approximation: Avicenne," *Arabic Sciences and Philosophy*, 10 (2000), 223–257.

Rāzī, Fakhr al-Dīn al-. *Al-Mabāḥith al-Mashriqiyyah*, ed. Muhammad al-Mu'tasim biLlah al-Baghdadi, 2 vols. Beirut: Dar al-Kitab al-Arabi, 1990.

al-Maṭālib al-ʿĀliya, ed. Ahmad Hijazi al-Saqa, 9 vols. Beirut: Dar al-Kitab al-Arabi, 1987.

Muḥaṣṣal Afkār al-Mutaqaddimīn wa-l-Mutaʾakhkhirīn, ed. Abd al-Rauf Said. Cairo: Maktabat al-Kulliyāt al-Azhariyya, n.d.

al-Tafsīr al-Kabīr, 32 vols. Beirut: Dar Ihya al-Turath al-Arabi, 1996.

Reid, Thomas. *An Inquiry into the Human Mind on the Principles of Common Sense* [1764]: *A Critical Edition*, ed. Derek Brookes. University Park, PA: Penn State University Press, 1997.

Rescher, N. "al-Fārābī on the Question: Is Existence a Predicate?," in *Studies in the History of Arabic Logic*, 39–42. Pittsburgh, PA: University of Pittsburgh Press, 1963.

"The Concept of Existence in Arabic Logic and Philosophy," in *Studies in Arabic Philosophy*. Pittsburgh, PA: University of Pittsburgh Press, 1966.

Richardson, Kara. "Avicenna's Conception of the Efficient Cause," *British Journal for the History of Philosophy*, 21.2 (2013), 220–239.

"Causation in Arabic and Islamic Thought," *The Stanford Encyclopedia of Philosophy* (Winter 2015 Edition), ed. Edward N. Zalta: https://plato.stanford.edu/archives/win2015/entries/arabic-islamic-causation/.

Rizvi, Sajjad H. "An Islamic Subversion of the Existence-Essence Distinction? Suhrawardī's Visionary Hierarchy of Lights," *Asian Philosophy*, 9.3 (1999), 219–227.

"Mullā Ṣadrā and Causation: Rethinking a Problem in Later Islamic Philosophy" *Philosophy of East and West*, 55.4 (2005), 570–583.

Mullā Ṣadrā Shirazi: His Life, Works and the Sources for Safavid Philosophy. JSS Supplements 18. Oxford: Oxford University Press, 2007.
"Roots of an Aporia in Later Islamic Philosophy: the Existence-Essence Distinction in the Philosophies of Avicenna and Suhrawardī," *Studia Iranica*, 29 (2000), 61–108.
The Stanford Encyclopedia of Philosophy (Summer 2009 Edition), ed. Edward N. Zalta: https://plato.stanford.edu/archives/sum2009/entries/Mullā-Ṣadrā/.
Rosen, E. *Copernicus and the Scientific Revolution*. Malabar, FL: Krieger Publishing Co., 1984.
Roxanne, Marcotte. "Suhrawardī," *The Stanford Encyclopedia of Philosophy* (Fall 2016 Edition), ed. Edward N. Zalta: https://plato.stanford.edu/archives/fall2016/entries/suhrawardī/.
Rudolph, Ulrich. *Al-Māturīdī and the Development of Sunnī Theology in Samarqand*, trans. Rodrigo Adem. Boston, MA: Brill, 2014.
Ruffus, Anthony and Jon McGinnis, "Willful Understanding: Avicenna's Philosophy of Action and Theory of the Will," *Archiv für Geschichte der Philosophie*, 97.2 (2015), 160–195.
Rūmī, Jalāl al-Dīn, *Dīwān Shams-i Tabrīzī*, ed. B. Furūzānfar, 10 vols. Tehran: University of Tehran Press, 1957–1967.
The Mathnawī of Rūmī, ed. and trans. R. A. Nicholson, 8 vols. London: Luzac, 1925–1940.
Russell, Robert J. "Does the 'God Who Acts' Really Act? New Approaches to Divine Action in the Light of Science," *Theology Today*, 54.1 (1997), 43–65.
Russell, Robert J., Nancey Murphy, and Arthur Peacocke, eds, *Chaos and Complexity: Scientific Perspectives on Divine Action*. Vatican City State: Vatican Observatory Publications, 1995.
Ryan, Todd. "Hume's Argument for the Temporal Priority of Causes," *Hume Studies*, 29.1 (2003), 29–41.
Sabūnī, Aḥmad ibn Muḥammad al-. *Maturidiyye Akaidi (al-Bidāya fī Uṣūl al-Dīn)*, Turkish trans. Bekir Topaloğlu. Istanbul: Diyanet İşleri Başkanlığı, n.d.
Sabzawārī, Mulla Hādī. *The Metaphysics of Sabzawari*, trans. M. Mohaghegh and T. Izutsu. New York: Caravan Books, 1977.
Sadr, Muhammad Baqr al-. *Our Philosophy*, trans. Shams C. Inati. CreateSpace Independent Publishing, 2014.
Ṣadrā, Mullā. *al-Ḥikmat al-Muta'āliya fi-l-Asfār al-'Aqliyya al-Arba'a*, ed. R. Lutfi et al., 3rd ed. Beirut: Dar lhya al-Turath al-Arabi, 9 vols, 1981.
Ḥuduth al-'Ālam. ed. S. H. Musaviyan. Tehran: Bunyad-i Hikmat-i Islami-yi Sadra [Sadra Islamic Philosophy Research Institute], 1959.
Īqāẓ al-Nā'imīn. ed. Mohammed Khansari; Tehran: SIPRIn, 1384/2005.
Kitāb al-Mashā'ir, trans. Seyyed Hossein Nasr, ed. intr. and annot. Ibrahim Kalın. Provo, UT: Brigham Young University Press, 2014.
The Wisdom of the Throne (al-Ḥikmat al-'Arshiyya), trans. James Winston Morris. Princeton, NJ: Princeton University Press, 1981.
Salmon, Wesley C., ed. *Zeno's Paradoxes*. Indianapolis, IN and New York: The Bobbs-Merrill Company, Inc., 1970. Reprinted in paperback in 2001.
Santayana, George. *Skepticism and Animal Faith*. New York: Dover, 1955.

Saritoprak, Zeki. "Bediüzzaman Said Nursi," in *The Islamic World*, ed. Andrew Rippin, 396–402. London and New York: Routledge, 2008.

"Said Nursi," in *Bibliographies in "Islamic Studies,"* ed. Andrew Rippin. New York: Oxford University Press, 2011.

Saunders, Nicholas. *Divine Action and Modern Science*. Cambridge, UK: Cambridge University Press, 2002.

"Does God Cheat at Dice? Divine Action and Quantum Possibilities" *Zygon*, 35.3 (2000), 541–542.

Schacht, Joseph. "New Sources for the History of Muhammadan Theology," *Studia Islamica*, 1 (1953), 23–42.

"Theology and Law in Islam," in *Theology and Law in Islam*, ed. G. E. von Grunebaum, 3–23. Wiesbaden: Otto Harrassowitz, 1971.

Schmidtke, S. *Theologie, Philosophie und Mystik im zwölferschiitischen Islam des 9./15.Jahrhunderts: die Gedankenwelten des Ibn Abi Gumhur al-Ahsai (um 838/1434-35-nach 905/1501)*. Leiden: Brill, 2000.

Serdar, Ziauddin. *Explorations in Islamic Science*. London: Mansell Publishing Ltd, 1989.

Setia, Adi. "Atomism Versus Hylomorphism in the *Kalām* of al-Fakhr al-Dīn al-Rāzī," *Islam & Science*, 4.2 (2006), 113–140.

"Fakhr al-Dīn al-Rāzī on Physics and the Nature of the Physical World: A Preliminary Survey," *Islam & Science*, 2.2 (2004), 161–180.

Shahrastānī, ʿAbd al-Karīm al-. *al-Milal wa-l-Niḥal*, ed. Muhammad Sayyid Kilani. Cairo: Mustafa al-Babi al-Halabi, 1961.

Nihāyat al-Iqdām, ed. Alfred Guillaume. London: Oxford University Press, 1934.

Shamsi, F. A. "Ibn Sina'Arguments Against Atomicity of Space," *Islamic Studies*, 23.2 (1984), 83–102.

Sirhindī, Aḥmad. *Maktubāt*, vols 1–2, trans. Kasim Yayla. Istanbul: Merve Yayinlari, 1999.

Sorabji, Richard. *Animal Minds and Human Morals: The Origins of the Western Debate*. Ithaca, NY: Cornell University Press, 1993.

Matter, Space, and Motion: Theories in Antiquity and their sequel. London: Duckworth and Ithaca, NY: Cornell University Press, 1988.

Necessity, Cause and Blame: Perspectives on Aristotle's Theory. London: Duckworth, 1980.

Stavrineas, Stasinos. "Nature as a principle of change," in *Aristotle's* Physics: *A Critical Guide*, ed. Mariska Leunissen, 46–65. Cambridge, UK: Cambridge University Press, 2015.

Street, Tony. "Concerning the Life and Works of Fakhr al-Din al-Razi," in *Islam: Essays on Scripture, Thought and Society, a Festschrift in honour of Anthony H. Johns*, 135–146. Leiden: Brill, 1997.

Suhrawardī, *L'archange empourpré: quinze traités et récits mystiques*, trans., intro., and notes H. Corbin. Paris: Fayard, 1976.

The Philosophy of Illumination: A New Critical Edition of the Text of Hikmat al-Ishraq, with English trans., notes, commentary, and intro. J. Walbridge and H. Ziai. Provo, UT: Brigham Young University Press, 1999.

Swerdlow N. and O. Neugebauer, *Mathematical Astronomy in Copernicus's De Revolutionibus*, 2 vols. New York: Springer-Verlag, 1984.

Taftazānī, Sa'd al-Dīn. *Sharḥ al-Talwīh 'ala Tawḍih li Matni al-Tankīh fi Uṣūl al-Fiqh*. Beirut: Dar al-Kutub al-Ilmiyyah, n.d.

Tahānawī, Muḥammad ibn 'Ali. *Kashshāf Iṣṭilaḥāt al-Funūn*, ed. Ali Dahruj. Beirut: Maktabat Lubnan, 1996.

Tracy, Thomas F. "Particular Providence and the God of the Gaps" in *Chaos and Complexity: Scientific Perspectives on Divine Action*, ed. R. Russell, N. Murphy, and A. Peacocke, 291–324. Vatican: Vatican Observatory and Berkeley, CA: The Center for Theology and the Natural Sciences, 1995.

"Theologies of Divine Action," in *The Oxford Handbook of Religion and Science*, ed. Philip Clayton and Zachary Simpson, 596–611. New York: Oxford University Press, 2006.

Ṭūsī, Naṣīr al-Dīn. *Talkhīṣ al-Muḥaṣṣal*, ed. Abdullah Nurani. Muassasa-i Motalaat-i Islami Daneshgah-i McGill Şuba-i Tahran, 1980.

Ṭūsī's Commentary on Ibn Sīnā's Pointers and Reminders (Sharḥ al-Ishārāt), ed. S. Dunyá, 4 vols. Cairo: 1957–1960.

Türker, Ömer. "Introduction," in *Sharḥ al-Mawāqif*. Turkish trans. Ömer Türker. Istanbul: Türkiye Yazma EserlerKurumu Başkanlığı, 2015.

Van Ess, Josef. *Theologie und Gesellschaft im 2. und 3. Jahrhundert Hidschra. Eine Geschichte des religiosen Denkens im fruhen Islam*, 6 vols. Berlin: Walter de Gruyter, 1991–1997.

Walbridge, John. *The Leaven of the Ancients: Suhrawardī and the Heritage of the Greeks*. Albany: State University of New York Press, 2000.

Walker, I. "The Problem of Evil and the Activity of God." *New Blackfriars*, 62 (1982): 441–463.

Wallis, R. T. *Neoplatonism*, 2nd ed. London: Duckworth, 1995.

Waterlow, Sarah. *Nature, Change, and Agency in Aristotle's Physics*. Oxford: Clarendon Press, 1982.

Watt, W. Montgomery. *Islamic Creeds: A Selection*. Edinburgh: Edinburgh University Press, 1994.

"Some Muslim Discussions of Anthropomorphism," in *Early Islam*, 86–93. Edinburgh: Edinburgh University Press, 1990.

Wensinck, A. J. *The Muslim Creed*. New Delhi: Oriental Books Reprint Corporation, 1979.

La Pensee de Ghazālī. Paris: Libr. d'Amérique et d'Orient A. Maisonneuve, 1950.

White, M. J. *The Continuous and the Discrete: Ancient Physical Theories from a Contemporary Perspective*. Oxford: Clarendon Press, 1992.

Whitehead, A. N., *Process and Reality*, corrected edn., ed. David R. Griffin and Donald W. Sherburne. New York: Free Press, 1978.

Wiles, M. *Reason to Believe*. London: SCM Press, 1999.

Williams, Wesley. "Aspects of the Creed of Imam Ahmad ibn Hanbal: A study of Anthropomorphism in Early Islamic Discourse," *International Journal of Middle East Studies*, 34 (2002), 441–463.

Wisnovsky, Robert. "Avicenna and the Avicennian Tradition," in *The Cambridge Companion to Arabic Philosophy*, ed. P. Adamson and R. C. Taylor, 92–136. Cambridge, UK: Cambridge University Press, 2005.

"Avicenna's Islamic Reception," in *Interpreting Avicenna: Critical Essays*, ed. Peter Adamson, 190–213. Cambridge, UK: Cambridge University Press, 2013.

Avicenna's Metaphysics in Context. Ithaca, NY: Cornell University Press, 2013.
"Final and Efficient Causality in Avicenna's Cosmology and Theology," *Quaestio*, 2 (2002), 97–124.
"Notes on Avicenna's Concept of Thingness," *Arabic Sciences and Philosophy*, 10 (2000), 181–221.
Wolfson, Harry Austryn. "Ibn Khaldun on Attributes and Predestination," *Speculum*, 34.4 (1959), 585–597.
"Muʿammar's Theory of *Maʿnā*," in *Arabic and Islamic Studies in the Honor of Hamilton A.R. Gibb*, ed. George Makdisi, 673–688. Leiden: Brill, 1965.
The Philosophy of Kalam. Cambridge, MA: Harvard University Press, 1976.
Yazdi, M. H. *The Principles of Epistemology in Islamic Philosophy: Knowledge by Presence*. Albany: State University of New York Press, 1992.
Yazicioglu, Umeyye Isra. *Understanding the Qurʾanic Miracle Stories in the Modern Age*. University Park, PA: Penn State University Press, 2013.
Zarkān, Muhammad Salih al-. *Fakhr al-Dīn al-Rāzī wa Arāʾuhu al-Kalāmiyyah wa-l-Falsafiyyah*. Beirut: Dar al-Fikr, 1963.
Ziai, H. "The Illuminationist Tradition," in *History of Islamic Philosophy*, ed. S. H. Nasr and O. Leaman, 465–496. London: Routledge, (2003) [1996].
Knowledge and Illumination: A Study of Suhrawardī's Hikmat al-Ishraq. Atlanta, GA: Scholars Press, 1990.
"Mullā Ṣadrā," in *History of Islamic Philosophy*, ed. S. H. Nasr and O. Leaman, 635–642. London: Routledge, 1996.

Index

Abū Hanifa, 35
accidents (a'rāḍ), 22, 30–34, 37–38, 68, 80, 122, 131, 136–137, 143, 152–154, 162–163, 173–174, 179, 229, 256, 260
accidental lights, 101–103
accountability, 3, 71, 146
acquisition, 12, 34–38, 72–73, 104, 128, 133, 160–161, 214–215, 220, 225, 260
active intellect (*al-'aql al-fa'āl*), 174, 177
actual indivisibility, 77
actuality, 11, 26, 46, 49, 51, 53, 55, 65, 75, 88–90, 98–99, 165, 172, 184, 186–188, 199, 227
adab, 123, 215
aesthetics, 209, 214, 225–226
aether, 212
agency, 10, 13, 16, 34, 36–37, 58, 63, 67, 69, 71, 83, 90, 99, 104, 110, 121, 126, 135, 139, 148–149, 152, 156, 186, 189, 191, 193, 199, 264
Aḥmad ibn Ḥanbal, 18
Ali Sedad, 201, 272
al-Idrāq, 26
al-juz' alladhī lā yataqassam, 29
Almagest, 175
Alousi, H. M., 23, 30, 262
Altaie, Mohammed B., 239
amrun iḍāfiyyun, 247
angelic intermediation, 62
anteriority/posteriority, 166
anthropic intermediation, 62
anthropocentrism, 238
anthropomorphism, 19, 232, 236
apophatic theology, 48
appearance of habit, 248
arbitrariness, 86, 95, 97, 156, 173, 260
arbitrary king, 130, 241, 248
argument from consciousness, 227
argument from spatiotemporal continuity, 229
argument from will, 228
Aristotelian logic, 3, 81
Aristotelianism, 3–4, 6, 10–14, 40, 44, 48, 50, 61–62, 81, 83, 85, 88–89, 92, 98–99, 131, 136, 159, 169, 172–173, 179, 181, 189, 201, 207, 243, 256–257, 259
Aristotle, 10–11, 44, 50, 59, 74, 76, 85, 92–93, 96, 126, 156, 170, 175, 181, 207, 258, 263–267, 276–277
aṣālat al-māhiyya, 101, 112
Asfār, 93, 184–185, 188–191, 195, 197, 199, 275
Ash'arī, ix, 18–25, 27, 30, 32–34, 36–37, 163, 220, 263, 266–267
Ash'arite occasionalism, 3, 13–14, 16, 27, 36, 38, 61–62, 67, 84, 86–87, 99, 123, 125, 127, 142, 153, 157, 163, 168, 173, 181–182, 200, 230, 243, 255–256
Ash'arite theologians, 1, 4, 14, 16, 18–20, 22, 27–28, 30, 33, 35, 37, 61, 213, 225, 230
Ash'arite theology, 13, 16, 31, 38, 60, 63, 73–74, 154, 159, 166, 239
astronomy, 81, 169, 171, 174–175, 181, 243, 276
Atatürk, M. Kemal., 201
atomism, 5, 13, 30–31, 33, 38, 60–61, 69, 73–75, 77, 79–80, 103, 120–121, 143, 154, 162, 179, 181, 201–202, 210–211, 226, 256, 265–266

atomism of time, 33
atomistic cosmology, 6, 20, 32
authorization (*tafwīḍ*), 35
autonomy, 12, 232, 248–249
Avicennian natural philosophy, 14, 159, 173, 181
awareness of Being, 250, 252
al-awwal, 42, 47

Bāqillānī, 19–23, 26–28, 30–33, 35–36, 73, 228, 242
barzakh, 111, 125
being *qua* being, 49
Berkeley, 84, 207, 233, 249, 263, 272, 277
Berkeleyan immaterialism, 249
bestowal of existence, 48, 52, 59, 185, 194, 196, 257–258, 260
bestower of existence, 92
Bigliardi, Stefano, 238
bi-lā kayfa, 18
Breath of the Merciful, 121, 157
British emprícism, 207
Büchner, F. Ludwig, 201
Burckhardt, Titus, 237

causal activity, 48, 88, 95, 111, 115, 135, 140, 142, 184, 244, 257–259
causal disproportionality, 5, 202
causal necessity, 62, 84, 87, 123, 161, 213, 240, 255
cause and effect, 2–3, 6, 15, 24, 27, 31, 38, 63, 68–70, 83, 87, 124–126, 142, 160, 168, 171, 181, 200, 202–203, 206, 213–214, 216–217, 220, 222, 224–225, 227, 229–230, 240–242, 244–245, 247–249, 253, 256
celestial intellects, 91, 99, 141, 156, 179, 259
celestial motion, 43
celestial spheres, 43, 54, 171, 175–178, 243
chain of causality, 3
Chaos theory, 233
chaotic systems, 234–235
Chittick, William, 116, 119–121, 123–124, 131, 135, 213, 264, 268
classical mechanics, 233
Clayton, Philip, 227, 234–235, 241, 264, 267, 277
cleavage of the moon, 87
coercion, 12
co-eternity, 57, 151, 164
colonialism, 236
colorless light, 106
composition of points, 78
comprehensive existence, 137, 141
computability of chaotic systems, 233
Comte, August, 201
conceptual indivisibility, 77
concrete indivisibility, 77
conjunction, 6, 27–28, 37–38, 52, 68, 72, 92, 159–160, 174, 181, 191, 203, 214, 240, 242, 244–245, 255, 260
constant conjunction, 38, 68, 242, 260
constant re-creation, 32, 60, 120–121, 154, 187, 210, 259
constellation, 174
contingency, 2
contingent, 2, 44, 93, 100–101, 103, 105, 108, 110, 128, 136–137, 140, 143, 146, 151, 153, 185–186, 195–196, 198
contingent existent, 45
continuous creation, 5, 89, 136, 141, 143, 154
cosmological presumptions of modern science, 237
cosmology, 11, 13, 29, 33, 37–38, 62, 69, 123, 126, 131, 143, 162, 169, 172–175, 177, 181, 200, 255–256, 278
creation ex nihilo, 64
criticism of atomism, 69

deferent, 171, 175
demonstrability, 62
determinism, 37, 41, 88, 95, 130, 220, 222
deterministic interpretation (of quantum theory), 235
deterministic worldview, 96
Dhanani, Alnoor, 30–33, 73, 76, 265
Dilthey, Wilhelm, 251
Ḍirār ibn ʿAmr, 32
directedness of consciousness, 250
discrete/continuous world, 13, 30, 32–33, 76–77, 80, 123, 163, 181, 210, 212, 255
disproportionality of cause and effect, 15, 125, 202, 211, 224–225, 227–230, 256
divine action, 60, 66, 212, 234, 244
divine agency, 63, 67
divine attributes, 6, 13, 16–17, 19–20, 29, 46, 48, 59–60, 63, 66–67, 70, 113, 125, 137–138, 144–145, 157, 164, 189–191, 200, 203, 208, 213, 255
divine command, 3, 167

divine freedom, 6, 13, 27, 29, 53–54, 64, 70, 113, 115, 127–128, 138, 157, 167–168, 173, 191, 219, 260
divine habits, 5, 28, 87, 155
divine intellect, 151
divine names, 117–122, 125, 127–128, 132, 137, 145–147, 151, 202, 212, 217–218, 224, 230, 236
divine presence, 3, 205
Divine Self-Disclosure, 15
divine speech, 19
DNA molecule, 233
drinking (alcohol), 26
dual causality, 49
dualism, 127, 144, 260
dunameis, 207
dusky substance, 108, 114
dynamic systems, 234
dynamis panton, 10

eccentric, 175
economics, 3
Elmalılı Hamdi Yazir, 201
emanation, 5, 10, 41, 43, 48–49, 52, 57, 64, 69, 89, 99, 105, 108, 141, 143, 156–157, 173–174, 176, 194, 197
emanationism, 56, 136, 140–141, 156–157, 258–259
emergence theory, 234–235
empiricism, 3, 207, 243
epicycles, 175
epistemology, 3, 6, 47, 113, 168–169, 181, 237, 239
equant, 175
erosion of light, 102
eschatology, 3, 6, 14, 24, 168, 181
essence (*māhiyya*), 4, 6, 12–13, 40, 44, 53–54, 58, 100, 250
Euclidian geometry, 4, 13, 61, 73, 79–80, 201, 256
Europe, 201
evil, 23, 34–35, 43, 46, 118, 167–168, 197, 214–215, 248
evolutionary trajectory, 233
existence (*wujūd*), 4, 6, 12–13, 40, 44, 53, 90, 100, 127, 137, 141, 192, 250, 253, 257, 259
existentiation, 55, 57, 89, 121, 129, 131, 136, 138–139, 141–142, 147–149, 151, 154, 156, 194–196, 198, 259
expansion of existence, 93, 137, 143, 185, 197, 199, 260
expedient truth, 173
externalization (*ẓuhūr*), 26
extramental reality, 3

al-Fā ʿil al-Mukhtār, 168, 177–178
Fārābī, 18, 46, 52, 91, 104, 132, 140, 265, 274
Faṣl al-Maqāl, 89, 269
Fazlur Rahman, 189, 192, 198
Feyerabend, Paul, 236
final cause, 11, 57
fire and burning, 26
First Intellect, 50, 140–141
fixed archetypes, 14, 116, 118, 129–131, 134, 137, 147–148, 151, 154
Flashes (Lem'alar), 202, 204–205, 273
formation of mountains, 177–178
four causes, 10
four elements, 179
fragrance of existence, 150, 259
Frank, Richard M., 20, 23, 25, 31, 33, 41, 208
free will, 1, 14, 24, 80, 129, 220, 223, 232, 247–248, 254, 256, 260
free-fall of a stone, 225
French occasionalism, 228
fünūn-u cedīde (Tr.), 201
Fuṣūṣ al-Ḥikam, 118, 144, 146–148, 151, 185, 268
al-Futūḥāt al-Makkīyya, 116, 118, 268

General Divine Action, 231
general expanding existence (*al-wujūd al-ʿām al-munbasiṭ*), 148
genetic mutations, 233
geology, 182
geometrical indivisibility, 77
Geulincx, Arnold, 35, 228
ghayr majʿūl, 138–139
Ghazālī, ix, 1, 4, 14, 22, 26, 35, 41, 43, 60–69, 71, 80–81, 84, 86–88, 91, 98–99, 101, 104, 132, 170–172, 176, 180, 213, 228, 239, 241, 256, 259, 262, 266–268, 271–273, 277
gift of existence, 53–54
Gimaret, Daniel, 23–24, 27, 33, 35, 267–268
giver of existence, 49–50, 53, 55, 59, 98–99, 185, 249, 257

gloomy essences, 5, 102, 105–108, 111, 115, 258
gnomon, 75
Goldziher, Ignaz, 18
Golshani, Mahdi, 238–239, 245, 264, 267
gradational metaphysics, 7, 14, 54, 100, 103, 105, 107, 115, 128, 132, 149, 190–191
grammar, 19
gravitational acceleration, 226
Greeks, 106, 171, 175, 191, 265, 277
Griffel, Frank, 26, 42, 63, 240, 267
Griffin, David Ray, 169, 227, 241
Guenon, Rene, 237
Guessoum, Nidhal, 237–238, 245, 264, 267
Guiderdoni, Bruno, 238–239, 264

ḥādith, 19, 160, 163
haecceity, 47, 55
Hanbalites, 18
ḥaqq, 30, 53, 55, 118
hayūlā, 49, 143, 157, 174, 179
Heidegger, 246, 250, 252, 268
hierarchy, 119, 173, 191, 237
ḥikma, 24, 36, 167, 170, 181
Ḥikmat al-Ishrāq, 101, 103, 112
Hishām ibn Ḥakem, 33
Holy Effusion (*al-fayḍ al-muqaddas*), 148
homogenous atoms, 31, 80, 133, 179
Hudhayl, 17, 29, 33, 266
ḥulūl, 137
human autonomy, 3
human volition, 71
Hume, 84, 207, 241, 268, 275
ḥusn, 23, 167
Husserl, Edmund, 250, 268
hyle, 143, 153, 156–157, 174, 179
hylomorphic criticism, 256
hylomorphism, 4, 60–62, 69, 80–81, 153, 180–181
hypotenuse, 74

Ibn al-Haytham, 175
Ibn Fūrak, 2, 23, 26–28, 30, 33, 36, 268
Ibn Ḥazm, 2, 22, 29–31, 36, 268
Ibn Humām, 221, 247, 268
Ibn Khaldūn, 242, 268, 272
Ibn Maymūn (Maimonides), 28, 30, 36–38, 268
Ibn Rushd, 1, 4, 14, 41, 65, 83–84, 86–88, 90–92, 94–95, 97–99, 132, 136, 173, 177, 188, 240–241, 244, 249, 253, 257, 259, 268
Ibn Sīnā, 1, 4, 13, 40–52, 54–61, 63, 69, 73–77, 79–80, 83–84, 91, 98–100, 104, 109, 115, 132, 136, 140, 145, 153, 169–170, 180, 201, 244, 249, 253, 256–259, 266, 268–270, 277
Ibn ʿArabī, 1, 4–5, 14, 59, 84, 93, 116–133, 135–137, 143–144, 148, 154, 157, 187–188, 192, 198–199, 201, 210–211, 213–214, 230, 250, 253, 256, 259, 268, 270
Identity, 84
idolatry, 35
Iḥyā', 68
Illuminationism, 4
illusion, 34, 70, 76, 123, 125–126, 213, 215, 220, 248
imaginary suns, 209
imkān, 22, 29, 56, 58, 118, 160, 172, 255
immateriality of the soul, 180
impossibility, 44, 79, 142, 241
impossible existent (*mumtaniʿ al-wujūd*), 45
in-betweenness, 75
inbisāṭ al-wujūd, 93, 137, 185, 197
incorporeal light, 102–103, 108, 114
independence, 108, 114, 121, 163, 203–204
indeterminacies, 233
indeterministic interpretations (of quantum theory), 235
indistinguishability, 240
individuation of light, 106–107
indivisible point, 78–79
infinite density, 234
infinite divisibility, 76, 78
infinite regress, 145
initial conditions, 233
instantaneous velocity, 226
instantiation, 147
intellectual volition, 54
intercessory prayer, 232
interconnectivity, 232
intermediation, 62, 84, 91, 99, 115, 140–142, 156–157, 203, 244–245, 258–259
Iqtiṣād, 22, 67–68, 266
irāda, 17, 64, 128, 165
ishrāqiyyūn, 4, 257
Islamic occasionalism, 15, 240, 243–248, 253, 260
Islamic philosophy, 4–5, 100

Islamization of science, 237
Ismail al-Faruqi, 236
istimrār al-ʿāda, 241
istiʿdād, 169, 174, 179
ittiḥād, 137
Izutsu, T., 46, 102, 116, 118–119, 121–123, 184, 214, 269, 275

jabr, 35
Jabrī, Mohammad A. al-, 27
Jāḥiẓ, 24, 26, 33, 269
Jamal al-Din Afghani, 236
jawhar, 29–30, 49, 103, 143, 162, 179–180
Jubbāʾī, 17, 20, 24, 262
judgement, 3, 36, 85
Jurjānī, 1–2, 4–5, 14, 61, 80, 82, 93, 159–164, 166–168, 170, 172–173, 175, 177–178, 180–181, 201, 241, 256, 269
justice, 3, 6, 23–24, 41, 232
Juwaynī, 19, 21–24, 27–28, 30–33, 35–36, 73, 176, 228, 263, 269
juzʾ, 29, 136

kalām, 15, 40, 61, 159, 165, 202, 230
Kalın, Ibrahim, 192
Kant, 216, 223, 242, 252
kasb, 12, 34–38, 104, 128, 133, 160, 260
kenotic accounts, 236
Khayyāṭ, 24–25, 270
Kinematic equations, 225
Kitāb al-Mashāʿir, 183, 192, 275
Kogan, Brian, 41, 88, 97, 270
Kuhn, Thomas, 236
kull, 136

Lakatos, Imre, 236
laws of nature, 28, 206, 210, 232, 235, 239–241, 244–245, 254
Letters (Mektubat), 204, 211, 273
Levinas, Emmanuel, 250, 252
light analogy, 5
light in itself, 101, 113
Light of Lights, 101–102, 104–109, 111–115, 258
loci, 31, 118, 120, 137, 168, 200, 202, 211, 213, 217, 225–226, 230
locus of contact, 78–79
logic, 3, 7, 19, 27, 30, 34, 81, 159–160, 168, 176–178, 180, 208, 226, 240, 244–245
logical impossibilities, 27, 144, 165, 172
lower-level structures, 234
luminosity, 108, 110, 113–114
luminous object, 127

Makdisi, George, 16, 18, 25, 278
makhlūq, 17
Malebranche, 181, 228, 271–272
Maqālāt, ix, 18, 22–25, 29, 33–34, 36–37, 263
maqdūrāt, 34
Marmura, Michael, 22, 40–43, 47, 62, 64, 67–68, 213, 266, 269
mashshāʾiyyūn, 4, 257
Maṭālib, 77–79, 81, 274
materialism, 201
mathematical formulas, 17, 225, 227, 235
mathematicity, 209, 226, 230, 236
Mathnawī, 1, 124, 129, 275
maʿnā, 25
mechanism, 238
mental causation, 27
mental constructions, 3, 227, 243
mental existence, 184, 194, 206–207
metaphysical assumptions of science, 239
metaphysical causality, 40, 48, 50, 52–56, 59, 99, 115, 249–250, 253, 257–259, 261
metaphysical cause, 99
metaphysical framework, 4, 6, 40, 122, 135, 174–175, 177, 241–242, 247, 257
metaphysics of causation, 15
methodological naturalism, 238
Miftāḥ Ghayb, 93, 136, 274
miracles, 28, 62, 72–73, 83, 87, 155, 157, 168, 218–219, 230, 232, 235, 238–240, 242, 244–245
mirror, 118, 127, 205, 210, 212, 217, 219, 225, 229
Mishkāt al-Anwār, 101, 267
modern science, 159, 201, 237, 256
modulation, 190–191, 193
moral agency, 3, 12
morality, 6, 38, 126, 210, 261
morphē, 181
Morris, James W., 116, 187, 268, 272, 275
most beautiful names (*asmā al-ḥusnā*), 117
Most Holy Effusion (*al-fayḍ al-aqdas*), 148
motion and rest, 11, 22, 38, 48–49, 52, 59, 70, 249–250, 257
muḥāl, 22, 44
Muhammad Abduh, 236
muḥaqqiqīn, 197
Muḥaṣṣal, 70–72, 76–77, 79, 81, 274
mujāwara, 27, 31, 37–38, 159, 255

mukhaṣṣiṣ, 32, 165, 176
multiplicity of eternals, 17, 164
mumkin al-wujūd, 45, 100
mumkināt, 22, 176, 241
murādāt, 34
murajjih, 80, 95, 136, 154, 159, 176, 255
musabbab, 2
mustard seed, 77
mutakallimūn, 4, 162, 179
Muʿammar ibn ʿAbbad al-Sulamī, 17
Muʿtazilites, 1–2, 4, 13, 16–21, 23–25, 28–30, 33–35, 38, 40, 52, 127–128, 133, 160, 163–164, 166–167, 180, 220, 238
mystics, 1, 3, 6, 135, 192, 195, 249, 255, 257

Nafas al-Raḥmān, 121, 148
nafs, 136, 173–174, 180
naqḍ al-ʿāda, 27
natural phenomena, 10, 27, 62, 123–124, 173, 178, 205–206, 214, 216, 219, 232, 239, 246–247, 250, 252
natural philosophy, 14, 24, 159, 169–171, 173, 178, 181, 206, 256
naturalism, 238
naẓar, 27
Naẓẓām, 23–25, 30, 33, 262
Necessary Existent, 42, 44–47, 51, 53, 55, 58, 66, 100, 102, 112, 174, 262
necessary relation, 28–29, 60, 69, 87, 169, 180–181, 242
negative causality, 111
Neoplatonism, 4, 7–9, 13, 40–41, 48, 61, 186, 277
non-deterministic relation, 95
nonexistence (*ʿadam*), 19
non-linear systems, 233
nullification of the habits, 27
Nursi, ix, 1, 4–5, 15, 61, 80, 125, 133, 200–205, 207, 209, 212, 214, 216–217, 219–225, 227–228, 230, 236, 244, 247, 256, 268, 270, 273, 276

observation, 68
occasionalist accounts, 4–5, 12, 261
occasionalist critique, 83
occasionalist logic, 248
occasionalist worldview, 6, 13, 60, 80
omnibenevolent, 209
omnipotence, 2–3, 22
omnipresence, 3, 10
omniscience, 3, 130
ontology, 14, 54, 100, 102–105, 107, 115, 125, 127–128, 189–192, 199, 210
optimum, 23, 264
orthodoxy, 17, 62

panentheism, 234
paradigm shift, 234
paradox, 76
Parmenides, 7–9
participatory account of causality, 5, 14, 44, 83, 88, 100, 128, 139, 152, 257
particular providence, 232
particularization, 64, 147–148, 151, 194
particularization problem, 64
particulars, 101, 112, 136, 166, 173
passage of time, 77
passivity, 62, 84, 121
Peacocke, Arthur, 233–234, 275
people of nature (*ahl al-ṭibaʿ*), 26
Perennialism, 237
Peripatetic school, 4
perspectivalism, 193
pervasion of existence, 137, 185, 197
phenomenology, 250–253
phenomenology of causality., 250
philosophia naturalis, 169
philosophy of science, 5, 14, 69, 80, 82, 159, 181, 201, 236
physical causality, 11, 40, 49–50, 52, 59, 99, 250, 253, 258, 261
physical laws, 202, 205, 207–208, 210, 218, 227, 240
physics, 4, 76, 81, 169–171, 179, 181, 233, 243
pietistic courtesy, 168
Plato, 7–10, 44, 175, 186, 264, 273
Platonic Forms, 7
Plotinus, 8–10, 186, 246, 264
point, 77
Polanyi, Michael, 236
politics, 3, 261
Polkinghorne, John, 233–234
Popper, Karl, 236
positivism, 201
potency, 49, 51, 56, 88, 90
potentiality, 10–11, 26, 46, 50–51, 55, 58, 65, 80, 83, 88–91, 95–96, 98–99, 119, 165, 184, 188, 258, 266
predestination, 3, 41

predictability, 14, 27, 70, 116, 124, 126, 131, 172, 216, 219–220, 242
pre-eternity, 64, 69, 80, 88, 212
pre-modern science, 237
preparedness (*isti'dād*), 131, 260
preponderance, 4, 21, 38, 61, 63, 65, 71, 73, 80, 83, 89, 95, 99, 134, 136, 141, 143, 154, 157, 159, 165, 173, 176–178, 182, 229, 255, 260
preponderance without reason, 4, 61, 63, 71, 73, 80, 83, 89, 134, 136, 159, 173, 182, 255, 260
preponderer, 32, 71
primacy of existence, 45, 192
primary matter (*hylē*), 181
principality of essence, 101, 112
principium tertii exclusi, 248
privation, 43, 45, 51, 110, 184
probabilistic laws, 233
process, 14, 116, 120, 122–124, 126, 186
prophetology, 6, 14, 24, 168–169, 181, 242
Proximate Light, 107–108, 114
proximity, 27–28, 31, 35, 37–38, 159–160, 174, 203, 255
Ptolemy, 14, 81, 159, 169–173, 175, 181, 201, 243, 256
pure act, 11, 83, 88, 90, 94–96, 99, 186, 188, 258
pure actuality, 51, 90
pure existence, 45–46, 48, 51–54, 58–59, 64, 83, 88, 90, 94, 99, 122, 136, 184–185, 188, 192, 197, 258
pure goodness, 136
pure intellect, 47, 54, 96
pure light, 101, 114, 145
pure potentiality, 51
Pythagorean Theorem, 74

Qāḍī 'Abduljabbār, 2, 18, 22–23, 26–29, 34, 36, 274
qadīm, 19, 36, 89, 150, 164
qawābil, 92, 112, 141, 186
Qayṣarī, 1, 4–5, 14, 59, 115, 134–136, 143–156, 185, 192, 198–199, 253, 258–259, 274
quantum mechanics, 232, 235
quantum system, 233
quantum theory, 233
quasi-physical force, 233
qudra, 17, 35, 160
question of Being, 251–252
quiddity, 66, 69, 194
Qūnawī, 1, 4–5, 14, 59, 84, 93, 115, 134–143, 150, 154–155, 157, 185, 192, 198–199, 253, 258–259, 274
Qur'an, 2, 23–24, 86, 102, 117–119, 213, 236

Rays (Şualar), 224, 273
Rāzī, 1, 4, 13, 43, 60–61, 69–73, 76–77, 79–81, 201, 228, 256, 274, 276, 278
receptivity, 56, 109, 112, 186
re-creation frequency, 76
regulative idea, 124, 126, 216, 218
Reid, Thomas, 206, 223, 241, 273
relational, 116, 119, 122, 124–126, 188, 221, 247
relational metaphysics, 14
relationality, 118, 122, 127, 129
relative matter, 220–221, 247
relatively absolute, 151
Relativization of science, 237
religion and science, 1, 3, 15, 235–237, 239, 250
representational thinking, 251, 253
revelation, 3–4, 19, 63, 168
Risale- i Nur Collection, 202, 204, 224, 268
rituals, 3
Rizvi, Sajjad, 192
Rūmī, 124, 129, 275

sabab, 2, 26
Ṣadr al-Sharī'ah, 247
Sadr, Muhammad Baqr al-, 206
Ṣadrā, 1, 4–5, 15, 59, 93, 183–199, 250, 253, 259, 264, 270, 274–275, 278
Santayana, George, 229, 275
sarayān al-wujūd, 93, 137, 185, 197
school of *wujūdiyya*, 143, 156–157, 258
Schuon, Fritjhof, 237
scientific methodology, 3, 231, 238, 240, 242–244
scientific models, 5, 14, 61, 81, 256
scientific reductionism, 234
second intellect (*al-'aql al-thānī*), 177
secondary causality, 5, 62, 70, 123–125, 136, 140–142, 200, 202–204, 213–216, 218, 229, 245, 248, 259
secondary intelligible (*ma'qūl thānī*), 192
self-awareness, 54, 113
self-imposed habits, 6, 27, 70, 181, 200, 205–206, 216, 240, 245

Seyyed Hossein Nasr, 183, 192, 238, 270, 275
Shahrastānī, 18, 21–24, 32–34, 37, 176, 276
Sharḥ al-Mawāqif, 93, 159–160, 172, 241, 268–269, 277
Sharḥ Fuṣūṣ, 144, 146–148, 151, 185, 268
Sharīʿa, Ṣadr al-, 220, 247
al-Shifāʾ al-Ilāhiyyāt, 42–44, 46–51, 53, 55, 57, 269
shirk, 35–36, 164
Shiʿites, 18, 164
simplicity, 57, 66, 69, 91, 94, 97, 145, 184–185, 188, 194, 258
skepticism, 81, 84, 201, 241–243, 253
societies of theophanies, 14, 126, 128
solar system, 175
sovereignty, 6, 23, 70, 105, 137, 203, 207, 211
Special Divine Action, 231
sphere, 78
subatomic particles, 233
substantial motion (*ḥaraka jawharīya*), 187
Sufi metaphysicians, 84, 99, 184–185, 257, 259
iSufi metaphysics, 4–5, 11, 14–15, 94, 120, 135, 202, 209, 211–212, 218, 224, 230
Sufism, 46, 62, 116, 118–119, 121–123, 214, 269
Suhrawardī, 1, 4–5, 14, 46, 50, 59, 100–101, 103, 105–108, 110, 112–115, 190–192, 199, 250, 253, 258, 262, 267, 271, 273–278
superposition, 233
syllogism, 3, 81
system biology, 234

ṭabīʿa, 24, 29
ṭafra, 33
al-Tafsīr al-Kabīr, 70, 274
Tahāfut, 22, 63–65, 67–69, 104, 132, 170, 172–173, 176–177, 180, 241, 267, 269
Tahāfut al-Tahāfut, 84
takhṣīṣ, 21, 177, 220
Talkhīṣ al-Muḥaṣṣal, 27, 277
tarjīh, 38, 64–65, 69, 71, 80, 95, 136, 141, 143, 154, 159, 165, 176, 255
tawḥīd, 17
tawlīd, 27, 29, 161
taʾwīl, 19
taʿaddud al-qudamāʾ, 17
teleology, 28, 167
temporal posteriority, 151
tenth intellect, 174
terrestrial bodies, 174, 177
test, 70
the Philosophers, 4, 14, 22, 56, 63–67, 80, 85, 90–92, 97–98, 136, 139–141, 143–144, 152–153, 155, 164, 167, 169–170, 173–177, 179–180, 182, 189, 196–197, 243, 256–257, 267–268
theodicy, 3, 14–15, 232, 248, 254, 260
theology of *possibility*, 16, 31–32, 37–38, 63, 255, 260
theophanic individualities, 116, 126, 128
theophany, 116, 119–120, 122–126, 128, 194
theories of causality, 3, 15, 40, 62, 157
theory of *aḥwāl*, 19
theory of latency (*kumūn*), 26
theosophy, 4, 120
thinking that recalls (*das andenkende denken*), 251
Turkish Republic, 201
Ṭūsī, 27, 43, 58, 138, 269, 277
two dates, 71, 80
two-dimensionality of causality, 250

uncaused cause, 12, 37, 46, 52, 57–58, 113, 130, 247
unity of existence (*wahdat al-wujūd*), 127
universals, 3, 101, 136
unmoved mover, 11
upper-level occurrences, 234

vacuum, 31, 33
veil, 70, 123, 125, 128, 133, 193, 202–204, 208, 213, 215, 217, 219, 224, 250
velocity, 76, 226
void, 73–75, 85

wāḥid, 47, 91–93, 132, 141, 166
wājib, 45, 71, 101, 150, 167
wājib al-wujūd, 45, 100–101
Wāsil ibn ʿAṭāʾ, 17
wave-function, 233
Wensinck, A. J., 18, 61, 277

Whitehead, Alfred N., 169, 223, 241, 246, 277
Wisnovsky, Robert, 40, 44–45, 58–59, 277
with/without intermediation, 140, 142
Wolfson, H. A., 25, 62, 243, 278
Words (Sözler), 125, 203–204, 214, 219, 221–222, 225–226, 273
working hypotheses, 173, 182
world of command (Tr. *alem-i emr*), 222
world of creation (Tr. *alem-i halk*), 222
wujūd al-ʿām, 137
wujūd's infinity, 148, 151, 155, 192, 258–259

Ziauddin Sardar, 236

ʿAlī Qushjī, 171, 243
ʿilla, 2, 26, 29, 42, 52, 181
ʿilm, 17, 27

Printed in the United States
by Baker & Taylor Publisher Services